MW00650588

Ecumenism
and Interreligious Dialogue

SEMESTER EDITION

[DID-uh-kay]

The *Didache* is the first known Christian catechesis. Written in the first century, the *Didache* is the earliest known Christian writing outside of Scripture. The name of the work, "*Didache*," is indeed appropriate for such a catechesis because it comes from the Greek word for "teaching," and indicates that this writing contains the teaching of the Apostles.

The *Didache* is a catechetical summary of Christian Sacraments, practices, and morality. Though written in the first century, its teaching is timeless. The *Didache* was probably written by the disciples of the Twelve Apostles, and it presents the Apostolic Faith as taught by those closest to Jesus Christ. This series of books takes the name of this early catechesis because it shares in the Church's mission of passing on that same Faith, in its rich entirety, to new generations.

Below is an excerpt from the *Didache* in which we see a clear example of its lasting message, a message that speaks to Christians of today as much as it did to the first generations of the Church. The world is different, but the struggle for holiness is the same. In the *Didache*, we are instructed to embrace virtue, to avoid sin, and to live the Beatitudes of our Lord.

My child, flee from every evil thing, and from every likeness of it. Be not prone to anger, for anger leads the way to murder; neither jealous, nor quarrelsome, nor of hot temper; for out of all these murders are engendered.

My child, be not a lustful one; for lust leads the way to fornication; neither a filthy talker, nor of lofty eye; for out of all these adulteries are engendered.

My child, be not an observer of omens, since it leads the way to idolatry; neither an enchanter, nor an astrologer, nor a purifier, nor be willing to took at these things; for out of all these idolatry is engendered.

My child, be not a liar, since a lie leads the way to theft; neither money-loving, nor vainglorious, for out of all these thefts are engendered.

My child, be not a murmurer, since it leads the way to blasphemy; neither self-willed nor evil-minded, for out of all these blasphemies are engendered.

But be meek, since the meek shall inherit the earth.

Be long-suffering and pitiful and guileless and gentle and good and always trembling at the words which you have heard.[1]

The *Didache* is the teaching of the Apostles and, as such, it is the teaching of the Church. Accordingly, this book series makes extensive use of the most recent comprehensive catechesis provided to us, the *Catechism of the Catholic Church*. The *Didache* series also relies heavily on Sacred Scripture, the lives of the saints, the Fathers of the Church, and the teaching of Vatican II as witnessed by the pontificates of St. John Paul II, Benedict XVI, and Francis.

1. "The Didache," *Ante-Nicene Fathers*, vol.7. tr. M.B. Riddle. ed. Alexander Roberts, James Donaldson, and A. Cleveland Coxe (Buffalo, NY: Christian Literature Publishing Co., 1886).

Ecumenism
and Interreligious Dialogue

Author: Eric Sammons
Publisher: Rev. James Socias

MIDWEST THEOLOGICAL FORUM
Downers Grove, Illinois

Published in the United States of America by

Midwest Theological Forum
4340 Cross Street, Suite 1
Downers Grove, IL 60515

Tel: 630-541-8519
Fax: 331-777-5819
mail@mwtf.org
www.theologicalforum.org

Revised First Edition
ISBN Hardcover 978-1-936045-97-6
ISBN Paperback 978-1-939231-82-6

Author: Eric Sammons
Publisher: Rev. James Socias
Editor in Chief: Jeffrey Cole

Contributing Editor: Gerald Korson
Other Contributors: Suzan Sammons
Design and Production: Marlene Burrell, Jane Heineman of April Graphics, Highland Park, Illinois

Acknowledgements

Excerpts from the English translation of the *Catechism of the Catholic Church* for the United States of America, copyright ©1994, United States Catholic Conference, Inc.—Libreria Editrice Vaticana. Used with permission.

Excerpts from the English translation of the *Catechism of the Catholic Church: Modifications from the Editio Typica*, copyright ©1997, United States Catholic Conference, Inc.—Libreria Editrice Vaticana. Used with permission.

Scripture quotations are from the Catholic Edition of the *Revised Standard Version of the Bible*, copyright ©1965, 1966, National Council of the Churches of Christ in the United States of America. Used by permission. All rights reserved.

Excerpts from the *Code of Canon Law, Latin/English Edition*, are used with permission, copyright ©1983 Canon Law Society of America, Washington, DC.

Citations of official Church documents from Neuner, Josef, SJ and Dupuis, Jacques, SJ, eds., *The Christian Faith: Doctrinal Documents of the Catholic Church*, 5th ed. (New York: Alba House, 1992). Used with permission.

Excerpts from *Vatican II: The Conciliar and Post Conciliar Documents, New Revised Edition* edited by Austin Flannery, OP, copyright ©1992, Costello Publishing Company, Inc., Northport, NY, are used with permission of the publisher, all rights reserved. No part of these excerpts may be reproduced, stored in a retrieval system, or transmitted in any form or by any means—electronic, mechanical, photocopying, recording or otherwise, without express written permission of Costello Publishing Company.

Library of Congress Cataloging-in-Publication Data

Sammons, Eric, author.
Ecumenism and interreligious dialogue / Eric Sammons. — First edition.
pages cm. — (The Didache series)
Includes index.
ISBN 978-1-936045-97-6
1. Church — Unity — Textbooks. 2. Christian union — Textbooks. 3. Ecumenical movement — Textbooks.
4. Catholic Church — Doctrines — Textbooks. 5. Church history — Textbooks. 6. Christianity and other religions — Textbooks.
7. Religions — Textbooks. I. Title.
BV601.5.S26 2014
262.001'1 — dc23

2013032011

The Subcommittee on the Catechism, United States Conference of Catholic Bishops, has found that this catechetical high school text, copyright 2020, is in conformity with the *Catechism of the Catholic Church* and that it fulfills the requirements of Elective Course E of the *Doctrinal Elements of a Curriculum Framework for the Development of Catechetical Materials for Young People of High School Age.*

In accordance with c. 824, permission to publish is granted on July 5, 2013, by Most Reverend Francis J. Kane, Vicar General of the Archdiocese of Chicago. Permission to publish is an official declaration of ecclesiastical authority that the material is free from doctrinal and moral error. No legal responsibility is assumed by the grant of this permission.

Printed in Canada

TABLE OF CONTENTS

TABLE OF CONTENTS

TABLE OF CONTENTS

TABLE OF CONTENTS

ABBREVIATIONS USED FOR THE BOOKS OF THE BIBLE

OLD TESTAMENT

Genesis	Gn	Tobit	Tb	Ezekiel	Ez
Exodus	Ex	Judith	Jdt	Daniel	Dn
Leviticus	Lv	Esther	Est	Hosea	Hos
Numbers	Nm	1 Maccabees	1 Mc	Joel	Jl
Deuteronomy	Dt	2 Maccabees	2 Mc	Amos	Am
Joshua	Jos	Job	Jb	Obadiah	Ob
Judges	Jgs	Psalms	Ps	Jonah	Jon
Ruth	Ru	Proverbs	Prv	Micah	Mi
1 Samuel	1 Sm	Ecclesiastes	Eccl	Nahum	Na
2 Samuel	2 Sm	Song of Songs	Sg	Habakkuk	Hb
1 Kings	1 Kgs	Wisdom	Wis	Zephaniah	Zep
2 Kings	2 Kgs	Sirach	Sir	Haggai	Hg
1 Chronicles	1 Chr	Isaiah	Is	Zechariah	Zec
2 Chronicles	2 Chr	Jeremiah	Jer	Malachi	Mal
Ezra	Ezr	Lamentations	Lam		
Nehemiah	Neh	Baruch	Bar		

NEW TESTAMENT

Matthew	Mt	Ephesians	Eph	Hebrews	Heb
Mark	Mk	Philippians	Phil	James	Jas
Luke	Lk	Colossians	Col	1 Peter	1 Pt
John	Jn	1 Thessalonians	1 Thes	2 Peter	2 Pt
Acts of the Apostles	Acts	2 Thessalonians	2 Thes	1 John	1 Jn
Romans	Rom	1 Timothy	1 Tm	2 John	2 Jn
1 Corinthians	1 Cor	2 Timothy	2 Tm	3 John	3 Jn
2 Corinthians	2 Cor	Titus	Ti	Jude	Jude
Galatians	Gal	Philemon	Phlm	Revelation	Rev

GENERAL ABBREVIATIONS

AG — *Ad Gentes Divinitus* (Decree on the Church's Missionary Activity)

CA — *Centesimus Annus* (On the Hundredth Anniversary)

CCC — *Catechism of the Catholic Church*

CDF — Congregation for the Doctrine of the Faith

CIC — Code of Canon Law (*Codex Iuris Canonici*)

CPG — *Solemn Profession of Faith*: Credo of the People of God

CT — *Catechesi Tradendæ* (On Catechesis in our Time)

DCE — *Deus Caritas Est* (God is Love)

DD — *Dies Domini* (The Lord's Day)

DH — *Dignitatis Humanæ* (Declaration on Religious Freedom)

DoV — *Donum Vitæ* (Respect for Human Life)

DV — *Dei Verbum* (Dogmatic Constitution on Divine Revelation)

DS — Denzinger-Schonmetzer, *Enchiridion Symbolorum, definitionum et declarationum de rebus fidei et morum* (1985)

EV — *Evangelium Vitæ* (The Gospel of Life)

FC — *Familiaris Consortio* (On the Family)

GS — *Gaudium et Spes* (Pastoral Constitution on the Church in the Modern World)

HV — *Humanæ Vitæ* (On Human Life)

IOE — *Iura et Bona* (Declaration on Euthanasia)

LE — Laborem Exercens (On Human Work)

LG — *Lumen Gentium* (Dogmatic Constitution on the Church)

MF — *Mysterium Fidei* (The Mystery of Faith)

PH — *Persona Humana* (Declaration on Sexual Ethics)

PL — J.P. Migne, ed., *Patrologia Latina* (Paris: 1841-1855)

PT — *Pacem in Terris* (On Establishing Universal Peace)

QA — *Quadragesimo Anno* (The Fortieth Year)

RP — *Reconciliatio et Pœnitentia* (On Reconciliation and Penance)

RH — *Redemptor Hominis* (The Redeemer of Man)

SC — *Sacrosanctum Concilium* (The Constitution on the Sacred Liturgy)

SRS — *Sollicitudo Rei Socialis* (On Social Concerns)

SS — *Spe Salvi* (In Hope We Are Saved)

USCCB — United States Conference of Catholic Bishops

VS — *Veritatis Splendor* (Splendor of the Truth)

Preface

ot too long ago the majority of Catholic young people in the U.S. went to Catholic schools, lived in largely Catholic neighborhoods, and generally associated only with other Catholic youth. Today such a situation is increasingly rare. Living in a society growing ever more diverse and secular, Catholics routinely interact with non-Catholics: Protestant Christians, Jews, Orthodox Christians, Muslims, Hindus, and those of other religions or no religion at all. Such interaction leads naturally to legitimate and important questions: When it comes to questions about God, who is right? How are we to follow God? What is the meaning of life? And, perhaps most pressing to many, will my non-Catholic friends go to heaven when they die?

As we will learn this semester, these are vital questions, and they have answers. It is all too common today to relegate such questions to the area of "personal opinion" and to pretend that there are no right or wrong answers. But God, as we will see, has revealed himself and his plan for our salvation, and he established the Catholic Church so we can follow that plan better.

Although the Catholic Church enjoys the fullness of truth, this does not negate the value of other religions and their search for truth. The sincere seeking of truth—in accordance with right reason and natural law—points us toward the way that brings life. Yet Jesus Christ said that he is the Way, the Truth and the Life (Jn 14: 6), and he prayed that "all may be one" through believing in him (Jn 17: 21). Ecumenism and interreligious dialogue are the effort of the Church to engage other Christians and those who follow other religions in a dialogue that, we hope and pray, leads to Christ who is the Truth and the Church he founded in order to allow the Holy Spirit to bring all people into communion with God and with each other.

The work of ecumenism is also part of the New Evangelization that the Church has promoted in recent years. The New Evangelization is the call for all Catholics, especially those who have drifted from the faith or been ill catechized, to seek a deeper relationship with the Lord—both in knowledge and in love. By virtue of this deeper relationship, then, Catholics will want to engage with non-Catholics in discovering both the ways we mutually accept the truth and the ways we differ.

What does all this mean in the life of one Catholic student? Hopefully, by deepening your knowledge both of the Church's role in the Revelation of God as well as the beliefs and practices of non-Catholic faiths, you can engage more fruitfully your non-Catholic friends in a pursuit of the truth. This will involve a proclamation of the truths of the Catholic Faith, a recognition of the truths proclaimed by other faiths, and a charitable and honest explanation of where Catholic belief differs from non-Catholic. In other words, you'll be able to discuss effectively with your friends matters of the highest importance—after all, what is more important than God and our eternal destination?—without it becoming a messy argument that serves only to divide and harm relationships.

The existence of religions in the world is a clear sign of the innate desire in every human heart to know about things transcendent: God, life everlasting, good and evil, sin and redemption. But God in his infinite mercy has not left us to grasp for that knowledge without any help: He sent his Son to reveal himself to us and to establish a Church. It is the responsibility of all Catholics, through word and deed, to assist the Church in her ecumenical mission and to help our fellow religious seekers to follow the path that leads to eternal life.

Eric Sammons
June 29, 2013
Solemnity of Saints Peter and Paul, Apostles

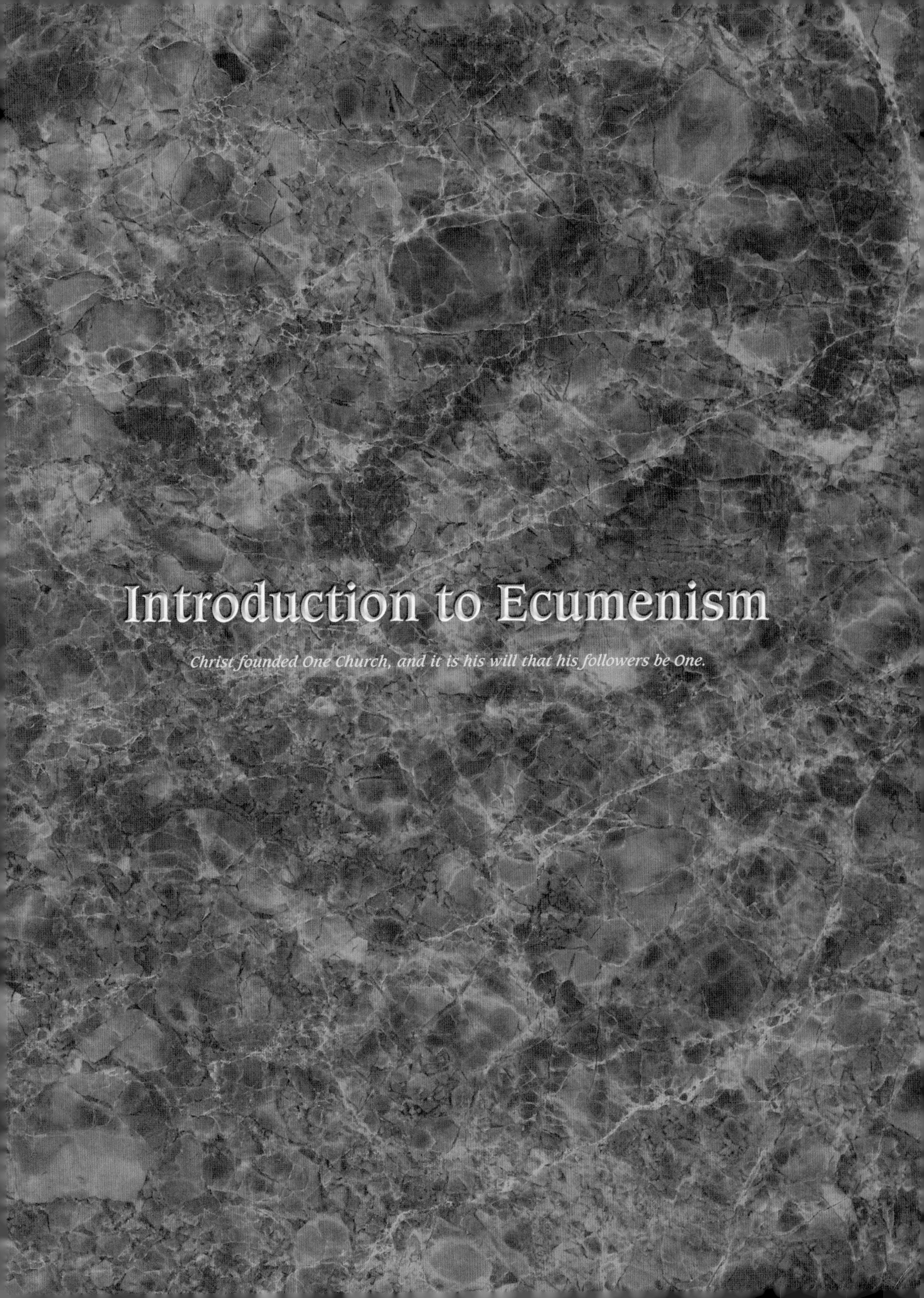

Introduction to Ecumenism

Christ founded One Church, and it is his will that his followers be One.

Ecumenism and Interreligious Dialogue

INTRODUCTION

Introduction to Ecumenism

"That they may all be one; even as thou, Father, art in me, and I in thee, that they also may be in us, so that the world may believe that thou hast sent me." (Jn 17: 21)

Everyone loves a joyful reunion. Perhaps you have experienced a family reunion in which relatives from far and wide come together as one for a happy celebration—to celebrate nothing more than the simple fact of being a family. The various members of an extended family might differ from one another in terms of their education, employment, social standing, interests, hobbies, and other facets of their lives, but the commonality they share as members of the same family is stronger than their differences. They strive to create a family atmosphere that reflects the love they have for one other while avoiding those things that might cause needless conflicts.

That is not to say that there is never any friction whenever family members gather. Even among smaller family groups, including at Christmas and other holiday gatherings, people can get into disagreements or get on one another's nerves. There are also families where the divisions run so deep that some members have lost the will to get together anymore. There is great pain in families in which brothers and sisters, aunts and uncles, or sons and daughters have separated themselves from their families to the point where a true family reunion seems impossible. Many a tear is shed and many a heart aches over the loved ones who choose not to be present at a family celebration. Hardly a family is spared this grief at one time or another.

The Last Supper (detail) by West.
"That they may all be one" (Jn 17: 21).

The Church is like the home of a loving father whose doors are open wide, welcoming all the members of his family to gather in peace, joy, and unity. Jesus Christ, the Son of God, came to save all of us from the clutches of sin and to gather all people into the one Family of God: his Mystical Body, the Church. During his earthly ministry, Christ founded his Church to guide all people in the truth and to communicate his truth throughout the world and throughout all time.

Despite his intention, Christ knew that the same power of sin that had separated humanity from God would also separate members of the human family from one another. Even among those who believed in Christ and sought to follow him, divisions would arise. It pained Our Lord greatly to know that his people would remain divided despite all he had said and done for us in order to unite us as one people.

Even on the very night before he was to be crucified, Christ prayed to his heavenly Father for the unity of his people:

I do not pray for these only, but also for those who believe in me through their word, that they may all be one; even as thou, Father, art in me, and I in thee, that they also may be in us, so that

Jerusalem, Jerusalem by Tissot.
"O Jerusalem, Jerusalem,... How often would I have gathered your children together as a hen gathers her brood under her wings." (Mt 23:37)

> the world may believe that thou hast sent me. The glory which thou hast given me I have given to them, that they may be one even as we are one, I in them and thou in me, that they may become perfectly one, so that the world may know that thou hast sent me and hast loved them even as thou hast loved me. (Jn 17: 20-23)

Christ earnestly desired that all his followers be united as closely with one another as he is united to his Father. Yet, even the books of the New Testament, written a generation or so after Christ had ascended into heaven, indicate divisions forming within the ranks of Christian believers.

As history has unfolded, the Church founded by Christ has experienced wounds to her unity again and again as groups of believers have broken away to form separate faith communities. Many of these communities have divided further and splintered repeatedly, creating more and more communities independent of one another. Far from achieving and maintaining the unity so ardently desired by Christ, the body of believers who claim to be his followers has been severely fragmented.

Modern-day Christianity is marked by three primary groups: One group is the Catholic Church with the Pope—the direct successor of St. Peter, whom Christ established as the earthly head of his Church—as her chief shepherd. Another group includes the various Orthodox Churches, most of which broke away from the Catholic Church between the fifth and eleventh centuries. Yet another group includes Protestant denominations, which according to the *World Christian Encyclopedia* (2001) number in the tens of thousands and all of which trace their histories as far back as the sixteenth century. A not insignificant percentage of this last group is the many independent, nondenominational communities and "megachurches."

Despite the appearance of such Christian diversity, the fact remains that Christ founded only one Church. It is his stated will that all his disciples be united as one Church. The task of healing the divisions and separations that afflict Christianity with the aim of restoring true unity as one Church is called *ecumenism*.

WHAT IS ECUMENISM?

Ecumenism, the subject of this textbook, is an unfamiliar word to many people. Most people have heard of or read an announcement for a prayer service or gathering described as *ecumenical,* and people sometimes reference an *ecumenical movement.* All of these terms are closely related.

The word "ecumenism" comes from the Greek *oikoumene,* which means "the whole (inhabited) earth." As you can imagine from the aforementioned overview of the diversity of Christian communities, the task of restoring unity amid so many divisions is a daunting one, yet it remains your obligation and the obligation of every Christian to seek that unity, however elusive it may seem. Something that is *ecumenical* is designed with an eye toward bringing Christians together.

Archbishop of Canterbury Dr. Rowan Williams and Pope Benedict XVI at an ecumenical celebration and evening of prayer at Westminster Abbey, September 17, 2010, with representatives from all the main Christian churches including the Greek Orthodox, Coptic, and Free Churches.

Rightly understood, ecumenism focuses not so much on what divides Christians from one another but on what already unites us: the elements of belief that all Christians tend to share in common. Considered in a certain sense, unity can be seen as a gift from God that we already possess in a limited way, a gift that we must recognize and accept in order to strengthen and perfect it. St. Peter urged all disciples of Christ to "have unity of spirit, sympathy, love of the brethren, a tender heart and a humble mind."[1] St. Paul taught that the faithful are united through the Death and Resurrection of Christ: "If we have been united with him in a death like his, we shall certainly be united with him in a resurrection like his."[2] This unity comes through *Baptism*: "By one Spirit we were all baptized into one body—Jews or Greeks, slaves or free—and all were made to drink of one Spirit."[3] Belief in God, faith in the risen Christ, openness to the Holy Spirit, Baptism, and reverence for Sacred Scripture are among the core beliefs all Christians share in common.

There is a saying—though often attributed to St. Augustine, the great fourth-century theologian, but of much later origin—that aptly expresses the aims of Christian unity. It is referred to here in the words of St. John XXIII:

> **The common saying, expressed in various ways and attributed to various authors, must be recalled with approval: in essentials, unity; in doubtful matters, liberty; in all things, charity.** (*Ad Petri Cathedram,* 1959)

What are these "essentials" in which we must find our unity? To understand this better, we must recognize that the Christian faith is our response to what God has revealed to the world, a Revelation that took place over the course of many centuries and found its complete fulfillment in Jesus Christ. It is important, then, that we first look more closely at history—not just Christian history but the story of humanity and God's relationship with the human race. We call this story *salvation history.*

SOME GUIDING PRINCIPLES OF ECUMENISM

1. Christ founded One Church, and it is his will that his followers be One.

"Before offering himself up as a spotless victim upon the altar, Christ prayed to his Father for all who believe in him: 'that they all may be one; even as thou, Father, art in me, and I in thee, that they also may be one in us, so that the world may believe that thou has sent me'"[4] (*Unitatis Redintegratio,* 2).

2. **In the course of Church history, certain divisions have arisen between the followers of Christ for which both sides were to blame.**

However, "even in the beginnings of this one and only Church of God there arose certain rifts,[5] which the Apostle strongly condemned.[6] But in subsequent centuries much more serious dissensions made their appearance and quite large communities came to be separated from full communion with the Catholic Church—for which, often enough, men of both sides were to blame" (*UR* 3).

3. **While the sole Church of Christ subsists in the Catholic Church governed by the Pope and the bishops united to him, there are many elements of sanctification and truth in the Churches and ecclesial communities of our separated brethren.**

While "the sole Church of Christ...subsists in (*subsistit in*) the Catholic Church...governed by the successor of Peter and by the bishops in communion with him"[7] (CCC 816), there are "'many elements of sanctification and truth'[8]...found outside the visible confines of the Catholic Church" (CCC 819). Furthermore, the "[Holy] Spirit uses these Churches and ecclesial communities as a means of salvation, whose power derives from the fullness of grace and truth that Christ entrusted to the Catholic Church" (CCC 819).

Some non-Catholic communities have preserved Apostolic Succession and valid Sacraments and are, therefore, true "churches." Others have failed to preserve Apostolic Succession and thus lack a valid episcopate and Eucharist and, therefore, are referred to as "ecclesial communities."

"The Churches which, while not existing in perfect communion with the Catholic Church, remain united to her by...apostolic succession and a valid Eucharist, are true particular Churches[9] (*Dominus Iesus*, 17).

"On the other hand, the ecclesial communities which have not preserved the valid Episcopate and the genuine and integral substance of the Eucharistic mystery,[10] are not Churches in the proper sense; however, those who are baptized in these communities are, by Baptism, incorporated in Christ and thus are in a certain communion, albeit imperfect, with the Church"[11] (*DI* 17).

4. **All Christians should long for unity.**

"All [Christians] however, though in different ways, long for the one visible Church of God, a Church truly universal and set forth into the world that the world may be converted to the Gospel and so be saved, to the glory of God" (*UR* 1).

The Church exhorts all of the faithful to promote Christian unity.

"The Sacred Council exhorts all the Catholic faithful to recognize the signs of the times and to take an active and intelligent part in the work of ecumenism" (*UR* 4).

5. **Unity among Christians makes the preaching of the Gospel more effective.**

The Church seeks to heal the divisions that exist among Christians as such is the will of Christ. Such unity gives a sign to the world and makes more effective the preaching of the Gospel to every creature. (cf. *UR* 1)

6. **The Catholic Church is enriched by the natural, historical, and cultural patrimony of her separated brethren. The Church must preserve unity in essential matters but promote legitimate diversity.**

Such divisions impoverish the catholicity of the Church, who consequently lacks the natural, historical, and cultural patrimony that could be contributed by her separated brethren. This is especially the case with the great liturgical traditions present in the Eastern Churches but is also the case with all of the ecclesial communities. (cf. *UR* 4)

7. **The Church is Holy. Her members, however, are on a journey toward perfect holiness and, thus, are in constant need of purification and reform. Catholics have a responsibility both to know and to live their own faith.**

The Church, united with Christ and sanctified by him, is Holy (cf. CCC 824), and "through him and with him she becomes sanctifying" (CCC 824). She is "the holy People of God"[12] and "her members all called 'saints'"[13] (CCC 823). Though the Church is Holy, "in her members perfect holiness is something yet to be acquired" (CCC 825). Insofar as she is comprised of human members, the Church is in constant need of purification and reform, especially in regard to those sins and offenses committed against her separated brethren.

Conversion and holiness of life are essential for ecumenism.

"All the faithful should remember that the more effort they make to live holier lives according to the Gospel, the better will they further Christian unity and put it into practice. For the closer their union with the Father, the Word, and the Spirit, the more deeply and easily will they be able to grow in mutual brotherly love" (*UR* 7). This change of heart and holiness of life, along with public and private prayer for the unity of Christians, should be regarded as the soul of the whole ecumenical movement, and merits the name, "spiritual ecumenism" (*UR* 8).

8. Catholics must seek to understand their separated brethren and, in a spirit of charity, to share the truths of the Catholic faith with them.

"We must get to know the outlook of our separated brethren. To achieve this purpose, study is of necessity required, and this must be pursued with a sense of realism and good will. Catholics, who already have a proper grounding, need to acquire a more adequate understanding of the respective doctrines of our separated brethren, their history, their spiritual and liturgical life, their religious psychology and general background" (*UR* 9).

In ecumenical dialogue, Catholics must seek to explain the faith in a manner that our separated brethren can understand and in a way that removes obstacles. Catholics, however, must remain firm in the truth, which is the objective.

"The way and method in which the Catholic faith is expressed should never become an obstacle to dialogue with our brethren. It is, of course, essential that the doctrine should be clearly presented in its entirety. Nothing is so foreign to the spirit of ecumenism as a false irenicism, in which the purity of Catholic doctrine suffers loss and its genuine and certain meaning is clouded. At the same time, the Catholic faith must be explained more profoundly and precisely, in such a way and in such terms as our separated brethren can also really understand" (*UR* 11).

"In ecumenical dialogue, Catholic theologians standing fast by the teaching of the Church and investigating the divine mysteries with the separated brethren must proceed with love for the truth, with charity, and with humility" (*UR* 11). Truth is the objective.

9. "Worship in common... is not to be considered as a means to be used indiscriminately for the restoration of Christian unity.

"There are two main principles governing the practice of such common worship: first, the bearing witness to the unity of the Church, and second, the sharing in the means of grace. Witness to the unity of the Church very generally forbids common worship to Christians, but the grace to be had from it sometimes commends this practice. The course to be adopted, with due regard to all the circumstances of time, place, and persons, is to be decided by local episcopal authority, unless otherwise provided for by the Bishops' Conference according to its statutes, or by the Holy See" (*UR* 8).

10. Christ established St. Peter and his successors as the leader of and sign of unity for his Church.

Among the doctrines most distinctive to the Catholic Church is the primacy of the Pope as the Successor of St. Peter, who was intended by Christ to be the visible head of all Christians. Without accepting his ministry, Christians will never attain the kind of unity that God willed for his Church, which is a sign and sacrament of unity.

ENDNOTES – INTRODUCTION

1. 1 Pt 3:8.
2. 1 Rom 6:5.
3. 1 Cor 12:13.
4. Jn 17:21.
5. Cf. 1 Cor 11:18-19; Gal 1:6-9; 1 Jn 2:18-19.
6. Cf. 1 Cor 1:11 sqq; 11, 22.
7. *LG* 8 § 2.
8. Ibid.
9. Cf. *UR* 14, 15; Congregation for the Doctrine of the Faith, Letter *Communionis Notio*, 17: AAS 85 (1993), 848.
10. Cf. *UR* 22.
11. Cf. ibid., 3.
12. *LG* 12.
13. Acts 9:13; 1 Cor 6:1; 16:1.

CHAPTER 1

God Reveals His Plan of Salvation

God desires that all of humanity be united in communion with him and with one another forever. Everyone—Jews and Gentiles, people of all nations, races, tongues—is invited to enter into this communion.

Ecumenism and Interreligious Dialogue

CHAPTER ONE

God Reveals His Plan of Salvation

INTRODUCTION

Salvation history can be described as the story of God's reaching out to man and of man's response to God.

Every human person searches for God, whether he or she realizes it or not. Endowed as we are with a rational intellect, the human person is a natural philosopher, able to consider questions both abstract and profound. Men and women since the dawn of time have asked these kinds of questions:

- Why are we here?
- Is there more to the world than what we see?
- Is there something beyond this world?
- Who or what created the universe? And us?
- If someone created us, then what does he expect from us?
- Is there a God? If so, who is God?
- Does he care about us?

God the Father with Sts. Mary Magdalene and Catherine of Siena by Bartolomeo.

The very fact that we ask these questions demonstrates that we were made for something more than this world. A dog or bumblebee or blade of grass does not ask such questions; only human persons look beyond what the physical senses can perceive and ponders their very existence and purpose. For this reason, because we seek answers to such questions, we can say that a human being is fundamentally a *religious being*:

> The desire for God is written in the human heart, because man is created by God and for God; and God never ceases to draw man to himself. Only in God will he find the truth and happiness he never stops searching for.... In many ways, throughout history down to the present day, men have given expression to their quest for God in their religious beliefs and behavior: in their prayers, sacrifices, rituals, meditations, and so forth. These forms of religious expression, despite the ambiguities they often bring with them, are so universal that one may well call man a *religious being*. (CCC 27-28)

Religion is our attempt to seek out God, to understand his *mystery*. This involves engaging in religious activities—communication with spiritual beings, the offering of sacrifice, and the like—but also the use of the mind and *natural reason* to determine if there is a God. St. Paul wrote: "Ever since the creation of the world [God's] invisible nature, namely, his eternal power and deity, has been clearly perceived in the things that have been made."[1] In other words, creation itself—with its magnificence and order—proclaims that there is a Creator, a *Someone* who created everything.

This knowledge, however, alone is unfulfilling. Mere acknowledgment of the fact that there is a Creator does not satisfy our longing for something more. We wonder: Is God like us? Does he love us? How can I please him or get to know him better? Does God hold the keys to my happiness and fulfillment? Inevitably, we find that our attempts to know more about him quickly fall short. We must recognize that our ability to know God on our own is quite limited and incomplete. We need God to reveal himself to us.

In this chapter, we will explore:

- ✠ How and why God reveals himself to us;
- ✠ God's self-Revelation through his covenants in the Old Testament; and
- ✠ The fullness of God's self-Revelation in Jesus Christ.

GOD REVEALS HIMSELF TO US

Although natural reason helps us know that there is a God and discern something about his attributes, on our own we cannot come to know him well or intimately, his full identity. But we are not lost, for God has chosen to *reveal* himself to us in a way that we can understand. This self-Revelation of God to humanity is called *Divine Revelation.*

Sermon on the Mount by Yelin.
God has revealed himself in words.
"Let your light so shine before men, that they may see your good works and give glory to your Father who is in heaven." (Mt 5:16)

HISTORICITY OF THE BIBLE

Sacred Scripture is a main source of our knowledge of Divine Revelation, and it tells us the story of salvation history. But how do we know the Bible is accurate? Can we trust that what the Bible says is historically true? To answer this question briefly, let us just examine the historicity of one section of the Bible: the four Gospels.

First, it is important to remember the difference between analyzing something scientifically and analyzing something historically. When analyzing a scientific theory, we must test it over and over again under certain conditions and then use our senses to observe the result. Only after we will have done so can we declare something to be a scientific fact. But this cannot be done for events in the past. For example, no living person has seen or heard George Washington, yet it would be foolish to deny his existence. We can look at the historical records—eyewitness accounts, writings about him and writings attributed to him, the consequences of his life—in order to assess the historicity of claims made about this person. In many ways, proving a historical claim is similar to the job of a jury at a legal trial: Jurors must analyze all the evidence—much of it based on eyewitness testimony—and then come to a conclusion.

Second, in examining the historicity of the Gospels, we must understand the purpose of the Gospel writings themselves. St. Luke began his Gospel with a succinct description of his purpose:

> Inasmuch as many have undertaken to compile a narrative of the things which have been accomplished among us, just as they were delivered to us by those who from the beginning were eyewitnesses and ministers of the word, it seemed good to me also, having followed all things closely for some time past, to write an orderly account for you, most excellent Theophilus, that you may know the truth concerning the things of which you have been informed. (Lk 1: 1-4)

St. John was even more explicit as to why he wrote his Gospel:

> Jesus did many other signs in the presence of the disciples, which are not written in this book; but these are written that you may believe that Jesus is the Christ, the Son of God, and that believing you may have life in his name. (Jn 20: 30-31)

The Gospel writers did not write their accounts in order to create a historical proof for twenty-first century people; they wrote their accounts so that people in their time would come to accept the truth about Jesus Christ and believe that he is the Son of God. They were serious about history, but their overriding purpose was *theology*. In other words, these are not news reports; rather, they are writings that convey historical events in a way that presents theological truths. For example, a Gospel writer might have changed the order of events to express a theological truth more clearly. Or, for a similar purpose, he might have related, one after another, teachings of Christ that were originally given over an extended period of time. These actions are not anti-historical; they put historical truth at the service of theological truth.

Furthermore, the life of Christ is more attested—by a significant order of magnitude—than that of any other ancient figure. We have thousands of extant copies of the Gospels from ancient times, far more than any other ancient historical document. We have multiple extrabiblical references to the life of Christ from near-contemporary sources. We have later events, such as the rise of Christianity, that can only be explained reasonably by the existence of Christ as described in the Gospels.

Unlike ancient legends, the Christian faith is founded on historical facts. God became a specific man at a specific time in a specific place. We can be confident that the historical record clearly shows that these facts can be trusted.

Moses Crossing the Red Sea by Raphael.
God has revealed himself through deeds.
"Thus the LORD saved Israel that day from the hand of the Egyptians;...and the people feared the LORD; and they believed in the LORD and in his servant Moses." (Ex 14:30-31)

Salvation history is filled with fumbling efforts to find God, but for his part God has been pursuing us methodically, offering us a relationship with him so we might come to know him. We are like small children who become fascinated with a display of toys and become separated from our father. When we realize that we are alone, we have no idea where our father is and no way to find him. What we do not realize is that our father has been tirelessly searching for us as well, long before we even knew we were lost.

> By natural reason man can know God with certainty, on the basis of his works. But there is another order of knowledge, which man cannot possibly arrive at by his own powers: the order of divine Revelation.[2] Through an utterly free decision, God has revealed himself and given himself to man. This he does by revealing the mystery, his plan of loving goodness, formed from all eternity in Christ, for the benefit of all men. God has fully revealed this plan by sending us his beloved Son, our Lord Jesus Christ, and the Holy Spirit. (CCC 50)

How has God revealed himself? Through both *deeds* and *words*. Through mighty deeds he has acted to change the course of history and to bring people to knowledge of him. Through words he has spoken to us through human beings so that we might know the truth about him. These deeds and words act together to reveal the identity of God:

> This plan of revelation is realized by deeds and words having an inner unity: the deeds wrought by God in the history of salvation manifest and confirm the teaching and realities signified by the words, while the words proclaim the deeds and clarify the mystery contained in them. By this revelation then, the deepest truth about God and the salvation of man shines out for our sake in Christ, who is both the mediator and the fullness of all revelation. (*Dei Verbum*, 2)

We see that God has not left us to our limitations, to a life of frustration and loneliness. Instead, he has reached out to us to unveil his identity and to form a relationship with us in a long process that has occurred throughout history.

> God communicates himself to man gradually. He prepares him to welcome by stages the supernatural Revelation that is to culminate in the person and mission of the incarnate Word, Jesus Christ. (CCC 53)

In short, God revealed himself over a period of time. This gradual unveiling is the essential story of salvation history because, by revealing himself to us, God invites us to salvation, into communion with him. The history of humanity—from our creation to the end of time—is a history of God drawing us closer to himself so we might know him better.

It might seem odd that God works in such a way. Why did he not reveal himself all at once? We might imagine God simply appearing majestically in the sky for all to see, introducing himself in no uncertain terms and laying out exactly what he expects of us. Who could resist such a show of power? Or if he truly wants to save us, why does he not just repeal the Ten Commandments and announce that everyone will be with him in heaven forever?

There are a couple of reasons for this. The first is that God gave us the gift of free will. We have the freedom to choose whether to believe in him or not, the freedom to choose good or evil. He will not force us to love him, to obey him, to have faith in him. He will not force us into eternal happiness in heaven. He simply surrounds us with his love and invites us to respond to that love so we might freely choose the salvation that he offers to us.

The second reason speaks to our human experience. Consider how our human relationships take time to unfold. We come to know others gradually, learning more and more about them as we spend more time with them. When you meet someone new at school or work, you know very little about that person. You learn his name and a few facts about his life, and perhaps you will recognize him the next time you run into him. By his clothes and his manner of speaking, you might make certain assumptions about him, but your knowledge is limited and might even be faulty.

The Annunciation by Albani.
"In the sixth month the angel Gabriel was sent from God to a city of Galilee named Nazareth, to a virgin betrothed to a man whose name was Joseph, of the house of David; and the virgin's name was Mary." (Lk 1:26-27)

Over time you get to know him better, especially as he reveals himself to you: his likes and dislikes, his family background, and his views on the world. Whereas in the beginning you knew certain facts about him, you have gradually come to know him deeper and deeper in a much more personal way. Human beings do not come to this knowledge immediately or through some shortcut; it takes time.

The same is true of our knowledge of God. And in the case of God, whose perfection and mystery is infinitely beyond human imagination, our task of coming to know God more deeply is a never-ending process.

> St. Irenæus of Lyons repeatedly speaks of this divine pedagogy using the image of God and man becoming accustomed to one another: The Word of God dwelt in man and became the Son of man in order to accustom man to perceive God and to accustom God to dwell in man, according to the Father's pleasure.[3] (CCC 53)

Thus, God reveals himself throughout the course of salvation history—a *pedagogy* by which, step by step, he unlocks the mystery of himself to the human race. This Divine Revelation can be divided into two main steps: history before the coming of his Son, during which God prepared his people for the Redeemer as related in the Old Testament, and the Revelation of the Word made flesh as expressed in the New Testament.

Creation of the Sun, Moon, and Planets by Michelangelo.
We cannot assume that the author of Genesis meant a literal 24-hour day when he described Creation occurring over a period of seven "days."

REVELATION IN THE OLD TESTAMENT

GOD THE CREATOR

The questions that we are considering here—Who is God? Why are we here?—have been asked since the beginning of time. The Bible, in fact, begins by addressing them. Its first book, Genesis, speaks to these fundamental issues in its first three chapters, the familiar story of the creation of the world and the sin of Adam and Eve, the first man and woman. These chapters also reveal some profound truths about God and about our world.

We frequently hear about a supposed conflict between religion and science, or between faith and reason. It is especially manifested in debates between creationists and evolutionists. If you were to listen only to popular accounts, you might believe that there are only two kinds of people: those who believe God created the world in seven, twenty-four-hour days a few thousand years ago and those who believe that all species, including human beings, evolved over millions of years with absolutely no divine guidance. In order to believe the story of creation in Genesis, this thinking goes, you have to reject science, and if you believe in the findings of science, then the Bible has nothing meaningful to say about creation. But this betrays a fundamental misunderstanding of both science and the Revelation.

Even in the earliest days of the Church, Christians questioned whether the creation narrative in Genesis should be taken literalistically. For example, in the fourth century, St. Augustine wrote that our twenty-four-hour days "indeed recall the days of creation, but without in any way being really similar to them."[4] In other words, we cannot assume that the Sacred Author of Genesis meant a literal, twenty-four-hour day when he described creation occurring over a period of seven "days."

Remember: Just because a written account is not meant to be taken *literalistically* does not preclude it from conveying a *literal truth*. If a husband were to write in a poem about his wife that "her eyes shine like the stars," we understand him to mean—the *literal* truth he wishes to convey—that he finds her eyes beautiful, even if *literalistically* her eyes were not as luminous as all the stars in the Milky Way galaxy. In order to understand any passage of the Bible, we must first understand why the author wrote it and what truths he wanted to convey. In the creation narrative, the author is in part addressing and critiquing other ancient religions' creation narratives, and he is relating fundamental truths about God and our relationship with him. Here are some of the truths that we can glean from the Creation narrative in Genesis:

- ✠ **God created the world out of nothing.** Most other creation accounts speak of some triumph of one god over other gods that resulted in the formation of the world out of preexisting matter. Genesis, however, emphasizes that God created the world by his own power *ex nihilo* ("out of nothing").
- ✠ **Creation is good.** One of mankind's mistaken ideas is that matter is evil and only the spirit is good. Genesis rebukes this idea head-on: Everything God created is good, and any evil in the world is due to our (or the angels') rejection of God.
- ✠ **Human beings are unique and bear a resemblance to God.** Although Genesis makes clear the infinite gap between God and man, it also emphasizes that, unlike the rest of physical creation, men and women are made "in the image and likeness of God."[5] That does not mean we look like God, but that he endowed us with characteristics in his likeness, such as an intellect, free will, and an immortal soul. Because of this likeness, we have the potential for a unique relationship with God.
- ✠ **The universe is ordered.** Genesis reveals that, when God created the world, it was "without form and void."[6] Over the next six "days," God solved this problem and gave the world both form (days 1-3) and content (days 4-6). The idea that the world is orderly (with "form") is really a presupposition of all science, for if the universe were not orderly, we could not study it and draw conclusions from what we see. Although Genesis is not a science book, it implicitly proclaims the importance of science.

ORIGINAL SIN

The original goodness and order of creation did not last. Our first parents' peace with God was disrupted when they, misusing their gift of free will, chose to sin against God. Because of that sin of disobedience, evil entered into the world. Sin and evil corrupted their relationship with God and the relationships among all members of the human race.

> **The serpent was more subtle than any other wild creature that the LORD God had made. He said to the woman, "Did God say, 'You shall not eat of any tree of the garden'?" And the woman said to the serpent, "We may eat of the fruit of the trees of the garden; but God said, 'You shall not eat of the fruit of the tree which is in the midst of the garden, neither shall you touch it, lest you die.' "But the serpent said to the woman, "You will not die. For God knows that when you eat of it your eyes will be opened, and you will be like God, knowing good and evil." So when the woman saw that the tree was good for food, and that it was a delight to the eyes, and that the tree was to be desired to make one wise, she took of its fruit and ate; and she also gave some to her husband, and he ate. Then the eyes of both were opened, and they knew that they were naked; and they sewed fig leaves together and made themselves aprons. And they heard the sound of the LORD God walking in the garden in the cool of the day, and the man and his wife hid themselves from the presence of the LORD God among the trees of the garden.** (Gn 3:1-8)

Evil is not a creation of God but results from the abuse of human freedom. The sin of Adam and Eve is called *Original Sin*, and it has affected all of humanity in all generations.

Eve, the Serpent, and Death (detail) by Baldung.

Paradise by Cranach the Elder.
Man's peace with God was disrupted when our first parents chose to sin against God. But God will not abandon us to our fallen state of existence. He will send someone to save us from the power of evil.

Why would the sin of our first parents be transmitted to the rest of humanity? The original holiness and justice experienced by Adam and Eve was given not only to them as individuals but to their very human nature—to all of humanity. When they chose to sin, their sin wounded our human nature:

> By yielding to the tempter, Adam and Eve committed a *personal sin*, but this sin affected *the human nature* that they would then transmit *in a fallen state*.[7] It is a sin which will be transmitted by propagation to all mankind, that is, by the transmission of a human nature deprived of original holiness and justice. (CCC 404)

Scripture also reveals something else about the Fall of man: God's refusal to abandon the human race to their sinful and fallen state.

> **The LORD God said to the serpent, "Because you have done this, cursed are you above all cattle, and above all wild animals; upon your belly you shall go, and dust you shall eat all the days of your life. I will put enmity between you and the woman, and between your seed and her seed; he shall bruise your head, and you shall bruise his heel."** (Gn 3:14-15)

This is called the *Protoevangelium* ("First Gospel"), the first promise of "Good News." God will not abandon us to our fallen state of existence but will send someone—the seed of a woman—who will crush the head of the Evil One and save us from the power of evil. This is where God's plan of salvation history commences. The *Protoevangelium* also reveals an important attribute of God: He is a loving Creator who cares deeply for his creation, most especially for humanity, whom he earnestly desires to reconcile to himself.

It is, nonetheless, not only the actions of God after the Fall that reveal aspects of God's nature. Creation itself is the first Revelation of the *Triune God* as it originates in the Father and is brought into being by the Word, Jesus Christ, through the power of the Holy Spirit.

> Creation is the foundation of "all God's saving plans," the "beginning of the history of salvation"[8] that culminates in Christ. Conversely, the mystery of Christ casts conclusive light on the mystery of creation and reveals the end for which "in the beginning God created the heavens and the earth": from the beginning, God envisaged the glory of the new creation in Christ.[9] (CCC 280)

We will continue to see this pattern throughout the Old Testament: As God reveals himself gradually through time, he always directs his people toward his ultimate Revelation, his Son, Jesus Christ.

GOD REVEALED IN HIS PROMISES AND COVENANTS

One key way to follow salvation history when reading the Bible, especially the Old Testament, is to take note of the various promises and *covenants* that God made with his people through his chosen representatives. Promises and covenants are fundamental ways by which God reveals himself.

Most people understand what a promise is, but the idea of *covenant* might be a bit foreign. In many ways a covenant is like a promise. The difference is that a covenant is always a mutual agreement between two persons or parties and is solemnly ratified, usually with an oath or vow.

After the Fall God prepared the world for the Redeemer by entering into covenants with his Chosen People. The covenants of the Old Testament were alliances, or solemn commitments, between God and a particular person, people, or nation. These include the covenants God made with Noah, Abraham, and Moses.

Every biblical covenant has a specific scope, a set of people to whom the covenant applies. Although God's plan from the beginning was to save all people—and he has never wavered on this—he began this work on a small scale and gradually expanded the scope of his promises to encompass more and more people. Thus, God first formed a particular people, his *Chosen People*, who in turn were intended to grow and become his witnesses to all nations, with the eventual goal of gathering all people into one body.

As our discussion of salvation history continues, we will see how God gradually restored and repaired his relationship with humanity through promises to Adam and David and his covenants with Noah, Abraham, and Moses. But the greatest covenant he established was through his beloved Son, Jesus Christ. In this truly "new" covenant, God set up a permanent covenant between all people and himself. Christ himself made it clear that the Eucharist is a sign of this Covenant at the Last Supper:

> **[Jesus] took bread, and when he had given thanks he broke it and gave it to them, saying, "This is my body which is given for you. Do this in remembrance of me." And likewise the cup after supper, saying, "This cup which is poured out for you is *the new covenant* in my blood. (Lk 22:19-20, emphasis added)**

The *New Covenant* in Christ is the "new and everlasting covenant" that fulfills all previous covenants and promises because Christ is the fulfillment of all Divine Revelation.

Before considering the New Covenant, however, let us hearken back to God's promises and covenants in the Old Testament, which generally were communicated through certain leaders he himself had chosen.

The Last Supper (detail) by Bloch.
The New Covenant in Christ is the "new and everlasting covenant" that fulfills all previous covenants.

The Creation of Adam in the Garden of Eden by Brueghel the Younger.
The covenants of the Old Testament were alliances, or solemn commitments, between God and a particular person, people, or nation.

GOD'S PROMISE TO ADAM

We have already discussed the first promise God made to all people in the preceding section: the *Protoevangelium*. Although in Genesis it was God speaking to the serpent about the "seed" of "the woman" who would "bruise" the head of the serpent, the promise implicitly extends to all people to whom the promised "seed" would bring redemption from sin.

Even in the early Church, scholars began to recognize how this promise was fulfilled in Jesus Christ, the Son of God, who came to redeem the world. The Blessed Virgin Mary, chosen by God to bear the Christ Child, came to be known as the "New Eve" because, through her obedience to God in bringing his Son into the world, she helped bring salvation to humanity, effectively reversing the sin of the first Eve. As St. Peter Chrysologus wrote in the fifth century, "Christ was born of a woman so that just as death came through a woman, so through Mary, life might return."[10]

In the writings of St. Paul, Christ in a similar way is linked to Adam, for through the Sacrifice of Christ we are able to conquer sin and be raised to new life:

> **"The first man Adam became a living being"; the last Adam became a life-giving spirit. But it is not the spiritual which is first but the physical, and then the spiritual. The first man was from the earth, a man of dust; the second man is from heaven. As was the man of dust, so are those who are of the dust; and as is the man of heaven, so are those who are of heaven. Just as we have borne the image of the man of dust, we shall also bear the image of the man of heaven.** (1 Cor 15: 45-49)

The *Catechism of the Catholic Church* says of the *Protoevangelium*:

> The Christian tradition sees in this passage an announcement of the "New Adam" who, because he "became obedient unto death, even death on a cross," makes amends superabundantly for the disobedience of Adam.[11] Furthermore many Fathers and Doctors of the Church have seen the woman announced in the *Protoevangelium* as Mary, the mother of Christ, the "new Eve." Mary benefited first of all and uniquely from Christ's victory over sin: she was preserved from all stain of original sin and by a special grace of God committed no sin of any kind during her whole earthly life.[12] (CCC 411)

This promise in the *Protoevangelium* set the stage for the rest of the Old Testament promises and covenants. Each would be designed to unify the people of God and prepare them for the coming of the Redeemer, Jesus Christ.

Noah Sacrificing after the Deluge by West.
God's covenant with Noah and his descendants was a renewal of the command to Adam and Eve to have dominion over creation, with the specific admonition not to shed one another's blood.

GOD'S COVENANT WITH NOAH

The story of Noah is a familiar one. With the world inundated by sin, God decided to destroy the earth in a flood, saving only the righteous Noah and his family. Following God's instructions to build an ark and to take aboard specimens from all the animals, Noah and his family survived the torrential rains that fell for forty days and forty nights.

After the waters began to recede and the Ark had landed on high ground, Noah disembarked with his family and offered a sacrifice of burnt offerings to God in adoration and thanksgiving. These sacrifices came from among the "clean animals" that Noah had taken aboard the Ark, thus serving as a type of the Sacrifice of Christ, who was the sinless and perfect Lamb of God.

God was pleased with Noah's offering and made a covenant with Noah, promising never again to punish the world in this way. As a sign, he placed the rainbow in the sky.

> **When the LORD smelled the pleasing odor, the LORD said in his heart, "I will never again curse the ground because of man, for the imagination of man's heart is evil from his youth; neither will I ever again destroy every living creature as I have done."** (Gn 8: 21)

At the beginning of salvation history, God entrusted the world to Adam. In this second beginning, God repeated this loving gesture with Noah, blessing his family and instructing them to "be fruitful and multiply, and fill the earth," just as he had told our first parents.[13] The goods of creation would be a great blessing for Noah and his descendants so long as they remained faithful to God's commandments.

God's covenant with Noah and his descendants was a renewal of the command to Adam and Eve to have dominion over creation, adding the specific admonition not to shed one another's blood.

> **"Every moving thing that lives shall be food for you; and as I gave you the green plants, I give you everything. Only you shall not eat flesh with its life, that is, its blood. For your lifeblood I will surely require a reckoning; of every beast I will require it and of man; of every man's brother I will require the life of man. Whoever sheds the blood of man, by man shall his blood be shed; for God made man in his own image."** (Gn 9: 3-6)

Salvation history reveals that God never ceases to love his people. No matter how evil their behavior, he continues to give them another chance.

TYPOLOGY

alvation history is replete with "types." A *type*, sometimes called a prefiguration, is a person, place, event, or institution in the Bible that foreshadows future and greater realities that God will reveal to his people. Types help prepare God's people for his later works and allow us to understand more deeply his previous works. These types are not simply "prophecies," as that word is commonly used, which tell of future events; rather, they reflect the deeper themes of God's plan of salvation.

For example, Isaac is a type of Christ. If we look at the story of the sacrifice of Isaac in Genesis 22, we can see a number of parallels to the life of Christ. Isaac is the "beloved son" of his father,[15] which foreshadows the Baptism and Transfiguration of Our Lord, when God the Father calls Christ his "beloved son."[16] There are many more connections, and the following chart shows several:

LIKENESS	ISAAC	CHRIST
Beloved son	Gn 22: 2	Mt 3: 17; 17: 5
Son of Abraham	Gn 21: 3	Mt 1: 1
Offered in sacrifice by his loving father	Gn 22: 2	Mt 27: 35; Mk 15: 24; Lk 23: 33
Sacrifice on Mt. Moriah, later location of Jerusalem	Gn 22: 2 (cf. 2 Chr 3: 1)	Mt 16: 21-23
Carried wood to his sacrifice	Gn 22: 6	Jn 19: 17
Bound to the wood	Gn 22: 9	Jn 19: 18-19
Resurrected or saved from the sacrifice	Gn 22: 4 (cf. Heb 11: 17-19)	Mt 16: 21; 17: 23; 20: 19

These similarities are not mere coincidences; they help our understanding of each event. The anguish of Abraham at having to sacrifice his beloved son helps us to understand more deeply the sacrifice by God the Father in allowing his beloved Son to be crucified for our sake. The Resurrection of Christ shows us the great faith of Abraham, for, as the Epistle to the Hebrews reveals, "[Abraham] considered that God was able to raise men even from the dead; hence, figuratively speaking, he did receive him back" (Heb 11:19).

Typology helps us to unlock the mysteries of the Bible. By seeing the rhythms within God's plan of salvation, we are able to understand more deeply the persons and events within it.

Isaac Bears the Wood for His Sacrifice by Tissot.

> After the unity of the human race was shattered by sin God at once sought to save humanity part by part. The covenant with Noah after the flood gives expression to the principle of the divine economy toward the "nations," in other words, towards men grouped "in their lands, each with [its] own language, by their families, in their nations."[14] (CCC 56)

With Noah, this second chance took the form of a covenant that revealed God's mercy.

Though the covenant that God made with Noah did not remove the effects of Original Sin—our desire to sin (*concupiscence*) and death—God did urge Noah and his descendants to be faithful to his laws, which were intended to lead people to lives of blessing and prosperity. Though the Flood gave us a new beginning in our relationship with God, this "cleansing" only temporarily arrested the spread of evil. Only Christ's definitive Sacrifice on the Cross defeats evil once and for all.

GOD'S COVENANT WITH ABRAHAM: THE PROMISE OF A GREAT NATION

The remainder of Genesis deals with the four generations of patriarchs: Abraham, Isaac, Esau, and Jacob (later renamed Israel) and the twelve sons of Jacob, the progenitors of the Twelve Tribes of Israel.

A *patriarch* is a father figure of an extended family, or clan, that may include a multitude of servants or slaves needed to tend large herds and flocks. The constant need to feed and water these animals made life in the Hebrews' patriarchal system necessarily nomadic.

The first biblical patriarch in Genesis was the leader of one of these family units. God's plan for our salvation began to take definite shape when God revealed himself to Abram, whom he later renamed Abraham. Abraham is called the "father of faith,"[17] for he followed God in spite of hardship and difficulty. God had a definitive plan for Abraham and promised him that it would be through his descendants that his plan of salvation for the whole human race would be accomplished.

> **The LORD said to Abram, "Go from your country and your kindred and your father's house to the land that I will show you. And I will make of you a great nation, and I will bless you, and make your name great, so that you will be a blessing. I will bless those who bless you, and him who curses you I will curse; and by you all the families of the earth shall bless themselves." So Abram went, as the LORD had told him.** (Gn 12:1-4a)

Abraham, Sarah, and the Angel by Provost. Abraham is called the "father of faith," for he followed God in spite of hardship and difficulty.

In this message to Abraham, God promised, "All the families of the earth shall bless themselves." That is, God's offer of salvation eventually would be extended to all peoples; it would not always be limited to a certain race or tribe. The promise made to Abraham passed on to his son Isaac, and then to Isaac's son Jacob, whom God later renamed Israel. Jacob then had twelve sons, among them his particular favorite, Joseph.

The biblical narrative of Joseph is also well known: Joseph's brothers were so jealous of him that they sold him into slavery—some of them wanted to murder him outright—but told his father that he had been killed by wild beasts. Joseph's captors eventually took him to Egypt, where he found favor with the

Joseph Explains the Dreams of Pharaoh by Guignet.
"Then Joseph said to Pharaoh,'...It is as I told Pharaoh, God has shown to Pharaoh what he is about to do. There will come seven years of great plenty throughout all the land of Egypt, but after them there will arise seven years of famine, and all the plenty will be forgotten in the land of Egypt;...for it will be very grievous.'" (Gn 41:25-31)

Egyptian king, or *Pharaoh*, because God had given him the gift of interpreting dreams. Eventually, he was put in charge of all Egypt. When a famine struck the land—which Joseph had predicted—Egypt was prepared with storehouses of grain because of Joseph's foresight. His family came to Egypt to buy grain, and Joseph eventually revealed himself as their lost brother. Pharaoh invited Joseph's family to live in Egypt, where they prospered.

In time the descendants of Jacob (Israel) grew numerous and became known as the Israelites. They were divided into Twelve Tribes after the twelve sons of Jacob. These tribes functioned almost like provinces within the people of Israel. Here we see God's plan more completely: He would use the nation of Israel as the means by which "all the families of the earth" shall be blessed.

Their prosperity in Egypt came to an end after a later Pharaoh, fearful of the Israelites' great numbers, enslaved them and forced them into labor. They remained in that state until God called another patriarch, Moses, to lead his people out of their slavery.

GOD'S COVENANT WITH MOSES: THE TEN COMMANDMENTS

God's plan of salvation and his self-Revelation took a significant leap with Moses. God revealed to Moses both fundamental truths about himself and the particular laws governing how he expected his people to live.

One of the most important events in all human history is the encounter between Moses and God in the burning bush:

> [The voice] said, "I am the God of your father, the God of Abraham, the God of Isaac, and the God of Jacob."...And now, behold, the cry of the people of Israel has come to me, and I have seen the oppression with which the Egyptians oppress them. Come, I will send you to Pharaoh that you may bring forth my people, the sons of Israel, out of Egypt." But Moses said to God, "Who am I that I should go to Pharaoh, and bring the sons of Israel out of Egypt?" He said, "But I will be with you; and this shall be the sign for you, that I have sent you: when you have brought forth the people out of Egypt, you shall serve God upon this mountain." Then Moses said to God, "If I come

Moses and the Burning Bush by Raphael.
Even the grammar of I AM WHO I AM conveys God's eternity as one who is always in the present and has always existed.

to the people of Israel and say to them, 'The God of your fathers has sent me to you,' and they ask me, 'What is his name?' what shall I say to them?" God said to Moses, "I AM WHO I AM." And he said, "Say this to the people of Israel, 'I AM has sent me to you.'" (Ex 3: 6, 9-14)

When Moses asked God for his name, he responded: "I AM WHO I AM." By saying this, God revealed that he is not like the pagan "gods" of other nations, manmade idols with familiar names as well as humanlike faults and weaknesses. Nor is he just one "god" out of many. No; God is one God, ineffable, whose very name supersedes all comprehension and defies description. In fact, he is existence itself...he simply "is who is." Even the grammar of I AM WHO I AM conveys his eternal nature as one who is always in the present and has always existed.

This Revelation was a major breakthrough in the history of religion. No longer could God be thought of as kind of "national god." Every one of the pagan peoples who populated the world at that time had its own deity or deities. The God of Israel had revealed himself as above all things and the source of all things.

God, nonetheless, was not finished revealing himself to Moses. He also wanted to communicate what it meant to live an authentically human life. Through Moses, God formed the people of Israel into a tight-knit nation and unveiled a system of morality and a system of worship reflected in the *Ten Commandments* (or *Decalogue*) and the *Mosaic Law.*

These two pillars of the Law—morality and worship—would shape the people of Israel throughout her history. They would set Israel apart from the other nations, calling them to be an example by which all peoples would come to know the Lord. They were to be a holy and priestly people.

> **After the patriarchs, God formed Israel as his people by freeing them from slavery in Egypt. He established with them the covenant of Mount Sinai and, through Moses, gave them his law so that they would recognize him and serve him as the one living and true God, the provident Father and just judge, and so that they would look for the promised Savior.**[18] (CCC 62)

TEN COMMANDMENTS

COMMANDMENT (Exodus 20:1-17)	CCC Reference
1. I am the LORD your God, who brought you out of the land of Egypt, out of the house of bondage. You shall have no other gods before me. You shall not make for yourself a graven image, or any likeness of anything that is in heaven above, or that is in the earth beneath, or that is in the water under the earth; you shall not bow down to them or serve them. (Ex 20:1-5)	CCC 2084-2141
2. You shall not take the name of the LORD your God in vain. (Ex 20:1-5)	CCC 2142-2167
3. Remember the sabbath day, to keep it holy. Six days you shall labor, and do all your work; but the seventh day is a sabbath to the LORD your God; in it you shall not do any work. (Ex 20:8-10)	CCC 2168-2195
4. Honor your father and your mother, that your days may be long in the land which the LORD your God gives you. (Ex 20:12)	CCC 2197-2257
5. You shall not kill. (Ex 20:13)	CCC 2258-2330
6. You shall not commit adultery. (Ex 20:14)	CCC 2331-2400
7. You shall not steal. (Ex 20:15)	CCC 2401-2463
8. You shall not bear false witness against your neighbor. (Ex 20:16)	CCC 2464-2513
9. You shall not covet your neighbor's house; you shall not covet your neighbor's wife, or his manservant, or his maidservant, or his ox, or his ass, or anything that is your neighbor's. (Ex 20:17)	CCC 2514-2533
10. You shall not covet…anything that is your neighbor's…. You shall not desire your neighbor's house, his field, or his manservant, or his maidservant, or his ox, or his ass, or anything that is your neighbor's. (Ex 20:17)	CCC 2534-2557

Adoration of the Golden Calf by Poussin.
The Book of Leviticus, along with much of the Book of Deuteronomy, details regulations and norms regarding the proper worship of God.

> Israel is the priestly people of God, "called by the name of the LORD," and "the first to hear the word of God,"[19] the people of "elder brethren" in the faith of Abraham. (CCC 63)

We often think of Moses as simply the lawgiver, the one through whom God gave the Ten Commandments and other moral teachings. But if we examine the *Pentateuch* (the first five books of the Old Testament) carefully, we see that it is dominated by rules and regulations surrounding when and how to worship. In fact, when God first established a covenant with Moses, founded on the covenant with Abraham, he told Moses: "If you will obey my voice and keep my covenant, you shall be my own possession among all peoples; for all the earth is mine, and you shall be to me a *kingdom of priests* and a holy nation."[20]

God's Chosen People were being formed in such a way that they would all be priests who worshiped God in all things. Israel, however, proved to be an unfaithful people. While Moses was on the mountain receiving God's Revelation, many of the people fell into the practice of idolatry, forging a golden calf as a false god for their worship, an act that had the collaboration even of Aaron, Moses' brother. Because of this, God designated the men of the Tribe of Levi to be his priestly order to govern and lead the worship of Israel.[21] The Book of Leviticus, along with much of Deuteronomy, details regulations and norms regarding the Levites' worship of God.

GOD'S PROMISE TO DAVID

Sadly, idolatry and unfaithfulness would continue to occur throughout Israel, even among many of her leaders, and the people of Israel would fail to live up to God's laws and his plans for them. But God did not abandon his people, regardless of their sins; in fact, he continued to reveal himself to them and and renew his covenant with his people precisely in response to these great falls. Like a doctor who prescribes more medicines the sicker a patient becomes, God intervened more and more in order to lead Israel on the road to salvation.

This infidelity to God's covenant had a corrupting effect throughout Israel. Ruled first by Joshua, successor to Moses, and then by a series of judges, the nation became bitterly divided along tribal lines.

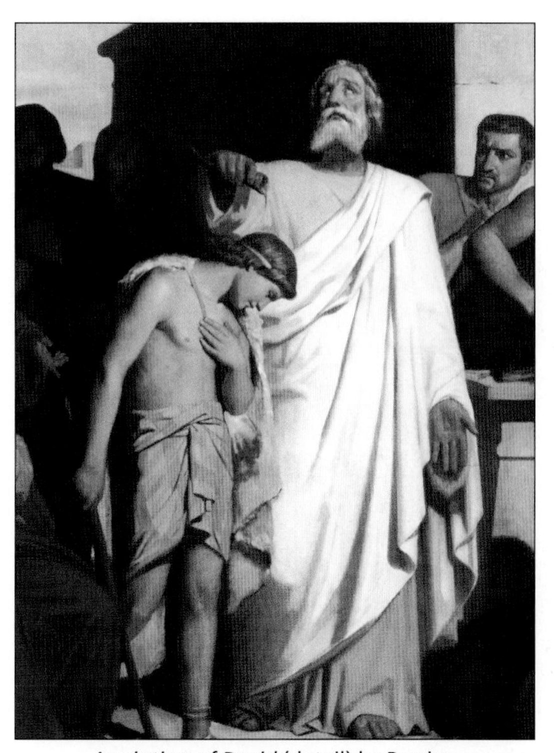

Anointing of David (detail) by Barrias.
"And the LORD said, 'Arise, anoint him; for this is he.'
Then Samuel took the horn of oil,
and anointed him in the midst of his brothers;
and the Spirit of the LORD came mightily upon David
from that day forward." (1 Sm 16: 12-13)

In a desperate bid to restore unity, the people of Israel petitioned God to anoint for them a king to rule them like other nations.[22]

God acceded to their wish and had his prophet Samuel anoint Saul as the first King of Israel. The tribes, however, failed to unite under Saul, and Saul fell into sin. God then chose David to succeed him.

David was a king "after [God's] own heart."[23] After some struggles, David succeeded in uniting all the tribes into one nation. He established Jerusalem as the capital and decided to build a temple there. God made David and his heirs "sons of God"[24] who would have everlasting reign over the earth:

> **When your days are fulfilled and you lie down with your fathers, I will raise up your offspring after you, who shall come forth from your body, and I will establish his kingdom. He shall build a house for my name, and I will establish the throne of his kingdom for ever. I will be his father, and he shall be my son. When he commits iniquity, I will chasten him with the rod of men, with the stripes of the sons of men; but I will not take my steadfast love from him, as I took it from Saul, whom I put away from before you. And your house and your kingdom shall be made sure for ever before me; your throne shall be established for ever." (2 Sm 7: 12-16)**

Like the other promises and covenants that God had established with Israel, this "house" pointed to a final covenant that would fulfill all the promises that God had made to his people. Although beloved by God, David would not be the complete fulfillment of God's plans, as he, too, struggled with sin. It would take a descendant of his to bring this plan to final perfection. Through his promises to David, God prepared the world for the fullness of his Revelation so that those who are open to him might accept it.

FROM DAVID TO THE MESSIAH

As a loving Father, God continually intervened in the life of the Israelites to help them follow his will. Even though the history of the Old Testament shows continual failures to be faithful to God on the part of his people, God did not reject them or turn his face away from them. Instead, God used those failures as means to reveal his love and mercy more deeply.

David's son and successor as king, Solomon, would complete the building of the Temple. It appeared that God's promises to Israel were coming to fulfillment. But then everything went wrong: Solomon and the people, influenced by their pagan neighbors, dabbled again in idolatry, and a war broke out that divided the kingdom. The ten tribes in the north called their kingdom Israel, while the two southern tribes around the capital of Jerusalem called their kingdom Judah. From this latter name the religion of the Chosen People became known as Judaism, and the people became known as Jews.

In the eighth century BC, the Northern Kingdom fell to Assyria, and the people of the ten tribes there were exiled or assimilated into the dominating pagan culture. In the sixth century BC, Judah fell to Babylon, and Jerusalem and the Temple were destroyed and defiled. After two generations of exile, however, the people were allowed to return to reestablish the Jewish state. A few centuries later the Greeks conquered Judah, and later still Judah would came under the rule of the Roman Empire. This painful history—the divided kingdom, the loss of the Northern Kingdom, the conquest of Jerusalem, the

Jeremiah Lamenting the Destruction of Jerusalem by Ebert.
"The LORD is good to those who wait for him, to the soul that seeks him.
It is good that one should wait quietly for the salvation of the LORD." (Lam 3: 25-26)

experience of exile, and oppression by foreign occupiers—served to increase the longing of Israel for the redemption promised by God.

Throughout this period of history, God sent a number of *prophets* to the Chosen People to reveal the truth about him. These prophets—Isaiah, Jeremiah, Elijah, and others—always directed Israel back to obedience to God's Commandments and to the proper worship of him. They also reminded Israel that God would fulfill his promises one day and encouraged them to remain faithful to his covenants. God brought salvation to them eventually through his promised Redeemer.

REVELATION IN THE NEW TESTAMENT

CHRIST, THE FULLNESS OF REVELATION

We see how God's plan of salvation is progressive, leading humanity step by step into a deeper knowledge of him. Over time, God revealed to the world his plan for us: that we would become children of God, royal priests who would be a blessing to the world and would be able to overcome the power of sin and death. And in the fullness of time, God sent his Son, Jesus Christ, to fulfill this plan.

> "When the time had fully come, God sent forth his Son, born of a woman, born under the law, to redeem those who were under the law, so that we might receive adoption as sons."[25] This is "the gospel of Jesus Christ, the Son of God":[26] God has visited his people. He has fulfilled the promise he made to Abraham and his descendants. He acted far beyond all expectation—he has sent his own "beloved Son."[27] (CCC 422)

All of salvation history is directed toward and fulfilled by Jesus Christ. He is the true Son of God, the one by whom all the nations will be blessed. He is the climax of the story of God's love for the world.

> **He is the image of the invisible God, the first-born of all creation; for in him all things were created, in heaven and on earth, visible and invisible, whether thrones or dominions or principalities or authorities—all things were created through him and for him.**

> **He is before all things, and in him all things hold together.**
> **He is the head of the body, the church; he is the beginning, the first-born from the dead, that in everything he might be pre-eminent.**
> **For in him all the fulness of God was pleased to dwell.** (Col 1:15-19)

The identity of Jesus Christ as the Son of God is revealed through a series of events in Christ's life. When the Archangel Gabriel announced to the Blessed Virgin Mary that she was to bear a Son, he proclaimed that this child was like no other child born of woman:

> **"Do not be afraid, Mary, for you have found favor with God. And behold, you will conceive in your womb and bear a son, and you shall call his name Jesus. He will be great, and will be called the Son of the Most High;**
> **and the Lord God will give to him the throne of his father David,**
> **and he will reign over the house of Jacob for ever;**
> **and of his kingdom there will be no end."** (Lk 1:30-33)

At the beginning of Christ's public ministry, following his baptism by John the Baptist, his identity was affirmed again by a direct Revelation of God the Father:

> **When Jesus was baptized, he went up immediately from the water, and behold, the heavens were opened and he saw the Spirit of God descending like a dove, and alighting on him; and lo, a voice from heaven, saying, "This is my beloved Son, with whom I am well pleased."** (Mt 3:16-17)

Simon Peter, the leader of the Apostles and their spokesman, received a Revelation of the identity of Christ when he asked his closest followers, "Who do you say that I am?"

> **Simon Peter replied, "You are the Christ, the Son of the living God." And Jesus answered him, "Blessed are you, Simon Bar-Jona! For flesh and blood has not revealed this to you, but my Father who is in heaven."** (Mt 16:16-17)

Baptism of Christ by Grebber.
"This is my beloved Son,
with whom I am well pleased."

The word *Christ* means "the Anointed One." A scriptural anointing meant to be smeared literally with sacred oil. In the Old Testament prophets anointed the divinely appointed Kings of Israel with oil, and after each anointing the king received the Spirit of God so as to enable him to fulfill his sacred mission. They were sometimes called "the anointed." Where the Old Testament offers prophecies of "the anointed one," Christians see these as indicating the coming of the *Messiah* (Hebrew for "the Anointed One"), the Redeemer, who will be anointed with the Spirit of God by God himself. So when Simon Peter called Jesus "the Christ," he was announcing his faith in Jesus as the Messiah, the Anointed One foretold by the prophets.

By calling Jesus the "Son of the Living God," Simon Peter professed belief in his divinity: Jesus is the true Son of God. Christ's response affirmed the truth of what he had just professed.

Christ also made his own proclamation of his identity: "Before Abraham was, I am,"[28] and, "I and the Father are one."[29] He also frequently referred to God as his Father and addressed God directly with that term. Through these Revelations we see that Christ is more than just another prophet, or another priest, or another king. He is God the Son, who is the preeminent Priest, Prophet, and King, the one to whom all previous priests, prophets, and kings were directed. He is the fullness of Revelation.

> For a Christian, believing in God cannot be separated from believing in the One he sent, his "beloved Son," in whom the Father is "well pleased"; God tells us to listen to him.[30] The Lord himself said to his disciples: "Believe in God, believe also in me."[31] We can believe in Jesus Christ because he is himself God, the Word made flesh: "No one has ever seen God; the only Son, who is in the bosom of the Father, he has made him known."[32] Because he "has seen the Father," Jesus Christ is the only one who knows him and can reveal him.[33] (CCC 151)

All the Revelations of God in the Old Testament were true, but they were incomplete. They revealed aspects of God's nature, but much of God's mystery remained hidden. With Christ, we can now see God, for Christ reveals him completely. One attribute of God that was hidden in the Old Testament but revealed in Christ is that God is a Trinity of Persons.

The Holy Trinity (detail) by Cairo.
The doctrine of the Blessed Trinity shapes and defines all of our dealings with God.

CHRIST REVEALS THE TRINITY, A SIGN OF UNITY

By sending his Son, God also revealed the central mystery about himself, the central mystery of our faith: the *Blessed Trinity*.

Christ, the Son of God and Second Person of the Trinity, revealed to us more of his Father, the First Person of the Trinity, as well as the Holy Spirit, the Third Person of the Trinity, whom he promised to send[34] after he ascended to the Father. At Pentecost, just as Christ had promised, the Holy Spirit descended upon the Apostles.[35] So the Father sent the Son to redeem the world, and the Son sent the Holy Spirit to sanctify and guide the Church in his truth. This dual "sending" in history reflects the eternal relations within the Godhead itself: The Father generates the Son, and from the Father and the Son the Holy Spirit proceeds.

An important concept arises from these truths: God is One, but he is not alone; he is a *communion* of Persons. Father, Son, and Holy Spirit live eternally in perfect union and yet distinct in three divine Persons.

The Trinity is a doctrine unique to Christianity. Human reason alone cannot deduce the doctrine of the Trinity; God must reveal it to us. Human efforts to understand divine realities have posited that there are many gods (*polytheism*) or that there is only one God (*monotheism*), but never could we have conceived of the mystery of the Blessed Trinity. It is a truth that cannot be fully grasped but must be accepted on faith.

THE EPIPHANY OF OUR LORD

Immediately after the Fall of our first parents, God began to put into place his plan for our salvation. This plan, like the mustard seed in Christ's parable (cf. Mt 13: 31-32), began small and grew over time. Eventually, it encompassed the whole world. First, God chose Abraham and his family to be the ones in whom the promise of salvation would reside. For centuries, God worked with the Chosen People to prepare the world for the coming of his Son.

The Jewish people conceived of the world as separated into two groups: Jews and Gentiles. Gentiles were simply non-Jews and, therefore, not recipients of God's promises. But even in the Old Testament we see traces of God's plan to extend his salvation to all peoples. For example, the Lord told the prophet Isaiah that he would be a prophet not just to the Israelites. Rather, God told him, "I will give you as a light to the nations, that my salvation may reach to the end of the earth" (Is 49: 6). This prophecy comes to its fulfillment in Jesus Christ. With the advent of Christ, God's plan extends to all peoples, regardless of their nationality or race. Christ is "a light for revelation to the Gentiles" (Lk 2: 32) by which God's love is manifested to all the nations.

Adoration of the Magi (detail) by Lorenzo.

On January 6, or the nearest Sunday in some dioceses, the Church celebrates this "manifestation" in a special way. The Epiphany of the Lord commemorates the public manifestation of Christ, including the event when the Magi—who were Gentiles—recognized the universal kingship of Christ. Led by God through their study of the stars, these men came from afar to offer gifts of gold, frankincense, and myrrh to the newborn king. They did not know the ancient Jewish prophecies, so they had to ask King Herod where the King of the Jews would be born. They were not members of the Chosen People. God chose them as the first non-Jews to adore his Son. In this way, he manifested his plan of salvation beyond the Jewish people to all nations.

This doctrine of the Blessed Trinity shapes and defines all our dealings with God. As St. John the Apostle put it simply, "God is love":[36] the love of the Father for the Son and the Son for the Father. This love is so real that from it proceeds another Person, the Holy Spirit. Human families model this reality in a limited way: A husband and a wife love each other so much that their expression of love produces a child. Of course, in the mystery of the Trinity, the Holy Spirit exists eternally, and the generation of a human child does not fully reflect this.

> The mystery of the Most Holy Trinity is the central mystery of Christian faith and life. It is the mystery of God in himself. It is therefore the source of all the other mysteries of faith, the light that enlightens them. It is the most fundamental and essential teaching in the "hierarchy of the truths of faith."[37] The whole history of salvation is identical with the history of the way and the means by which the one true God, Father, Son and Holy Spirit, reveals himself to men "and reconciles and unites with himself those who turn away from sin."[38] (CCC 234)

Salvation history itself is an expression of the Blessed Trinity: God is a loving Father who created the human race and raised us up to be his sons and daughters. He sent his Son, Jesus Christ, God the Son, to be our model and to save us from our sins. Finally, he sent his Holy Spirit to the world to guide his people until the end of time. At all times, God is guiding his wayward children lovingly back to himself.

THE END OF PUBLIC REVELATION

Since Jesus Christ is the fullness of God's Revelation, there is no need for further public revelation after the death of his Apostles, who lived and traveled with Christ and learned from him directly. All that is necessary for our salvation has been given to us; nothing further can be added.

> "The Christian economy, therefore, since it is the new and definitive Covenant, will never pass away; and no new public revelation is to be expected before the glorious manifestation of our Lord Jesus Christ."[39] (CCC 66)

The completion of Divine Revelation, however, does not mean that we have a complete understanding of that Revelation, for finite human reason can never complete the task of unlocking the mysteries of the infinite God. The *Catechism* continues:

> Yet even if Revelation is already complete, it has not been made completely explicit; it remains for Christian faith gradually to grasp its full significance over the course of the centuries. (CCC 66)

It is the task of Christians to understand more deeply and to follow the Revelation given by God in Jesus Christ. This is not a task only for a certain time, or only for certain people. It is a task for all the People of God until Christ will come again in glory at the end of time.

The Vision of St. John (detail) by Cano. St. John the Evangelist, the Beloved Disciple, was the last Apostle to die and the only Apostle who was not martyred. He died peacefully ca. AD 100.

Put more simply: Although God has already revealed everything he wishes to reveal to the world, his faithful on earth are still seeking to understand his Revelation in a deeper and more complete way. This is why Christ established his Church, gave his Church the authority to teach in his name, and sent his Holy Spirit upon the Church: "When the Spirit of truth comes, he will guide you into all the truth."[40]

CONCLUSION

Every person knows, in the depths of his or her heart, that he or she is made for more than this world. All that we see around us, while beautiful and glorious in many respects, is imperfect. We yearn for something beyond what we see; we yearn for *someone* beyond ourselves. We were created for God, and, as St. Augustine famously wrote, "Our hearts are restless until they rest in Thee."[41] But God did not leave us alone in our yearnings; he did not abandon us to this imperfect world. Since our original rejection of him, he has been gradually preparing everyone to be reconciled to him and to have a clear path to eternal bliss with him. This is the plan of salvation.

Initiated right after the Fall, it began with the *Protoevangelium*—the "First Gospel"—and continued with God's covenants with his people through Noah, Abraham, and Moses. God then directed his people through the *prophets*, always pointing them to the eventual perfect climax of his plans—the sending of his beloved Son, Jesus Christ. In Christ, God's plan reaches its fulfillment, and the Revelation of God's identity as a Trinity of Divine Persons is given to us. After the Ascension of Christ into heaven, God sent his Holy Spirit to guide us into an ever deeper understanding of his Revelation until the end of time.

Who is God, then? He is a Father who loves us so dearly that he was willing to sacrifice his beloved Son to save us from our own sins. He is not a distant God but one who reveals himself to us intimately for the sake of our salvation.

CHALLENGES

How can we say that the Church, the Sacrament of Salvation, was part of God's plan from the beginning?

Christians of the first centuries said, "The world was created for the sake of the Church."[42] God created human beings so that they might live in perfect communion with him, sharing in his divine life. This original state of communion with God—enjoyed by our first parents—prefigures the Church. That communion, however, was broken by Original Sin, our first parents' free decision to disobey God.

Christ Handing the Keys to St. Peter (detail) by Rubens. Christ established a hierarchy and a Magisterium, led by St. Peter and his successors, that would be guaranteed always to proclaim the truth under the guidance of the Holy Spirit.

After the Fall of Adam and Eve, God immediately desired to save us and began to reveal his plan of salvation. He promised a Redeemer, the seed of the woman, who would "bruise" the head of the serpent (cf. Gn 3:15). He began to call his people together, to "regather" them into one. He began to reveal himself, making covenants and promises with his chosen patriarchs and leaders in order to form them into a communion with himself and with one another, instructing his people in the moral law that they were to follow. In this way, he formed the People of Israel, who also prefigure the Catholic Church, which was instituted by Christ, the Son of God and Redeemer of the world.

The Church established by Christ is more than just the regathering of God's faithful people. She is the Sacrament of Salvation. Christ gave the Church the sacred responsibility of continuing his mission of salvation on earth, teaching the Gospel to the ends of the earth, and making disciples of all nations, "baptizing them in the name of the Father and of the Son and of the Holy Spirit."[43] The Church is not an exclusive club of the "select." Everyone—Jews and Gentiles, people of all nations, races, and tongues—is invited to enter into this communion. God desires that all people be united in communion with him and with one another forever.

To accomplish this, Christ founded his Church and empowered her with the means to bring about this communion. He established a hierarchy and a Magisterium, led by St. Peter and his successors, that would be guaranteed to proclaim the truth always under the guidance of the Holy Spirit. He instituted a ministerial priesthood that would dispense his divine life through the Sacraments, particularly Baptism, which cleanses us of Original Sin and fills us with sanctifying grace, and the Eucharist, by which we share in his Body and Blood. In this way, members of the Church comprise the Mystical Body of Christ. They are united to Christ, the Head of his Mystical Body, and with one another.

The Church on earth, part of the Mystical Body of Christ, prefigures the Church as it exists for all eternity in heaven: the perfect communion of the blessed in heaven with God the Father, the Son, and the Holy Spirit.

As we can see, then, the Catholic Church is at once both the remedy for the fallen state of sinful humanity and the original plan that God had in mind. The Catholic Church exists for the simple reason that every human person is created by God to be united both to God and, through him, with others. The Church, which is the Family of God, makes this communion possible.

PILLARS OF THE FAITH

POPE BENEDICT XVI

Long before he was elected to the papacy in 2005, Joseph Cardinal Ratzinger—later elected Pope Benedict XVI—had long been regarded as one of the premier theologians of the Church in the modern era.

Born in Marktl am Inn, Germany, in 1927, Joseph Ratzinger was ordained to the priesthood in 1951 and earned his doctorate in theology two years later. He went on to teach theology at leading German universities for two decades and served as a *peritus*, or expert advisor, to Josef Cardinal Frings during the sessions of the Second Ecumenical Council of the Vatican, 1962-1965. He was named Archbishop of Munich and Freising by St. Paul VI in 1977.

Four years later, St. John Paul II named him prefect of the Congregation for the Doctrine of the Faith and of the International Theological Commission, and in this position he became the pontiff's most trusted advisor. He presided over the preparation of the new *Catechism of the Catholic Church* and presented the volume to the Pope in 1992 after six years of collaborative work. He continued to serve as the Vatican's chief of doctrine until the death of St. John Paul II and his own election in 2005 as the 264th successor to St. Peter as Bishop of Rome. He resigned the papacy in 2013.

The theological reflections offered by Benedict XVI throughout his life have been profound and wide-ranging, but one particular topic he has explored is that of the relationship between the covenants of the Old Testament and the New Covenant in Christ. In his 1998 book *Many Religions—One Covenant: Israel, the Church and the World*, he wrote of a "theology of covenant" that forever links the covenant with Abraham with the Christian covenant.

Pope Benedict XVI.
The theological reflections offered by Pope Benedict throughout his life have been profound and wide-ranging.

The covenant that God made with the people through Moses in the Mosaic Law was intended to be provisional, or temporary, as God gradually formed his Chosen People. The people of Israel, however, broke this covenant by continually falling into sin and idolatry—the worship of false gods—and thus often seemed to lose the blessings that God had promised through the covenant that they had broken.

Continued

POPE BENEDICT XVI

Continued

When Christ celebrated his Last Supper with the Apostles, he said the chalice was a "new covenant in my blood" (Lk 22: 20). These words recall the Old Testament prophecy of Jeremiah, who prophesied that God would establish a "new covenant" for the people of Israel to replace the one "which they broke." Through this new covenant, the people would know God and he would "forgive their iniquity" (Jer 31: 31-34). Yet, that does not mean there is some kind of dividing line between the Old and New Covenant: Cardinal Ratzinger referred to a "dynamic unity" in salvation history in which the "eternally valid" covenant of Abraham is now perfectly fulfilled in Christ.

So there is a continuity among the covenants. Just as Christ said he came "not to abolish but to fulfill" the Law and the prophets (Mt 5: 17), so, too, does his New Covenant fulfill rather than void the Old Covenant.

This is a very important point when it comes to dialogue between Jews and Christians. This "theology of covenant" looks at the blessings of Israel not as something that was taken away from the Chosen People but as something that came to its fulfillment in Christ according to God's plan of salvation. The covenant with Abraham is enshrined and perfected in the New Covenant in Christ. The promised blessing of a "multitude of nations" is fulfilled in Christ and his Church, which proclaims the Gospel message throughout the world so that every person has the opportunity to become a member of the People of God, the "children of Abraham." Whereas once there was one Chosen People, the people of Israel, who enjoyed God's favor, there is today only one People of God—the Church, the Body of Christ—into which Jew and Gentile alike is welcome. As the future Pope wrote in *Many Religions—One Covenant*, "The mission of Jesus is to unite Jews and pagans into a single People of God."

Indeed, this also has implications for unity among Christians as well as in outreach to people of every faith or even no faith. Christ should be seen not as roadblock to unity but as its very pathway. All are called into the one People of God, for it is through Christ that "the God of Israel has become the God of the nations," wrote Cardinal Ratzinger. As St. Paul wrote to the Ephesians:

> [Christ] is our peace, who has made us both one, and has broken down the dividing wall of hostility, by abolishing in his flesh the law of commandments and ordinances, that he might create in himself one new man in place of the two, so making peace, and might reconcile us both to God in one body through the cross, thereby bringing the hostility to an end. (Eph 2: 14-16)

In gratitude for his pontificate, Pope Emeritus Benedict XVI received an icon of *Our Lady of Humility* from Pope Francis.

SUPPLEMENTARY READING

God Chose to Reveal Himself and to Make Known His Will

2. In His goodness and wisdom God chose to reveal Himself and to make known to us the hidden purpose of His will (see Eph 1: 9) by which through Christ, the Word made flesh, man might in the Holy Spirit have access to the Father and come to share in the divine nature (see Eph 2: 18; 2 Pt 1: 4). Through this revelation, therefore, the invisible God (see Col 1: 15; 1 Tm 1: 17) out of the abundance of His love speaks to men as friends (see Ex 33: 11; Jn 15: 14-15) and lives among them (see Bar 3: 38), so that He may invite and take them into fellowship with Himself. This plan of revelation is realized by deeds and words having an inner unity: the deeds wrought by God in the history of salvation manifest and confirm the teaching and realities signified by the words, while the words proclaim the deeds and clarify the mystery contained in them. By this revelation then, the deepest truth about God and the salvation of man shines out for our sake in Christ, who is both the mediator and the fullness of all revelation.

— Second Ecumenical Council of the Vatican, Dogmatic Constitution on Divine Revelation *Dei Verbum*, no. 2

Saving Ecumenism from Itself

The Fathers of the Second Ecumenical Council of the Vatican found ways of showing how that Church could and should pursue ecumenism. Four important insights, all expressed by Vatican II, undergirded the commitment of Catholics to this new apostolate.

First of all, the scandal of Christian division posed difficulties for the Catholic Church's own missionary work. It was a stumbling block that impeded what the council called "the most holy cause of proclaiming the gospel to every creature." Non-Christians often reacted to missionary efforts with the feeling that, before asking them to convert, the missionaries ought to agree among themselves about what Christianity is. Why should the past quarrels among European or American Christians, some asked, be visited upon young churches from other parts of the world? Did it make any sense for an African, for example, to join the Swedish Lutheran Church or to become a Southern Baptist?

In the second place, the Catholic Church recognized that the divisions among Christians impoverished her catholicity. She lacked the natural and cultural endowments that other Christians could have contributed if they were united with her. Catholicity required that all the riches of the nations should be gathered into the one Church and harvested for the glory of God.

Third, the fullness of Christianity in Catholicism did not imply that all other churches were devoid of truth and grace. For all their differences, they shared considerable commonalities in faith, worship, and ministerial order. The council taught, in fact, that non-Catholic churches and communions were "by no means deprived of significance and importance for the mystery of salvation" because the Holy Spirit could use them as instruments of grace. Vatican II, therefore, represents a sharp turn away from the purely negative evaluation of non-Catholic Christianity that was characteristic of the previous three centuries.

And fourth, the Catholic Church, insofar as she was made up of human members and administered by them, was always in need of purification and reform. Through ecumenical contacts, other Christian communities could help her to correct what was amiss, to supply what was lacking, and to update what was obsolete....

John Paul II consistently opposed styles of ecumenism that seemed to aim at settling for a least common denominator. In an address to the Roman Curia on June 28, 1980, he laid down the principle that "the unity of Christians cannot be sought in a 'compromise' between the various theological positions, but only in a common meeting in the most ample and mature fullness of Christian truth." In his encyclical *Ut Unum Sint* he proposed a better alternative. After stating that "the unity willed by God can be attained only by the adherence of all to the content of revealed truth in its entirety," he

SUPPLEMENTARY READING Continued

went on to say that dialogue is not merely an exchange of ideas but also, in some way, "an exchange of gifts." Later, in the same encyclical, he wrote: "Communion is made fruitful by the exchange of gifts between the churches insofar as they complement each other." In these words he called for a new chapter in the history of ecumenism....

With this mentality, Catholics would want to hear from the churches of the Reformation the reasons they have for speaking as they do of Christ alone, Scripture alone, grace alone, and faith alone, while Catholics tend to speak of Christ and the Church, Scripture and tradition, grace and cooperation, faith and works. We would want to learn from them how to make better use of the laity as sharers in the priesthood of the whole People of God. We would want to hear from evangelicals about their experience of conversion and from Pentecostals about perceiving the free action of the Holy Spirit in their lives. The Orthodox would have much to tell about liturgical piety, holy tradition, sacred images, and synodical styles of polity. We would not want any of these distinctive endowments of other ecclesial families to be muted or shunted aside for the sake of having shared premises or an agreed method.

Conversely, Catholics would not hesitate to go into the dialogue with the full panoply of beliefs, sustained by our own methods of certifying the truth of revelation. We are not ashamed of our reliance on tradition, the liturgy, the sense of the faithful, and our confidence in the judgment of the Magisterium.

One of the doctrines most distinctive to the Catholic Church is surely the primacy of the pope as the successor of Peter—a primacy that the First Vatican Council set forth in clear, uncompromising language. Because Catholics cherish this doctrine, we should not be content to keep it to ourselves. The successor of Peter, we believe, is intended by Christ to be the visible head of all Christians. Without accepting his ministry, Christians will never attain the kind of universal concord that God wills the Church to have as a sign and sacrament of unity. They will inevitably fall into conflict with one another regarding doctrine, discipline, and ways of worship. No church can simply institute for itself an office that has authority to pronounce finally on disputed doctrines. If it exists at all, this office must have been instituted by Christ and must enjoy the assistance of the Holy Spirit. The Petrine office is a precious gift that the Lord has given us not only for our own consolation but as something to be held in trust for the entire *oikoumene*.

—Avery Cardinal Dulles, "Saving Ecumenism from Itself," *First Things*, (New York, New York: The Institute on Religion and Public Life), December 2007

St. Peter by Rubens.
"One of the doctrines most distinctive to the Catholic Church is surely the primacy of the pope as the successor of Peter." —Avery Cardinal Dulles

VOCABULARY

BAPTISM
First of the Seven Sacraments; it gives access to the other Sacraments; first and chief Sacrament of the Forgiveness of Sins because the baptized Christian receives the remission of both personal sins and Original Sin. It incorporates the recipient into the Church, the Mystical Body of Christ.

BLESSED TRINITY
The mystery of one God in three Persons: Father, Son, and Holy Spirit.

CHOSEN PEOPLE
The name given to the people of Israel, the Israelites or Jews, to emphasize their unique relationship to God. They did not become his people because they earned it but because God chose them out of all the peoples to be his own.

CHURCH
The name given the assembly of people whom God has called together from the ends of the earth. This word has three meanings: the people that God gathers together, the local church (diocese), and the liturgical assembly. Also, the name given to a building used for public Christian worship.

CHRIST
From the Greek *christos*, "the anointed one." Used in reference to Jesus because he accomplished perfectly the divine mission of Priest, Prophet, and King.

COMMUNION
From the Latin for "mutual participation" or "oneness together": in the sense of Holy Communion, the reception of the Body and Blood of Christ in the Eucharist; in the sense of fellowship, the bond of union with Christ and all baptized, faithful Christians in the Church.

CONCUPISCENCE
The disordered human appetites or desires that remain even after Baptism due to the temporal consequences of Original Sin and which constitute an inclination to sin. This is often used to refer to desires resulting from strong sensual urges or attachment to things of this world.

COVENANT
A solemn agreement between people or between God and man involving mutual commitments and guarantees.

DIVINE ECONOMY
God's activity in creating and governing the world, particularly with regard to his plan for the salvation of the world in the Person and work of Jesus Christ, a plan which is being accomplished through his Body—the Church—in her life and Sacraments.

ECUMENICAL MOVEMENT
A movement of people that seeks unity among all Christians. The modern ecumenical movement was started in the early twentieth century and now includes Catholic, Orthodox, and Protestant Christians.

ECUMENISM
The task of healing the divisions and separations that afflict Christianity and restoring true unity as one Church.

EX NIHILO
Latin for "out of nothing." God created all things *ex nihilo*—there was nothing in existence except God before he began creation.

VOCABULARY Continued

ISRAELITES
The people chosen by God to be his people and inherit the promises of Abraham. This people is named after Israel (Jacob), from whose twelve sons the tribes of Israel descend. Judah is the son or tribe of Israel from whom the Jews descended and who retained the knowledge of God's laws.

MESSIAH
Hebrew for "anointed." This is used in reference to Jesus because he accomplished perfectly the divine mission of priest, prophet, and king, signified by his being anointed as Christ.

MONOTHEISM
The belief in only one God.

MOSAIC LAW
The Law given to Moses, primarily in the Ten Commandments.

MYSTERY
A divinely revealed truth whose very possibility cannot be rationally conceived before it is revealed and, after revelation, whose inner essence cannot be fully understood by the finite mind. Also, in Eastern Christianity, the name for a Sacrament.

NATURAL REASON
The ability of the human mind to deduce and learn from observation. Each person is given natural reason and can use it to determine that there is one God who created everything.

ORIGINAL SIN
Adam and Eve's abuse of their human freedom in disobeying God's command. As a consequence, they lost the grace of original holiness and justice, and became subject to the law of death; sin became universally present in the world; every person is born into this condition. This sin separated mankind from God, darkened the human intellect, weakened the human will, and introduced into human nature an inclination toward sin.

PATRIARCH
In Scripture, a father who leads a family or tribe. Abraham and his descendants, the founders of Israel, are known as the patriarchs.

PEDAGOGY
The method one uses to teach. "God communicates himself to man gradually. He prepares him to welcome by stages the supernatural Revelation that is to culminate in the person and mission of the incarnate Word, Jesus Christ." (CCC 53)

PENTATEUCH
Greek for "of five books." The five books of Moses (the first five of the Old Testament): Genesis, Exodus, Leviticus, Numbers, and Deuteronomy.

PHARAOH
In ancient times, the king of Egypt; often worshiped as a god by the Egyptian people.

POLYTHEISM
The belief that there are multiple gods. Most religions throughout history have been polytheistic.

PRIVATE REVELATION
A revelation made in the course of history which neither adds to, nor forms part of, the Deposit of Faith; rather, it helps people live out the faith more fully. Some (e.g., Fatima and Lourdes) have been recognized by the Church as authentic.

PROPHET
From the Greek *prophetes*, meaning one who speaks for. One who speaks to the people for God.

PROTOEVANGELIUM
From the Greek *proto* meaning "first" and *evaggelos* meaning "bringing good news." The first message of good news—the first Gospel—is Genesis 3:15 in which the promise of the Messiah and Redeemer is foretold.

PUBLIC REVELATION
Revelation given by God that applies to all peoples and is directly related to man's salvation. All Revelation found in Scripture and Sacred Tradition is public revelation.

VOCABULARY Continued

SALVATION HISTORY
The history of God's work in this world to save the human race. Due to Original Sin, all men and women were separated from God. However, God intervened in the world to restore man to himself. The climax of salvation history is the life, Death, and Resurrection of Jesus Christ.

TEN COMMANDMENTS
The Decalogue. The fundamental laws given by God at Mt. Sinai that govern divine and human relations.

THEOLOGY
The study of God and Divine Revelation.

TRINITY
See Blessed Trinity.

TRIUNE GOD
A description denoting that there is one God in three Persons. The three Persons of God are Father, Son, and Holy Spirit.

TYPE
An event or person in Scripture that points forward to a later event or person. The type has similar virtues or other qualities as its fulfillment. For example, the sacrifice of Isaac is a type for the sacrifice of Christ.

TYPOLOGY
The study of types in Scripture. The typology found in the Old Testament points to the New Testament fulfillment, which shows the unity of the divine plan of salvation.

The Resurrected Christ by Rosa.
"For what will it profit a man, if he gains the whole world and forfeits his life? Or what shall a man give in return for his life? For the Son of man is to come with his angels in the glory of his Father, and then he will repay every man for what he has done. Truly, I say to you, there are some standing here who will not taste death before they see the Son of man coming in his kingdom." (Mt 16:26-28)

STUDY QUESTIONS

1. What is ecumenism?
2. What does it mean to say that man is a religious being?
3. What is religion?
4. What is Divine Revelation?
5. How has God revealed himself?
6. What is salvation history?
7. Why does God reveal himself gradually over time?
8. When did God first promise that he would save us?
9. When did God's plan of salvation begin to take definite shape?
10. Who did God reveal himself as to Moses? What "name" did he give himself?
11. On what two pillars did God form Israel?
12. What did God do when his people fell?
13. Why were prophets sent by God?
14. What is the "fullness of time"?
15. What was St. Peter's reply to Christ's question, "Who do you say that I am?"
16. Who is the fullness of Revelation?
17. What does the Blessed Trinity say about who God is?
18. How do human families model the Blessed Trinity?
19. Has public revelation ended, and if so, when did it end?

PRACTICAL EXERCISES

1. In your Bible read about the establishment of one of the covenants listed in the chapter. List a way this covenant prefigured Christ's New Covenant. Quote the passage in which God gives a person that covenant.

2. Read the Second Vatican Council document *Dei Verbum* and write a one-page summary of it.

3. The Blessed Trinity is an eternal communion of Persons, which on earth is reflected in the Church and the family. Give at least one example of how each of these earthly communions reflects the Trinitarian communion of Persons.

FROM THE CATECHISM

28 In many ways, throughout history down to the present day, men have given expression to their quest for God in their religious beliefs and behavior: in their prayers, sacrifices, rituals, meditations, and so forth. These forms of religious expression, despite the ambiguities they often bring with them, are so universal that one may well call man a *religious being*:

> From one ancestor [God] made all nations to inhabit the whole earth, and he allotted the times of their existence and the boundaries of the places where they would live, so that they would search for God and perhaps grope for him and find him—though indeed he is not far from each one of us. For "in him we live and move and have our being."[44]

423 We believe and confess that Jesus of Nazareth, born a Jew of a daughter of Israel at Bethlehem at the time of King Herod the Great and the emperor Caesar Augustus, a carpenter by trade, who died crucified in Jerusalem under the procurator Pontius Pilate during the reign of the emperor Tiberius, is the eternal Son of God made man. He "came from God,"[45] "descended from heaven,"[46] and "came in the flesh."[47] For "the Word became flesh and dwelt among us, full of grace and truth; we have beheld his glory, glory as of the only Son from the Father.... And from his fullness have we all received, grace upon grace."[48]

424 Moved by the grace of the Holy Spirit and drawn by the Father, we believe in Jesus and confess: "You are the Christ, the Son of the living God."[49] On the rock of this faith confessed by St. Peter, Christ built his Church.[50]

ENDNOTES – CHAPTER ONE

1. Rom 1:20.
2. Cf. *Dei Filius*: DS 3015.
3. St. Irenæus, *Adv. hæres*. 3, 20, 2: PG 7/1, 944; cf. 3, 17, 1; 4, 12, 4; 4, 21, 3.
4. Gen. Litt., 4:27.
5. Cf. Gn 1:26.
6. Gn 1:1.
7. Cf. Council of Trent: DS 1511-1512.
8. *GCD* 51.
9. Gn 1:1; cf. Rom 8:18-23.
10. *Sermon* 99.5.
11. Cf. 1 Cor 15:21-22, 45; Phil 2:8; Rom 5:19-20.
12. Cf. Pius IX, *Ineffabilis Deus*: DS 2803; Council of Trent: DS 1573.
13. Gn 9:1.
14. Gn 10:5; cf. 9:9-10, 16; 10:20-31.
15. Gn 22:2.
16. Lk 3:22; Mt 17:5.
17. Cf. Gal 3:7.
18. Cf. *DV* 3.
19. Dt 28:10; Roman Missal, Good Friday, General Intercession VI; see also Ex 19:6.
20. Ex 19:5-6, emphasis added.
21. Ex 32:27-29.
22. 1 Sm 8:1-22.
23. 1 Sm 13:14.
24. Ps 2:7.
25. Gal 4:4-5.
26. Mk 1:1.
27. Mk 1:11; cf. Lk 1:55, 68.
28. Jn 8:58.
29. Jn 10:30.
30. Mk 1:11; cf. 9:7.
31. Jn 14:1.
32. Jn 1:18.
33. Jn 6:46; cf. Mt 11:27.
34. Cf. Jn 16:5-14.
35. Cf. Acts 2:1-13.
36. 1 Jn 4:8.
37. *GCD* 43.
38. *GCD* 47.
39. *DV* 4; cf. 1 Tm 6:14; Ti 2:13.
40. Jn 16:13.
41. *Confessions*, 1, 1.
42. *Pastor Hermæ*, Vision 2, 4, 1: PG 2, 899; cf. Aristides, *Apol.* 16, 6; St. Justin, *Apol.* 2, 7: PG 6, 456; Tertullian, *Apol.* 31, 3; 32, 1: PL 1, 508-509.
43. Mt 28:19.
44. Acts 17:26-28.
45. Jn 13:3.
46. Jn 3:13; 6:33.
47. 1 Jn 4:2.
48. Jn 1:14, 16.
49. Mt 16:16.
50. Cf. Mt 16:18; St. Leo the Great, *Sermo* 4, 3: PL 54, 150-152; 51, 1: PL 54, 308-309; 62, 2: PL 54, 350-351; 83, 3: PL 54, 431-432.

CHAPTER 2

The Church as the Sacrament of Salvation

The Church is a sign of God's Kingdom in the world and a sign of the Kingdom of Heaven.

Ecumenism and Interreligious Dialogue

CHAPTER TWO

The Church as the Sacrament of Salvation

INTRODUCTION

In many and various ways God spoke of old to our fathers by the prophets; but in these last days he has spoken to us by a Son, whom he appointed the heir of all things, through whom also he created the world. (Heb 1:1-2)

We read in the previous chapter how salvation history is fundamentally about God gradually calling his people together into unity. Although God selected particular men to serve as mediators of his covenants, those covenants were always made not with a single person but with a group of people. This group of people, in turn, witnessed to the rest of humanity God's holiness and love. God's plan from the beginning has always been to save the entirety of the human race, and he worked through a particular part of the human race to make that happen. This Chosen People gradually grew to encompass more and more people as God revealed himself to the world progressively.

Over the course of this chapter, we will begin by exploring the divine foundation of the Catholic Church, namely:

- ✠ God the Father planned the Church, the Sacrament of Salvation, from the beginning of time.
- ✠ The Church was prefigured in the People of Israel.
- ✠ The Church was divinely instituted by Jesus Christ, God's own Son.
- ✠ The Church is guided, sustained, and sanctified by the Father through the Son and Holy Spirit.
- ✠ The Church is the Body of Christ, with Christ as the Head and the faithful as members of the Body.

We will also discuss the role of the Church in proclaiming what God has revealed:

- ✠ Christ founded his Church upon the Apostles and entrusted them to preach the Gospel that he had taught them.
- ✠ The Apostles have handed down this role and the authority of proclaiming God's Revelation to the Popes and bishops in an unbroken line of succession.
- ✠ The Pope and bishops today continue their ministry of teaching God's Revelation faithfully.

Feed My Lambs by Tissot.
Christ founded his Church upon the Apostles and entrusted them to preach the Gospel that he had taught them.

St. Peter's Square filled with the People of God.
The *visible dimension* of the Church is seen in people united around the teaching of the Apostles, the Sacraments, and the hierarchical order of Pope and bishops.

THE CHURCH: SACRAMENT OF SALVATION

The Seven Sacraments are visible signs by which God confers his grace; in a similar manner, the Church a visible sign of God's grace. She is the Sacrament of Salvation because she is both the sign and the means of God's salvation for all people. She is also the Sacrament of Communion because she gathers all people into communion with God and with one another. As the *Catechism* teaches:

> "The Church, in Christ, is like a sacrament—a sign and instrument, that is, of communion with God and of unity among all men."[1] The Church's first purpose is to be the sacrament of the *inner union of men with God*. Because men's communion with one another is rooted in that union with God, the Church is also the sacrament of the *unity of the human race*. In her, this unity is already begun, since she gathers men "from every nation, from all tribes and peoples and tongues";[2] at the same time, the Church is the "sign and instrument" of the full realization of the unity yet to come. (CCC 775)

The New Testament word communion—in Latin, *communio*; in Greek, *koinonia*—expresses the essential core of the Church's mystery.[3] In communion there is a *vertical dimension*: man's communion with God who is "above" us; it also has a *horizontal dimension*: our communion with the other members of Christ's faithful in a relationship of radical equality.[4]

What does this mean? Recall that the Church is both a visible reality and an invisible reality. For the Church to be a sign it must be visible, and the Church is a visible, human institution. The Church's communion is sacramental, then, because she is a visible sign of an invisible reality. The *visible dimension* is seen in people united around the teaching of the Apostles, the Sacraments, and the hierarchical order of Pope and bishops. The *invisible dimension* is our intimate communion with the Holy Trinity and the other members of Christ's Church on earth, in heaven, and in purgatory.

We can point to the Pope, bishops, priests, deacons, members of religious orders, and a vast number of lay people who are members of the Church. We can see church buildings and all the other properties that she operates directly or indirectly, including schools, hospitals, soup kitchens, and orphanages. The Church has a visible government and her own laws. She has a visible liturgy and a vast literature, which includes the Sacred Scriptures. And she has a 2000-year history that can be studied.

All these exist as instruments to carry out God's intention to share his divine life with all people: "At the end of time...all the just, from Adam and 'from Abel, the just one, to the last of the elect,' will be gathered together with the Father in the universal Church" (*LG* 2). All the Church's visible means and activities exist to accomplish what is essentially invisible to us now: communion with God and with one another.

THE CHURCH: PLANNED FROM THE BEGINNING OF CREATION

God created human persons to live in communion both with him and with one another. In his infinite wisdom, by a plan that remains a great mystery to the human mind, he created the entire universe for us and chose to raise humanity up to share in his own divine life in communion with him. This communion already prefigures the Church, the gathering of his people into one body, which will be perfected at the end of time.[5]

> Christians of the first centuries said, "The world was created for the sake of the Church."[6] God created the world for the sake of communion with his divine life, a communion brought about by the "convocation" of men in Christ, and this "convocation" is the Church. The Church is the goal of all things,[7] and God permitted such painful upheavals as the angels' fall and man's sin only as occasions and means for displaying all the power of his arm and the whole measure of the love he wanted to give the world... (CCC 760)

The gift of grace offers us a share in God's divine life. Baptism, by which we enter the Church, confers upon us sanctifying grace that cleanses us of all sin, including Original Sin, by which our first parents lost the state of grace in which they were created. The Church, by way of her Sacraments and moral teachings, presents us with the means to cooperate with this free gift of grace throughout our lives so we may be saved and enter into perfect communion with God for all eternity.

As the *Catechism* teaches, quoting St. Clement of Alexandria: "Just as God's will is creation and is called 'the world,' so his intention is the salvation of men, and it is called 'the Church.'"[8]

THE CHURCH: PREFIGURED IN THE PEOPLE OF ISRAEL

After our original communion with God was broken by sin, God immediately began to repair this communion, to regather his people.[9] The Chosen People, who gathered as Israel, therefore prefigures the formation of the Church.

The Israelites' Camp and Wilderness Tabernacle at Mount Sinai.
God set apart one people to be a light to the world.

> The gathering together of the People of God began at the moment when sin destroyed the communion of men with God, and that of men among themselves. The gathering together of the Church is, as it were, God's reaction to the chaos provoked by sin. (CCC 761)

The remote preparation for this regathering began when God called Abraham and promised to make him the father of a great nation. With Jacob, whom God renamed Israel, and through his twelve sons, God gave his people their identity. With Moses and the liberation of Israel from captivity in Egypt, a nation was created to serve God in both right living and right worship. God set apart one people to be a light to the world so all would see the proper way to honor and serve him.

With Moses in the wilderness, the people of Israel ratified the covenant that God had offered them: "By this election, Israel is to be the sign of the future gathering of all nations."[10] The people, as the People of God, had accepted their special communion with God and with one another.

God is a God of infinite mercy. Although the Israelites turned away from him frequently, he did not

Joshua Passing the River Jordan with the Ark of the Covenant by West.
The people of Israel, as the People of God, had accepted their special communion with God and with one another.

abandon them. He continued to mold them, sending prophets to announce to them the ways of God. Eventually, he formed them into a kingdom, first under Saul, but then more definitively under David and his son Solomon. He promised David that his kingdom would reign forever and that his son would rule forever.

Yet, his people were not faithful, and the prophets pointed out how Israel had broken the covenant. God's people failed to live up to their great calling: to become who they were called to be. The people began to worship foreign gods and disobey the Ten Commandments. Eventually, ruin came to the kingdom, and the Israelites were conquered and exiled.

Even then, God did not forget his promises to them. God, in his faithfulness, one day offered a new and eternal covenant, the prophets announced. It was not to be David's immediate son Solomon who was to rule forever but a future descendant, a "son of David"—and that would be Jesus Christ, the Son of God born of the Blessed Virgin Mary, a descendant of David.

The Church founded by Christ in the New Testament is that New Covenant, the fulfillment of the People of God formed as the nation of Israel in the Old Testament. The Church can therefore be called the Fulfillment of Israel, as she fulfills the promises and covenants that God made to his people.

To "fulfill" means to complete, to bring something to its ultimate goal. As God worked through Israel to bring salvation to the world, so now he works through the Church. The mission of Christ was not to reject the Old Testament or to abolish it; rather, he came to bring it to completion. Christ said, "Think not that I have come to abolish the law and the prophets; I have come not to abolish them but to fulfill them."[11] The coming of Christ must not cause us to forget or reject the Old Testament—"the law and the prophets," as the Scriptures that had already been written were called in the Gospels—for it is the very foundation of the New Testament.

THE CHURCH: FOUNDED BY JESUS CHRIST

When God, in the fullness of time, entered decisively into history at the Incarnation to bring about our salvation, he again sent a mediator who would be the instrument of his covenant with a people. But this time he did not select a human person; he sent his own divine Son to take on our human nature—become part of the human family—and to form the new people of God, the Church.

> It was the Son's task to accomplish the Father's plan of salvation in the fullness of time. Its accomplishment was the reason for his being sent.[12] "The Lord Jesus inaugurated his Church by preaching the Good News, that is, the coming of the Reign of God, promised over the ages in the scriptures."[13] To fulfill the Father's will, Christ ushered in the Kingdom of heaven on earth. The Church "is the Reign of Christ already present in mystery."[14] (CCC 763)

Salvation comes to the world through the Church, the people formed by Christ for this mission. Far from being an "accident" of history, the Church is the reason that Christ came. The Church is a sign of God's Kingdom in the world and a sign of the Kingdom of Heaven, and she is given the sacred duty to proclaim the coming of the Kingdom of God and to draw all people to Christ. The members of the Church are the "seed and beginning of the Kingdom," the "little flock" who "form Jesus' true family."[15]

The Twelve Tribes of Israel that came forth from the twelve sons of Jacob formed the foundation upon which God built the nation of Israel in the Old Testament. In the New Testament Christ built his Church on the foundation of the Twelve Apostles: "Truly, I say to you, in the new world, when the Son of man shall sit on his glorious throne, you who have followed me will also sit on twelve thrones, judging the twelve tribes of Israel"[16]:

> The Lord Jesus endowed his community with a structure that will remain until the Kingdom is fully achieved. Before all else there is the choice of the Twelve with Peter as their head.[17] Representing the twelve tribes of Israel, they are the foundation stones of the new Jerusalem.[18] The Twelve and the other disciples share in Christ's mission and his power, but also in his lot.[19] By all his actions, Christ prepares and builds his Church. (CCC 765)

We will return to the topic of the structure of the Church and the role of the Apostles later in this chapter.

Christ's Charge to Peter by Raphael.
In the New Testament Christ built his Church on the foundation of the Twelve Apostles.

THE CHURCH: GIVEN DIVINE ASSISTANCE FROM THE BLESSED TRINITY

Ever since Christ's *Ascension* into heaven, his work on earth has been the work of the Church. Before Christ entered into his Passion, he promised the Apostles that he would send the "Counselor, the Holy Spirit" who would "teach you all things, and bring to your remembrance all that I have said to you."[20] The Holy Spirit would be the guide who would lead Christ's Church to all truth as well as help her grow in holiness.

At Pentecost, the fulfillment of this promise came to pass:

> **When the day of Pentecost had come, they were all together in one place. And suddenly a sound came from heaven like the rush of a mighty wind, and it filled all the house where they were sitting. And there appeared to them tongues as of fire, distributed and resting on each one of them. And they were all filled with the Holy Spirit and began to speak in other tongues, as the Spirit gave them utterance.** (Acts 2:1-4)

The Descent of the Holy Spirit at Pentecost in effect revealed the Church by animating the Church, which inspired and empowered the Apostles to understand and to take on their sacred mission courageously. The Holy Spirit transformed a small group of frightened men into bold witnesses of the faith who, for the sake of Christ, persevered joyfully through hardships and sufferings. They did this in order to proclaim the Good News that Jesus Christ had died and risen for the salvation of the world.

Pentecost (detail) by Juan de Flandes.
The descent of the Holy Spirit at Pentecost in effect revealed the Church by animating the Church.

It seems impracticable, in the days leading up to Pentecost, that this seemingly insignificant group of ordinary men—who had trades and families of their own before leaving them to follow Christ—would become some of the most influential men who ever lived. Yet, that's what happened. The only explanation is the power of the Holy Spirit in their lives. The Holy Spirit is the "soul" of the Body of Christ, the Church, who gives her life and direction so as always to remain firmly in the truth of God's Revelation.

We see, then, that the Church enjoys divine assistance from all three Persons of the Blessed Trinity: The Father sent the Son, the Son established the Church, and the Father and Son sent the Holy Spirit so the Church can carry out her divine mission to the world.[21]

THE CHURCH: THE MYSTICAL BODY OF CHRIST

The salvation of humanity comes to us through the life, Death, and Resurrection of Christ. By becoming man, the Son of God made his earthly Body the means by which people can come to a union with God. And after his Ascension it is still the Body of Christ—the Church—that is the path to salvation in this world. As members of the Body of Christ, we are united intimately to one another. St. Paul explained,

> **As in one body we have many members, and all the members do not have the same function, so we, though many, are one body in Christ, and individually members one of another. Having gifts that differ according to the grace given to us, let us use them: if prophecy, in proportion to our faith; if service, in our serving; he who teaches, in his teaching; he who exhorts, in his exhortation; he who contributes, in liberality; he who gives aid, with zeal; he who does acts of mercy, with cheerfulness.** (Rom 12:4-8)

ST. PAUL, APOSTLE

How many Apostles were there? The first number that probably comes to mind is "twelve." After all, at the beginning of his public ministry, Christ selected twelve men to be Apostles, and that was no arbitrary number: the Twelve Apostles are the New Testament fulfillment of the Old Testament Twelve Tribes of Israel. Chosen by Christ himself, these twelve men lived and traveled with him during his public ministry and were his witnesses after his Resurrection. In fact, after Judas Iscariot had taken his own life, the remaining eleven were inspired to replace him as soon as possible, selecting St. Matthias to fill Judas's vacant "office" (Acts 1:15-26).

Yet, there is another man called "apostle" who did not follow Christ during his earthly ministry and was not among his chosen Twelve: St. Paul, the "Apostle to the Gentiles."

St. Paul, when he was known as Saul, was a Pharisee who persecuted the young Christian Church ferociously because he thought her Faith was a dangerous subversion of Judaism by errant Jews. But the ninth chapter of Acts recounts the turning point of his life—an event that would change the world: En route to persecute more Christians, Saul received his calling directly from Christ:

> As [Saul] journeyed he approached Damascus, and suddenly a light from heaven flashed about him. And he fell to the ground and heard a voice saying to him, "Saul, Saul, why do you persecute me?" And he said, "Who are you, Lord?" And he said, "I am Jesus, whom you are persecuting; but rise and enter the city, and you will be told what you are to do." The men who were traveling with him stood speechless, hearing the voice but seeing no one. (Acts 9:3-7)

One of the defining characteristics of every Apostle is that he encountered the risen Christ (cf. Acts 1:22). This would seem to limit the number of potential Apostles to those who had followed Christ during his earthly ministry. However, St. Paul was given a unique gift in that he witnessed the risen Christ *after* his Ascension into heaven. Because of this grace, he is considered an Apostle just as much as the other Twelve.

St. Paul by Castillo.
St. Paul, Apostle to the Gentiles,
became the Church's greatest evangelist.

After his dramatic conversion, St. Paul became the Church's greatest evangelist, traveling throughout the Roman Empire in an effort to bring people to Christ. His letters to various local churches and fellow disciples make up the bulk of the New Testament. His influence on the early Church is inestimable.

In the Church every member—from the Pope to a newly baptized infant—has a role to play, but all these roles are united in one purpose: the salvation of souls. Furthermore, we are united in one Body with Christ as the Head:

> **[Christ] is the head of the body, the church; he is the beginning, the first-born from the dead, that in everything he might be pre-eminent. For in him all the fulness of God was pleased to dwell, and through him to reconcile to himself all things, whether on earth or in heaven, making peace by the blood of his cross.** (Col 1:18-20)

The Holy Spirit unites the diverse members of the Church from different cultures and backgrounds into one unified Body. And by that Spirit the Church brings salvation to the world.

The *Catechism* states it this way:

> Believers who respond to God's word and become members of Christ's Body, become intimately united with him: "In that body the life of Christ is communicated to those who believe, and who, through the sacraments, are united in a hidden and real way to Christ in his Passion and glorification."[22] This is especially true of Baptism, which unites us to Christ's death and Resurrection, and the Eucharist, by which "really sharing in the body of the Lord,...we are taken up into communion with him and with one another."[23] (CCC 790)

One of the greatest theologians and philosophers of Christian history, St. Thomas Aquinas, described it simply: "Head and members form as it were one and the same mystical person."[24] The Church as the Mystical Body of Christ is a true mystery, one that we must accept on faith: By the Sacraments of the Church, we become intimately united to Christ and to one another in an utterly incomprehensible way.

THE CHURCH: FOUNDED UPON THE APOSTLES

As you might expect, God revealed himself gradually to his people, sent his Son to establish his people as a Church, and then sent the Holy Spirit to guide the Church in truth for a special purpose. The Church is endowed with a sacred mission: to preach the Good News of Jesus Christ and proclaim salvation to the world.

To accomplish this, Christ established a structure for his Church, founding her upon his inner circle of friends, the Apostles. The Apostles and their successors continued Christ's work of salvation after his Ascension and will continue it until the end of time, when he will return in glory.

> In the office of the apostles there is one aspect that cannot be transmitted: to be the chosen witnesses of the Lord's Resurrection and so the foundation stones of the Church. But their office also has a permanent aspect. Christ promised to remain with them always. The divine mission entrusted by Jesus to them "will continue to the end of time, since the Gospel they handed on is the lasting source of all life for the Church. Therefore,...the apostles took care to appoint successors."[25] (CCC 860)

To these Apostles Christ revealed himself in a deeper way than he revealed himself to the crowds who came to hear him preach. Although he taught the people many things, he reserved special instruction to the Apostles themselves: "Privately to his own disciples he explained everything."[26] They were, after all, his chosen witnesses

The Transfiguration by Carracci.
Christ revealed himself to the Apostles in a deeper way than he revealed himself to the crowds who came to hear him preach.

whom he sent out to preach his Gospel. We find many instances in the Gospels where Christ spoke to the Apostles alone, teaching them deeper truths and answering their questions.

While he appointed twelve Apostles, to one of them he gave primacy over the others. That man was Simon Peter.

St. Peter Is Given the "Keys to the Kingdom of Heaven"

Scripture tells us that Christ, in making Simon Peter the head of his Church, gave him the "keys to the kingdom of heaven."[27] These words were highly significant in light of the Old Testament.

When God established a kingdom for Israel, he also established the office of prime, or chief, minister, a high official who had authority over the kingdom. The symbol of this authority was the "key of the house of David," which would be given to him by the king.

A *prime minister* is someone who is granted the authority of an ultimate ruler such as a king or queen. The power wielded by a prime minister is not his or her own; it flows from the ultimate ruler. When a prime minister speaks, he or she speaks in the name of the king. The keys given to the prime minister of the Kingdom of Israel, then, was a symbol of his granted authority. The prophet Isaiah speaks of the succession of one prime minister, Shebna, to the next prime minister, Eli'akim. God told Shebna:

> **In that day I will call my servant Eliakim the son of Hilkiah, and I will clothe him with your robe, and will bind your girdle on him, and will commit your authority to his hand; and he shall be a father to the inhabitants of Jerusalem and to the house of Judah. And I will place on his shoulder the key of the house of David; he shall open, and none shall shut; and he shall shut, and none shall open.** (Is 22: 20-22)

Eliakim, although not the king, had complete authority to determine who could enter the "house of David"; he was vested with the keys of the kingdom.

This office of prime minister provides a model for the role of St. Peter, whom Christ established as the head of his Church, which is continued today in the office of the Pope. We see this office continue in the New Testament when Christ gives the *keys of the kingdom* to St. Peter:

St. Peter Preaching in the Presence of St. Mark by Fra Angelico.
"The Lord Jesus endowed his community with a structure that will remain until the Kingdom is fully achieved." (CCC 765)

[Jesus] said to them, "But who do you say that I am?" Simon Peter replied, "You are the Christ, the Son of the living God." And Jesus answered him, "Blessed are you, Simon Bar-Jona! For flesh and blood has not revealed this to you, but my Father who is in heaven. And I tell you, you are Peter, and on this rock I will build my church, and the powers of death shall not prevail against it. I will give you the keys of the kingdom of heaven, and whatever you bind on earth shall be bound in heaven, and whatever you loose on earth shall be loosed in heaven." (Mt 16:15-19)

WHY ST. PETER IS "THE ROCK"

The life of St. Peter is truly remarkable. Although he was born and raised a humble Galilean fisherman named Simon, he was chosen by Christ to be "the rock" on which the Lord would build his Church, the New People of God (*see* Mt 16:15-19).

The name "Peter" is not really a name but rather the Greek *petra*, "rock." While it appears obvious from the English translation of these verses that the Apostle Simon is being named the "rock" on which Christ will build his Church, most non-Catholics dispute this interpretation, basing their disagreement on certain variations in the Greek text in which the New Testament was originally written. The key words in Greek are italicized here:

> "You are **Petros**, and on this **petra** I will build my church." (Mt 16:18)

Petros is the Greek word for "little rock" or "pebble," whereas *petra* is the Greek word for "rock" or "stone." Therefore, some claim that the Apostle Simon was not the rock to which Christ was referring but his profession of faith, or Christ himself, that is really the "rock." There are at least three problems with this interpretation.

First, claiming that St. Peter is not the "rock" flies in the face of the obvious meaning of Christ's words. Christ renamed Simon, which in the Bible implies a new mission in life (for example, God renamed Abram as Abraham). If Simon himself was not the "rock," why rename him at all? Why not just keep his name Simon and say that his profession of faith was the "rock?"

Apostle Peter (detail) by Mengs.

Second, Christ and St. Peter spoke in the Aramaic language. The account found in St. Matthew's Gospel is a translation written in Greek. In the original Aramaic, the word *Cephas* ("rock") would have been used in both instances with no distinction of the size of the stone.

Finally, a deeper understanding of the Greek language helps us to more clearly understand this passage. In Greek, as in many languages (but not in English), nouns are masculine, feminine, or neuter. The Greek word *petra* (rock) is feminine. However, Christ is using the word "rock" as a new name for Simon, and a man cannot have a feminine name, so using the masculine form of the word would be natural, which is *Petros*. Thus, the difference between the two Greek words is not a difference in meaning but simply a difference in gender.

The Apostle St. Peter is truly the "rock" on which Christ built his Church.

Thus, the Apostle St. Peter was given a leadership role in the New People of God, the Church: He was given the "keys to the kingdom of heaven," allowing him to rule with the authority of the King himself, the Son of David—Jesus Christ.

> The Lord Jesus endowed his community with a structure that will remain until the Kingdom is fully achieved. Before all else there is the choice of the Twelve with Peter as their head.[28] Representing the twelve tribes of Israel, they are the foundation stones of the new Jerusalem.[29] The Twelve and the other disciples share in Christ's mission and his power, but also in his lot.[30] By all his actions, Christ prepares and builds his Church. (CCC 765)

Thus, the basic structure of the Church is not manmade; neither is it something that can be changed or adjusted to fit human whims. It is divinely instituted by Jesus Christ himself as the fulfillment of a plan begun at the foundations of the world.

The Primacy of St. Peter

Aside from Christ, no one comes to the fore in the Gospels quite like St. Peter. It seems that at every major event of Christ's adult life we find nearby this Galilean fisherman. And Christ speaks to none of the other Apostles quite like the way he speaks to St. Peter, giving him specific duties and authority that he does not grant the others.

The New Testament presents St. Peter as preeminent; he is mentioned much more than any other Apostle or disciple, he is always mentioned first when grouped with other Apostles, and he is always shown to be their leader. For example, note the language St. Matthew used to list the Apostles:

Christ's Charge to Peter by Veronese. One of St. Peter's primary tasks was to help keep the other Apostles from falling away.

> The names of the twelve apostles are these: first, Simon, who is called Peter, and Andrew his brother; James the son of Zebedee, and John his brother; Philip and Bartholomew; Thomas and Matthew the tax collector; James the son of Alphaeus, and Thaddaeus; Simon the Cananaean, and Judas Iscariot, who betrayed him. (Mt 10: 2-4)

The other Apostles are simply listed, but St. Matthew points out that "Simon, who is called Peter" is "first." St. Peter is not just listed first by happenstance; the language of Scripture is precise, and here it is making clear that he has a leadership position among the Apostles.

At the Last Supper, this special role for St. Peter is made even clearer. Christ proclaimed,

> "Simon, Simon, behold, Satan demanded to have you, that he might sift you [plural, the Apostles] like wheat, but I have prayed for you [singular, Peter] that your faith may not fail; and when you have turned again, strengthen your brethren." (Lk 22: 31-32)

Note the distinction between the two instances of "you" in this passage: Christ told St. Peter that Satan wants to sift all the Apostles like wheat, but he then said that he prayed only for St. Peter. In addition, he told only St. Peter to strengthen his brethren, that is, the other Apostles. Undeniably, Christ was giving him a special ministry. One of St. Peter's primary tasks was to help keep the other Apostles from falling away.

In the last chapter of the Gospel of St. John, three times Christ asked St. Peter if he loved him.[31] Recall that he had recently denied three times that he even knew Christ. When St. Peter affirmed that he loved Christ, Christ's response was not the expected "I forgive you" or "I love you." Instead he told St. Peter to "feed" or "tend" the Lord's sheep. He is to be a shepherd of Christ's flock. Here, too, it is clear that Christ was giving St. Peter a specific ministry in the Church, one not shared by any of his companions.

St. Peter as the "Rock"

But the clearest sign of St. Peter's special ministry in the Church is his very name. Although his given name was Simon, Christ himself changed his name to "Peter," which means "rock," thus signifying his role in the Church.

From the Gospel narrative "upon this rock" (Mt 16:15-19), we can glean several truths:

- ✠ **Christ established a Church.** This passage makes it abundantly clear that Christ intended to and did establish a Church.
- ✠ **Christ established a *visible* Church.** Some non-Catholic Christians claim that the Church is "invisible," meaning that it has no visible structure or *hierarchy* with authority over its members, and only God knows its membership. As we read in the previous chapter, the Church was prefigured at the beginning of time and was present "invisibly" in the regathering of the people of Israel; now, with the dramatic event at Caesarea Philippi, Christ established the Church in its visible dimension. Christ took a real person—Simon—and made him the rock (Peter) on which the Church would be built. By the fact that Christ established St. Peter as the head of the Church in such a public way, it is clear that this Church and its hierarchy would be visible to all.
- ✠ **Christ gave St. Peter certain authority over this visible Church.** Christ established a hierarchical Church with someone to govern it. By giving St. Peter the "keys of the kingdom," he was giving him a unique authority in the Church. Likewise, the power to bind and loose, which was extended also to the other Apostles later in the Gospels, denotes a position of authority in the Church community.

St. Peter Enthroned by Guido of Siena.
Christ took a real person—Simon—and made him the rock (Peter) on which the Church would be built.

Appearance on the Mountain in Galilee (detail) by Duccio.
After his Resurrection, Christ continued to explain his Revelation to the Apostles and commanded them to go out as his emissaries in the wider world.

THE APOSTLES ENTRUSTED TO SPREAD THE GOSPEL

In the New Testament the Apostles are presented as having pivotal importance. Throughout most of the Gospels, they were clearly ignorant of Christ's intentions and mission, yet the Lord poured himself out to them continually, teaching them, admonishing them, and promising them great responsibilities and powers in his future kingdom. They were with him throughout his public ministry, and Christ was careful to pass on his teachings to them. After his Resurrection, Christ continued to explain his Revelation to them and commanded them to go out as his emissaries in the wider world.

His parting instructions, which we read in the previous chapter, bear repeating here. Before Christ ascended to his Father, he told his Apostles:

> **"All authority in heaven and on earth has been given to me. Go therefore and make disciples of all nations, baptizing them in the name of the Father and of the Son and of the Holy Spirit, teaching them to observe all that I have commanded you; and lo, I am with you always, to the close of the age." (Mt 28:18-20)**

With these words, sometimes called the "Great Commission," Christ commanded his Apostles to make disciples, entrusting to them two primary tasks: administering the Sacraments ("baptizing") and proclaiming his Revelation ("teaching"). This was to be their task until the "close of the age"—until the end of time.

At Pentecost, as we read earlier in this chapter, the Holy Spirit empowered the Apostles to begin to carry out this sacred mission on their own for the first time. The followers of Christ were not called to focus solely on their own holiness in order to be a sign for the rest of the world like the Israelites were called to do; rather, filled as they were with the Holy Spirit, the People of God became a missionary people, evangelizing the whole world with the Gospel just as Christ had instructed them to do.

> The whole Church is apostolic, in that she remains, through the successors of St. Peter and the other apostles, in communion of faith and life with her origin: and in that she is "sent out" into the whole world. All members of the Church share in this mission, though in various ways. "The Christian vocation is, of its nature, a vocation to the apostolate as well." Indeed, we call an apostolate "every activity of the Mystical Body" that aims "to spread the Kingdom of Christ over all the earth."[32] (CCC 863)

Throughout the Old Testament the Lord promised that eventually all peoples would be blessed through Israel—that through the example of Israel's faithfulness to the covenant, all nations would come to adore the Lord. However, they were never commanded to go out actively to bring others into the Family of God. After Pentecost, we see clearly that the mission of God's People was changed: St. Peter and the Apostles were sent out to accomplish the conversion of the whole world, preaching to the ends of the earth the Good News about Jesus Christ.

During the earthly life of Christ, the Apostles were far from impressive, showing at different times such defects as pride, self-interest, slowness in understanding, and cowardice. Yet, after the coming of the Holy Spirit at Pentecost, they were transformed into bold proclaimers of Christ's Resurrection. They proclaimed a Faith that spread eventually throughout the world. One of the great proofs of the truth of Christianity is the humanly unexplainable transformation of these common men.

The important role of the Apostles continues to be demonstrated in the Acts of the Apostles, which tells the story of the early Church. To be more accurate, it relates primarily the story of two Apostles: St. Peter, the first head of the Church, and St. Paul, whose missionary zeal among non-Jews earned him the moniker "Apostle to the Gentiles." The Apostles are shown to be the foundation of the Church, the primary means by which Christ's Revelation is passed on to the world.[33] This book includes the conversion story of St. Paul, a Pharisee and persecutor of Christians who was transformed by the power of Christ to become his greatest evangelizer.

Take some time to read the Acts of the Apostles. You will see that the Church is not inward looking but always looking beyond her boundaries to reach those still outside.

APOSTOLIC SUCCESSION

According to Christ's instructions, the Apostles were to continue the mission of Christ on earth until his glorious return at the end of time. Yet, human mortality presented a problem: The Apostles themselves were not to live forever. How were they to carry out Christ's command until the end of the world?

The Apostles tackled that situation almost immediately after the Ascension. One of the original Twelve, Judas Iscariot, who had betrayed Christ, had died. That left only eleven Apostles rather than the Twelve, who represent the Twelve Tribes of Israel.

St. Matthias by Martini.
With the appointment of St. Matthias to succeed Judas Iscariot, a model for Apostolic Succession was created.

Immediately following the Ascension of Our Lord at the beginning of Acts, we find the Eleven together in prayer in the Upper Room. St. Peter declared: "One of the men who have accompanied us during all the time that the Lord Christ went in and out among us, beginning from the baptism of John until the day when he was taken up from us—one of these men must become with us a witness to his resurrection."[34]

The office of Apostle required a replacement, one who could be a "witness to his Resurrection" and fulfill the command of Christ to make disciples by administering the Sacraments and proclaiming God's Revelation in Jesus Christ. So the Apostles chose St. Matthias and appointed him as the successor of Judas Iscariot.

St. Matthias was entrusted with the same task as the first Apostles. In this way, a model for succession was created: When an Apostle had died, another man was to take his place in the ministry. These successors are the bishops, who continue the task of the Apostles to administer the Sacraments and hand on Revelation.

Today we have far more than twelve Catholic bishops in the world. As the Church rapidly grew and expanded throughout the region, the Apostles had to appoint more bishops to minister to the ever more numerous faithful, and these bishops were not necessarily personal witnesses to the Resurrection. These bishops ordained other bishops, and the process has continued since apostolic times. Because of this line of succession, today's Catholic bishops trace their authority and office directly to the Apostles. Therefore, they are true successors to the Apostles, and are thus charged and empowered to continue the Apostles' sacred mission given to them by Christ.

As the Fathers of the Second Ecumenical Council of the Vatican proclaimed:

> [The] divine mission, entrusted by Christ to the apostles, will last until the end of the world,[35] since the Gospel they are to teach is for all time the source of all life for the Church. And for this reason the apostles, appointed as rulers in this society, took care to appoint successors....They therefore appointed such men, and gave them the order that, when they should have died, other approved men would take up their ministry.[36]
>
> Among those various ministries which, according to tradition, were exercised in the Church from the earliest times, the chief place belongs to the office of those who, appointed to the episcopate, by a succession running from the beginning,[37] are passers-on of the apostolic seed.[38] Thus, as St. Irenaeus testifies, through those who were appointed bishops by the apostles, and through their successors down in our own time, the apostolic tradition is manifested[39] and preserved.[40] (*Lumen Gentium*, 20)

In other words, the task of faithfully transmitting the Revelation of God to future generations is given to the bishops, including the Pope, who is the Bishop of Rome. *Apostolic Succession* is a great gift to the faithful, for it allows every follower of Christ to know with confidence the teachings of Jesus Christ.[41]

THE TRANSMISSION OF DIVINE REVELATION

The Catholic Church, then, in and through the Pope and the bishops in communion with him, is in turn entrusted with continuing the mission that Christ gave to his Apostles so all people may come to a saving knowledge of God's plan of salvation. So how did the Apostles, and later the bishops, hand on what had been entrusted to them? The same way any information is handed on to future generations: through spoken word, written word, and living witness.

The Four Evangelists by Bloemaert.
Left to right: St. Luke with the Ox, St. Mark with the Lion, St. John with the Eagle, St. Matthew with the Angel. Through their lives, writings, and preaching, the Apostles handed on the Revelation given to them by Christ to the next generation of believers.

The Apostles committed their lives to teaching others about the Gospel of Christ: They preached far and wide, some wrote down accounts of our salvation through Christ, and they lived out the New Commandment of Christ for all to see. Through their lives, writings, and preaching, the Apostles handed on the Revelation given to them by Christ to the next generation of believers. This is still how bishops hand on Revelation from generation to generation.

We refer to the sacred writings of Revelation as the Bible, or *Sacred Scripture*, and we refer to the teachings handed down from the time of the Apostles to the present as *Sacred Tradition*. These two elements together, Scripture and Tradition, are called the *Deposit of Faith*. Together they provide the means by which God's Revelation is passed on to us.

AUTHORS OF THE NEW TESTAMENT

The New Testament is a collection of various letters, historical accounts, and other writings. But who exactly are the authors of the New Testament?

The most prolific New Testament author is St. Paul. Of the twenty-seven books of the New Testament, thirteen are attributed to him: Romans, 1 and 2 Corinthians, Galatians, Ephesians, Philippians, Colossians, 1 and 2 Thessalonians, 1 and 2 Timothy, Titus,

St. Paul by Andrea di Bartolo. Thirteen books of the New Testament are attributed to St. Paul.

and Philemon. These Epistles were written between the late '40s and mid-'60s of the first century. Although all these writings have been associated with St. Paul since that time, some scholars in modern times have disputed the Pauline authorship of some of these letters.

The Apostle St. John is associated with five New Testament writings: the Gospel of St. John, the three Epistles bearing his name, and the Book of Revelation. As with St. Paul's writings, some scholars dispute his authorship of these works, but tradition has always connected him to these writings.

St. Luke, the physician-disciple of St. Paul, wrote the Gospel of St. Luke and the Acts of the Apostles. Although in our modern Bibles these two books are separated by the Gospel of John, St. Luke originally wrote them as a two-volume work.

The Apostle St. Peter is associated with the two Epistles bearing his name: 1 and 2 Peter. Many scholars believe that 1 Peter was originally a homily preached by him at an early Easter Vigil and later written down in letter form.

The Epistle to the Hebrews has no attribution; its authorship has long been debated. Some claim that St. Paul wrote it, others associate it with one of St. Paul's disciples, but it seems unlikely we will ever make a definite determination.

Of the remaining letters in the New Testament, one was written by St. James, the first Bishop of Jerusalem, and the other by the Apostle St. Jude.

The first two Gospels in the New Testament have traditionally been associated with the names they bear: St. Matthew and St. Mark. St. Matthew's Gospel was written to new converts to Christianity from Judaism, while St. Mark's was a compilation of the teachings of St. Peter.

Of course, this has been an accounting of the *human* authors of the New Testament, but there is another author of each of these twenty-seven books: the Holy Spirit. As inspired works, we believe that the Holy Spirit, while allowing for the human initiative and individuality of each author, guided the writing of each work to convey what he wanted these authors to transmit. Each book was originally written for an ancient people, yet, through the inspiration of the Holy Spirit, each was also written for us today.

There exists a close connection and communication between sacred tradition and Sacred Scripture. For both of them, flowing from the same divine wellspring, in a certain way merge into a unity and tend toward the same end. For Sacred Scripture is the word of God inasmuch as it is consigned to writing under the inspiration of the divine Spirit, while sacred Tradition takes the word of God entrusted by Christ the Lord and the Holy Spirit to the Apostles, and hands it on to their successors in its full purity, so that led by the light of the Spirit of truth, they may in proclaiming it preserve this word of God faithfully, explain it, and make it more widely known.

Consequently it is not from Sacred Scripture alone that the Church draws her certainty about everything which has been revealed. Therefore both sacred tradition and Sacred Scripture are to be accepted and venerated with the same sense of loyalty and reverence.[42] (*Dei Verbum*, 9)

THE ROLE OF THE HOLY SPIRIT

How can we be sure that what has been passed on to us is truly God's Revelation in "its full purity"? How do we know that it has not been corrupted over the generations, with manmade traditions and doctrines added onto the true Gospel of Jesus Christ or key elements stripped away?

Pentecost by Maino.
The Holy Spirit guides the Church to all truth.

Christ promised his followers that this would not happen. He promised to be with his disciples until the end of time.[43] The Church's ability to teach and live the life of Christ through the Sacraments would be guided by Christ's presence for all ages.

Furthermore, recall how Christ, when he made St. Peter the "rock" upon which he would build his Church and gave him the "keys of the kingdom of heaven," stated that "the gates of hell shall not prevail" against the Church.[44] If the "gates of hell" were able to prevail against the Church, then she would no longer be able to teach the life-giving words of Christ or would teach them incorrectly. But Christ bestowed upon his Church—founded on St. Peter, the Rock—the grace to withstand such powers and thus the ability to teach correctly what Christ himself had revealed.

That takes us back to the guidance of the Holy Spirit, whom Christ called the "Spirit of truth."[45] The Holy Spirit guides the Church to all truth; he enables the Church to proclaim without fail God's truth and to pass on his Revelation. This great gift of the Church ensures that all people will have the opportunity to hear the truth as Christ proclaimed it.

THE MAGISTERIUM, INTERPRETER OF GOD'S REVELATION

How does the Holy Spirit guide and protect the passing on of God's Revelation through Scripture and Tradition? Does he tell each Christian what is true and what is false? Does he announce to the world the proper understanding of a passage of Scripture or a received tradition? No, the Holy Spirit guides the *Magisterium*, or teaching office, of the Church so she can be the authoritative interpreter of God's Revelation.

The Magisterium is composed of the Pope and the bishops united with him, who are charged with the office of teaching authoritatively. They have succeeded St. Peter and the Apostles in their roles as authentic interpreters of the Word of God. We see this teaching office interpreting the Word of God throughout Church history, starting even in the time of the Apostles themselves.

> "The task of giving an authentic interpretation of the Word of God, whether in its written form or in the form of Tradition, has been entrusted to the living teaching office of the Church alone. Its authority in this matter is exercised in the name of Jesus Christ."[46] This means that the task of interpretation has been entrusted to the bishops in communion with the successor of Peter, the Bishop of Rome. (CCC 85)

In the early Church one of the great debates was the degree to which the first Christians had to follow the ritual laws of the *Old Covenant*. If a non-Jew were to be baptized a Christian, did he or she also have to be circumcised and follow all the ritual laws found in the Old Testament? This was a serious debate that threatened to divide the Church. But in Acts we see how the Church—through her teaching office—resolved this issue:

St. Peter Preaching After Pentecost by Masolino. The Catholic faithful are charged with listening to the voice of the Magisterium.

> Some men came down from Judea and were teaching the brethren, "Unless you are circumcised according to the custom of Moses, you cannot be saved." And when Paul and Barnabas had no small dissension and debate with them, Paul and Barnabas and some of the others were appointed to go up to Jerusalem to the apostles and the elders about this question.
>
> The apostles and the elders were gathered together to consider this matter. And after there had been much debate, Peter rose and said to them, "Brethren, you know that in the early days God made choice among you, that by my mouth the Gentiles should hear the word of the gospel and believe. And God who knows the heart bore witness to them, giving them the Holy Spirit just as he did to us; and he made no distinction between us and them, but cleansed their hearts by faith. Now therefore why do you make trial of God by putting a yoke upon the neck of the disciples which neither our fathers nor we have been able to bear? But we believe that we shall be saved through the grace of the Lord Jesus, just as they will." (Acts 15:1-2, 6-11)

We see clearly the model for resolving disputes that arise in the interpretation of God's Word: The Apostles gathered in council with the Pope (St. Peter) and made a decision that is binding on the whole Church. This is the Magisterium in action.

Later in Church history, as we will see in the next chapter, councils made declarations on the divinity of Christ, the humanity of Christ, the canon of Scripture, and other important issues. These were all instances of Christ's promise that the "Spirit of truth" would guide the Church to "all the truth."

> "Yet this Magisterium is not superior to the Word of God, but is its servant. It teaches only what has been handed on to it. At the divine command and with the help of the Holy Spirit, it listens to this devotedly, guards it with dedication and expounds it faithfully. All that it proposes for belief as being divinely revealed is drawn from this single deposit of faith."[47] (CCC 86)

The Catholic faithful are charged with listening to the voice of the Magisterium as they would to the Apostles, or to Christ himself, as they speak in the name of Christ:

> Mindful of Christ's words to his apostles: "He who hears you, hears me,"[48] the faithful receive with docility the teachings and directives that their pastors give them in different forms. (CCC 87)

This "docility," as we will see later, does not imply an inert experience of the Catholic faith. Rather, the full embrace and knowledge of the teachings of the Church provide the fuel meant to empower the faithful not only to live out their own lives as Christians but also to serve as solid witnesses to the faith as they share the faith with others.

CONCLUSION

From the beginning of time God planned and formed a people to be his own. Initially, his people were the descendants of Abraham, Isaac, and Jacob: the people of Israel. But with the coming of his Son, Jesus Christ, the Church—the fulfillment of Israel—became his people and has reached to the ends of the world. Instituted by Christ himself, the Church was born by the Holy Spirit at Pentecost. Every baptized person becomes a member of this Church, called to a specific task and vocation within it.

> Christ, having been lifted up from the earth has drawn all to Himself.[49] Rising from the dead[50] He sent His life-giving Spirit upon His disciples and through Him has established His Body which is the Church as the universal sacrament of salvation. Sitting at the right hand of the Father, He is continually active in the world that He might lead men to the Church and through it join them to Himself and that He might make them partakers of His glorious life by nourishing them with His own Body and Blood. (*Lumen Gentium*, 48)

Our Lord gave to the Church the responsibility of proclaiming the Revelation of God and of spreading the Gospel faithfully to the ends of the earth. No task is nobler or more important to the salvation of the world. Every member of the Church is called to proclaim this Gospel, but to the successors of the Apostles—the Pope and the bishops united to him—is entrusted the sacred task of ensuring an authentic proclamation of God's Revelation. The Magisterium is guided by the Holy Spirit in the task of teaching and guarding the Deposit of Faith, that is, the Revelation preserved in Scripture and Tradition.

The Resurrection by Tintoretto.
"Rising from the dead He sent His life-giving Spirit upon His disciples and through Him has established His Body which is the Church as the universal sacrament of salvation." (*LG* 48)

CHALLENGES:

Isn't one faith or religion just as good as any other?

This question may sound like an expression of religious tolerance, but in reality it reflects what could be a certain relativism or even agnosticism. The question is relativistic in that it implies that religious truth is entirely a subjective experience, a matter of personal preference; it is agnostic in that it suggests that we cannot really know which religious claims are valid and which are not either because there is no such thing as objective truth or because we cannot discover objective truth with any degree of certainty.

The Ascension by Copely.
The Church knows that she holds the truths revealed by God, but she also defends human freedom as one of God's greatest gifts.

The fact is that objective truth does exist and that truth is knowable. Not only has God endowed the human person with knowledge of his existence and the natural law "written on the human heart," he has revealed himself also throughout salvation history, thus giving us a certainty of truth through faith. The fullness of his Revelation and the truth that he has communicated is found in the Catholic Church. Christ instituted this Church and commissioned her to teach that truth and Revelation throughout all time.

That does not mean that the Orthodox Churches, Christian ecclesial communities, and even non-Christian religions are without value. To the contrary, the Church recognizes that there are elements of holiness and truth in many different religious traditions. Those Churches and ecclesial communities that are in partial or imperfect communion with the Catholic Church likewise share a substantial portion of the truths taught by the Church. Other religious traditions, both offshoots of Christianity and various religions originating in the Far East or Middle East, also reflect elements of truth when their beliefs and moral values correspond with the Catholic faith.

Thus, it is incorrect to claim that one faith or religion is "just as good" as any other. Religious faith is about the search for truth, and the Catholic Church is endowed with this truth through the Revelation that is given to us from God. Therefore, it can readily be stated that the Catholic faith has the fullness of truth. Others can be good to the degree that they share in this truth.

To make such a statement can seem arrogant or triumphalistic, and we want to avoid sounding that way. To be fair, such an acknowledgment really underlines our personal sinfulness: How often do we, as professed Catholics, fail to live up to the truths we profess? How often do we allow a lapse in our prayer life, our moral choices, or our lived witness to what we say we believe? Knowing the truth brings with it a great responsibility to live that truth and to share that truth with others. If we claim to be Catholic, then we must live as good and faithful Catholics.

Sharing the truth with others in a nontriumphalistic way, guided by humility, requires a deep respect for the beliefs of others. The Church knows that she holds the truths revealed by God, but she also defends human freedom as one of God's greatest gifts. No one can impose a particular religious belief on another; therefore, we must always recognize the sincere faith that others embrace even when it is not our own. That is why the ecumenical and interfaith dialogues in which the Church engages non-Catholics are always characterized by deep respect even as we continue to strive for the full unity of all humanity under God through his Church.

PILLARS OF THE FAITH

STS. PETER AND PAUL

Sts. Peter and Paul are the two greatest figures of the early Church, the men most responsible for shaping and expanding the reach of the Gospel in the known world. St. Peter was the first head of the Church by virtue of having been appointed by Christ himself, and St. Paul of Tarsus is perhaps the greatest missionary in the history of the Church.

Earlier in this chapter we read about the dramatic conversion of Saul, the name by which St. Paul was known before he became a Christian. You might well imagine how Christians and their leaders might have been a little wary of St. Paul's story of having accepted Christ, fearing a trap. After all, Saul had used duplicitous means to root out Christians and have them arrested, imprisoned, beaten, or even killed, as in the case of St. Stephen (Acts 6:1-8:1).

However, St. Paul began to preach openly that Jesus was the Christ, the Son of God. He was even imprisoned himself for being a Christian, but escaped with the help of other believers. One of them, Barnabas, brought St. Paul to Jerusalem to meet with St. Peter and the Apostles. There St. Paul presented his "gospel which I preach among the Gentiles, lest somehow I should be running or had run in vain" (Gal 2:2) to ensure that what he was teaching was in line with what the Apostles were teaching, with the result that "those who were in repute"—the highest teaching authority—"added nothing" to what he had taught.

For a time, St. Paul preached right along with them in Jerusalem. Then St. Paul returned to

Apostles Peter and Paul by El Greco. The men most responsible for shaping and expanding the reach of the Gospel in the known world.

his home city of Tarsus, where he continued to preach to both Jews and Gentiles. Increasingly, St. Paul focued on converting the Gentile (non-Jewish) peoples, which earned him the moniker "Apostle to the Gentiles."

Because the Christian faith was still closely associated with the Jewish religion, there was an opinion among some, referred to as the "circumcision party," that in order to become a disciple of Christ, a person first had to become a Jew. Pagans who converted, in this thinking, would have to be circumcised and to observe the Jewish dietary laws. But St. Paul opposed this point of view, believing

Continued

STS. PETER AND PAUL

Continued

it to be an unnecessary burden since Christ had freed his people from such constraints of the Old Law.

The debate raged for years and was finally settled, by the guidance of the Holy Spirit, at the Council of Jerusalem. St. Peter, having previously received a vision about the suitability of lifting Jewish dietary laws (Acts 10), ruled on behalf of St. Paul's position, and St. James spoke for the others in ratifying St. Peter's judgment. A letter was sent among the churches that placed no such circumcision requirement on the Gentiles but only suggested that they abstain from meat that had been sacrificed to pagan idols and avoid immorality (Acts 15). Jewish Christians and Gentile Christians were equals in the faith.

Eventually, both Sts. Peter and Paul would die in Rome as martyrs during the bloody persecution of Christians there. Yet, Christianity would survive on the power of their witness to the faith. Harkening to the legendary twin founders of pagan Rome, Romulus and Remus, the early Christians considered Sts. Peter and Paul the founders of a new, Christian Rome. St. Irenæus, a Church Father and second-century bishop, described the local church in Rome as "the very great, the very ancient, and universally known Church founded and organized at Rome by the two most glorious apostles, Peter and Paul" (*Against Heresies III*, Chapter 3, 2).

This foundation by the leading Apostles gave support to the recognition of the Church of Rome as the leading church in all of Christendom. Likewise, it united for all time the work and ministry of the two chief Apostles, Sts. Peter and Paul. To this day these Apostles are commemorated together on June 29, their shared feast day.

Interestingly, considering the topic of this text, when the Week of Prayer for Christian Unity was first instituted, two minor feasts related to Sts. Peter and Paul "bookended" the week: the Feast of St. Peter's Confession was celebrated on January 18 (it was later merged with another feast by St. John XXIII in 1960), while the Feast of the Conversion of St. Paul is celebrated on January 25.

The Martyrdom of St. Paul by Tintoretto. Both Sts. Peter and Paul died in Rome as martyrs during the bloody persecution of Christians there.

SUPPLEMENTARY READING

Sacred Tradition and Sacred Scripture Flow from the Same Divine Wellspring

There exists a close connection and communication between sacred tradition and Sacred Scripture. For both of them, flowing from the same divine wellspring, in a certain way merge into a unity and tend toward the same end. For Sacred Scripture is the word of God inasmuch as it is consigned to writing under the inspiration of the divine Spirit, while sacred tradition takes the word of God entrusted by Christ the Lord and the Holy Spirit to the Apostles, and hands it on to their successors in its full purity, so that led by the light of the Spirit of truth, they may in proclaiming it preserve this word of God faithfully, explain it, and make it more widely known. Consequently it is not from Sacred Scripture alone that the Church draws her certainty about everything which has been revealed. Therefore both sacred tradition and Sacred Scripture are to be accepted and venerated with the same sense of loyalty and reverence.[51]

— Second Ecumenical Council of the Vatican, Dogmatic Constitution on Divine Revelation *Dei Verbum*, no. 9

The Nativity by Bicci di Lorenzo. St. Paul VI proclaimed the Mother of Christ the Mother of the Church.

The Blessed Virgin Mary, Mother of the Church

If we are aware of this task, then we seem to understand better what it means to say that the Church is a mother[52] and also what it means to say that the Church always, and particularly at our time, has need of a Mother. We owe a debt of special gratitude to the Fathers of the Second Vatican Council, who expressed this truth in the Constitution *Lumen Gentium* with the rich Mariological doctrine contained in it.[53] Since [St.] Paul VI, inspired by that teaching, proclaimed the Mother of Christ "Mother of the Church,"[54] and that title has become known far and wide, may it be permitted to his unworthy Successor to turn to Mary as Mother of the Church at the close of these reflections which it was opportune to make at the beginning of his papal service. Mary is Mother of the Church because, on account of the Eternal Father's ineffable choice[55] and due to the Spirit of Love's special action,[56] she gave human life to the Son of God, "for whom and by whom all things exist"[57] and from whom the whole of the People of God receives the grace and dignity of election. Her Son explicitly extended his Mother's maternity in a way that could easily be understood by every soul and every heart by designating, when he was raised on the Cross, his beloved disciple as her son.[58] The Holy Spirit inspired her to remain in the Upper Room, after our Lord's Ascension, recollected in prayer and expectation, together with the Apostles, until the day of Pentecost, when the Church was to be born in visible form, coming forth from darkness.[59] Later, all the generations of disciples, of those who confess and love Christ, like the Apostle John, spiritually took this Mother to their own homes,[60] and she was thus included in the history of salvation and in the Church's mission from the very beginning, that is from the moment of the Annunciation. Accordingly, we who form today's generation of disciples of Christ all wish to unite ourselves with her in a special way. We do so with all our attachment to our ancient tradition and also with full respect and love for the members of all the Christian Communities.

SUPPLEMENTARY READING Continued

We do so at the urging of the deep need of faith, hope and charity. For if we feel a special need, in this difficult and responsible phase of the history of the Church and of mankind, to turn to Christ, who is Lord of the Church and Lord of man's history on account of the mystery of the Redemption, we believe that nobody else can bring us as Mary can into the divine and human dimension of this mystery. Nobody has been brought into it by God himself as Mary has. It is in this that the exceptional character of the grace of the divine Motherhood consists. Not only is the dignity of this Motherhood unique and unrepeatable in the history of the human race, but Mary's participation, due to this Maternity, in God's plan for man's salvation through the mystery of the Redemption is also unique in profundity and range of action.

We can say that the mystery of the Redemption took shape beneath the heart of the Virgin of Nazareth when she pronounced her "fiat." From then on, under the special influence of the Holy Spirit, this heart, the heart of both a virgin and a mother, has always followed the work of her Son and has gone out to all those whom Christ has embraced and continues to embrace with inexhaustible love. For that reason her heart must also have the inexhaustibility of a mother. The special characteristic of the motherly love that the Mother of God inserts in the mystery of the Redemption and the life of the Church finds expression in its exceptional closeness to man and all that happens to him. It is in this that the mystery of the Mother consists. The Church, which looks to her with altogether special love and hope, wishes to make this mystery her own in an ever deeper manner. For in this the Church also recognizes the way for her daily life, which is each person.

— St. John Paul II, encyclical *Redemptor Hominis*, no. 22

Annunciation by Poussin.
"We can say that the mystery of the Redemption took shape beneath the heart of the Virgin of Nazareth when she pronounced her 'fiat.'" (*RH* 22)

VOCABULARY

APOSTOLIC SUCCESSION
The handing on of ecclesiastical authority from the Apostles to their successors, the bishops, through the laying on of hands.

ASCENSION
Forty days after his Resurrection, the entry of Christ's humanity into divine glory.

CIRCUMCISION
The ritual excision of the foreskin designated as the visible sign of God's covenant with Abraham and his descendants. Circumcision set the People of God apart from other nations.

COUNCIL
Synod. A formal meeting of bishops (sometimes with other ecclesiastics) convened for regulation or discipline in the Church. Especially in the early Church, councils were held to clarify points of Christian doctrine. The Council of Jerusalem is recounted in Acts 15; the First Ecumenical Council was held in Nicæa in 325.

DEPOSIT OF FAITH
The heritage of faith contained in Sacred Scripture and Tradition, handed on in the Church from the time of the Apostles, from which the Magisterium draws all that it proposes for belief as being divinely revealed.

HIERARCHY
Greek for the "sacred rule." The Apostles and their successors, the bishops, to whom Christ gave the authority to teach, sanctify, and rule in his name.

KEYS OF THE KINGDOM
The power to bind and loose given by Christ to St. Peter. The badge of the office of prime minister in the Davidic kingdom.

MAGISTERIUM
The name given to the teaching authority of the Church, entrusted to the Pope and the bishops in communion with him.

MISSIONARY
One who goes out to preach the Gospel to those who do not yet follow it.

OLD COVENANT
The Mosaic Law, encapsulated as the Ten Commandments, and its stipulation from God to the Israelites that "I will be your God, and you will be my people" (Jer 7:23).

PRIME MINISTER
A servant of the king who oversees all the affairs of the kingdom; the king's most trusted advisor.

SACRAMENT
An efficacious sign of grace, instituted by Christ and entrusted to the Church, by which divine life is dispensed through the work of the Holy Spirit. There are seven Sacraments.

SCRIPTURE, SACRED
Bible. The books that contain the truth of God's Revelation and were composed by human authors inspired by the Holy Spirit. The Bible contains both the forty-six books of the Old Testament and the twenty-seven books of the New Testament.

SYNAGOGUE
A Jewish house of meeting. Sacrifices could be offered only at the Temple in Jerusalem, but Jews all over the world went to local synagogues to worship and to hear the Scriptures read and interpreted.

TRADITION, SACRED
From the Latin for "handed down," this refers to a teaching, whether written or oral, entrusted by Christ to the Apostles and their successors, and which has been transmitted to each generation of Christians through Apostolic Succession.

STUDY QUESTIONS

1. Why did God anoint mediators?
2. What is the foundation of the New Testament?
3. What was the Son's task in the world?
4. What is the path to salvation in this world?
5. How does the Holy Spirit reorient the People of God?
6. What is the role of a prime minister? Who has a similar role in the Catholic Church?
7. What is the Great Commission?
8. Name two ways the Church is "apostolic."
9. How did the mission of God's people change after Pentecost?
10. What did the Holy Spirit do for the disciples on Pentecost?
11. What was a duty of the Apostles? (Hint: Why did Judas need a replacement?)
12. What are two means by which God's Revelation is passed on?
13. Who guides the Church to all truth?
14. What is the Magisterium?
15. How does the Church resolve disputes that arise in matters of Church teaching?

PRACTICAL EXERCISES

1. Revelation is given to us and handed on through Scripture, Tradition, and the Magisterium. Give a brief description of each of these three and tell how each helps us understand God's Revelation.

2. A Protestant friend says that only the Bible is needed to understand God and his Revelation. Tell how you would explain the Church's role and authority in understanding Divine Revelation.

3. Many people think a Church is not necessary for following Christ. What are three reasons the Church is essential for truly living a Christian life?

4. A friend tells you that it doesn't really matter what Church you go to; all that matters is that you love Christ and have him in your heart. How do you answer?

FROM THE CATECHISM

759 "The eternal Father, in accordance with the utterly gratuitous and mysterious design of his wisdom and goodness, created the whole universe and chose to raise up men to share in his own divine life,"[61] to which he calls all men in his Son. "The Father...determined to call together in a holy Church those who should believe in Christ."[62] This "family of God" is gradually formed and takes shape during the stages of human history, in keeping with the Father's plan. In fact, "already present in figure at the beginning of the world, this Church was prepared in marvelous fashion in the history of the people of Israel and the old Alliance. Established in this last age of the world and made manifest in the outpouring of the Spirit, it will be brought to glorious completion at the end of time."[63]

766 The Church is born primarily of Christ's total self-giving for our salvation, anticipated in the institution of the Eucharist and fulfilled on the cross. "The origin and growth of the Church are symbolized by the blood and water which flowed from the open side of the crucified Jesus."[64] "For it was from the side of Christ as he slept the sleep of death upon the cross that there came forth the 'wondrous sacrament of the

FROM THE CATECHISM Continued

whole Church.'"[65] As Eve was formed from the sleeping Adam's side, so the Church was born from the pierced heart of Christ hanging dead on the cross.[66]

857 The Church is apostolic because she is founded on the apostles, in three ways:

— she was and remains built on "the foundation of the Apostles,"[67] the witnesses chosen and sent on mission by Christ himself;[68]

— with the help of the Spirit dwelling in her, the Church keeps and hands on the teaching,[69] the "good deposit," the salutary words she has heard from the apostles;[70]

— she continues to be taught, sanctified, and guided by the apostles until Christ's return, through their successors in pastoral office: the college of bishops, "assisted by priests, in union with the successor of Peter, the Church's supreme pastor":[71]

> You are the eternal Shepherd
> who never leaves his flock untended.
> Through the apostles
> you watch over us and protect us always.
> You made them shepherds of the flock
> to share in the work of your Son....[72]

ENDNOTES – CHAPTER TWO

1. *LG* 1.
2. Rev 7:9.
3. Bishops of the United States of America, September 16, 1987, n. 1: "Insegnamenti di Giovanni Paolo II" X, 3 (1987), p. 553.
4. Ratzinger, Joseph, *Letter to the Bishops of the Catholic Church on some Aspects of the Church, Understood as Communion,* 3.
5. Cf. CCC 759.
6. *Pastor Hermæ*, Vision 2, 4, 1: PG 2, 899; cf. Aristides, *Apol.* 16, 6; St. Justin, *Apol.* 2, 7: PG 6, 456; Tertullian, *Apol.* 31, 3; 32, 1: PL 1, 508-509.
7. Cf. St. Epiphanius, *Panarion* 1, 1, 5: PG 41, 181C.
8. Clement of Alex., *Pæd.* 1, 6, 27: PG 8, 281; cf. CCC 760.
9. Cf. CCC 761.
10. CCC 762; Cf. Ex 19:5-6; Dt 7:6; Is 2:2-5; Mi 4:1-4.
11. Mt 5:17.
12. Cf. *LG* 3; *AG* 3.
13. *LG* 5.
14. *LG* 3.
15. Cf. CCC 764; Lk 12:32; Mt 10:16; 26:31; Jn 10:1-21; Mt 12:49.
16. Mt 19:28.
17. Cf. Mk 3:14-15.
18. Cf. Mt 19:28; Lk 22:30; Rev 21:12-14.
19. Cf. Mk 6:7; Lk 10:1-2; Mt 10:25; Jn 15:20.
20. Jn 14:26.
21. Cf. CCC 767-768.
22. *LG* 7.
23. *LG* 7; cf. Rom 6:4-5; 1 Cor 12:13.
24. St. Thomas Aquinas, *STh* III, 48, 2.
25. *LG* 20; cf. Mt 28:20.
26. Mk 4:34.
27. Mt 16:19.
28. Cf. Mk 3:14-15.
29. Cf. Mt 19:28; Lk 22:30; Rev 21:12-14.
30. Cf. Mk 6:7; Lk 10:1-2; Mt 10:25; Jn 15:20.
31. Jn 21:15-19.
32. *AA* 2.
33. Cf. CCC 858.
34. Acts 1:21-22.
35. Cf. Mt 28:20.
36. S. Clem. Rom., *ad Cor.* 44, 2; ed. Funk, I, p. 154 s.
37. Cfr. Tertull., *Præscr. Hær.* 32; PL 2, 52 s.; S. Ignatius M., *passim.*
38. Cfr. Tertull., *Præscr. Hær.* 32; PL 2, 53.
39. Cfr. S. Irenæus, *Adv. Hær.* III, 3, 1; PG 7, 848 A; Harvey 2, 8; Sagnard, p. 100 s.: *manifestatam.*
40. Cfr. S. Irenæus, *Adv. Hær.* III, 2, 2; PG 7, 847; Harvey 2, 7; Sagnard, p. 100:. *custoditur,*., cfr. ib. IV, 26, 2; col. 1053, Harvey 2, 236, necnon IV, 33, 8; col. 1077; Harvey 2, 262.
41. Cf. CCC 861-862.
42. First Vatican Council, Dogmatic Constitution on the Catholic Faith, Chap. 2, "On Revelation": Denzinger 1786 (3005).
43. Mt 28:20.
44. Mt 16:18-19.
45. Jn 16:13.
46. *DV* 10 § 2.
47. *DV* 10 § 2.
48. Lk 10:16; cf. *LG* 20.
49. Cf. Jn 12:32.
50. Cf. Rom 6:9.
51. First Vatican Council, Dogmatic Constitution on the Catholic Faith, Chap. 2, "On Revelation": Denzinger 1786 (3005).
52. Cf. *LG* 63-64; AAS 57 (1965) 64.
53. Cf. Chapter VIII, 52-69; AAS 57 (1965) 58-67.
54. St. Paul VI: *Closing Address at the Third Session of the Second Vatican Ecumenical Council,* November 21, 1964: AAS 56 (1964) 1015.
55. Cf. *LG* 56: AAS 57 (1965) 60.
56. Ibid.
57. Heb 2:10.
58. Cf. Jn 19:26.
59. Cf. Acts 1:14; 2.
60. Cf. Jn 19:27.
61. *LG* 2.
62. *LG* 2.
63. *LG* 2.
64. *LG* 3; cf. Jn 19:34.
65. *SC* 5.
66. Cf. St. Ambrose, *In Luc.* 2, 85-89: PL 15, 1666-1668.
67. Eph 2:20; Rev 21:14.
68. Cf. Mt 28:16-20; Acts 1:8; 1 Cor 9:1; 15:7-8; Gal 1:1; etc.
69. Cf. Acts 2:42.
70. Cf. 2 Tm 1:13-14.
71. *AG* 5.
72. *Roman Missal*, Preface of the Apostles I.

Ecumenism and Interreligious Dialogue

CHAPTER 3

The Church as the Sacrament of Communion

The Eucharist is the source of communion among the members of the Church.

Ecumenism and Interreligious Dialogue

CHAPTER THREE

The Church as the Sacrament of Communion

INTRODUCTION

"I do not pray for these only, but also for those who believe in me through their word, that they may all be one; even as thou, Father, art in me, and I in thee, that they also may be in us, so that the world may believe that thou hast sent me. The glory which thou hast given me I have given to them, that they may be one even as we are one, I in them and thou in me, that they may become perfectly one, so that the world may know that thou hast sent me and hast loved them even as thou hast loved me." (Jn 17: 20-23)

In the previous chapter we reviewed the divine origins of the Church and how she fit into God's plan of salvation. Jesus Christ, the Son of God, established one Church, the fulfillment of Israel, on the foundation of the Twelve Apostles, with St. Peter as primary among the Apostles. He commissioned his Church under the leadership of the Apostles to teach and baptize all nations, bringing everyone into the Church that he established. This sacred mission continues today and through the end of time through Apostolic Succession and under the guidance and empowerment of the Holy Spirit.

This one Church established by Christ is the Catholic Church. However, while the Catholic Church has more than one billion members, there are almost as many people in the world who profess faith in Christ but do not belong to the Catholic Church. These divisions in Christianity are far from the unity Christ willed for his Church. The work toward full Christian unity is called ecumenism.

Throughout this book we will be using a number of terms that may seem familiar to us but perhaps need to be defined more fully for greater clarity. In the first two chapters of this text, we have already made use of three of these terms with some frequency: *church*, *Christian*, and *communion*.

In this chapter, we will explore:

- ✠ What is a Church?
- ✠ How is the Church a Sacrament of Communion?
- ✠ What is Apostolic Succession, and why is it important?
- ✠ What does it mean to say that the fullness of truth "subsists in" the Catholic Church?
- ✠ What are the four marks of the Catholic Church?
- ✠ What does it mean to be called a Christian?
- ✠ What does it mean to be in full communion with the Catholic Church?
- ✠ What is imperfect, or partial, communion?
- ✠ What are some of the ways in which full communion can be ruptured?
- ✠ How is the Eucharist related to communion?
- ✠ Is there salvation outside the Church?

According to Catholic doctrine and tradition, a church is a Christian community that has maintained Apostolic Succession. Many of the organized Christian faith groups that we commonly call churches are more properly called *ecclesial* communities.

ECCLESIOLOGY OF COMMUNION

The Church as the Sacrament of Communion

The Church is the Sacrament of Communion because she is both the sign and the means by which God brings people into communion with himself and with each other through the grace of the Sacraments. Every person enters into the Church's communion by faith and by Baptism.[1] Through Baptism the faithful are incorporated into a Body—the Church—which the risen Lord builds up and sustains through the Eucharist. The Eucharist, the root and center of the community, is the source of communion among the members of the Church, uniting each one of them with Christ himself:

> **Because there is one bread, we who are many are one body, for we all partake of the one bread. (1 Cor 10:17)**
>
> **When we share in the Body and Blood of Christ we become what we receive.**[2]

The Eucharist is not simply some "thing" that makes communion happen. The Eucharist is literally Jesus Christ himself. God himself is the source and instrument of communion between him and his people.

What is the Church?

The word *church* has several shades of meaning. Sometimes "the Church" refers to the entire body of baptized Christian believers—Catholics, Orthodox, and Protestants of all denominations. Other times it refers to all baptized Christians in union with the Pope (the Catholic Church). When we speak in certain other contexts, such as when we discuss what "the Church" teaches, we refer to her Magisterium or hierarchy. It also is common to speak of individual "churches," as in the local church or diocese, or even to identify a particular parish ("I attend St. Teresa of Avila Church"). The term is applied commonly to almost every non-Catholic Christian denomination ("Susan is a member of the Presbyterian Church").

Furthermore, you will see in common usage that the word "church" is sometimes capitalized. When used in a title such as "The Orthodox Church in America," it is capitalized because it is part of a formal title. The term "church" is also capitalized when referring to the Catholic Church such as "a member of the Church through Baptism." However, it is not capitalized when it refers informally to multiple church communities or to a church building. This usage—followed in this book—helps to distinguish between the different meanings of "church."

Although we tend to label every Christian denomination as a "church," many of the organized Christian faith groups that we commonly call churches, in fact, are more properly called *ecclesial* communities. You may have noticed already in this text that we have referred to the Protestant denominations in this manner.

Importance of Apostolic Succession

Pope Francis leaves the Sistine Chapel after his election by the College of Cardinals on March 13, 2013 to be the Apostolic Successor of St. Peter, the 266th Pope of the Roman Catholic Church, and the Bishop of Rome. The bishops of the Catholic Church trace their office in an unbroken line back to the original Twelve Apostles.

According to Catholic doctrine and tradition, a church is a Christian community that has maintained Apostolic Succession, that is, it has received its teaching and ministerial authority in a direct line handed down from Christ and his Apostles. The leaders of a church, in other words, must be true successors of the Apostles.

As we read in the previous chapter, the bishops of the Catholic Church trace their office in an unbroken line back to the original Twelve Apostles. We see in the Acts of the Apostles that St. Peter and the other Apostles already were appointing successors to continue and extend the ministry commissioned to them by Christ. These leaders were called bishops, who in turn handed on their authority to other men through the *laying on of hands*, consecrating them to the fullness of the Sacrament of *Holy Orders*.

Why is Apostolic Succession important? It is important because, through this same Sacrament of Holy Orders, bishops are empowered to ordain men to the ministerial priesthood, and these priests are in turn empowered to celebrate the Eucharist, whereby they validly consecrate ordinary bread and wine so they become the true Body and Blood of Christ. Without Apostolic Succession, there would be no validly ordained bishops, no validly ordained priests, and no valid Sacrament of the Eucharist.

In the documents of the *Second Ecumenical Council of the Vatican* (1962-1965), the Council Fathers—the Catholic bishops of the world, who in communion with the Pope exercise the Magisterium—used the term "church" in reference to the Eastern Orthodox communities. They did so because the Orthodox bishops have maintained Apostolic Succession despite having rejected papal authority. The Orthodox Churches thus retain a valid priesthood and a valid Eucharist. Even though the Catholic and Orthodox Churches are divided from one another on particular issues, they share in the continued ministry handed on from the Apostles. The Council documents describe the Orthodox Churches as "the separated Churches."

On May 15, 2009 Pope Benedict XVI met with the Patriarch of Jerusalem Theophilos III at the Greek Orthodox Patriarchate in the Old City of Jerusalem during his eight day pilgrimage to the Holy Land.

The Protestant and Anglican communities that arose out of the *Reformation* of the sixteenth century as well as the Christian communities that developed in later years, however, lack these necessary elements required to be considered true churches. They either deny the need for Apostolic Succession or have redefined the term in a way that is incompatible with what the Catholic and Orthodox Churches teach. Their leaders are not in a "line" of succession dating to the Apostles. Lacking that, they have neither validly ordained clergy nor a valid Eucharist. Applying the term "ecclesial communities" to these Protestant denominations signifies their dignity as true Christians and, at the same time, distinguishes them from those who have valid Apostolic Succession and a valid Eucharist.

As a 2007 statement from the Congregation for the Doctrine of the Faith explained:

> According to Catholic doctrine, these Communities do not enjoy apostolic succession in the sacrament of Orders, and are, therefore, deprived of a constitutive element of the Church. These ecclesial Communities which, specifically because of the absence of the sacramental priesthood, have not preserved the genuine and integral substance of the Eucharistic Mystery cannot, according to Catholic doctrine, be called "Churches" in the proper sense.[3]

Fullness of Truth "Subsists in" the Catholic Church

Nevertheless, the same document explains that there is much the Catholic Church shares in common with these Protestant ecclesial communities. These communities, the statement says, contain "numerous elements of sanctification and of truth." These elements permit the Holy Spirit to use those communities as "instruments of salvation" that can draw Christians within those communities toward the fullness of the Church founded by Christ, which "subsists in" (exists fully and completely in) the Catholic Church. The Pontifical Council for Promoting Christian Unity explains:

> Catholics hold the firm conviction that the one Church of Christ subsists in the Catholic Church "which is governed by the successor of Peter and by the Bishops in communion with him."[4] They confess that the entirety of revealed truth, of sacraments, and of ministry that Christ gave for the building up of his Church and the carrying out of its mission is found within the Catholic communion of the Church.[5]

Catholics ought not consider this status as members of the true Church with excessive pride, however, as even everyone within the Catholic Church is in need of drawing into closer communion and closer fidelity to the faith. The document goes on to state:

> Certainly Catholics know that personally they have not made full use of and do not make full use of the means of grace with which the Church is endowed. For all that, Catholics never lose confidence in the Church. Their faith assures them that it remains "the worthy bride of the Lord,

ceaselessly renewing herself through the action of the Holy Spirit until, through the cross, she may attain to that light which knows no setting."[6] Therefore, when Catholics use the words "Churches," "other Churches," "other Churches and ecclesial Communities" etc., to refer to those who are not in full communion with the Catholic Church, this firm conviction and confession of faith must always be kept in mind.[7]

The Four Marks of the Church

This "confession of faith" is aptly capsulated in the creed, a statement of fundamental beliefs, that is prayed in the Mass. In this creed the Catholic faithful affirm belief in "one, holy, catholic, and apostolic church." These four attributes are often called the *marks of the Church*; in other words, they are the defining characteristics by which the Church can be recognized.

Icon depicting the First Ecumenical Council of Nicæa, AD 325, called by Emperor Constantine to unite the Christian empire, which was divided over Arianism. The council concluded with the Nicene Creed proposed by St. Athanasius.

These four marks were first expressed at the First Ecumenical Council of Constantinople AD 381 and inserted as a point of belief into the creed that had been formulated at the Council of Nicæa AD 325.

We have already discussed to some degree the nature of these four marks:

- **The Church is One** because there is only one Lord, one Church, one Baptism, one faith, one Body of Christ.[8]
- **The Church is Holy** because she is of divine origin; Christ sacrificed himself to sanctify her, and the Holy Spirit continues to give her life and holiness; she remains perfect despite being made up of sinners.[9]
- **The Church is Catholic** (universal) because she is the one Body of Christ and in her sacred mission she extends her invitation to salvation to the entire world, to every human person. The term "Catholic Christian," in fact, was first applied to members of the Church in the fourth century in order to distinguish the true Church from the Arians and other breakaway sects that represented some of the first breaches of Christian unity.
- **The Church is Apostolic** because she was founded upon the Apostles and continues to receive her authority from them by way of a true Apostolic Succession, passed down through the laying on of hands in the Sacrament of Holy Orders.

Although the Orthodox Churches as well as the Anglicans and certain other Protestant ecclesial communities recite the same *Nicene-Constantinopolitan Creed* in their liturgies, they tend to interpret the meaning of these four marks differently. The Catholic Church alone has the fullness of all four marks, while the other Christian churches and ecclesial communities variously share in some, but not all, of these marks. As the Second Vatican Council taught:

> **The one Church of Christ which in the Creed we profess as one, holy, catholic and apostolic,[10]... subsists in the Catholic Church, which is governed by the successor of Peter and by the Bishops in communion with him,[11] although many elements of sanctification and of truth are found outside of its visible confines. (*Lumen Gentium*, 8)**

The Baptism of Christ by Patinir.
To be a Christian means simply to have received a valid Baptism.

WHAT IS A CHRISTIAN?

Note that within the ecclesial communities that are not regarded as "churches," the members are still considered Christians. To be a Christian means simply to have received a valid Baptism. As long as a person is baptized with water, with the intention of "doing what the Church does" by baptizing, and accompanied by the *Trinitarian formula* ("...in the name of the Father, and of the Son, and of the Holy Spirit"), that individual has been validly baptized. Most Baptisms that take place in Protestant communities are recognized as valid by the Catholic Church.

Baptism has many salutary effects, not the least of which is the forgiveness of sins and the giving of sanctifying grace. Through Baptism, the baptized person also is incorporated into the Church and becomes a member of the Body of Christ.[12]

It is therefore the means by which one enters the Church. It is our birth into the Family of God and new life in Christ, a sharing in his Death and Resurrection. As St. Paul writes,

> **Do you not know that all of us who have been baptized into Christ Jesus were baptized into his death? We were buried therefore with him by baptism into death, so that as Christ was raised from the dead by the glory of the Father, we too might walk in newness of life.** (Rom 6: 3-4)

Thus incorporated into Christ, the baptized "have a right to be called Christians."[13] They become children of God and partakers of the divine nature. All Christians belong to God's family; all Christians belong to the Church, the People of God. Because of this, all the baptized share a certain communion with Christ and with one another.

> The comparison of the Church with the body casts light on the intimate bond between Christ and his Church. Not only is she gathered *around him*; she is united *in him*, in his body. (CCC 789)

THE MEANING OF COMMUNION

In this text we have spoken of several types of communion:

- ✠ Communion among the three Persons of the Blessed Trinity;
- ✠ Our communion with God;
- ✠ Our communion with other Christians;
- ✠ The communion of the bishops with the Pope; and
- ✠ Holy Communion, reception of the Sacrament of the Holy Eucharist.

Although each of these uses describes a different form of communion, each pertains to the fundamental definition of communion.

Supper at Emmaus by Pontormo. *Communion* refers to being united together.

The word "communion" comes from the Latin words *communio*, which means "sharing in common," and *communis*, "participation by all." It is the word biblical translators used for the Greek term *koinonia,* which is often translated as "fellowship." In both terms, we can more or less perceive the words "common" and "union." "Communion," then, refers to being united together.

With that in mind, let us look again at the five types of communion mentioned above.

- ✠ The communion of the Blessed Trinity is a perfect communion: The three Persons are in perfect union in one God.
- ✠ Our communion with God relates to our relationship with him. Our first parents, Adam and Eve, enjoyed communion with God, but sin broke that communion. The more we seek holiness through living the faith and doing God's will, the stronger our communion with him will be.
- ✠ As noted earlier, the Christian faithful on earth, by virtue of Baptism, share degrees of communion with one another. The more closely we are united in faith, the greater our communion with one another will be.
- ✠ The Catholic bishops, as successors of the Apostles, share a communion in faith with the Pope, the successor of St. Peter, primary among the Apostles. They share a common mission given to them by Christ to carry on his own mission of teaching the Good News of salvation.
- ✠ The Sacrament of the Holy Eucharist is called Holy Communion because of the sign and effect of the Sacrament. When Catholics receive the Eucharist at Mass, it is a sign of their communion with Christ, his Church, and with one another, and it also strengthens these bonds of communion. By receiving the true Body and Blood of Christ, we become incorporated more deeply into his Body, the Church.[14]

Central to this chapter is the communion among baptized Christians. Since there is only one Church established by Christ but numerous Christian churches and ecclesial communities separated by differences in belief and practice, then what kind of "communion" do Christians really share? Clearly not all Christians are in communion with the Catholic Church and with one another to the same degree. How can we best describe the relationship among these various faith groups amid so much division?

The answer is that we speak of these relationships in terms of whether they are in *full communion* or *imperfect communion* with the Catholic Church.

WHAT DOES IT MEAN TO BE IN FULL COMMUNION?

The true Church founded by Christ, we have noted, "subsists...in the Catholic Church" (*LG* 8). To "subsist in" means to exist in all truth and totality. The Catholic Church, therefore, has the fullness of truth taught by Christ. Other churches and ecclesial communities possess that truth to a greater or lesser degree depending upon how much of the essence of the faith they hold in common with the Catholic Church.

Non-Catholic Christians—those who do not embrace the fullness of truth taught by the Catholic Church—share a certain communion with the Catholic Church by virtue of Baptism, but they possess this communion in an incomplete way. They are incorporated into the Church, yet they are not in full communion with the Church. As the *Catechism of the Catholic Church* teaches:

> Baptism constitutes the foundation of communion among all Christians, including those who are not yet in full communion with the Catholic Church: "For men who believe in Christ and have been properly baptized are put in some, though imperfect, communion with the Catholic Church. Justified by faith in Baptism, [they] are incorporated into Christ; they therefore have a right to be called Christians, and with good reason are accepted as brothers by the children of the Catholic Church."[15] "Baptism therefore constitutes the *sacramental bond of unity* existing among all who through it are reborn."[16] (CCC 1271)

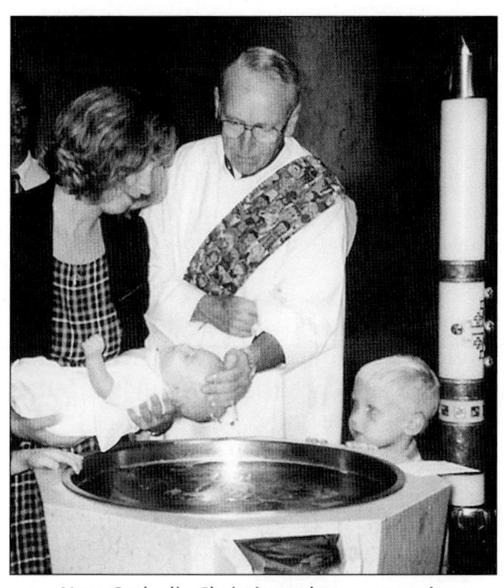

Non-Catholic Christians share a certain communion with the Catholic Church by virtue of Baptism.

Baptism in itself does not indicate full communion with the Church founded by Christ. At the same time, full communion with the Catholic Church is not possible without Baptism.

The official ecclesiastical law of the Church, compiled in the *Code of Canon Law*, tells us how full communion is defined:

> Those baptized are fully in the communion of the Catholic Church on this earth who are joined with Christ in its visible structure by the bonds of the profession of faith, the sacraments, and ecclesiastical governance. (CIC, 205)

From this statement we can glean that in addition to Baptism there are three essential aspects of full communion:

- Acceptance of a common profession of faith;
- *Eucharistic communion*; and
- Respect and obedience toward those in authority in the Church.

Let us look at each one of these aspects in turn, especially with regard to how they apply to each individual person.

Profession of Faith

One of the fundamental principles of Christianity is that God has revealed himself throughout history, most especially in his Son, Jesus Christ. To be a follower of Christ is to profess the faith as it has been handed on to his Church. Christ, before his Ascension, told his Apostles to "teach...them to observe all that I have commanded you" (Mt 28: 20); in other words, the Christian faith is not simply a matter of being baptized but includes an assent of the mind and will to the teachings of Christ and his Church.

In the case of most people, this profession of faith is first made for them by their parents. When a baby is baptized, he or she cannot make the assent of mind and will to Christ, so parents and sponsors (godparents) make this profession in his or her name. However, at some point, each baptized person must make a choice to accept the teachings of Christ and his Church as true and life-giving. Those who reject this profession of faith are not in full communion with the Church.

Eucharistic Communion

Since it is a gift from God rather than an act of man, full communion goes deeper than simply a profession of faith. It is not under our power that we remain in full communion; it is through the action of God in the Sacraments, most especially the Eucharist, the "sacrament of the Church's unity."

> *The unity of the Mystical Body: the Eucharist makes the Church.* Those who receive the Eucharist are united more closely to Christ. Through it Christ unites them to all the faithful in one body—the Church. Communion renews, strengthens, and deepens this incorporation into the Church, already achieved by Baptism. In Baptism we have been called to form but one body.[17] The Eucharist fulfills this call: "The cup of blessing which we bless, is it not a participation in the blood of Christ? The bread which we break, is it not a participation in the body of Christ? Because there is one bread, we who are many are one body, for we all partake of the one bread."[18] (CCC 1396)

Adoration of the Lamb (detail) by Van Eyck. Without the Eucharist, there is no Church, and without the Church there can be no full communion.

The *Catechism* goes further in describing how the Sacrament of the Eucharist enriches our communion with Christ and his Church:

> Believers who respond to God's word and become members of Christ's Body, become intimately united with him: "In that body the life of Christ is communicated to those who believe, and who, through the sacraments, are united in a hidden and real way to Christ in his Passion and glorification."[19] This is especially true of Baptism, which unites us to Christ's death and Resurrection, and the Eucharist, by which "really sharing in the body of the Lord,...we are taken up into communion with him and with one another."[20] (CCC 790)

It is the Eucharist that gives us the grace and strength to remain in communion with Christ and his Church, and it is the Eucharist that binds together Christ's followers as one Body. The Eucharist is so vital to this communion that we often call it just that: "communion." The Eucharist constitutes the Church; without the Eucharist, there is no Church, and without the Church there can be no full communion.

Obedience to Authority

Finally, full communion demands obedience to those in authority in the Church. Specifically, one must be in union with the successors of St. Peter and the Apostles—the Pope and the bishops united with him. Christ gave the Apostles his own authority over the Church (cf. Mt 16:18-19; 18:18), and in order to be in full communion with him, we must be united with those to whom he gave authority. Like the Old Testament People of God, those who are part of the Church are not individuals who determine truth on their own but instead a united Body that follows the authority of those given it by God. Christ told his disciples, "He who hears you hears me, and he who rejects you rejects me, and he who rejects me rejects him who sent me" (Lk 10:16). To reject legitimate authority in the Church is to reject Christ himself and to place oneself outside of full communion.

In summary, unless Baptism, profession of faith, Eucharistic communion, and obedience to Church authority are all in place, a Christian or Christian community is not in full communion with the Catholic Church.

Appearance While the Apostles Are at Table by Duccio.
"Afterward he appeared to the eleven themselves as they sat at table; and he upbraided them for their unbelief and hardness of heart, because they had not believed those who saw him after he had risen. And he said to them, "Go into all the world and preach the gospel to the whole creation. He who believes and is baptized will be saved; but he who does not believe will be condemned." (Mk 16: 14-16)

WHAT IS IMPERFECT COMMUNION?

Now that we have defined what full communion means, we can understand better what imperfect communion is. Simply put, imperfect communion describes those among the baptized who are not in full communion with the Catholic Church. Their communion is imperfect because of differences from the Catholic Church in doctrine, discipline, and/or ecclesiastical structure. Even so, the Catholic Church recognizes all baptized Christians as brothers and sisters in faith and as members of the Body of Christ.

There are two main groupings among those who are in imperfect communion with the Catholic Church: those communities with valid Apostolic Succession and a valid Eucharist, and those without these characteristics.

> "The Church knows that she is joined in many ways to the baptized who are honored by the name of Christian, but do not profess the Catholic faith in its entirety or have not preserved unity or communion under the successor of Peter."[21] Those "who believe in Christ and have been properly baptized are put in a certain, although imperfect, communion with the Catholic Church."[22] *With the Orthodox Churches*, this communion is so profound "that it lacks little to attain the fullness that would permit a common celebration of the Lord's Eucharist."[23] (CCC 838)

As we noted earlier and will explore further in the next chapter, the Orthodox Churches—predominantly based in the Middle East, Eastern Europe, and Asia, but with presences throughout much of the world—have a valid Eucharist and valid Apostolic Succession but are not presently in union with the Bishop of Rome, the Pope. As we will see, these Churches and the Catholic Church have much in common, and much work is being done to bring about reunion between them.

Chapter 5 will focus upon those Christian communities, usually called Protestant or Reformed communities, that broke away from the Catholic Church in the sixteenth century and later. These communities, for the most part, still administer valid Baptisms but do not enjoy a valid Eucharist or valid Apostolic Succession. As we read earlier in the chapter, these are called Christian ecclesial communities in order to distinguish them from Christian churches, which have retained these attributes.

Divisions in the Church

The divisions in Christianity are the result of sin both inside and outside the Church. Blame for our divisions cannot be placed solely on one set of people; these divisions came into being through the fault of many people, including some in Church leadership. Oftentimes, in fact, divisions will not be overcome until all parties take responsibility for the faults in their own communities and offer forgiveness for those times they have been wronged. The purpose of ecumenical dialogue is not to assign blame for these divisions but to work to overcome them.

Christ desired that all his followers would be united as one Body (cf. Jn 17: 21) in belief, practice, and love. This unity was to be expressed and given strength through sacramental communion. But over time many factors came into play to weaken and even destroy this unity.

The *Catechism* distinguishes three types of sin that can rupture full communion: *heresy*, *apostasy*, and *schism*. These are further defined in the *Code of Canon Law*:

> **Heresy is the obstinate denial or obstinate doubt after the reception of baptism of some truth which is to be believed by divine and Catholic faith; apostasy is the total repudiation of the Christian faith; schism is the refusal of submission to the Supreme Pontiff or of communion with the members of the Church subject to him. (CIC, 751)**

On December 7, 1965, St. Paul VI and Ecumenical Patriarch of Constantinople Athenagoras I issued the *Catholic-Orthodox Joint Declaration of 1965* rescinding the excommunications of the Great Schism of 1054.
"Through the action of the Holy Spirit those differences will be overcome through cleansing of hearts, through regret for historical wrongs, and through an efficacious determination to arrive at a common understanding and expression of the faith of the Apostles and its demands."

Of course, the source of all ruptures is sin, and each of these ruptures is a sin against the unity of the Church desired by Christ. We might think first of the sinfulness of someone who has been given the gift of faith but rejects or neglects that gift; however, sins committed by those within the Church may motivate people to leave its visible boundaries. Human pride by leaders in the Church may cloud their ability to see a path to the resolution of a crisis. Whatever the case may be, unity is a work of God, and division is the work of the fallen human race.

> **Even in the beginnings of this one and only Church of God there arose certain rifts, which the Apostle strongly condemned.[24] But in subsequent centuries much more serious dissensions made their appearance and quite large communities came to be separated from full communion with the Catholic Church—for which, often enough, men of both sides were to blame. (*Unitatis Redintegratio*, 3)**

In addition, we must distinguish the first protagonists in a division from those who inherit that division from their ancestors. Someone born into a community or church outside the Catholic Church did not choose his or her situation and, thus, should not be blamed for actively causing division among the Body of Christ.

> **The children who are born into these Communities and who grow up believing in Christ cannot be accused of the sin involved in the separation, and the Catholic Church embraces upon them as brothers, with respect and affection. (*Unitatis Redintegratio*, 3)**

THE EUCHARIST: SACRAMENT OF THE CHURCH'S UNITY

The role of the Eucharist in bringing about Christian unity is essential; by sacramentally uniting ourselves to Christ we are united as well with his Body, the Church. In fact, it has often been called the "Sacrament of the Church's Unity." The Eucharist both *represents* and *brings about* union. When people share the Eucharist, by that very fact they are in union with one another, but that union is also strengthened by the Eucharist; that is, the Eucharist brings about a divinely instituted union.

Sometimes people complain about the Catholic Church not allowing non-Catholics to receive Holy Communion at Mass.[25] At first glance this practice may seem divisive: If the Eucharist is the "Sacrament of the Church's Unity," why does the Church not allow everyone to receive it?

USCCB GUIDELINES FOR THE RECEPTION OF COMMUNION

FOR CATHOLICS

As Catholics, we fully participate in the celebration of the Eucharist when we receive Holy Communion. We are encouraged to receive Communion devoutly and frequently. In order to be properly disposed to receive Communion, participants should not be conscious of grave sin and normally should have fasted for one hour. A person who is conscious of grave sin is not to receive the Body and Blood of the Lord without prior sacramental confession except for a grave reason where there is no opportunity for confession. In this case, the person is to be mindful of the obligation to make an act of perfect contrition, including the intention of confessing as soon as possible (canon 916). A frequent reception of the Sacrament of Penance is encouraged for all.

FOR OUR FELLOW CHRISTIANS

We welcome our fellow Christians to this celebration of the Eucharist as our brothers and sisters. We pray that our common Baptism and the action of the Holy Spirit in this Eucharist will draw us closer to one another and begin to dispel the sad divisions that separate us. We pray that these will lessen and finally disappear, in keeping with Christ's prayer for us "that they may all be one" (Jn 17: 21).

Because Catholics believe that the celebration of the Eucharist is a sign of the reality of the oneness of faith, life, and worship, members of those churches with whom we are not yet fully united are ordinarily not admitted to Holy Communion. Eucharistic sharing in exceptional circumstances by other Christians requires permission according to the directives of the diocesan bishop and the provisions of canon law (canon 844 § 4). Members of the Orthodox Churches, the Assyrian Church of the East, and the Polish National Catholic Church are urged to respect the discipline of their own Churches. According to Roman Catholic discipline, the *Code of Canon Law* does not object to the reception of communion by Christians of these Churches (canon 844 § 3).

FOR THOSE NOT RECEIVING HOLY COMMUNION

All who are not receiving Holy Communion are encouraged to express in their hearts a prayerful desire for unity with the Lord Jesus and with one another.

FOR NON-CHRISTIANS

We also welcome to this celebration those who do not share our faith in Jesus Christ. While we cannot admit them to Holy Communion, we ask them to offer their prayers for the peace and the unity of the human family.

Communion of the Apostles (detail) by Signorelli. Both the Church and the Eucharist are called the Body of Christ.

Our actions say something about what we believe. Receiving the Eucharist at a Catholic Church means that one accepts the truth and reality of both the Eucharist and the Church that administers it. It means that one accepts that the Catholic Church is a divine institution founded by Christ and that Christ is truly and sacramentally present in that Eucharist. It is also an expression that the person receiving it is in communion with the Catholic Church. If one does not accept these realities and is not in communion with the Catholic Church, then to receive the Eucharist would be to express a falsehood publicly. The shared reception of the Eucharist represents a shared unity of belief—a unity that must exist before that shared communion can happen.

"If you are the body and members of Christ, then it is your sacrament that is placed on the table of the Lord; it is your sacrament that you receive. To that which you are you respond 'Amen' ('yes, it is true!') and by responding to it you assent to it. For you hear the words, 'the Body of Christ' and respond 'Amen.' Be then a member of the Body of Christ that your *Amen* may be true."[26] (CCC 1396)

But if this were the end of the story, then Christian unity would be nothing more than a man-made unity like that found in a political party or social club. The Eucharist is not merely the "prize" for agreeing to a certain set of principles. No; the Eucharist also mystically unites each who receives it into one Body—the Body of Christ. This is a union far beyond mere human unity.

Both the Church and the Eucharist are called the Body of Christ. This dual use of the term is not accidental; rather, it points to the deep reality that, although we who receive the Eucharist are many, we are all one Body, the Church. The Eucharist unites us mystically to Christ, and by doing so it unites us also to the Church.

"The Eucharist makes the Church" (CCC 1396). This encapsulates the reality of our unity. It is not a unity based on uniformity of thought, but based on our *union* with Christ. All members of the Church are united by Christ's Blood; the Church is the Family of God.

SALVATION OUTSIDE FULL COMMUNION WITH THE CHURCH

Christian faith ultimately is concerned with our salvation, our hoped-for eternal communion with God in heaven. It might be good to take a moment here to consider this question: If a Christian is in imperfect communion with the Church founded by Christ, what implications does this have for his or her salvation?

When people of differing religious beliefs discuss salvation, the questions can become more personal, more direct: Will *you* be saved? Do you have to agree with me (or my church) on certain essential issues in order to go to heaven? Must you follow the practices of my religion to be accepted by God?

Several of the Fathers of the Church repeated a teaching that may sound alarming to our ears today: "Outside the Church there is no salvation." On the surface, this can seem like a statement that only Catholics can be saved—a notion sure to rankle other Christians, non-Christians, and even Catholics who have friends and family members outside the communion of the Church. And this oft-quoted teaching has done just that through the centuries, used as a weapon to attack the Catholic Church as elitist and triumphalistic.

In truth, the statement is nothing of the sort. What it does mean is that all salvation comes through Christ and his Church, as the *Catechism* explains, citing the Second Vatican Council:

> Re-formulated positively, it means that all salvation comes from Christ the Head through the Church which is his Body:
>
> > Basing itself on Scripture and Tradition, the Council teaches that the Church, a pilgrim now on earth, is necessary for salvation: the one Christ is the mediator and the way of salvation; he is present to us in his body which is the Church. He himself explicitly asserted the necessity of faith and Baptism, and thereby affirmed at the same time the necessity of the Church which men enter through Baptism as through a door. Hence they could not be saved who, knowing that the Catholic Church was founded as necessary by God through Christ, would refuse either to enter it or to remain in it.[27] (CCC 846)

The *Catechism* goes on to note that this affirmation is not aimed toward "those who, through no fault of their own, do not know Christ and his Church."[28]

Yet, the assertion that the Catholic Church is the one true Church often raises concerns about salvation. Catholics who are involved in religious discussions with non-Catholics will often be faced with the question, "Do you believe that non-Catholics cannot be saved?" The *Catechism of the Catholic Church* addresses this question in the context of the necessity of Baptism.

> Baptism is necessary for salvation for those to whom the Gospel has been proclaimed and who have had the possibility of asking for this sacrament.[29] The Church does not know of any means other than Baptism that assures entry into eternal beatitude; this is why she takes care not to neglect the mission she has received from the Lord to see that all who can be baptized are "reborn of water and the Spirit." *God has bound salvation to the sacrament of Baptism, but he himself is not bound by his sacraments.* (CCC 1257)

Baptism of the Ethiopian by Rembrandt. The Church states that she knows no other way by which a person can receive salvation than Baptism.

So we see that the Church affirms, in keeping with the teachings of Christ, that Baptism is necessary for salvation. Emphasizing that every Catholic is bound to share his or her Catholic faith with others, the Church states that she knows no other way by which a person can receive salvation than Baptism. However, the *Catechism* also includes this important sentence: "*God has bound salvation to the sacrament of Baptism, but he himself is not bound by his sacraments.*" In other words, we are only aware of one means to salvation—Baptism—therefore, we are bound to receive it if we want to be saved. At the same time, God—being All-powerful and All-loving—can do as he pleases, and we must recognize that God is free to work in ways we may not understand.

The *Catechism* continues:

> The Church has always held the firm conviction that those who suffer death for the sake of the faith without having received Baptism are baptized by their death for and with Christ. This *Baptism of blood*...brings about the fruits of Baptism without being a sacrament. (CCC 1258)

Martyrs for Christ, even if they have not yet been baptized, are also saved; they have received a "baptism by blood." One who gives his life for Christ will surely be received by him after his death.

> For *catechumens* who die before their Baptism, their explicit desire to receive it, together with repentance for their sins, and charity, assures them the salvation that they were not able to receive through the sacrament. (CCC 1259)

Good Friday Morning: Jesus in Prison by Tissot. Just as Christ prayed to his heavenly Father that "they may be one," united in faith, so, too, did he pray that none may be lost.

Those who had planned to be baptized but died before they could receive it may also receive salvation through their desire to be united to the Lord.

And finally,

> "Since Christ died for all, and since all men are in fact called to one and the same destiny, which is divine, we must hold that the Holy Spirit offers to all the possibility of being made partakers, in a way known to God, of the Paschal mystery."[30] Every man who is ignorant of the Gospel of Christ and of his Church, but seeks the truth and does the will of God in accordance with his understanding of it, can be saved. It may be supposed that such persons would have *desired Baptism explicitly* if they had known its necessity. (CCC 1260)

So the Church makes clear that salvation is at least possible even for those who have not been baptized with water. If such a person is saved, it is not *because* of their ignorance, but *in spite* of it. Our heavenly Father looks mercifully upon everybody's desire for the truth and practice of charity.

The Church, in fact, prays that all may be saved:

> The Church prays that no one should be lost: "Lord, let me never be parted from you." If it is true that no one can save himself, it is also true that God "desires all men to be saved" (1 Tm 2: 4), and that for him "all things are possible" (Mt 19: 26). (CCC 1058)

Just as Christ prayed to his heavenly Father that "they may be one," united in faith, so, too, did he pray that none may be lost. The two desires are really one in the same: The mission of the Church to bring about the unity of all people is also the mission of the Church to bring the Good News of salvation to the entire world.

CONCLUSION

Our Lord Jesus Christ—the Good Shepherd—established his Church as one flock. This Church, which has Christ as its cornerstone, was built on St. Peter and entrusted to the Apostles, who were to teach all nations, "administer the Sacraments, and rule the Church in love" (*UR* 2). The authority given them by Christ was in turn passed on to their successors—the Pope, the successor of St. Peter, and the bishops, successors of the Apostles—in order to be a source of unity and to continue the salvific mission of Christ in the world until he comes again.

> We believe that Our Lord entrusted all the blessings of the New Covenant to the apostolic college alone, of which Peter is the head, in order to establish the one Body of Christ on earth to which all should be fully incorporated who belong in any way to the people of God. (*Unitatis Redintegratio*, 3)

Christ desired that his followers model a unity so strong as to reflect the very unity among the three Persons of the Blessed Trinity. Yet, sadly, history has repeatedly witnessed divisions in the Body of Christ. From the time of Sts. Peter and Paul all the way up to our day, those who claim to follow Christ have not been of "one faith."[31]

> The divisions among Christians prevent the Church from attaining the fullness of catholicity proper to her, in those of her sons who, though attached to her by Baptism, are yet separated from full communion with her. (*Unitatis Redintegratio*, 4)

In recent decades awareness has grown among Christians that they must work to bring about full communion between all who bear the name "Christian." The Catholic Church, which has defined exactly what full communion entails, is vital to this effort, praying and working earnestly for the day when all Christians will enjoy the fullness of unity intended by Christ.

CHALLENGES:

Isn't it more important to show tolerance and not say that the Catholic faith is better than any other?

This is related to the Challenges question at the end of the previous chapter. Would we not be more "tolerant" of other beliefs if we did not proclaim that the fullness of truth is found in the Catholic Church?

The two positions are not mutually exclusive. We can do both: proclaim the truth and be tolerant of others. The best way is to be mindful always of the innate dignity of every human person.

We must respect other persons fully, their right to form religious opinions, their duty to seek the truth, and their obligation to follow their sincerely formed consciences. People of all faiths, all walks of life, and all strata of human existence are loved by God, and he desires that everyone respond to his call to communion. We must remain mindful that we are all worthy of God's love and of the human dignity with which he has endowed us.

Parable of the Lost Sheep by Soord. Our Lord Jesus Christ, the Good Shepherd, established his Church as one flock. We are all worthy of God's love and of the human dignity with which he has endowed us.

Because we love and live in the truth, however, we cannot be tolerant of untruth, of falsehood. Once we begin to tolerate falsehood, we are on the road to the notion that "one faith or religion is just as good as another"—the challenge we countered in the previous chapter. Instead, it is because of the very dignity of the human person that we must *counter* falsehood: Everyone has a right to be presented with the truth, and everyone is called to embrace that truth. Therefore, rather than "tolerate" untruth, we must present the truth out of sincere respect for the other person.

That does not mean we are allowed to be triumphalistic or uncharitable; that is not the example that Christ left us. Instead, Christ proclaimed the truth clearly and with great love. We must be charitable witnesses to Christ, for only in such charity do we show respect for the dignity of others. If we do not proclaim the truth in love, then we are not serving as good and faithful witnesses for Christ, let alone effective ones. We might even do harm to others by speaking the truth in an offensive and unattractive way, making repellant that which should command our love and awe.

It ought to be of some comfort for us to realize that the work of changing the hearts of others rests with the Holy Spirit. We can only be God's messengers and witnesses. Strictly speaking, it is not up to us to convert people to Catholicism. We only plant the seeds of faith by speaking the truth in love and let the Holy Spirit take over from there.

PILLARS OF THE FAITH

HENRI CARDINAL DE LUBAC, SJ

Henri Cardinal de Lubac, SJ, was a leading theologian of the twentieth century who pioneered a fresh understanding of the relationships among the Christian churches.

Born in Cambrai, France, in 1896, he joined the Society of Jesus (Jesuits) in Lyon in 1913 and served in the French army during World War I, suffering severe wounds in combat. He was educated at the Jesuit Houses of study at Jersey and Fourviere and was ordained a priest in 1927.

De Lubac studied in Rome until 1929, and then he taught the history of religion at a theological seminary in Lyon for the next thirty-two years. During this time he also translated early Christian manuscripts and battled against the Nazi threat and anti-Semitism (bigotry against Jews) through his writings and through participation in Resistance movements. He was a *peritus*, or expert advisor, at the Second Ecumenical Council of the Vatican (1962-1965). He was named a cardinal in 1983 by St. John Paul II and passed away in 1991.

Henri Cardinal de Lubac, SJ (1896-1991)
De Lubac was a *peritus* (Latin for "expert") at the Second Vatican Council and a member of its Theological Commission.

One of de Lubac's key proposals had to do with the role of the Eucharist in Church unity. He explained famously that the first millennium of Christianity was characterized by the concept that "the Eucharist makes the Church," but in the second millennium the emphasis was that "the Church makes the Eucharist."

While both statements are true, properly understood, de Lubac believed that the Church over the centuries had perhaps neglected the first of these ideas.

To say that "the Eucharist makes the Church" illustrates how the sharing of the Eucharist, the Body and Blood of Christ, is what unites the Church, or brings it into communion. The faithful everywhere around the world, wherever the Eucharist is celebrated, are intimately bonded in community with one another. This was a key teaching among the Fathers of the Church, the great leaders of Christianity whose thoughts and writings helped shape the Church over her first several centuries of existence.

Continued

HENRI CARDINAL DE LUBAC, SJ

Continued

The Last Supper by Ribalta.
The Church "makes the Eucharist" every time a bishop or priest celebrates the Mass.

In the second millennium, Church reflection and popular piety turned increasingly to the Real Presence of Christ in the Eucharist—the doctrine that the Body and Blood of Christ are truly present in the Eucharist under the appearance, or form, of ordinary bread and wine. Attention was then more heavily turned toward this Real Presence and how the bishop or priest celebrating Mass is empowered to change the Eucharistic species into Christ's Body and Blood. The Church, from this perspective, "makes the Eucharist" every time a bishop or priest celebrates the Mass.

But in the course of this, de Lubac said, we lost sight of the idea of how the Eucharist "makes the Church." In other words, by focusing more on how the Church turns bread into the Body of Christ and of how the recipient benefits spiritually from receiving Christ in Holy Communion, we did not reflect so much on how the Eucharist turns the Church community itself into the Body of Christ!

The concept is vital to any hopes of ecumenism among Christians because it understands the Eucharist as the key to Christian unity. Any discussion of how the various churches and ecclesial communities can reconcile with the Catholic Church necessarily centers on seeing the Eucharist for what it is: the Body of Christ, made by the Church, which itself has the power to make us into one community, the one People of God, the Church, the Body of Christ.

In his encyclical *Spe Salvi*, Pope Benedict XVI cited excerpts from Henri de Lubac's 1938 book *Catholicism: Christ and the Common Destiny of Man.*

SUPPLEMENTARY READING

The People of God: Christ's Faithful

204 §1. The Christian faithful are those who, inasmuch as they have been incorporated in Christ through baptism, have been constituted as the people of God. For this reason, made sharers in their own way in Christ's priestly, prophetic, and royal function, they are called to exercise the mission which God has entrusted to the Church to fulfill in the world, in accord with the condition proper to each.

§2. This Church, constituted and organized in this world as a society, subsists in the Catholic Church governed by the successor of Peter and the bishops in communion with him.

205. Those baptized are fully in the communion of the Catholic Church on this earth who are joined with Christ in its visible structure by the bonds of the profession of faith, the sacraments, and ecclesiastical governance.

206 §1. Catechumens, that is, those who ask by explicit choice under the influence of the Holy Spirit to be incorporated into the Church, are joined to it in a special way. By this same desire, just as by the life of faith, hope, and charity which they lead, they are united with the Church which already cherishes them as its own.

§2. The Church has a special care for catechumens; while it invites them to lead a life of the gospel and introduces them to the celebration of sacred rites, it already grants them various prerogatives which are proper to Christians.

—*Code of Canon Law*, cann. 204-206

The Church, A Mystery of Communion

3. The concept of *communion* lies *"at the heart of the Church's self-understanding,"*[32] insofar as it is the Mystery of the personal union of each human being with the divine Trinity and with the rest of mankind, initiated with the faith,[33] and, having begun as a reality in the Church on earth, is directed towards its eschatological fulfilment in the heavenly Church.[34]

If the concept of *communion*, which is not a univocal concept, is to serve as a key to ecclesiology, it has to be understood within the teaching of the Bible and the patristic tradition, in which *communion* always involves a double dimension: the *vertical* (communion with God) and the *horizontal* (communion among men). It is essential to the Christian understanding of *communion* that it be recognised above all as a gift from God, as a fruit of God's initiative carried out in the paschal mystery. The new relationship between man and God, that has been established in Christ and is communicated through the sacraments, also extends to a new relationship among human beings. As a result, the concept of *communion* should be such as to express both the sacramental nature of the Church while *"we are away from the Lord,"*[35] and also the particular unity which makes the faithful into members of one and the same Body, the Mystical Body of Christ,[36] an organically structured community,[37] *"a people brought into one by the unity of the Father and of the Son and of the Holy Spirit,"*[38] and endowed with suitable means for its visible and social union.[39]

4. *Ecclesial communion is at the same time both invisible and visible.* As an invisible reality, it is the communion of each human being with the Father through Christ in the Holy Spirit, and with the others who are fellow sharers in the divine nature,[40] in the passion of Christ,[41] in the same faith,[42] in the same spirit.[43] In the Church on earth, there is an intimate relationship between this invisible communion and the visible communion in the teaching of the Apostles, in the sacraments and in the hierarchical order. By means of these divine gifts, which are very visible realities, Christ carries out in different ways in history his prophetical, priestly and kingly *function* for the salvation of mankind.[44] This link between the invisible and visible elements of ecclesial communion constitutes the Church as the *Sacrament* of salvation.

From this sacramentality it follows that the Church is not a reality closed in on herself; rather, she is permanently open to missionary and ecumenical endeavour, for she is sent to the world to announce and witness, to make present and spread the mystery of communion which is essential to her: to gather together all people and all things into Christ;[45] so as to be for all an *"inseparable sacrament of unity."*[46]

—Ratzinger, Joseph Cardinal, *Letter to the Bishops of the Catholic Church on Some Aspects of the Church Understood as Communion*, Congregation for the Doctrine of the Faith, May 28, 1992

VOCABULARY

APOSTASY
The total repudiation of the Christian faith. Apostasy involves a choice—a conscious and full decision to leave Christianity.

CHRISTIAN
A baptized person; through Baptism one is incorporated into Christ through grace and is made a member of his Mystical Body, the Church.

CODE OF CANON LAW
An updated and systematic compilation of the laws of the Church. The present code was revised in 1983. The Eastern Catholic Churches are governed by a separate code of law.

ECCLESIAL COMMUNITIES
A name given to those Christian groups that do not enjoy Apostolic Succession and, therefore, have no valid Sacraments other than Baptism and Matrimony. This term respects their organization as pointing towards the Church, but also respects the fact that a valid Eucharist is necessary for a valid church.

EUCHARISTIC COMMUNION
Being in union with Christ and other Catholics through the reception of the Eucharist.

FORM
The necessary ritual words and signs that accompany a Sacrament.

FULL COMMUNION
The state of being completely and mystically united to Christ's Body, the Catholic Church. The four essential aspects to full communion are (1) Baptism; (2) acceptance of a common profession of faith; (3) Eucharistic communion; and (4) respect and obedience towards those in authority in the Church.

HERESY
The obstinate denial or doubt, after Baptism, of a truth that must be believed by the Catholic faithful. Heresy involves the choice to deny a Catholic truth. Not understanding a truth is not heresy.

IMPERFECT COMMUNION
The state of being united to the Catholic Church in an imperfect way. This term describes the Christian churches and ecclesial communities, which have valid Baptism but are lacking in one or more of the essential aspects of full communion.

LAYING ON OF HANDS
The ritual act, going back to the Old Testament, whereby men were consecrated for sacred duties. From the New Testament onward, it has been the action used to ordain men to the priesthood in the Sacrament of Holy Orders.

MARKS OF THE CHURCH
Key characteristics of the Church as described in the Nicene-Constantinopolitan Creed: The Church is one, holy, catholic, and apostolic.

MATTER
That part of a Sacrament with which or to which something is done in order to confer grace. Examples include water (Baptism), bread and wine (Eucharist), and Sacred Chrism and the laying on of a hand (Confirmation).

NICENE-CONSTANTINOPOLITAN CREED
Statement of foundational Christian beliefs composed at the First Council of Nicaea (AD 325) and later revised at the Council of Constantinople (AD 381).

PROFESSION OF FAITH
A synthesis or summary of the Faith professed by Christians. Professions of Faith are also known as "symbols of faith" or "creeds," derived from the Latin *credo*, meaning "I believe." The most common creeds are the Apostles' Creed and the Nicene Creed.

REAL PRESENCE
The unique and true presence of the Body, Blood, Soul, and divinity of Christ in the Eucharist under the appearances of bread and wine. The Church invites the faithful to deepen their faith in the Real Presence of Christ through worship and communion in the Eucharistic liturgy, and through acts of adoration outside of Mass.

VOCABULARY Continued

REFORMATION
Movement of the sixteenth century that included teachings contrary to Catholic teaching and resulted in the schism of the Protestant and Anglican ecclesial communities from the Catholic Church.

SACRAMENT OF HOLY ORDERS
The Sacrament of Apostolic Ministry by which the mission entrusted by Christ to his Apostles continues to be exercised in the Church through the laying on of hands, which leaves a sacramental character on the soul.

SACRAMENT OF THE CHURCH'S UNITY
A name given to the Eucharist to highlight its power to unite disparate peoples. This title points to another: communion.

SCHISM
A breach of the unity of the visible Church; the refusal to submit to the Pope or be united with the Church in communion with him.

SECOND VATICAN COUNCIL
An Ecumenical Council, called by St. John XXIII, held from 1962 to 1965. Its decisions have had a major impact on the Church in the modern world.

SEPARATED BRETHREN
The term often used by Catholics and the Church to refer to those Christians who are not fully members of the Catholic Church. It emphasizes that they truly are brothers and sisters in the faith, but that they are currently outside of full communion.

TRINITARIAN FORMULA
"In the name of the Father, and of the Son, and of the Holy Spirit." "The essential rite of Baptism consists in immersing the candidate in water or pouring water on his head, while pronouncing the invocation of the Most Holy Trinity: the Father, the Son, and the Holy Spirit" (CCC 1278).

STUDY QUESTIONS

1. What defines a church?
2. Why is valid Apostolic Succession essential to be considered a church?
3. What does it mean to say that the fullness of truth "subsists" in the Catholic Church?
4. What are the four marks of the Church?
5. What defines a Christian?
6. Describe several senses of the word "communion."
7. What are the essential aspects of full communion?
8. How does the Eucharist help maintain full communion?
9. What are the names of the three main groupings of Christians?
10. Why are some groups outside full communion called "Churches" while others are not?
11. What are the three types of ruptures to full communion?
12. How does someone born into a community outside full communion differ from one who initially causes a division?
13. Why does the Catholic Church not allow members of ecclesial communities to receive the Eucharist?

PRACTICAL EXERCISES

1. The four aspects of full communion are:
   1) Baptism
   2) Acceptance of a common profession of faith
   3) Eucharistic Communion
   4) Respect and obedience towards those in authority in the Church

   Tell how each is essential for full communion.

2. A non-Catholic friend attends Mass with you. When you explain that he cannot receive Communion, he's offended. How do you respond?

3. What is the proper attitude a Catholic should take toward a friend who is not a Christian or does not believe in God? Discuss.

FROM THE CATECHISM

787 From the beginning, Jesus associated his disciples with his own life, revealed the mystery of the Kingdom to them, and gave them a share in his mission, joy, and sufferings.[47] Jesus spoke of a still more intimate communion between him and those who would follow him: "Abide in me, and I in you....I am the vine, you are the branches."[48] And he proclaimed a mysterious and real communion between his own body and ours: "He who eats my flesh and drinks my blood abides in me, and I in him."[49]

788 When his visible presence was taken from them, Jesus did not leave his disciples orphans. He promised to remain with them until the end of time; he sent them his Spirit.[50] As a result communion with Jesus has become, in a way, more intense: "By communicating his Spirit, Christ mystically constitutes as his body those brothers of his who are called together from every nation."[51]

836 "All men are called to this catholic unity of the People of God....And to it, in different ways, belong or are ordered: the Catholic faithful, others who believe in Christ, and finally all mankind, called by God's grace to salvation."[52]

837 "Fully incorporated into the society of the Church are those who, possessing the Spirit of Christ, accept all the means of salvation given to the Church together with her entire organization, and who—by the bonds constituted by the profession of faith, the sacraments, ecclesiastical government, and communion—are joined in the visible structure of the Church of Christ, who rules her through the Supreme Pontiff and the bishops. Even though incorporated into the Church, one who does not however persevere in charity is not saved. He remains indeed in the bosom of the Church, but 'in body' not 'in heart.'"[53]

881 The Lord made Simon alone, whom he named Peter, the "rock" of his Church. He gave him the keys of his Church and instituted him shepherd of the whole flock.[54] "The office of binding and loosing which was given to Peter was also assigned to the college of apostles united to its head."[55] This pastoral office of Peter and the other apostles belongs to the Church's very foundation and is continued by the bishops under the primacy of the Pope.

882 The *Pope*, Bishop of Rome and Peter's successor, "is the perpetual and visible source and foundation of the unity both of the bishops and of the whole company of the faithful."[56] "For the Roman Pontiff, by reason of his office as Vicar of Christ, and as pastor of the entire Church has full, supreme, and universal power over the whole Church, a power which he can always exercise unhindered."[57]

The Last Supper (detail) by Bouveret.
All members of the Church are united by Christ's Blood; the Church is the family of God.

ENDNOTES – CHAPTER THREE

1. Cf. Eph 4:4-5; Mk 16:16.
2. St. Leo the Great, *Sermo* 63, 7.
3. *Responses to Some Questions Regarding Certain Aspects of the Doctrine of the Church*, Fifth Question.
4. *LG* 8.
5. *Directory for the Application of Principles and Norms on Ecumenism*, 17.
6. *LG* 9.
7. Ibid.
8. Cf. CCC 866.
9. Cf. CCC 867.
10. Cfr. *Symbolum Apostolicum*: Denz. 6-9 (10-13); Symb. Nic.-Const.: Denz. 86 (150), coll. *Prof. fidei Trid.*: Denz. 994 et 999 (1862 et 1868).
11. *Dieitur. Saneta (catholica apostolica) Romana Eccelesia.*: in *Prof. fidei Trid.*, 1. c. et Concl. Vat. I, Sess. III, *Const. dogm. de fide cath.*: Denz. 1782 (3001).
12. Cf. CCC 1267.
13. *UR* 3.
14. Cf. CCC 1396.
15. *UR* 3.
16. *UR* 22 § 2.
17. Cf. 1 Cor 12:13.
18. 1 Cor 10:16-17.
19. *LG* 7.
20. *LG* 7; cf. Rom 6:4-5; 1 Cor 12:13.
21. *LG* 15.
22. *UR* 3.
23. St. Paul VI, Discourse, December 14, 1975; cf. *UR* 13-18.
24. Cf. 1 Cor 1:11 sqq; 11, 22.
25. NB. "Catholic ministers administer the sacraments of penance, Eucharist, and anointing of the sick licitly to members of Eastern Churches which do not have full communion with the Catholic Church if they seek such on their own accord and are properly disposed. This is also valid for members of other Churches which in the judgment of the Apostolic See are in the same condition in regard to the sacraments as these Eastern Churches" (CIC, 844 § 3).
26. St. Augustine, *Sermo* 272: PL 38, 1247; cf. CCC 1396.
27. *LG* 14; cf. Mk 16:16; Jn 3:5.
28. CCC 847-848.
29. Cf. Mk 16:16.
30. *GS* 22 § 5; cf. *LG* 16; *AG* 7.
31. Eph 4:5.
32. St. John Paul II, *Address to the Bishops of the United States of America*, 16-IX-1987, n. 1: "Insegnamenti di Giovanni Paolo II" X, 3 (1987) p. 553.
33. 1 Jn 1:3: "*that which we have seen and heard, we proclaim also to you, so that you may have fellowship with us; and our fellowship is with the Father and with his Son Jesus Christ.*" Cf. also 1 Cor 1:9; St. John Paul II, Ap. Exh. *Christifideles Laici*, 30-XII-1988, n. 19; Synod of Bishops (1985), *Relatio Finalis*, II, C), 1.
34. Cf. Phil 3:20-21; Col 3:1-4; *LG* 48.
35. 2 Cor 5:6. cf. *LG* 1.
36. Cf. *ibidem*, no. 7; Pope Pius XII, Enc. *Mystici Corporis*, 29-VI-1943: AAS 35 (1943) pp. 200ff.
37. Cf. *LG* 11/a.
38. St. Cyprian, *De Oratione Dominica*, 23: PL 4, 553; cf. *LG* 4/b.
39. Cf. *LG* 9/c.
40. Cf. 2 Pt 1:4.
41. Cf. 2 Cor 1:7.
42. Cf. Eph 4:13; Phlm 6.
43. Cf. Phil 2:1.
44. Cf. *LG* 25-27.
45. Cf. Mt 28:19-20; Jn 17:21-23; Eph 1:10; *LG* 9/b, 13 and 17; Decr. *Ad Gentes*, nn. 1 and 5; St. Irenæus, *Adversus Hæreses*, III, 16, 6 and 22, 1-3: PG 7, 925-926 and 955-958.
46. St. Cyprian, *Epist. ad Magnum*, 6: PL 3, 1142.
47. Cf. Mk 1:16-20; 3:13-19; Mt 13:10-17; Lk 10:17-20; 22:28-30.
48. Jn 15:4-5.
49. Jn 6:56.
50. Cf. Jn 14:18; 20:22; Mt 28:20; Acts 2:33.
51. *LG* 7.
52. *LG* 13.
53. *LG* 14.
54. Cf. Mt 16:18-19; Jn 21:15-17.
55. *LG* 22 § 2.
56. *LG* 23.
57. *LG* 22; cf. *CD* 2, 9.

CHAPTER 4

Churches of the East

Over the centuries, human weakness and sin have repeatedly thwarted Christ's desire that all his followers be one.

Ecumenism and Interreligious Dialogue

CHAPTER FOUR

Churches of the East

INTRODUCTION

In the previous chapter we discussed what defines a Church, what is a Christian, differences between full and imperfect communion, and what elements are essential to true unity between the Catholic Church and the various Orthodox Churches and Christian ecclesial communities.

We can see that the division of Christianity today is not what Christ desired for the People of God, whom he wanted to gather into one Mystical Body. Over the centuries, human weakness and sin have repeatedly thwarted Christ's desire that all his followers be one. Sometimes it can seem that those who profess belief in Christ are divided beyond repair. And yet, in keeping with the stated will of Christ, every Christian has an obligation to work toward full Christian unity.

In studying the Churches of the East, we can distinguish between two main groupings: those in full communion, referred to collectively as the Eastern Catholic Churches, and those outside of full communion, such as the Eastern Orthodox Churches. The ecclesial communities that arose in the West following the Protestant Reformation will be presented in the next chapter.

In this chapter we will examine:

- ✠ The unity that existed in the early Church;
- ✠ The history of doctrinal controversy, heresy, unity, and division from the earliest days of the Church;
- ✠ What led to the schisms of the first millennium of Christianity;
- ✠ How political and cultural developments in Europe influenced relations between Christians in the East and the West;
- ✠ Similarities and differences between Catholic and Orthodox doctrine and practice; and
- ✠ The Eastern Catholic Churches.

Christ Pantocrator, Greek icon by Moskos.
Every Christian has an obligation to work toward full Christian unity.

St. Philip and St. James Altarpiece.
St. Philip was the first Christian to baptize a Gentile, and St. James was leader of the Church in Jerusalem.

UNITY AND TEACHING AUTHORITY IN THE EARLY CHURCH

In the first years of Christianity, after the Apostles began their evangelizing and sacramental ministry at Pentecost, the Body of Christian faithful were in full communion with one another. Scripture describes the peace and harmony that governed this early Christian community:

> **Those who received his word were baptized, and there were added that day about three thousand souls. And they devoted themselves to the apostles' teaching and fellowship, to the breaking of bread and the prayers.**
>
> **And fear came upon every soul; and many wonders and signs were done through the apostles.**
>
> **And all who believed were together and had all things in common; and they sold their possessions and goods and distributed them to all, as any had need.**
>
> **And day by day, attending the temple together and breaking bread in their homes, they partook of food with glad and generous hearts, praising God and having favor with all the people. And the Lord added to their number day by day those who were being saved.** (Acts 2: 41-47)

Scripture also tells us that controversies would soon follow. St. Paul's letters speak of rifts developing in the Church at Corinth. The epistles of Sts. Peter, John, and Jude make reference to false teachers who misled the faithful. They urged the Christians to hold fast to what they had been taught by the Apostles.

As we read in Chapter 2, the Apostles met in Jerusalem to discuss whether Gentiles had to follow the Mosaic Law, which would require males to undergo circumcision and all to follow such provisions as the dietary laws.

This meeting was pivotal because it is regarded as a precursor to the Ecumenical Councils of later years, and, like the election of St. Matthias as an Apostle to succeed Judas Iscariot, it was an early exercise of the Magisterium. Although there were later a few disagreements between St. Paul and the circumcision party, the question as a matter of Church teaching and policy was settled.

Throughout the early centuries of Christianity, the teaching authority of the Church—the Magisterium—would time and again be called upon to decide matters of confusion and disagreement. Thus would the Catholic unity of faith and practice be preserved. At the same time, Church resolutions on doctrinal controversies would sometimes be rejected by some Christians who would break away from the Church.

The Christian Martyrs' Last Prayer by Gerome.
During the first 300 years, the Church was focused not just on evangelization but also on mere survival.

THE FIRST THREE CENTURIES OF THE CHURCH

In order to understand the first major divisions that occurred within Christendom, we must first understand the context in which they developed.

Christ forewarned his disciples that following him would not be easy. And indeed it was a hard path the early disciples trod. Christians drew the ire of the Jewish leadership and eventually were cast out of the Temple, forbidden to worship with the Jews. In the Roman Empire there were occasional, regional persecutions of the Church in which Christians faced imprisonment or death when they refused to renounce their faith.

Blaming Christians for a fire that engulfed much of Rome, Emperor Nero ordered a wave of persecutions between AD 64 and 68 that claimed the lives of Sts. Peter and Paul. Following the death of St. Peter—who according to tradition was crucified upside-down at his own request since he believed himself unworthy to die as Christ had—the leadership of the Church passed to St. Linus, who is regarded as our second Pope after St. Peter. Apostolic Succession continued in this manner, with most of the early Popes dying martyrs' deaths.

Later emperors and regional Roman officials varied in their degree of contempt for Christianity, but persecutions escalated periodically—and sometimes Empire-wide—until the late third and early fourth centuries. Generally speaking, for about the first 300 years of the Church's existence, the Christian community was a persecuted minority sect in the Roman Empire. Although the laws against Christians were not consistently enforced, the penalty for being Christian at times included confiscation of property, imprisonment, or death. During this time, the Church was focused not just on evangelization but also on mere survival, and countless Christians suffered degrees of martyrdom.

Often buttressed by shared danger, the Church's unity during these three centuries was remarkable. Some discordant teachings and heresies were proposed during this era, but they developed fairly small followings, were readily opposed by bishops of nearby cities, the Pope, and other leaders; generally, these people died out or their followers were reconciled to the Church with time, even though some of their ideas were resurrected in later heresies. Eventually, however, more pressing disputes arose concerning the identity of Christ and the message of his Gospel that would require the Magisterium to formulate doctrine in a clearer and more definitive way.

CONSTANTINE AND THE ARIAN CRISIS (THIRD–FOURTH CENTURIES)

The last great Roman persecution of the Church came under Diocletian (AD 284-305), who also established a tetrarchy ("rule by four"), dividing the vast empire into East and West with a senior emperor (*augustus*) and a sub-emperor (*caesar*) in each. The system did not work very well or for very long, as there was fierce infighting for control of the empire within the tetrarchy.

In the early fourth century Emperor Constantine put a definitive end to Christian persecution in the West. Constantine is said to have experienced a conversion to the faith AD 312. Just as he was about to lead his troops into battle against the Eastern emperor, Maxentius, who challenged him for control of the entire empire, Constantine saw a vision of a brilliant cross in the sky bearing the inscription *In hoc signo vinces* ("In this sign you will conquer"). Despite being greatly outnumbered, Constantine and his army won, and he credited his victory to divine assistance from the God of the Christians. His Edict of Milan, endorsed also by Licinius, the new emperor in the East, restored civil rights to the Christian faithful. (Constantine himself, however, was not baptized until shortly before his death in 337.)

Now that it was safe to practice Christianity and survival was no longer an issue, the Church could turn more attention to working out theological questions openly. Before long, differences in doctrine that had lain dormant or simmered beneath the surface came to the forefront.

First Ecumenical Council of Nicæa, AD 325

Emperor Constantine and the Council of Nicæa. Manuscript illustration (ca. 825) showing the burning of Arian books with the caption: "Arian heretics condemned."

The first major conflict was the Arian heresy, or *Arianism*. In the late third century and into the fourth, a priest named Arius denied the divinity of Christ. He taught that Jesus had not always existed but was created by the Father before his Incarnation. He, therefore, is not equal to the Father but rather inferior to and subordinate to him. Arianism had many offshoots and forms and developed quite independently of Arius himself, but its key teaching was this direct challenge to the idea of the Blessed Trinity, particularly the coequality and coeternity of the Father and the Son.

In time, Arianism had taken hold even among some of the bishops and clergy to the point that Constantine[1] called for an *Ecumenical Council*, a gathering of all the bishops of the Church, for the purpose of debating and resolving the issue. Convened AD 325 in Nicæa and modeled on the Council of Jerusalem, the council proceedings resulted in a formal definition of the true divinity of Christ and his equality with the Father. The council condemned the central tenet of Arianism, clarifying that the Father and the Son were distinct Persons but describing their divine nature using the Greek *homoousios* (in Latin, *consubstantial*) meaning "of the same being," or "of the same substance." It also promulgated a "profession of faith," or creed.

The Nicene Creed states, in part:

> I believe in one God, the Father almighty, maker of heaven and earth, of all things visible and invisible. I believe in one Lord Jesus Christ, the Only Begotten Son of God, born of the Father before all ages. God from God, Light from Light, true God from true God, begotten, not made, consubstantial with the Father...

The Arians did not believe that the Son is "of the same substance" as the Father, and Arian factions pushed variously for language stating that he is "of a similar substance" or "of a dissimilar substance."

Both of these proposed expressions would have detracted from the idea that Jesus Christ is fully God and coequal with the Father.

Although Constantine hoped that this council would settle the debate and bring peace to the empire, the strife among Christians over doctrinal matters continued. Arian notions persisted despite the rebuff in the Nicene Creed. After Constantine died in 337, one of his sons and cosuccessors, Constantius II, used his power to support Arian bishops and spread Arian beliefs throughout the Empire in an effort to reverse the teachings of Nicæa.

Some Christians—including many bishops—rejected the decision of the First Ecumenical Council of Nicæa; some challenged the divinity of the Holy Spirit also. According to some Arian thought, the Holy Spirit was also a being created of the Father. The relationship of the Spirit to the Father and Son would take further councils to resolve and in fact later would become a major dividing point in East-West relations.

THE RISE OF CONSTANTINOPLE

During his momentous reign, Constantine had legalized Christianity and called the First Ecumenical Council of Nicæa, but he made yet another momentous decision that would impact Christianity and the world to the present day: Having reunited the Roman Empire under a single emperor once again, he moved its capital to the Eastern city of Byzantium (present-day Istanbul). He built the city into a bustling cultural and commercial metropolis and renamed it Constantinople in his own honor. This radical move shifted the balance of imperial power from the West, represented by the city of Rome, to the East, represented by the "New Rome," Constantinople.

First Ecumenical Council of Constantinople, AD 381

When Theodosius became emperor of the East AD 379, he took action against the increasing Arian influence in the Church, particularly in Constantinople itself, where the Arians were in substantial control. Theodosius declared Christianity, specifically the Christian faith as articulated at Nicæa, to be the official state religion of the Roman Empire. Then, in an effort to reconcile the increasing alienation between East and West caused in part by the Arian crisis, he called for an Ecumenical Council to be held in Constantinople AD 381.

St. Ambrose Converting Theodosius by Subleyras. Both St. Ambrose of Milan and Emperor Theodosius I fought continuously against Arianism and paganism.

At Constantinople the assembled bishops again condemned all heresies associated with Arianism. They also reaffirmed and expanded the creed formulated at Nicæa, including an elaboration on the Person of the Holy Spirit and an articulation, among other things, of what today we call the four marks of the Church ("one, holy, catholic, and apostolic"):

> I believe in the Holy Spirit, the Lord, the giver of life,
> who proceeds from the Father and the Son,
> who with the Father and the Son is adored and glorified,
> who has spoken through the prophets.
>
> I believe in one, holy, catholic, and apostolic Church.
> I confess one Baptism for the forgiveness of sins
> and I look forward to the resurrection of the dead
> and the life of the world to come. Amen.
> (Nicene-Constantinopolitan Creed)

In concert with the Council Fathers, Theodosius sought to replace the Arian bishops with bishops who accepted the doctrine of the Blessed Trinity. The Arians were suppressed, although they soon would surface yet again.

Mosaic in Hagia Sophia, former Eastern Orthodox cathedral and seat of the Patriarchate of Constantinople (537-1453). The Virgin Mary and Christ Child in the center; on the left stands Emperor Justinian I offering a model of the Hagia Sophia Church; on the right, Emperor Constantine I offering a model of the city of Constantinople.

Another important decree of the council, however, aggravated East-West tensions. The council, which was attended mostly by bishops from the East, declared that the bishop of Constantinople should be seen as second in honor to the Bishop of Rome. It called in effect for Constantinople to be recognized as a *patriarchate*, or one of the major governing centers of Christianity, a status previously accorded only to Rome, Alexandria, and Antioch. Constantinople, as the "New Rome" and center of the imperial government, was asserting herself as second in primacy only to Rome, the See of St. Peter.

This act was not accepted by the Pope (who did not attend the council) largely because it went against the Council of Nicæa, which had established Alexandria as second to Rome. It would be several years before the Western Church would recognize Constantinople as a patriarchate.

SCHISMS IN THE CHURCH (FIFTH CENTURY)

The Roman Empire was experiencing not only theological and ecclesial problems but also existential threats. Since about the mid-second century, the Empire had continually battled barbarians, including the Celts and Germanic tribes to the west, north, and south, and the Parthians to the southeast. These wars drained Roman military and economic resources, and with time the barbarians made major inroads by migrating into imperial territory, gradually reducing the size and power of the empire in the West.

Constantine and his immediate successors had reunited the empire under a single emperor for most of the fourth century, but later Theodosius again divided it into East and West, naming his two sons coemperors upon his death AD 395. Within eighty-five years, the barbarians, including many who had been recruited into the Roman army as mercenaries and through treaties, would all but take over the West. When the barbarian mercenaries overthrew the emperor and installed Odoacer as king of Italy AD 476, the Western half of the Roman Empire was no more.

SOME OTHER CONTROVERSIES IN THE EARLY CHURCH

Appolinarianism held that Christ had a human body and a human soul but that his rational mind was consumed into his divine nature. A variant of Monophysitism, it was condemned at the First Ecumenical Council of Constantinople AD 381.

Docetism denied the Incarnation, claiming instead that Jesus was a divine being who only appeared in human form like a phantasm. It was condemned at the First Ecumenical Council of Nicæa AD 325.

Donatism, a heresy originating in North Africa in the early fourth century, was a belief essentially in a Church of saints rather than sinners. Donatists held that a Christian who commits mortal sin after his or her Baptism cannot receive absolution. The issue came to a head during a time of religious persecution under the Emperor Diocletian, when the Donatists argued that forgiveness must be denied to Christians who made even a token denial of the faith in order to avoid persecution. They also believed that Sacraments administered by a sinful bishop or priest could not be valid and so "rebaptized" those Catholics who converted to the Donatist sect. After being repudiated by the Church, the Donatists set up their own rival church AD 316. St. Augustine's preaching won many Donatists back to the Church, but the sect continued for a few more centuries.

Gnosticism (from the Greek *gnosis*, "knowledge") took various forms but always claimed that salvation comes through esoteric knowledge. Some forms professed belief in two different gods who were in conflict, an evil god (Demiurge) and a good god. Matter (the physical world) was associated with the former and considered evil, while spirit, with the latter, was considered good. A number of false "gospels" and revelations were written in the first few centuries, often relating alleged conversations or visions of Jesus, the Blessed Virgin Mary, or other figures supposedly expressing Gnostic beliefs.

Manichæism was a gnostic variant that originated in the fourth century and persisted in the East into the Middle Ages. Strains of Gnosticism have continued to infect philosophies and ideologies until the modern day, especially in positing a spirit (good) versus matter (evil) dualism.

Hippolytus was a third-century priest who accused Pope Zephyrinus of the heresy of modalism. He also believed that adultery was unforgivable and criticized later Popes for granting absolution to people who were repentant for this sin. He was excommunicated and is sometimes considered the first "antipope," but he reconciled with the Church before his death as a martyr AD 235. He is recognized as a saint by both the Catholic and Orthodox Churches.

Marcionism was a heresy originating with Marcion, the wealthy son of a bishop. He was excommunicated AD 144 for teaching that the God of the Old Testament was a distinct and lesser deity than the God of the New Testament. He rejected the Old Testament and some of the books of the New Testament.

Monarchianism (from the Greek for "one ruler"), a heresy that developed in the second century, denied the Trinity. It appeared in two main forms. **Modalism** (also called **Sabellianism**, or "modalistic monarchianism") held that the Father, Son, and Holy Spirit were not distinct Persons of a Trinity but rather "modes," or expressions, of God. Sabellius, the leading proponent of this heresy, was excommunicated in 220. **Adoptionism** (or "dynamic monarchianism") held that Jesus was an ordinary human being whom God the Father "adopted" at some point in his life and made a "son of God." This idea was present also in some later forms of Arianism.

Continued

SOME OTHER CONTROVERSIES IN THE EARLY CHURCH

Continued

Montanism, started by a Christian convert named Montanus in the late second century, held to a very rigorous morality and taught that a Christian who fell from grace into sin could never be redeemed. Montanus and two women companions claimed to have received direct private revelations and to be the embodiment of the Holy Spirit.

Novatian was a priest and theologian of the third century who believed that it was an unforgivable sin for a Christian to renounce his or her faith (to *apostatize*) if threatened with persecution and that the Church had no power to grant them forgiveness. When St. Cornelius, another priest who believed that Christian *apostates* should be allowed to do penance and to be restored to full communion with the Church, was elected Pope in 251, Novatian gathered three bishops to consecrate himself as a rival "pope," thus forming his own church. He died in 258, but in the early fourth century his followers merged with the Donatists, with whom they were in substantial agreement, and persisted for several more centuries.

The Eastern half of the Roman Empire, which by historians is called the Byzantine Empire, remained strong. With so much of the turmoil centered in the West, there was less communication with the East, and Christian religious thought and traditions began to develop more independently of one another. As we will see, this lack of communications fostered some of the first schisms in the Church.

St. Athanasius by Coello. Throughout his life, St. Athanasius (296-373), bishop of Alexandria, was persistent and fearless in his fight against the Arian heresy.

The political changes that originated with Constantine and continued over the next few centuries widened the existing cultural gap between East and West. The East spoke Greek primarily, while Latin was spoken in the West. The West had often weak political leadership and a debilitated infrastructure, so the people looked to the Church to restore discipline and order in society. The East, on the other hand, enjoyed stable rule under the Byzantine emperors. Though not directly related to religious matters, such differences did lead to further weakening of the bonds between East and West. After we discuss the theological disputes that brought about schism in the fourth and fifth centuries, we will return to analyze further the impact of these East-West cultural differences.

It should be clear that many doctrinal, cultural, and political factors were involved in the divisions that arose among Christians in the East and the West. Ultimately, these factors—which we will visit in more detail—caused three major separations: the Nestorian crisis, the Monophysite crisis, and the final split between East and West.

The Nestorian Schism

By the early fifth century, a doctrinal debate had arisen in the Church over Christology. Christology is the theology of Christ. Who is he? Is he God, is he man? If he is both, how do his divinity and humanity relate to each other? The extensive debate and discord that these types of questions engendered finally came to a head.

During this time, a devotional title given to the Blessed Virgin Mary by many Greek-speaking Christians was *Theotokos* ("God-bearer"), which can be translated as "Mother of God." This title reflects more on Christ than on the Blessed Virgin Mary, for it is a declaration of who she carried in her womb: Jesus Christ, who is God himself.

A bishop named Nestorius objected to this title. He accepted the divinity of Christ, but he believed that the Blessed Virgin Mary was the mother only of Christ's humanity, not of his divinity. He suggested that she be called *Christotokos* ("Christ-bearer," or "Mother of Christ").

In response, the bishops of the Church gathered at the Ecumenical Council of Ephesus AD 431. It was there that the Council Fathers declared that the Blessed Virgin Mary is rightly called *Theotokos*. Their reasoning was this: A mother is not a mother of a person's nature; rather, she is the mother of the person. Christ is a divine *Person*, the Second Person of the Blessed Trinity, who is endowed with a *human nature* and a *divine nature*. So, if his Mother is the Mother of Christ, and he is a divine Person, then she is the Mother of this divine Person, who is God. This does not mean that the Blessed Virgin Mary existed before the Holy Trinity or gave birth to the eternal Godhead, but it does mean that she bore the divine Christ in her womb and gave birth to him. She was truly his Mother.

St. Cyril of Alexandria by Meneses.
St. Cyril was a central figure at the Ecumenical Council of Ephesus, which declared that the Blessed Virgin Mary is rightly called *Theotokos*.

Following the Ecumenical Council of Ephesus, many followers of *Nestorianism* were not satisfied. They fled the Roman Empire for the Persian Empire, encompassing approximately modern-day Iraq and Iran. Forty years later Emperor Zeno took a further step by expelling all Nestorians, as these Christians came to be known, from the Empire, forcing the rest of them to convert or to relocate to the Persian Empire.

Although these Christians rejected the declarations of the Ecumenical Council of Ephesus and broke communion with the larger Christian Church, they maintained valid Sacraments and Apostolic Succession. Thus began the first major separation among Christians. Although some later returned to union with Rome, this Church still exists today and is called the Assyrian Church of the East. Dialogue with these Christians has made much progress toward healing this schism.

The Monophysite Schism

Unfortunately, disagreements continued in the years following the Ecumenical Council of Ephesus. In her rejection of Nestorius's teachings, the Church emphasized the divinity of Christ. Whereas Nestorius sought to separate Christ's human nature from his divine nature, some Christians, especially in the regions around Alexandria, began to stress his divinity to the neglect of his humanity. They claimed that Jesus has only one nature—a divine nature—because his human nature was absorbed into his divine nature, sort of in the way a powder dissolves in water. This belief was called *Monophysitism*, from the Greek for "one nature." A small group of Monophysites held a council of their own in Ephesus in 449 confirming their teachings, but the Church, led by the Pope, rejected this council, calling it a "Robber Synod."

The Transfiguration, Greek icon. The Ecumenical Council of Chalcedon declared that Christ has two natures, perfect God and perfect man.

Two years later, in 451, a council was called in Chalcedon, which rejected Monophysitism and declared definitively that Christ is a divine Person with both a human nature and a divine nature, with the two natures united in what we call the *hypostatic union*:

> **Following the saintly fathers, we all with one voice teach the confession of one and the same Son, our Lord Jesus Christ: the same perfect in divinity and perfect in humanity, the same truly God and truly man, of a rational soul and a body; consubstantial with the Father as regards his divinity, and the same consubstantial with us as regards his humanity; like us in all respects except for sin; begotten before the ages from the Father as regards his divinity, and in the last days the same for us and for our salvation from Mary, the virgin God-bearer as regards his humanity; one and the same Christ, Son, Lord, only-begotten, acknowledged in two natures which undergo no confusion, no change, no division, no separation; at no point was the difference between the natures taken away through the union, but rather the property of both natures is preserved and comes together into a single person and a single subsistent being; he is not parted or divided into two persons, but is one and the same only-begotten Son, God, Word, Lord Jesus Christ, just as the prophets taught from the beginning about him, and as the Lord Jesus Christ himself instructed us, and as the creed of the fathers handed it down to us. (Declaration of the Council of Chalcedon)**

Many Christians, especially in Egypt, rejected the teachings of the Ecumenical Council of Chalcedon, held on to their belief in Monophysitism, and separated from the Church. Like those who had rejected the Ecumenical Council of Ephesus, they maintained valid Sacraments and Apostolic Succession even though they were outside full communion with the Church. Predominantly found in Egypt and other parts of Africa and the Middle East, these churches whose origins trace to the Monophysite heresy are known collectively as the Oriental Orthodox Churches. They are the Coptic Orthodox Church in Egypt, the Ethiopian Orthodox Church, the Eritrean Orthodox Church, the Armenian Apostolic Church, the Syriac Orthodox Church, and the Malankara Orthodox Syrian Church in India.

Most modern theologians looking back on this conflict conclude that the dispute was more over terminology than doctrine. The Christians who rejected Chalcedon did recognize both the humanity and divinity of Christ, but they felt that the words used by the Council Fathers at Chalcedon overemphasized his two natures, weakening the unity of Christ's Person (in fact, they thought that Chalcedon had endorsed the teachings of Nestorius by separating the two natures too radically). Followers of Chalcedon, on the other hand, thought that to reject the declarations of that council would be to declare that Christ's humanity was subsumed into his divinity.

In our day, dialogue between the Oriental Orthodox Churches and the Catholic Church has uncovered the fact that the actual *Christology* held by both groups is similar and, in fact, compatible. But full communion has not yet occurred, since many issues that have arisen in the 1500 years since Chalcedon still have to be resolved.

GROWING DIFFERENCES BETWEEN EAST AND WEST (AD 500-800)

In the centuries following the Ecumenical Council of Chalcedon, Christians in the East and the West drifted further apart. Their modes of politics and church governance, their culture and their languages, and even their theology diverged. Although there were difficulties, the Church in the East and the Church in the West remained in communion, even if that communion sometimes seemed tenuous and fragile.

Several factors during this period helped to define the growing differences.

The Barbarian Influence in the West

The encroachment of the Vandals, Celts, Goths, Visigoths, Franks, and other so-called barbarian peoples into the Roman Empire did more than occupy the military might of the West. As barbarian peoples migrated into Western Europe and were assimilated, they also had an impact on the broader culture. In the eyes of the Christians of the Eastern Roman Empire, this influence made the West decidedly less "cultured" and "civilized." Battles against the barbarian invasion also ruined the economy of the West, weakening its commercial power.

As the barbarian tribes conquered Western lands, there resulted a wide spectrum of different forms of government; some regions even fell into lawlessness. The Western emperor had less and less power and control over what was left of his half of the old Empire. With the decline and fall of the Western Roman Empire came a decline in Eastern regard for the Western Church.

Many of the barbarians, too, had been evangelized and converted to Christianity by Arians, which would keep the Arian controversy alive as these Germanic tribes conquered the West. This would lead bishops in the West to take actions that would offend the bishops of the East and fuel the fires that would lead to greater separation, as we will see later.

The Challenge of Different Languages and Theological Precision

St. John Chrysostom, 347-407, Archbishop of Constantinople, was an important Early Church Father. He is known for his eloquence in preaching and public speaking. He was given the Greek epithet *chrysostomos*, meaning "golden mouthed."

In the second half of the first Christian millennium, the West came to speak, write, and worship exclusively in Latin, while in the East the predominant language was Greek. There were few in the Church who could understand both languages perfectly. Naturally, communications among Christians of the East and West became more difficult and led easily to misunderstandings.

It is essential in theology that language be precise. One word translated into another language can take on a nuance that is unintended in the original tongue. We have already seen how language differences played a part in the Monophysite Schism.

In the West those theologians who wrote in Latin became the standard teachers of the faith, and none more so than St. Augustine, the great Latin doctor who lived AD 354-430. But in the East, St. Augustine was not as well known. Instead, the Church followed the lead of Greek-speaking theologians such as St. Gregory of Nazianzus, St. Basil, St. John Chrysostom, and St. Gregory of Nyssa.

Each of these great theologians, Latin or Greek, saw theological truths through different lenses. Some would focus more on one aspect of God's nature, others might contemplate another aspect. Over time these differences were exacerbated as their teachings became foundational to different schools of theological thought.

In addition, because of the broadening cultural and political chasm between East and West, the devotional and spiritual activities of the two cultures diverged. For example, although both East and West affirmed the traditional Trinitarian dogmas, Christians in the East emphasized the diversity of the three Persons of the Godhead (Father, Son, and Holy Spirit), whereas the West placed a greater emphasis on the unity of the Godhead—its one nature. Both are shared truths, but each brings a different perspective of that truth.

Church Structure

From the very beginning, Christians accepted that the Church was hierarchical, meaning it was ruled by a structure of authority, headed by the bishops as successors to the Apostles. There also was little dispute that the successors to St. Peter—the Pope, the Bishop of Rome—had primacy in the Church. That recognition was demonstrated even among bishops of the East from a very early date. When differences arose, it was not so much a question of *who* had primacy in the Church but *how* that primacy was to be properly exercised.

Another question of leadership involved the scope and autonomy of local bishops and churches. In the first centuries, the bishop of a city governed the Church in his locality with little interference from outside. Yet, in time, to meet the needs of the growing Church, this system developed as bishops collaborated with their fellow, nearby bishops in a coordinated way so the mission of the Church could be carried out effectively. Furthermore, there had to be a way to resolve appeals lodged against a bishop or disputes that might arise between neighboring churches.

One development that addressed the need for greater coordination of Church rule was the creation of *metropolitans*. A metropolitan is a bishop who has a degree of oversight over more than one diocese in his region. For example, if a Christian had a grievance against his local bishop, he could take his case to a metropolitan, who was usually a bishop of a nearby large city.

Eventually, as we read earlier, certain major cities became patriarchates, with the church in such a city ruled by a *patriarch*. A patriarch is a bishop who has authority over a large geographical section of the Church. By the beginning of the reign of the Emperor Constantine, the Church was administered by three patriarchates—Rome, Alexandria, and Antioch—with Rome having primacy and Alexandria as second to Rome. Later, Jerusalem and Constantinople would be added to the list of patriarchates.

However, the reasoning and theology behind these patriarchates gradually came to diverge between East and West. Early on, the Bishop of Rome was seen as having authority primarily due to his succession from the Apostles Sts. Peter and Paul, who were both martyred in Rome and, therefore, intrinsically connected to the city. This is why, as the patriarchate system developed, Rome was understood as having primacy over the others.

To Eastern minds, the governance of the Church also became closely associated with the governance of civil society. Since Rome was the capital and center of government for the Roman Empire, it was seen as natural that the Church herself should be governed from there. But after the capital of the empire had been moved to Constantinople, which grew in cultural prominence and political power, many saw the authority of the Bishop of Constantinople rise accordingly. This is why the East expected Constantinople, which now rivaled or even surpassed Rome in secular power and importance, to be recognized as a patriarchate, second only to Rome, as early as the late fourth century. Thus, the Patriarch of Constantinople, which had only a tenuous historical connection to an Apostle (St. Andrew), had great authority in the Church due to the political authority of the city rather than because of patrimony.

Rome also was the only patriarchate located in the West, whereas Alexandria and Antioch—and later, Jerusalem and Constantinople—were all situated in the East. While the East saw Rome as having primacy, they regarded it as a "primacy among equals" in the model of St. Peter, who was equal to the other Apostles but their leader by appointment from Christ. The Eastern Church and its patriarchates later came to conduct themselves with a fair degree of autonomy.

LITURGICAL RITES IN THE CHURCH

You do not have to study Eastern Christianity for long before you will come across the word "rite." You might find a reference to liturgies conducted according to the Maronite Rite, for example, or to differences between the Roman Rite and the Byzantine Rite. But what is a rite? There are actually several meanings to this word, all associated in some way with the liturgy and the Sacraments.

First, rite can refer to the liturgical actions associated with a Sacrament. For example, when we speak of the Rite of Baptism, we refer to all the prayers and actions involved when that Sacrament is administered.

The term is also used to refer to a liturgical tradition, which is the most relevant usage as far as ecumenism is concerned. In the Christian tradition many different liturgies have developed throughout the world. Each of these traditions revolves around the administration of the Sacraments and the prayer life of the faithful. So a rite, in this usage, includes all the connected liturgies in a specific tradition, such as the Roman Rite or the Byzantine Rite. It is important to remember that a rite in this context is not simply the Liturgy of the Eucharist—the Mass (Roman) or the Divine Liturgy (Byzantine)—but an entire liturgical tradition.

In the West there is one dominant rite—the Roman Rite—that is celebrated in various languages in almost all Roman Catholic churches throughout the Western world. Many might assume the same is true in the East, yet this is not the case. In the East numerous liturgical traditions have developed over the centuries with variations spread among the Churches. And this diversity is not limited to the variety of rites—a rite can vary from one church that celebrates it to the next. For example, the most predominant rite in the East is the Byzantine Rite, which is shared by a number of churches, including the Melkite, the Romanian and the Ukrainian. Within each church, however, this rite is used differently, with each church giving the rite its own distinctive celebration. Liturgical diversity is the norm in the East, although there is strong commonality as well.

Continued

The Divine Liturgy, Byzantine Catholic Church.
Liturgical diversity is the norm in the East, although there is strong commonality as well.

LITURGICAL RITES IN THE CHURCH

Continued

THE LITURGICAL RITES OF THE CATHOLIC CHURCH IN THE EAST AND WEST

CATHOLIC CHURCH IN THE WEST	
RITE	**CHURCH or GROUP**
Latin	Roman Rite (used throughout most of the Roman Catholic Church)
	Ambrosian Rite (Archdiocese of Milan, Italy)
	Bragan Rite (Archdiocese of Braga, Portugal)
	Mozarabic Rite (Archdiocese of Toledo, Spain)
	Dominican Rite (Dominican Order)
	Carmelite Rite (Carmelite Order)
	Carthusian Rite (Carthusian Order)
CATHOLIC CHURCHES IN THE EAST	
RITE	**CHURCH or GROUP**
Byzantine	Albanian Rite
	Belarusian Rite
	Bulgarian Rite
	Greek Rite
	Greek-Melkite Rite
	Hungarian Rite
	Italo-Albanian Rite
	Romanian Rite
	Russian Rite
	Ruthenian Rite
	Slovakian Rite
	Ukrainian Rite
Alexandrian	Coptic Rite
	Ethiopian Rite
Antiochene	Malankar Rite
	Maronite Rite
	Syriac Rite
Armenian	Armenian Rite
Chaldean	Chaldean Rite
	Malabar Rite

Early Church Fathers Icon.
By the beginning of the reign of the Emperor Constantine, the Church was administered by three patriarchates—Rome, Alexandria, and Antioch—with Rome having primacy and Alexandria as second to Rome.

In practice, however, even though the Bishop of Rome exercised the most sweeping authority over the Western Church due to its particular political and cultural situations, he always was considered a kind of "court of final appeal" over the entire Church, West and East. There are numerous instances in which an Eastern dispute was brought to the Bishop of Rome for resolution.

From this brief overview, we can see that the underlying causes of the separation between Western and Eastern Christendom—that is, between the Catholic Church and the Orthodox Church—were various and developed over a long period of time. These factors conspired with historical events to bring the differences to a divisive climax.

THE *FILIOQUE* CONTROVERSY (SEVENTH CENTURY–PRESENT)

When the Arian heresy was resurrected among the barbarian tribes, the Western Church faced a unique challenge. In order to combat this heresy, Christians in what is now Spain independently added a single Latin word to the Nicene-Constantinopolitan Creed (commonly called the Nicene Creed) in the fifth century. This word, *Filioque*, means "and the Son," and it was added after this phrase: "I believe in the Holy Spirit, the Lord and Giver of Life, who proceeds from the Father."

It may seem to be a minor distinction, but in the developing theologies of Western and Eastern Christianity it was an important one. The Christians who added the word *Filioque* wanted to emphasize the divinity of Christ by noting that he is equal to the Father. The *Filioque* addition clarifies that the Holy Spirit proceeds not just from the Father but from both the Father and the Son. There is scriptural support for *Filioque* in the Gospel of St. John, especially when Christ told his Apostles that he would send the Holy Spirit.[2] Although this phrase was not in the original Nicene Creed, in time this added word *Filioque* became more and more widely used in Latin liturgies in the Western Church even outside of the region where it first became popular. However, it was not added to the Creed in Rome until centuries later.

The Eastern Church, which recited the Nicene Creed in Greek and did not have to face the Arians at that time, did not add the term. Eventually, this difference in Nicene Creeds between East and West became a major point of contention, engendering intense debate between the two Churches by the eighth century.

The Eastern Church had a second major problem with *Filioque* that had nothing to do with theology. This second objection pertained to Church authority. The Eastern Church believed that a creed promulgated by an Ecumenical Council could only be changed by another Ecumenical Council such as in the way the First Council of Constantinople revised the Nicene Creed. The *Filioque* did not originate with an Ecumenical Council but with a local council of bishops in a particular and relatively small region and was simply adopted in other regions. No one else was consulted, least of all the bishops of the East.

The Western Church, however, grew to accept this addition to the Creed widely, especially after it was endorsed by the Pope. Thus, the controversy over the addition of *Filioque* to the Creed has its roots in both theological and church governance differences between East and West.

In the Latin Rite of the Catholic Church, *Filioque* is still part of the Creed today. At the same time, the Church also has come to accept the legitimacy of the Eastern tradition. In fact, the Catholic Church sees the two as complementary articulations in different words that emphasize different elements of related truths.

> At the outset the Eastern tradition expresses the Father's character as first origin of the Spirit. By confessing the Spirit as he "who proceeds from the Father," it affirms that he *comes from* the Father *through* the Son.[3] The Western tradition expresses first the consubstantial communion between Father and Son, by saying that the Spirit proceeds from the Father and the Son (*filioque*). It says this, "legitimately and with good reason,"[4] for the eternal order of the divine persons in their consubstantial communion implies that the Father, as "the principle without principle,"[5] is the first origin of the Spirit, but also that as Father of the only Son, he is, with the Son, the single principle from which the Holy Spirit proceeds.[6] This legitimate complementarity, provided it does not become rigid, does not affect the identity of faith in the reality of the same mystery confessed. (CCC 248)

Even with this increased acceptance of the Eastern tradition in the West, *Filioque* remains one of the most significant divisions between East and West today since many in the East feel its addition is both a theological error and a magisterial overstep. So, although some theologians do not believe it to be a church-dividing issue, others insist that it is an essential point of debate.

The Holy Trinity (detail) by Balen.
The addition of *Filioque* (*and the Son*) to the Nicene Creed clarifies that the Holy Spirit proceeds not just from the Father but from *both* the Father and the Son.

ICONOCLASTIC MOVEMENT (Eighth Century)

One of the most distinctive features of any Christian Church of the Byzantine tradition is the proliferation of icons. These mysterious paintings cover the walls and even the ceilings of Eastern churches and usually adorn the homes of the Eastern faithful. In fact, to many Western Christians, it is the icon that most identifies Eastern Christianity.

But what is an icon? The word "icon" is Greek for "image." Icons are two-dimensional images of holy people, places, and events. It may appear to be a form of painting, or just a type of religious artwork, but icons are much more than that. They are an aid to prayer, a means of helping us meditate and focus on something transcendent and holy.

In the Jewish tradition, sacred images are not permitted because of the Second Commandment: "You shall not make for yourself a graven image."[7] The prohibition was against the worship of false idols, such as the golden calf, but it came to be interpreted in an extreme way. Even among Christians, there are some who believe that all religious images are forbidden, even of Christ himself, because of this Commandment.

By the eighth century the icon tradition was becoming established in the East when the Byzantine emperors decided that the use of sacred images constituted an offense against the Second Commandment. These leaders put out an order that all religious images had to be destroyed. One emperor even convoked a local council of bishops to support his *iconoclast* (Greek for "image breaker") campaign. In the West, Pope Gregory III had condemned the iconoclast movement early on, but his strong position had little or no practical effect in the East.

But at the Second Ecumenical Council of Nicæa in 787, the last council considered Ecumenical by both Catholics and Eastern Orthodox Christians, the Church decreed that icons were licit and put an end to the movement. The Council Fathers based their reasoning on the Incarnation: In Christ, God became visible and physical to us, so created images that represent sacred things are acceptable in the Christian life. The crisis had been ended thanks largely to the intervention of the Western Church, but much damage had been done in the loss of sacred art.

Hagia Irene in Istanbul is a surviving witness to the Iconoclastic movement. It dates in its present form to the eighth century. Iconoclasts destroyed its frescoes, mosaics and icons, and a simple cross was placed above the main narthex where, in the Byzantine tradition, an image of the *Pantocrator* or *Theotokos* would have been present.

At Mass on Christmas Day 800 in St. Peter's Basilica, when Charlemagne knelt to pray, Pope Leo III crowned him *Imperator Romanorum* (Emperor of the Romans). In so doing, the Pope was effectively nullifying the legitimacy of Empress Irene of Constantinople. Charlemagne also supported the addition of *Filioque* in the Nicene Creed and defended iconography, both of which increased the division between East and West.

THE HOLY ROMAN EMPIRE (AD 800)

In the year 800 much of the territory of the former Western Roman Empire came under one rule when Pope Leo III crowned Charlemagne as emperor. Political power began to centralize again in the West under Charlemagne, but at no time was it ruled in such a centralized fashion as the Eastern Empire.

In this void the political power of the Bishop of Rome, the Pope, expanded. Already the spiritual leader in the West, the Pope was looked to by many people as a political leader as well. He became the unquestioned head of Western Christendom. While the Popes of this time asserted that their spiritual authority extended to Christians in the Byzantine Empire and beyond, in practice they had no means of enforcing that authority outside the boundaries of Western Europe. Thus, in practical terms, the Pope's rule was omnipresent to Western Christians and negligible to those in the East.

Charlemagne was a Catholic who sought to unify Western Europe in the faith, but he did so sometimes by military force. He even confronted the Muslims, adherents to the Islamic religion founded in Arabia in the early seventh century by Muhammad, who had conquered the Iberian Peninsula (present-day Spain and Portugal) in 711. Beginning with Charlemagne, the emperor was considered the protector of the Church and of the papacy, and papal patronage of the emperor would continue for centuries to follow.

As a result by 962, the Western European Empire would come to be known as the Holy Roman Empire. Under this system the Church prospered, and most of Western Europe was evangelized.

THE EXCOMMUNICATIONS OF AD 1054

In many history books you will see the year 1054 given as the date of the division between the Eastern and Western churches. The date provides a convenient reference point but hardly a definitive one.

The final breaking point between East-West relations arose over differences in liturgical practices. In the early eleventh century, Christians in southern Italy used the Eastern liturgy, including the custom of using leavened bread for the Eucharist. When Norman invaders arrived, they forced the faithful to adopt Latin practices, including the use of unleavened bread in the liturgy.

The bishop of the area appealed. Cardinal Humbert, one of the Pope's closest associates, responded that the custom of unleavened bread was proper and would continue to be enforced. The tensions escalated and began to include other disputes such as the nature of the authority of the Pope.

Eventually, Cardinal Humbert and a delegation from Rome went to Constantinople to resolve the problems. However, Cardinal Humbert was no diplomat, and the encounter with the Patriarch of Constantinople soon deteriorated. On July 16, 1054, he attended the Divine Liturgy at Hagia Sophia in Constantinople, where he denounced the Patriarch and delivered a decree of excommunication, dropping it on the high altar of the patriarchal church. In turn, the Patriarch excommunicated Cardinal Humbert and the delegates—but not the Pope, as some mistakenly believe. Technically, Cardinal Humbert did not have the authority to excommunicate in the Pope's name as Pope Leo IX had just died.

Although this dual *excommunication* is usually seen as the event that started the East-West schism, signs of unity persisted for a time after it. Even decades afterward, the Church in Constantinople included the Pope in her liturgical prayers, a gesture indicating full communion. And for centuries afterward many individual Catholic and Orthodox parishes still engaged in shared Eucharistic communion, apparently having no knowledge of a formal schism between East and West.

Nevertheless, these events do depict the breakdown in communion that had occurred between the two Churches. Instead of considering the universal Church as one Body, the East and the West came to view each other as separate entities. The dual excommunication event was a major and deeply symbolic milestone in the break between East and West.

THE SACK OF CONSTANTINOPLE (AD 1204)

During this time and in fact for more than two previous centuries, the Byzantine Empire had been fighting off repeated invasions by Muslim armies and, by the late eleventh century, was greatly weakened by war. After Muslims defeated the Byzantine army and had taken possession of Jerusalem, Emperor Alexis I appealed for help from the West. Only a few years afterward, with the stirring encouragement of Pope Bl. Urban II, Catholics of the Holy Roman Empire, from princes and priests to paupers, embarked on the first of several military *crusades* intended to liberate the Holy Land from Muslim rule. In the struggle against the advance of Islam, Western and Eastern Christians had found a common rival.

Near the end of the twelfth century, the Pope began to call for a Fourth Crusade in order to recapture Jerusalem, which had fallen back into Muslim hands. Most of the leaders of European countries ignored the call, dedicating their resources instead to internal matters that they considered more pressing. But

The Taking of Constantinople by Palma. Western European and Venetian crusaders looted, terrorized, and vandalized Constantinople for three days, during which many ancient Roman and Greek works of art were either stolen or destroyed.

During the sack of Constantinople, the famous bronze horses from the Hippodrome in Constantinople were looted by the Venetian Crusaders and sent back to Venice to adorn the facade of St. Mark's Basilica, where they stand majestically today.

an army was eventually gathered and set off in 1202. Pope Innocent III blessed the mission but expressly forbade the armies to attack any fellow Christians during this crusade.

Through a series of events, the crusading army ended up in Constantinople. Even though the Pope had forbidden it, the temptation to attack Constantinople was great, for then the leaders of the army could declare themselves rulers of the Byzantine Empire. The leaders of the army resolved to take control of Constantinople and set up a Latin Emperor. In April 1204, they breached the defenses of the city and invaded.

What occurred next was perhaps the most tragic event in the history of East-West relations. Although they had been threatened with excommunication, the invading armies spent three days ransacking the city—killing people, desecrating holy objects (including the Eucharist), and wreaking wanton destruction. Afterwards, they installed a Latin emperor, who ruled until 1261, when Byzantine armies succeeded in retaking Constantinople

These events deepened the divisions between East and West. What was before a disagreement over theology, culture, and politics became the basis for centuries of distrust toward all things Latin in the East.

"PAINFUL" MEMORIES, "DEEP REGRET"

Pope St. John Paul II in May 2001 addressed the responsibility of Catholics for the sack of Constantinople in AD 1204 and its impact on union between East and West. To His Beatitude Christodoulous, Archbishop of Athens and Primate of Greece, he noted:

Some memories are especially painful, and some events of the distant past have left deep wounds in the minds and hearts of people to this day. I am thinking of the disastrous sack of the imperial city of Constantinople, which was for so long the bastion of Christianity in the East. It is tragic that the assailants, who had set out to secure free access for Christians to the Holy Land, turned against their own brothers in the faith. The fact that they were Latin Christians fills Catholics with deep regret. How can we fail to see here the *mysterium iniquitatis* at work in the human heart? To God alone belongs judgement, and therefore we entrust the heavy burden of the past to his endless mercy, imploring him to heal the wounds which still cause suffering to the spirit of the Greek people.

ATTEMPTS AT REUNIFICATION

Even after these terrible events, there were attempts at reunification. On two occasions it seemed nearly accomplished.

Second Ecumenical Council of Lyon (AD 1274)

In 1274 the Second Ecumenical Council of Lyon sought to reunify the Catholic and Orthodox Churches with the cooperation of Byzantine Emperor Michael VIII Palaiologos. Eastern Orthodox delegates agreed to unity and even accepted the insertion of *Filioque* into the Nicene Creed.

When these delegates returned to the Eastern Empire with the news, however, they were met with strong opposition from many Orthodox clergy and faithful. Michael VIII worked hard to convince them, but he failed. After his death in 1282, his son and successor, Andronicus II, repudiated the council.

Eastern Bishop Mark of Ephesus.
Mark of Ephesus was the only Eastern bishop present at the Council of Florence to refuse to sign its decrees. He maintained that Rome was still in heresy and schism.

The Entry of Mehmet II into Constantinople by Constant.
At the age of 21, Mehmet II conquered Constantinople in 1453 and brought an end to the Byzantine Empire, transforming the Ottoman state into an empire. Istanbul's Fatih Sultan Mehmet Bridge is named after him.

Ecumenical Council of Florence (AD 1431)

In the fifteenth century Pope Eugene IV wanted earnestly to bring about a true reunion of all Christians. The armies of Islam had conquered much of the Byzantine Empire, and Constantinople itself was in danger of falling into Muslim hands. The Pope believed he could assist the Byzantine Empire and restore Christian unity.

In 1431 Pope Eugene IV called a council in Basel, although it was eventually moved to Ferrara and then to Florence. For the first time in centuries, the bishops of both the West and the East were invited to attend an Ecumenical Council. An Eastern delegation accepted the invitation, and hopes for reunion ran high.

The Council Fathers debated some of the doctrines and practices that divided East and West, including *Filioque*. In the end, it came to an agreement, with only the Eastern bishop Mark of Ephesus dissenting, and the Pope declared union in Christendom.

However, when the results of the council were announced in the East, they were not well received. Many in the East felt that their bishops had been pressured by the Byzantine emperor to accept Western teachings in order to obtain military assistance. Bishop Mark of Ephesus preached throughout the East against it. In the end those Eastern bishops who had accepted the Ecumenical Council of Florence were deposed, and its declarations were rejected in the East.

Military assistance from the West never arrived, and in 1453 the Byzantine Empire fell to Muslim invaders. Many Eastern Christians felt that the fall of Constantinople was divine punishment for the attempted reunion at Florence.

The schism between East and West was now firmly in place. Less than a century later, the Protestant Reformation would begin, and the Church founded by Christ would experience large-scale division once again. We will continue with the history of Christian division in the next chapter.

ST. JOSAPHAT OF POLOTSK: An Eastern Martyr for Ecumenism

St. Josaphat (1580-1623) may not rank among the better-known saints of the Catholic Church, but he is an important one in terms of ecumenism.

By the late sixteenth century, the schism between Eastern and Western Christianity had already existed for centuries. In a region that approximates present-day Belarus and Ukraine but was then part of the Polish-Lithuanian Commonwealth, the Christian churches were under the authority of the Patriarch of Constantinople. At a synod in 1595-1596, an Orthodox metropolitan in Kiev and five leading Orthodox bishops of the Ruthenian Church of the Rus led a drive to petition for reunification with the Catholic Church. The bishops approved the Union of Brest, and Pope Clement VIII approved the reunion soon afterward. These Christians who reunited with Rome retained their liturgical tradition and became known as the Ruthenian Catholic Church.

Not all the Orthodox in the region, however, were in agreement with the reunion plans. Even some of the bishops rebelled, particularly in the Ukraine region, which gave rise to a successful revolution for Ukrainian independence. There was open violence pitting Catholics against Orthodox, and many were killed in the process. Among these was St. Josaphat, who is called a martyr for Church unity because he died advocating peace and trying to bring Eastern Orthodox Christians into union with Rome.

Having entered the monastery in Vilna in 1604, St. Josaphat embraced the ecumenical effort with passion. He became abbot at Vilna and eventually was named a bishop, first of Vitebsk and later of Polotsk in 1617. At Polotsk he found a church in ruins in more ways than one: buildings in disrepair and many priests leading immoral lives. Within three years St. Josaphat rebuilt the church, publishing a catechism to be used in all churches, and demanded strict discipline of the clergy. All the while he kept preaching, teaching, and tending to the needs of the poor.

The Orthodox Church, however, set up their own rival bishops to attract Christians back from the Catholic faith. In time St. Josaphat saw his first diocese, Vitebsk, return to the Orthodox fold, and other towns followed suit. St. Josaphat also found opposition from his own Catholic community: Pope Clement had established that the Ruthenian Catholics ought to continue to use their own Byzantine Rite in the liturgy, but his people wanted to adopt the Roman Rite. People seemed unhappy on all sides.

St. Josaphat decided to return to Vitebsk to convince the people there to return to the Catholic Church even though he knew the violence of the separatists would put his very life in danger. He told the people, "You people want to kill me. You wait in ambush for me in the streets, on the bridges, on the highways, in the marketplace, everywhere. Here I am; I came to you as a shepherd. You know I would be happy to give my life for you. I am ready to die for union of the Church under St. Peter and his successor the Pope." He forbade Catholics to respond violently should an uprising occur, and he himself turned to prayer.

Unfortunately, the separatists turned to violence anyway. They came to St. Josaphat's residence and took hold of his friends and servants, beating them in the courtyard. When he came out to protest, he was beaten, hit with an ax, and shot in the head. His body was then dragged and thrown into a river.

It was the Jewish residents of Vitebsk who stepped into the situation in order to save the lives of St. Josaphat's friends and servants, and it was the Jews alone who mourned publicly the death of this great saint.

Yet, God has a way of turning great evil into great good. Bewildered and confused at the violence and murder, the people turned back to the Catholic faith, and even some of the rebellious bishops in the region followed suit. Later, in 1720, a large part of the Ukrainian Church reconciled with Rome, forming the Ukrainian Greek Catholic Church. St. Josaphat had helped bring about the unity he so dearly loved.

In 1867 St. Josaphat became the first canonized saint of the Eastern Catholic Churches.

Procession of the Palms in a Russian Orthodox Church on Palm Sunday. *The Great Entrance of the Divine Liturgy* commemorates the entry of the Lord into Jerusalem. The faithful take the palms and candles home and keep them in their icon corner as an *evloghia* (blessing).

Procession of the Palms in the Roman Catholic Church on Palm Sunday led by Pope Francis in St. Peter's Square. Palm Sunday commemorates the entrance of Jesus into Jerusalem, when palm branches were placed in his path. The Catholic Church considers the blessed palms to be sacramentals.

SIMILARITIES AND DIFFERENCES BETWEEN THE CATHOLIC CHURCH AND THE ORTHODOX CHURCHES

Although there are differences that prevent full communion, what Catholics and Orthodox share is far deeper than the things that divide them, and very strong ties exist between them. Consider the following:

Apostolic Succession. Like the Catholic Church, both the Oriental Orthodox Churches and the Eastern Orthodox Churches have bishops who are the direct successors of the Apostles. It is because of Apostolic Succession that the Orthodox communities are properly called "churches."

Valid Sacraments. Orthodox bishops maintain Apostolic Succession because they maintain valid ordinations, and these bishops—and the priests and deacons whom they ordain—therefore validly celebrate the Seven Sacraments. The Eucharist consecrated during an Orthodox liturgy, therefore, is the Body and Blood of Christ in exactly the manner as the Eucharist consecrated during a Catholic Mass. As any true unity depends on a shared Eucharist, the shared validity of the Sacraments is a major cause of hope for future union.

There are some distinctions in language and practice. The Eastern Orthodox and most Eastern Catholics generally refer to the Sacraments as "the Mysteries," and the Eucharistic liturgy is called the *Divine Liturgy*. Baptism is administered by immersion, and both Confirmation ("Chrismation") and the Eucharist (for which the Orthodox use leavened rather than unleavened bread) are administered at the time of Baptism by the bishop or priest, even with infants. Western Catholic practice with regard to infants and young children separates these three Sacraments in time, with first reception of the Eucharist usually delayed until the child reaches the age of reason and Confirmation often conferred in the adolescent years by a bishop.

Profession of Faith. The Orthodox and Catholic Churches share the same core doctrines, beliefs, and moral teachings. Aside from *Filioque*, the faithful of these Churches are in harmony on the truths enumerated in the Nicene-Constantinopolitan Creed. The foundational doctrinal declarations of the first seven Ecumenical Councils—on the Godhead, Jesus Christ, and the validity of holy images—are shared by both Catholics and Orthodox.

Acceptance of the early Ecumenical Councils. The Assyrian Church of the East accepts only the first two Ecumenical Councils, Nicæa (325) and Constantinople (381). The Oriental Orthodox Churches, which separated from the Catholic Church by rejecting the doctrinal definitions issued at the Ecumenical Council of Chalcedon in 451, accept only the three Ecumenical Councils that preceded it—Nicæa, Constantinople, and Ephesus (431). The Eastern Orthodox accept the first seven councils, the last being the Second Ecumenical Council of Nicæa (787).

The Eastern Churches did not participate in the later Ecumenical Councils called by the West. (Although Eastern bishops did attend the Ecumenical Council of Florence, the Orthodox do not consider it to be an Ecumenical Council because they did not accept its decisions.) The Eastern Churches believe that Councils conducted without the full participation of the Church's bishops in the East are not ecumenical and, therefore, neither valid nor binding.

In the West, however, where the Pope is understood to have the authority to call unilaterally for a council of the world's bishops, there continued to be Ecumenical Councils. The Second Vatican Council (1962-1965) is the twenty-first Ecumenical Council recognized by the Catholic Church.

Those councils held after the original seven—accepted by the West, rejected by the East—proclaimed many doctrines and practices that are binding on the Catholic Church but ignored by the Orthodox. A reunited Church would need to address the authority of those council resolutions.

The Immaculate Conception by Zurbaran. The Catholic Church and Orthodox Churches have different approaches concerning Marian dogmas.

Papal primacy and infallibility. The most serious of the differences between Orthodox and Catholic Churches concerns the role of the Pope. There are two specific doctrines concerning the papacy that the Orthodox reject: *infallibility* and *universal jurisdiction.*

Papal infallibility declares that the Pope, when teaching authoritatively to the whole Church on matters of faith or morals, is protected from error. This infallibility of the Pope is part of the general infallibility of the Church, which is led by the Holy Spirit to "all truth."[8] While Orthodox Christians accept the infallibility of the Church, they believe it can be exercised in an Ecumenical Council and not by the Pope on his own.

Catholic teaching states that the Bishop of Rome has full and complete authority over all Churches throughout the entire Church. This is called the universal jurisdiction of the Pope. In his role as the successor of St. Peter, he is given this jurisdiction in order to "strengthen the brethren."[9] The Orthodox Churches believe that though the Pope has a primacy in the Church as the Bishop of Rome, this primacy is largely honorary and carries no real authority over other bishops, especially bishops from the Eastern Patriarchates.

As for the leadership of the Oriental and Eastern Orthodox Churches, it is quite varied, as there are rifts in communion even within Orthodoxy. Eastern Orthodox Churches recognize a number of patriarchates and an *Ecumenical Patriarch*, the Patriarch of Constantinople, who enjoys a "primacy of honor" among the patriarchs; and yet there are other Orthodox Churches that operate independently. Oriental Orthodox Churches each have autonomous hierarchies.

Marian dogmas. Another theological difference lies in differing approaches to certain Marian dogmas. For example, the Catholic Church has declared that the Blessed Virgin Mary was conceived without Original Sin and calls this dogma the *Immaculate Conception*. The Orthodox believe that she was specially prepared for her role as the Mother of God and was sinless, but have a different understanding concerning Original Sin and its transmission.

STRUCTURE OF THE EASTERN ORTHODOX CHURCHES

Diversity is a key characteristic of the structure and life of the Orthodox Churches around the world. In general, the Western Church is not divided by national or cultural boundaries—it has a history of uniformity centered on the office of the papacy. Because of the history of the Orthodox Churches, however, national borders have been vitally important in their development, and the present structure of Orthodoxy stresses the independence of national Churches.

Pope Benedict XVI met with the Ecumenical Patriarch of Constantinople Bartholomew I in Istanbul in November 2006. They issued a *Joint Declaration* proclaiming the desire for Christian unity.

Orthodox Churches are either governed completely independently or are dependent upon another Orthodox Church. Typically, when the Orthodox establish a presence in a new territory, the fledgling Church is overseen by the founding Church. Once the new Church becomes established—which typically takes centuries—it becomes self-governing and is called *autocephalous* (Greek for "self-headed"). Sometimes there is a dispute among Orthodox Churches as to whether a Church is autocephalous, and these disputes can last a long time.

When a specific Church becomes prominent in influence or size within the family of Orthodox Churches, it can become a patriarchate, which means it is headed by a patriarch, the highest office within Orthodoxy. There are currently nine patriarchates in Eastern Orthodoxy, and fourteen or fifteen autocephalous Churches (there is disagreement on the status of the Orthodox Church in America).

As Ecumenical Patriarch the Patriarch of Constantinople is considered first in honor among the patriarchs. This position does not give him jurisdictional authority over the other Orthodox Churches, but it does give him a certain prestige which at times has been used to influence them. He is not by any means the equivalent of an "Orthodox Pope" since he does not have authority over bishops outside his own self-governed Church. Such a role is foreign to modern Orthodoxy.

Below is a current listing of all of Orthodoxy's autocephalous Churches. The last Church listed, the Orthodox Church in America, is considered autocephalous by the Russian Orthodox Church but not by Constantinople and some other Orthodox Churches. The Churches listed that are not patriarchates are self-governing but headed by an archbishop or metropolitan instead of a patriarch.

- Patriarchate of Constantinople
- Patriarchate of Alexandria
- Patriarchate of Antioch
- Patriarchate of Jerusalem
- Patriarchate of Moscow
- Patriarchate of Serbia
- Patriarchate of Romania
- Patriarchate of Bulgaria
- Patriarchate of Georgia
- Orthodox Church of Cyprus
- Orthodox Church of Greece
- Orthodox Church of Poland
- Orthodox Church of Albania
- Orthodox Church of the Czech and Slovak Republics
- Orthodox Church in America (status disputed)

Oriental and Eastern Orthodox Churches also accept the dogma of the *Assumption* of the Blessed Virgin Mary, which they call her Dormition ("falling asleep"). They believe that she died a physical death but that her body was resurrected and taken bodily into heaven three days later. Catholic belief does not specify whether she experienced death but only that she was assumed into heaven "when the course of her earthly life was completed."[10]

Discipline of priestly celibacy. In the early Church both married and unmarried men were ordained, although the Church generally required them (with the consent of their wife) to refrain from sexual relations after ordination. In the Western Church the priesthood increasingly came to comprise unmarried men, and the requirement for *celibacy* was made a universal discipline at the Second Lateran Council in 1139.

The Eastern Church, however, has always allowed married men to become priests. However, if a priest is widowed, he cannot remarry, and Orthodox bishops are required to be unmarried. In recent decades, under a special exception, or *indult*, the Catholic Church has ordained to the priesthood some married men who were Protestant clergymen before they converted to Catholicism. Furthermore, married men can usually be ordained as Eastern Catholic priests (as we will discuss later in this chapter).

Catholics and Orthodox share many of the same saints. This icon depicts three Doctors of the Western Church: St. Basil the Great, St. John Chrysostom, and St. Gregory of Nazianzus. In the Eastern Orthodox Churches they are known as the Three Holy Hierarchs.

Liturgy. As noted earlier, the Eastern Churches use several traditional rites or variants within those ritual traditions. The language of the Divine Liturgy has traditionally been the language of the original rite—Slavonic, Greek, and Syrian among them—although in recent years Orthodox communities in Western countries have been incorporating more of the local language as currently spoken, or *vernacular*, into the liturgy. The Roman Catholic Church used Latin as the liturgical language for many centuries but began using the vernacular as part of the reforms of the Second Vatican Council.

The Divine Liturgy has different prayers from the Mass but maintains the essential elements and a similar overall structure. Orthodox congregations traditionally stand throughout the service, occasionally prostrating themselves in worship. Orthodox Churches and liturgies make ample use of incense and iconography to facilitate worship, as we will discuss later.

Certain moral teachings. Several differences in moral teaching are also troublesome, especially in modern times. The Catholic Church, in keeping with Christ's teaching on the permanence of marriage (cf. Mt 19: 3-9), rejects the idea that a civil divorce can dissolve the marriage bond. She does, however, provide a formal process for annulment, a declaration by the Church that the conditions for a valid sacramental marriage never existed; a divorced man and woman are not free to remarry unless and until the Church has declared the marriage to be null. The Orthodox Churches, on the other hand, accept divorce as a matter of compassion for human frailty and allow for up to two subsequent marriages.

Some Orthodox Churches also have softened their teachings on contraception, allowing it in certain circumstances. The Catholic Church, following 2000 years of Christian teaching, rejects contraception because it violates the natural law and authentic human sexuality.

Spirituality. Furthermore, the spiritualties of the two Churches, which may appear on the surface to be very different, are actually complementary. Eastern Christian spirituality is richly theological with nothing incompatible with Catholic beliefs. A Catholic can read and benefit from the spiritual works of Eastern Orthodox writers.

Catholics and Orthodox share many of the same recognized saints, but Orthodox also have many saints of their own. The Orthodox observe a distinct liturgical calendar emphasizing different feasts. Furthermore, Orthodox Churches calculate the dating of Easter differently than the Catholic Church, so most years their celebration of this Feast of Feasts falls on a different Sunday than in the West.

IN FULL COMMUNION: EASTERN CATHOLIC CHURCHES

Parts of the Assyrian Church of the East, the Oriental Orthodox, and Eastern Orthodox Churches have over the years returned to full communion with the Catholic Church. These are known collectively as the Eastern Catholic Churches.

Although discussions between the leaders of the Catholic and Orthodox Churches did not occur after the Council of Florence, there were still occasional, local efforts to bring about full communion. In some areas missionaries from the Catholic Church worked to reunite local Orthodox Christians with the Catholic Church. In other cases an Orthodox bishop friendly to Rome would convert to Catholicism along with many of his flock. This led to the creation of the Eastern Catholic Churches.[11]

These Churches maintain the liturgy, spirituality, and teachings of their particular Eastern traditions but are now in full communion with the Pope and the Roman Catholic Church. Examples of such Churches include the Melkite Catholic Church, the Ukrainian Greek Catholic Church, and the Ruthenian Catholic Church.

The Maronite Catholic Church was never actually out of communion with Rome but simply was cut off from contact for several centuries. Situated in present-day Lebanon, the Maronites remained faithful despite pressure from Monophysites, emperors, and Muslim conquerors, and even Rome was not aware that this faithful Church existed. Crusaders from the West happened upon the Maronites in the late twelfth century, and the Maronite community provided support to the Crusaders' cause. Contact was reestablished, and the Maronites reaffirmed their unity with the Pope.

There are currently twenty-two Eastern Catholic Churches within the Catholic Church.

The Eastern Catholic Churches have had a difficult history. Most Orthodox do not consider them true Eastern Christians due to their allegiance to Rome. Yet, many Roman Catholics do not understand their relationship with these Churches, perhaps not even considering them truly Catholic due to their practice of Eastern forms of Christianity. Over the centuries, they have endured much hardship and suffering in their faithfulness to both communion with the Pope and their Eastern traditions.

Nevertheless, because the Eastern Catholic Churches are in full communion with the Pope, Roman Catholics may freely receive the Sacraments in Eastern Catholic Churches, and participation in an Eastern Catholic Divine Liturgy satisfies the obligation to attend Sunday Mass. The liturgies of the Eastern Catholic Churches involve many of several ancient rites and may use traditional or vernacular languages.

EASTERN CHRISTIAN LITURGY AND WORSHIP

In 987 the Russian czar Vladimir the Great sent emissaries to neighboring nations to study their various religious practices. His intention was to use the information they gathered to determine what religion his own country should practice.

The story goes that the envoys visited Muslims but found them to be without joy. They visited Jews but felt that their various trials in history, including losing Jerusalem, indicated that they were not favored by God. They visited Christians in Germany and found their religious practices acceptable but simple.

Then they visited Constantinople and the patriarchal church of Hagia Sophia, which at the time was the most magnificent church in Christendom. They arrived in the middle of a great liturgical celebration and were overwhelmed by the beauty and majesty of the Eastern liturgy. They declared, "We no longer knew whether we were in heaven or on earth." Shortly after their return, the czar converted to Christianity and instituted a Church under the authority of the Patriarch of Constantinople.

This story reflects the great importance that Eastern Christians place upon the liturgy. Like the Catholic Mass, the Orthodox Divine Liturgy is seen as a participation in the heavenly liturgy, the perfect communion of the divine life.

The Eastern liturgy, whether Orthodox or Eastern Catholic, is a feast for the senses; sight, sound, touch, smell, and taste are all directed toward the worship of God. The liturgy is a means for the faithful to offer up themselves to God and enter into the heavenly praise and worship of the Lord. Some key aspects of the Eastern liturgies include incense, music, icons, and processions.

Incense is an integral part of the Eastern liturgy, just as it was part of the Jewish liturgies of the Old Testament.[12] The burning of incense represents the raising of our prayers to God: "Let my prayer be counted as incense before thee."[13]

Iconostasis in the Greek Catholic Cathedral of Hajdudorog, Hungary.
For Eastern Christians icons are like windows into heaven.

Music is used frequently in the Eastern Christian liturgy. Bells figure prominently, and the bishops, priests, and deacons sing almost the entire liturgy with sung responses from the faithful; the whole liturgy has been described as "one song." This singing expresses the joy found in the worship of God: joy at the privilege of being able to stand in God's presence and even, in the Eucharist, to receive him.

Icons fill most churches of the Byzantine tradition, helping the faithful lift their gaze to heaven. Saints, Apostles, angels, our Blessed Mother, and the Lord are all represented. Often there is a screen or wall decorated with icons (the *iconostasis*) that separates the sanctuary from the nave, where the faithful assemble.

For most Christians in the West, religious images developed as a catechetical tool rather than as objects of devotion: They helped people to understand the faith more fully, especially those who were illiterate and could not read the Bible or other religious texts. But in the Byzantine tradition religious imagery took on a different purpose. Icons remind the worshipers of their unseen co-worshipers, the angels and saints of heaven who join in this earthly praise. They are like windows into heaven to remind all who see them that this earth is not their final home.

Processions also make up a key part of the Eastern liturgy. Processions are a visible and physical means to unite a community in prayer and to proclaim to the outside world the Christian faith. Before the reading of the Gospel and before the Eucharistic Prayer (in Greek, *anaphora*), the bishop, priests, deacons, subdeacons, and altar servers process around the inside of the church. In addition, on major feast days the whole congregation may join in a procession around the parish grounds or even the community.

CONCLUSION

Some Churches of the East are in full communion with the Catholic Church, as is the case with the Eastern Catholic Churches, while others possess an imperfect communion, for example, the Eastern Orthodox Churches. Although there are differences between the Catholic and Orthodox Churches, they share much in common, and there are strong ties between them.

There is much hope for reunion and work to end the division has been fervent in recent decades. In 1965 St. Paul VI and Constantinople Patriarch Athenagoras lifted the mutual excommunications of 1054 in a symbolic gesture representing the desire of both Churches to pursue reunion. Bishops, theologians, and lay scholars of both Churches have met many times since then to pursue reunion. Recent Popes, including St. John Paul II, Benedict XVI, and Francis, have seen working toward reunion with the Orthodox as a high priority of their pontificates. Furthermore, as modern society becomes more secular and anti-Christian, both Churches realize the benefit of working together for the common good throughout the world. Though tempered by a realistic view of the differences between the two Churches, the deep ties that bind them in terms of Sacraments, doctrine, and practice allow us to hope for the eventual healing of Church history's greatest schism.

The Churches in both East and West have venerable traditions of living the faith with courage and holiness. Both have also long blessed the world with holy Christians and administered the Sacraments wherever the faithful might be found. Although the approaches to spirituality and dogma are not identical between East and West, many have come to see these differing approaches as complementary rather than conflicting. St. John Paul II, who strongly desired union between Eastern and Western Christendom, used the imagery of "breathing with both lungs" to represent what would occur within the Church if Catholics and Orthodox were to reunite. His metaphor reveals both what we have lost by the schism and the vitality we stand to regain by reunion.

In speaking of Catholic relations with the Orthodox Churches, the Second Vatican Council stated:

> **It is the Council's urgent desire that, in the various organizations and living activities of the Church, every effort should be made toward the gradual realization of this unity, especially by prayer, and by fraternal dialogue on points of doctrine and the more pressing pastoral problems of our time.... if this cause is wholeheartedly promoted, the Council hopes that the barrier dividing the Eastern Church and Western Church will be removed, and that at last there may be but the one dwelling, firmly established on Christ Jesus, the cornerstone, who will make both one.**[14] (*Unitatis Redintegratio*, 18)

CHALLENGES:

What caused the various divisions in Christianity from the time of the Ecumenical Councils at Ephesus, Chalcedon, and up through the excommunications of AD 1054?

The schisms of the first eleven centuries of Christianity stemmed from controversies over doctrine and authority, but politics and cultures sometimes played contributing roles.

Most of the early Ecumenical Councils of the Church were convened specifically to deal with doctrinal questions that had cropped up over the course of time. In the first few centuries of the Church, theologians and bishops were presented with various heresies concerning the Person of Jesus Christ, the nature of the Blessed Trinity, and certain other mysteries of Divine Revelation. How best to articulate the truths of Revelation was a pressing question of the day. It is not surprising that, while such issues were being sorted out, various explanations and articulations were proposed that were at odds with one another.

In 1054 the Pope, St. Leo IX, sent a letter to the Patriarch of Constantinople, Michael Cerularius, that cited the *Donation of Constantine* to show that only the apostolic successor to Peter was the rightful head of the One Church. The Patriarch rejected the claim of papal primacy, and subsequently the One Church was split in two.

The fourth-century councils at Nicæa and Constantinople settled a number of theological questions about the nature of God and the Trinity—one of them being the co-equality of the three divine Persons as "consubstantial"—although some parties, such as the followers of Arius, still found reason to disagree.

By the early fifth century, these definitions raised another controversial question. The Blessed Virgin Mary, the mother of Christ, had become known in popular devotion as *Theotokos*, the Mother of God. But how could a mere human give birth to the eternal God? Would it not be more accurate to say that she is the mother of Jesus' humanity but not his divinity? That was the challenge raised by Nestorius. In effect, Nestorianism held that Christ had two natures and two "persons," or essences, rather than two natures united in one Person.

At the Ecumenical Council of Ephesus in 431, Nestorius's proposal was defeated. The Blessed Virgin Mary is indeed the Mother of God because, although Christ has both a human nature and a divine nature, he is only one divine Person. She truly bore this divine Person, who had both a divine and human nature, in her womb and delivered him in childbirth, so it is right to say she is the *Theotokos*.

Following the council, many Nestorians moved to the Persian Empire. A generation later, the Roman emperor deported any Nestorians who were still residing in the Roman Empire. Today, this church is called the Assyrian Church of the East.

Interior of Hagia Sophia in Istanbul (Constantinople). In this location on July 16, 1054, the papal legate Cardinal Humbert delivered a bull excommunicating the Patriarch of Constantinople. This act was probably invalid due to Pope Leo's death three months prior. The Patriarch responded with his own bull of excommunication against Humbert and the Pope, thus formalizing the Great Schism between East and West.

Another conflict soon surfaced. Nestorius had tried to separate Christ's humanity from his divinity; but now some believed the Church, after initially rejecting Nestorianism, was falling into Nestorius's heresy. In response, the Monophysites wanted to emphasize Christ's divinity over his humanity. Both views simply had difficulty reconciling how one person, even a divine Person, could have two natures and be both fully human and fully divine. So the bishops of the Church met again, this time at Chalcedon in 451, where they condemned Monophysitism and declared again that Christ has a divine nature and a human nature united in one divine Person. This was described as a *hypostasis*, or the hypostatic union.

Many Monophysites, especially in Egypt, rejected the Ecumenical Council of Chalcedon and broke away from full communion with the Church. This marked the beginning of the Oriental Orthodox Churches. Leaders of the Oriental Orthodox today say their position never embraced Monophysitism and instead feared that the language of Chalcedon was too close to the Nestorian position. Catholic-Oriental Orthodox dialogue in recent years has revealed that the Oriental Orthodox understanding of Christ is actually quite compatible with the Catholic.

The split between Western and Eastern Christianity—or what comes down to us today as the Catholic-Orthodox divide—resulted as much from political and cultural differences as from doctrinal disputes. There were language difficulties: Latin was spoken in the West and Greek in the East. The vastness of the Empire limited communication, so theology, spirituality, liturgy, and even ways of looking at the structure of the Church developed in different directions.

In the West the faithful recognized the Bishop of Rome as the Pope, the successor of St. Peter, to whom Christ had given the keys of the kingdom and thus endowed with the teaching and administrative authority over his Church. The East came to see the Pope as one of several patriarchs associated in a "primacy of equals" rather than the supreme authority. They also held to the importance of Ecumenical Councils, believing that no binding matters of faith could be decided without a council in which bishops throughout the world were participants.

A doctrinal issue arose when a local council in Spain inserted the word *Filioque* into the Creed, clarifying that the Holy Spirit proceeds from the Father "and the Son" (and not just from the Father *through* the Son, as was taught in the East). In time, the insertion was adopted throughout the West but rejected by Christians in the East. There were also differences of religious practice, for example, the West used unleavened bread for the Eucharist, while the East for the most part used leavened bread.

These two issues led to a disagreement between delegates from Rome and Constantinople in which each side excommunicated the other. This occurred in 1054, the year often regarded as the official beginning of the Great Schism.

PILLARS OF THE FAITH

STS. CYRIL AND METHODIUS

Today, schism between Catholics and Orthodox is a way of life. Christians in the West and the East have been estranged for over a millennium. There is no institutional memory of the Church "breathing with both lungs," as St. John Paul II described the united Church.

We may forget, then, that East and West were united for over 1000 years. During that time conflict and tension were common, yet collaboration and unity also existed among Christians in the East and the West. A great example of this union in the shared goal of preaching the Gospel can be found in the lives of the brothers Sts. Cyril and Methodius.

These two saints were born in Thessalonica in the ninth century, a time of significant tension between Rome and Constantinople. Although part of an influential political family, both chose to become monks. In 860 the two were sent by Patriarch Photius of Constantinople (and sometime adversary of the Bishop of Rome) as missionaries to a nomadic people in the region of the Caspian Sea. This mission was not a success, and they were soon afterwards sent to Moravia. As the sons of a Greek father and Slavic mother, they were acquainted with the language of the native people and worked to develop the Cyrillic alphabet (named for St. Cyril) by which Christian literature could be translated into the Slavonic language.

At this same time Germanic missionaries were also in Moravia, and they looked upon the brothers with suspicion, both for being from Constantinople and for not using the Latin language. The Germans persecuted Sts. Cyril and Methodius and worked to stop their mission. The brothers were called to Rome by Pope St. Nicholas I to defend their work, but before they arrived in the Eternal City, St. Nicholas had died. They met instead with his successor, Adrian II. Impressed with their endeavors and convinced of their orthodoxy, Pope Adrian sanctioned their work. He also endorsed their use of the Slavonic language in the liturgy. St. Cyril, however, was not able to return to Moravia, for he died in Rome.

Sts. Cyril and Methodius by Matejko. Sts. Cyril and Methodius represent both the conflict and collaboration between the Eastern and Western Churches.

Continued

STS. CYRIL AND METHODIUS

Continued

Soon afterwards, Pope Adrian erected an Archdiocese of Moravia and appointed St. Methodius as its first archbishop. In short order, however, Methodius was deposed by King Louis and the German bishops and sent to prison. Eventually, Pope John VIII (who had succeeded Adrian II) restored St. Methodius and once again sanctioned his work and the use of Slavonic in the liturgy. But even with these papal blessings Methodius still had many detractors. His struggles and labors eventually sapped his strength, and he died in 880.

Sts. Cyril and Methodius represent both the conflict and collaboration between the Eastern and Western Churches. Although they had to endure obstacles from other Christians in their apostolic work, they were supported and sanctioned by both Rome and Constantinople in a time of great tension between the two Churches. It takes sanctity to overcome human frailty, and Sts. Cyril and Methodius were saints who preached the Gospel of Jesus Christ regardless of the difficulty. They are models for Christians today who work to help the Church again "breathe with both lungs."

The Baska Tablet is one of the first discoveries of an inscription using the Glagolithic alphabet developed by Sts. Cyril and Methodius, dating from the year 1100. The inscribed stone slab records King Zvonimir's donation of a piece of land to a Benedictine abbey in the time of Abbot Drziha. The second half of the inscription tells how Abbot Dobrovit built the church along with nine monks.

SUPPLEMENTARY READING

The Traditions of East and West Are Complementary

"In the study of revealed truth East and West have used different methods and approaches in understanding and confessing divine things. It is hardly surprising, then, if sometimes one tradition has come nearer to a full appreciation of some aspects of a mystery of revelation than the other, or has expressed them better. In such cases, these various theological formulations are often to be considered complementary rather than conflicting."[15]

Pondering over the questions, aspirations and experiences I have mentioned, my thoughts turn to the Christian heritage of the East. I do not intend to describe that heritage or to interpret it: I listen to the Churches of the East, which I know are living interpreters of the treasure of tradition they preserve. In contemplating it, before my eyes appear elements of great significance for fuller and more thorough understanding of the Christian experience. These elements are capable of giving a more complete Christian response to the expectations of the men and women of today. Indeed, in comparison to any other culture, the Christian East has a unique and privileged role as the original setting where the Church was born. The Christian tradition of the East implies a way of accepting, understanding and living faith in the Lord Jesus. In this sense it is extremely close to the Christian tradition of the West, which is born of and nourished by the same faith. Yet it is legitimately and admirably distinguished from the latter, since Eastern Christians have their own way of perceiving and understanding, and thus an original way of living their relationship with the Savior. Here, with respect and trepidation, I want to approach the act of worship which these Churches express, rather than to identify this or that specific theological point which has emerged down the centuries in the polemical debates between East and West.

From the beginning, the Christian East has proved to contain a wealth of forms capable of assuming the characteristic features of each individual culture, with supreme respect for each particular community. We can only thank God with deep emotion for the wonderful variety with which he has allowed such a rich and composite mosaic of different tesserae to be formed.

— St. John Paul II, apostolic letter *Orientale Lumen*, no. 5

Eastern Catholic Churches and Ecumenism

The Eastern Churches in communion with the Apostolic See of Rome have a special duty of promoting the unity of all Christians, especially Eastern Christians, in accordance with the principles of the decree, "About Ecumenism," of this Sacred Council, by prayer in the first place, and by the example of their lives, by religious fidelity to the ancient Eastern traditions, by a greater knowledge of each other, by collaboration and a brotherly regard for objects and feelings.[16]

If any separated Eastern Christian should, under the guidance of the grace of the Holy Spirit, join himself to the unity of Catholics, no more should be required of him than what a bare profession of the Catholic faith demands. Eastern clerics, seeing that a valid priesthood is preserved among them, are permitted to exercise the Orders they possess on joining the unity of the Catholic Church, in accordance with the regulations established by the competent authority.[17]

— Second Ecumenical Council of the Vatican, Decree on the Catholic Churches of the Eastern Rite *Orientalium Ecclesiarum*, nos. 24-25

VOCABULARY

ARIANISM
Third- and fourth-century heresy formulated by Arius. This denied Christ's divinity, claiming he was not equal to the Father; rather, he was an exceptional creature raised to the level of "Son of God" because of his heroic fidelity to the Father's will and great holiness.

ASSUMPTION
The dogma that recognizes the Blessed Virgin Mary's singular participation in her Son's Resurrection by which she was taken up body and soul into heavenly glory when the course of her earthly life was finished.

AUTOCEPHALOUS
Literally, "self-headed." Describes an independently governed Orthodox Church.

CELIBACY
The state of one who has chosen to remain unmarried for the sake of the Kingdom of Heaven in order to give himself entirely to God and to the service of his people.

CHRISTOLOGY
The theology of Christ. Many of the debates of the early Church were over Christology: Who exactly is Jesus Christ? Is he God or just a creation? If he is God, is he also man? If so, how can someone be both God and man? These are immensely important questions, for they relate to whether or not Christ's Death and Resurrection are able to save us from our sins.

CHRISTOTOKOS
A Greek word meaning "Christ-bearer" or "Mother of Christ." It was the title the bishop Nestorius wanted to give to Mary, in order to avoid calling her the "Mother of God." While technically accurate, it is not complete, for it allows one to reject that Christ is a divine person, which ultimately rejects that he is the Second Person of the Blessed Trinity.

CONSUBSTANTIAL
A Latin translation of the Greek *homoousios*, meaning "one and the same essence." The three Persons of the Trinity—Father, Son, and Holy Spirit—share the same divine nature. This is affirmed of Christ in relation to the Father in the Nicene Creed: "I believe in one Lord Jesus Christ...consubstantial with the Father."

CRUSADES
From the Latin for "cross," this refers specifically to a series of eight defensive military expeditions between 1096 and 1270 undertaken by Christians to liberate the Holy Land from Muslims and to stop the expansion of Islam.

DIVINE LITURGY
The Eucharistic liturgy of the Eastern Churches, interchangeable with Mass in the Latin tradition.

ECUMENICAL PATRIARCH
This title was adopted by the Patriarch of Constantinople at a council in Constantinople in 587.

EXCOMMUNICATION
A censure by means of which a person is excluded from the communion of the faithful in response to "certain particularly grave sins" (CCC 1463). An excommunicated person is forbidden to have a ministerial role in the celebration of the Sacraments and other public ceremonies, to receive the Sacraments, or to exercise church offices or ministries (cf. CIC, 1331). Excommunication can be *latæ sententiæ* (i.e., automatic for certain intrinsically evil acts, such as abortion or the desecration of the Eucharist) or *ferendæ sententiæ* (i.e., imposed by ecclesiastical authority).

FILIOQUE
Latin for "and the Son." This addition to the Nicene-Constantinopolitan Creed expresses the double procession of God the Holy Spirit as from God the Father and God the Son. The bishops of the East refused the addition on both theological and church governance grounds, thus contributing to the Great Schism.

VOCABULARY Continued

HYPOSTATIC UNION
The revealed truth that Christ is one divine Person with both a divine nature and a human nature.

ICONOCLAST
Greek for "image breaker." A person who sees icons as occasions of idolatry and seeks to destroy them in a misguided attempt to purify Christian practice. This position was condemned at the Seventh Ecumenical Council (Nicæa) in 787.

IMMACULATE CONCEPTION
In light of God's free choice of the Blessed Virgin Mary from all eternity to be the Mother of his Son, it was ordained that from the first moment of her conception, Mary—by a singular grace of God and by virtue of the merits of Jesus Christ—was preserved from all stain of Original Sin. Believed from antiquity, this dogma was defined by Pope Bl. Pius IX in 1854.

INDULT
A special permission or privilege granted by a Church authority.

INFALLIBILITY
A charism (gift) of the Holy Spirit, given to the whole Church, that "preserve[s] the Church in the purity of the faith handed on by the apostles" (CCC 889). It takes several forms. The first form is the infallibility of the Pope: "The Roman Pontiff, head of the college of bishops, enjoys this infallibility in virtue of his office, when, as supreme pastor and teacher of all the faithful—who confirms his brethren in the faith—he proclaims by a definitive act a doctrine pertaining to faith or morals" (CCC 891). The second form is the infallibility of the body of bishops together with the Pope; they, too, are immune from error when they teach definitively about faith and morals, above all in an Ecumenical Council.

LEAVENED BREAD
Bread made with yeast. This is the type of bread used for the Eucharist in Orthodox and Eastern Catholic Churches.

METROPOLITAN
In the Latin Church, one who holds the rank of archbishop and presides over an ecclesiastical province.

MONOPHYSITISM
From the Greek for "single" and "nature." This heresy claims there is only one nature in Christ; any human nature he may have had was incorporated into his divine nature. It was condemned by both the Fourth Ecumenical Council (Chalcedon) in 451 and the Fifth Ecumenical Council (Second Council of Constantinople) in 553.

NESTORIANISM
Formulated by Nestorius in the fourth century, this heresy rightly claimed Christ was both human and divine but wrongly claimed he was neither fully human nor fully divine. Instead, Christ was a union of two natures, one human the other divine. This was condemned by the Third Ecumenical Council (Ephesus) in 431.

PATRIARCH (ORTHODOX)
A rank of bishop who rules an entire Orthodox Church. He is the bishop of the primary city within a Church's jurisdiction and has authority over the liturgy and other aspects of the life of that Church.

PATRIARCHATE
One of the recognized jurisdictions of the early Church, comprising Rome, Antioch, and Alexandria, with Rome having primacy; later, Constantinople and Jerusalem became patriarchates. Also, the several jurisdictions of modern Orthodox Churches.

PONTIFEX MAXIMUS
Title meaning "high priest" of the Roman pagan religion that was taken by Emperor Augustus. The title was later applied by the Catholic Church to the Pope.

VOCABULARY Continued

RITE
A formal act of public religious worship or other solemn observance.

SIGN OF THE CROSS
The act of tracing the Cross with the hand from the forehead to the breast and then from shoulder to shoulder. By the early third century, the practice of making the Sign of the Cross was deeply rooted in the Christian world.

THEOTOKOS
Greek for "God-bearer," often translated "Mother of God." Used since the early centuries of the Church, this title of Mary was defended by the Third Ecumenical Council (at Ephesus in AD 431).

UNIVERSAL JURISDICTION
Having authority over all peoples. The Catholic Church teaches that the Pope, by virtue of the ministry of St. Peter he exercises, has universal jurisdiction over all dioceses and parishes in the world. The Orthodox Churches reject this teaching.

UNLEAVENED BREAD
Bread made without yeast. This is the type of bread used for the Eucharist in the Catholic Church's Roman Rite.

Mosaic in Hagia Sophia (Istanbul, Turkey).
Byzantine Emperor Leo VI the Wise is shown bowing before Christ Pantocrator who holds a book with the text "Peace be with you. I am the light of the world." When Hagia Sophia became a mosque in 1453, the mosaics which date to the ninth and tenth centuries were covered with plaster due to Islam's ban on representational imagery. The mosque became a museum in 1935 and many of the mosaics were carefully restored. Restorers have attempted to maintain a balance between both Christian and Islamic cultures and some mosaics remain covered with Islamic calligraphy.

STUDY QUESTIONS

1. What was the Arian controversy?
2. What did the Council of Nicæa decree?
3. How did Constantine's move of the capital of the Empire affect Church history?
4. What is the Byzantine Empire?
5. What are some nonreligious factors in the split between East and West?
6. What are the three major schisms between East and West?
7. Why was the title *Theotokos* for Mary a Christological controversy?
8. How can Mary, a human person, be called the "Mother of God?"
9. What is the origin of the Assyrian Church?
10. What was the "Robber Synod?"
11. What is the origin of the Oriental Orthodox Churches?
12. Why do many Church historians today consider the schism resulting from the Council of Chalcedon to be more a result of differences in terminology than differences in doctrine?
13. How did cultural differences help lead to the Great East-West Split?
14. How did language differences help lead to the Great East-West Split?
15. What was the original reason for the addition Christians in the West made to the Nicene Creed?
16. What are metropolitans and patriarchs?
17. What are the five major patriarchates of the ancient Church?
18. How did the West and the East differently view the origin of the authority of the patriarchs?
19. What were the five major factors in the East-West Split?
20. Why did the Eastern Churches object to the addition of the *Filioque*?
21. Why does the Catholic Church see the two versions of the Nicene Creed as complementary today?
22. Why is the date 1054 considered as the date of the East-West split, and in what way is this an oversimplification?
23. Why did the Byzantine Emperor reach out to the Pope in the fifteenth century, and what was the Pope's response?
24. If the Council of Florence declared reunion between East and West, why did the reunion not actually happen?
25. What happened in 1453 that furthered the rift between East and West?
26. How did the Eastern Catholic Churches originate?
27. Why have the Eastern Catholic Churches had a painful history?
28. Why is the valid Eucharist of the Eastern Churches so important in the work of reunification?
29. What are some similarities between the Catholic and Orthodox Churches?
30. What is papal infallibility?
31. What is the universal jurisdiction of the Pope?
32. What is the Orthodox teaching on divorce?
33. How many Ecumenical Councils do the Orthodox accept as valid? How many do Catholics accept?
34. What did St. Paul VI and Patriarch Athenagoras do in 1965 to help the cause of reunion?

PRACTICAL EXERCISES

1. Attend the Divine Liturgy at and Eastern Catholic church. Compare and contrast it with the Mass in the Western Church. (N.B. Consult with your teacher or parish priest to ensure that the Divine Liturgy is indeed in an Eastern Catholic Church, i.e., in union with Rome.)

2. The Assyrian Church of the East and Oriental Orthodox Churches both trace their roots to schisms of the fifth century. Research one of these Churches. Who leads it today? Where is it based? How many people are in this Church? How many adherents live in your country?

3. Since 1980 an international dialogue between the Catholic Church and the Eastern Orthodox Churches has been underway, and since 2003 a dialogue with the Oriental Orthodox Churches to discuss their differences and similarities. Research these meetings. Where were they held? When was the last one? What topics have been discussed?

4. Give arguments for and against citing the year 1054 as marking the definitive split of East and West. Why are the dates 1204 and 1453 also important?

FROM THE CATECHISM

244 The eternal origin of the Holy Spirit is revealed in his mission in time. The Spirit is sent to the apostles and to the Church both by the Father in the name of the Son, and by the Son in person, once he had returned to the Father.[18] The sending of the person of the Spirit after Jesus' glorification[19] reveals in its fullness the mystery of the Holy Trinity.

245 The apostolic faith concerning the Spirit was confessed by the second ecumenical council at Constantinople (381): "We believe in the Holy Spirit, the Lord and giver of life, who proceeds from the Father."[20] By this confession, the Church recognizes the Father as "the source and origin of the whole divinity."[21] But the eternal origin of the Spirit is not unconnected with the Son's origin: "The Holy Spirit, the third person of the Trinity, is God, one and equal with the Father and the Son, of the same substance and also of the same nature...Yet he is not called the Spirit of the Father alone,...but the Spirit of both the Father and the Son."[22] The Creed of the Church from the Council of Constantinople confesses: "With the Father and the Son, he is worshipped and glorified."[23]

246 The Latin tradition of the Creed confesses that the Spirit "proceeds from the Father *and the Son (filioque).*" The Council of Florence in 1438 explains: "The Holy Spirit is eternally from Father and Son; He has his nature and subsistence at once (*simul*) from the Father and the Son. He proceeds eternally from both as from one principle and through one spiration....And, since the Father has through generation given to the only-begotten Son everything that belongs to the Father, except being Father, the Son has also eternally from the Father, from whom he is eternally born, that the Holy Spirit proceeds from the Son."[24]

247 The affirmation of the *filioque* does not appear in the Creed confessed in 381 at Constantinople. But Pope St. Leo I, following an ancient Latin and Alexandrian tradition, had already confessed it dogmatically in 447,[25] even before Rome, in 451 at the Council of Chalcedon, came to recognize and receive the Symbol of 381. The use of this formula in the Creed was gradually admitted into the Latin liturgy (between the eighth and eleventh centuries). The introduction of the *filioque* into the Nicene-Constantinopolitan Creed by the Latin liturgy constitutes moreover, even today, a point of disagreement with the Orthodox Churches.

FROM THE CATECHISM Continued

493 The Fathers of the Eastern tradition call the Mother of God "the All-Holy" (*Panagia*), and celebrate her as "free from any stain of sin, as though fashioned by the Holy Spirit and formed as a new creature."[26] By the grace of God Mary remained free of every personal sin her whole life long.

1233 Today in all the rites, Latin and Eastern, the Christian initiation of adults begins with their entry into the catechumenate and reaches its culmination in a single celebration of the three sacraments of initiation: Baptism, Confirmation, and the Eucharist.[27] In the Eastern rites the Christian initiation of infants also begins with Baptism followed immediately by Confirmation and the Eucharist, while in the Roman rite it is followed by years of catechesis before being completed later by Confirmation and the Eucharist, the summit of their Christian initiation.[28]

1399 The Eastern churches that are not in full communion with the Catholic Church celebrate the Eucharist with great love. "These Churches, although separated from us, yet possess true sacraments, above all—by apostolic succession—the priesthood and the Eucharist, whereby they are still joined to us in closest intimacy." A certain communion *in sacris*, and so in the Eucharist, "given suitable circumstances and the approval of Church authority, is not merely possible but is encouraged."[29]

During his visit to Athens, Greece, on May 4, 2001, St. John Paul II went to the Palace of the Archbishop of Athens and of all Greece, Archbishop Christodoulos. He addressed the Greek Orthodox authorities and the Holy Synod: "For all the occasions past and present, when sons and daughters of the Catholic Church have sinned by action or omission against their Orthodox brothers and sisters, may the Lord grant us the forgiveness we beg of him."

ENDNOTES – CHAPTER FOUR

1. Emperors convened some of the early councils because they recognized that a united Church was essential to an ordered society.
2. Jn 16:7.
3. Jn 15:26; cf. *AG* 2.
4. Council of Florence (1439): DS 1302.
5. Council of Florence (1442): DS 1331.
6. Cf. Council of Lyons II (1274): DS 850.
7. Ex 20:4-5.
8. Cf. Jn 16:13.
9. Cf. Jn 16:13.
10. CCC 974.
11. Although arguably there is a certain distinction between Eastern Catholic and Oriental Catholic Churches, in practice Church documents have used the terms "Eastern" and "Oriental" interchangeably in this regard.
12. Cf. Ex 30:1-10.
13. Ps 141:2.
14. Cf. Conc. Florentinum, Sess. VI (1439), *Definitio Laetentur caeli*: Mansi 31 1026 E.
15. *UR* 17.
16. *Ex tenore Bullarum unionis singularum Ecclesiarum orientalium catholicarum.*
17. *Obligatio synodalis quoad fratres seiunctos orientales et quoad omnes Ordines cuiuscumque gradus tum iuris divini tum ecclesiastici.*
18. Cf. Jn 14:26; 15:26; 16:14.
19. Cf. Jn 7:39.
20. Nicene Creed; cf. DS 150.
21. Council of Toledo VI (638): DS 490.
22. Council of Toledo XI (675): DS 527.
23. Nicene Creed; cf. DS 150.
24. Council of Florence (1439): DS 1300-1301.
25. Cf. Leo I, *Quam Laudabiliter* (447): DS 284.
26. *LG* 56.
27. Cf. *AG* 14; CIC, can. 851; 865; 866.
28. Cf. CIC, can. 851, 2o; 868.
29. *UR* 15 § 2; cf. CIC, can. 844 § 3.

CHAPTER 5

Ecclesial Communities in Western Christianity

All baptized Christians are in some way in communion with the Catholic Church, albeit an "imperfect communion."

Ecumenism and Interreligious Dialogue

CHAPTER FIVE

Ecclesial Communities in Western Christianity

INTRODUCTION

Following the schism between the East and the West, the next major division in Christendom occurred in the sixteenth century with the Protestant Reformation—in reality not so much a single movement as a collection of simultaneous and subsequent breaks from full communion with the Catholic Church.

Like the difficulties between East and West, these divisions involved not only theological differences but also politics and culture. The Pope and the Church were deeply involved in the society of the time. For leaders who opposed the policies and influence of the Bishop of Rome, the theological challenges posed by the sixteenth-century reformers provided an excuse to break free from papal influence. Because of these rapid and tumultuous events, Christianity in the West fragmented, creating divisions that exist to the present day.

In this chapter, we will explore:

- ✠ The historical context and background to the Reformation;
- ✠ The key figures, events, and principles involved in the Protestant and Anglican breaks from full communion;
- ✠ The divisions in Christianity that took place after the initial Reformation;
- ✠ Key similarities and contrasts among the beliefs and practices of the Protestant and Anglican ecclesial communities and the Catholic Church.

Palais des Papes (Papal Palace), Avignon, France.
During the Avignon Papacy (1309-1377) seven popes resided here from Clement V to Gregory XI. This immense Gothic building, with walls 17-18 feet thick, was built on a natural spur of rock, rendering it all but impregnable to attack.

THE CHURCH IN THE LATE MIDDLE AGES

In the history of religions, it seems that whenever faith and practice falter, scandal and division usually follow. We see this in the Old Testament when the infidelities of kings and people caused disunity resulting in a divided kingdom. We saw this also in the circumstances surrounding the schism between the Catholic and Orthodox Churches, where political rivalries and lack of charity created a break in communion that might otherwise have been prevented.

In the West, the time leading up to the sixteenth century was marked by repeated scandals which set the stage for widespread heresy and another major schism, or rather a rapid series of breakaways, from the Catholic Church.

The period of European history between the fall of Rome AD 476 and the conquest of Constantinople in 1453 is referred to as the *Middle Ages*. It was during this millennium that the Church came to exercise wider power and influence over the people of Western Europe, even in secular and political matters. At the same time, this power and influence was not always used wisely or effectively, which itself helped to sow seeds of discontent and mistrust that contributed to the later fragmentation of the Church.

Here we will briefly summarize some of the historical factors that shaped perceptions of the Church toward the end of the Middle Ages.

Church and State

Emperor Charlemagne by Durer. Charlemagne formalized the regions of modern-day central Italy, called the Papal States, which the Pope held as a temporal ruler.

We read in the previous chapter how, in barely a generation, the fourth-century Church was transformed from a minority group subject to intense persecution by the government to the official religion of the Roman Empire. Beginning with Constantine the Roman emperors always exercised a degree of authority in Church matters. This is not difficult to understand given the political reality of the time in which the emperor ruled all things within his realm.

After the fall of the Western half of the Roman Empire, Western Europe was left with a vacuum of authority that could adequately organize and govern the people. In fact, the Church was the only institution that could provide any sense of unity in what was left of the Empire, so the task fell to the Pope and bishops almost by default. As a result, the Church became involved in secular, political, and legal matters. For example, the Pope negotiated treaties with barbarian tribes, protected the people with armies, and provided a steady supply of food and services to the poor and suffering. Missionaries brought Christianity to the Germanic tribes, which helped unite the people of the West under the one Faith. As contemplative religious life developed, monastic communities copied Bibles, preserved records and libraries, and formed the first universities to educate the people. The Church, in so many ways through the Middle Ages, succeeded in preserving and developing Western Civilization.

Pope Leo III crowned Charlemagne, King of the Franks, as emperor in the year 800, thus formally and politically uniting most of Western Europe for the first time since the fifth century. Yet, the relationship between emperor and Pope was complex: The emperor was the protector of the Church, while the Pope lent a certain implicit divine approbation to the emperor's rule. Charlemagne also formalized the regions of modern-day central Italy, called the Papal States, which the Pope held as a temporal ruler. Thus, the Pope was the head of an independent, secular state, but he was also the spiritual and administrative leader of the Church throughout the Empire.

LATER PRE-REFORMATION HERESIES

emands for reform in the Catholic Church predated the Reformation by several centuries; for example, reforms were carried out within the monastic order at Cluny in the tenth and eleventh centuries with the aim of dealing with corruption and reducing the influence of the secular authorities in influencing monastic matters. New orders such as the Franciscans and Dominicans were founded to bring the Gospel to the faithful. However, other movements that sought reform ended up opposing the Church herself.

Peter Waldo assembled a group of laymen to lead a life of simple poverty and travel about preaching to the faithful in twelfth-century France. When they did not receive immediate and unconditional papal approval, they defied the Church and began to preach against her teachings and authority. They were condemned as heretics, but small pockets of the movement survived into the sixteenth century, at which time the Waldensians were assimilated into the Reformed ecclesial communities.

The calls for reform by these next two men are widely considered to have set the stage for the Reformation movements of the sixteenth century.

John Wycliffe was a fourteenth-century English theologian who opposed the practice of tributes paid to the Pope by the king of England. Later he came to oppose papal authority, denied the Real Presence of Christ in the Eucharist, and wrote an unauthorized translation of the Bible into English. Like the Waldensians, he sent out simple preachers, called Lollards, to spread his ideas. He, too, was finally condemned as a heretic, but only after his death.

Jan Hus, born in the late fourteenth century in Bohemia, was sympathetic to the writings of Wycliffe and openly supported his views. Hus rejected papal authority and spoke out strongly on the abuse of indulgences. He was excommunicated and burned at the stake for heresy in 1415—an act of inhumanity for which St. John Paul II issued a formal and public apology on behalf of the Church in 1999.

Western Schism: The Avignon Papacy (1309-1377)

As new nations formed and grew more powerful in Western Europe, kings began to assert themselves and even do battle with the Papal States. When a power struggle erupted between King Philip IV of France and Pope Boniface VIII around the turn of the fourteenth century—with the king opposing the papacy and the Pope declaring his own spiritual authority over the king's temporal authority—King Philip attacked Rome to arrest Pope Boniface, who was held prisoner for three days and severely beaten. He died not long after his release in 1303.

Two years later the cardinals elected Pope Clement V, a Frenchman, who moved the seat of the papacy to the French city of Avignon. Thereafter, six more Frenchmen would succeed him as Pope in what would become known as the Avignon Papacy. It signaled a time when the spiritual authority of the Pope was viewed as profoundly compromised by his subordination to the French crown.

The seven Popes who resided in Avignon between 1309 and 1377 tended to be worldly and financially corrupt. Many Catholics were not happy since they believed that the head of the Church belongs in Rome, the See of St. Peter. Largely through persuasion from St. Catherine of Siena, Pope Gregory XI decided to move the papacy back to Rome.

After Pope Gregory had died, the cardinals elected a Roman, Pope Urban VI. The powerful French cardinals, however, were unhappy with this choice and elected an *antipope*, Clement VII, installing him back in Avignon. Several more French antipopes succeeded him. While most nations of Europe remained loyal

Jan Hus at the Council of Constance by Lessing.
The main purpose of the Council of Constance (1414-1418) was to end the Western Schism involving three claimants to the papacy: Pope Gregory XII at Rome and antipopes Benedict XIII and John XXIII. The schism, which lasted more than forty years, resulted in untold confusion and a weakened Church, and paved the way for mass defections from the Church in the sixteenth century.

to Pope Urban, recognizing the validity of his election, a few favored the antipopes instead. (For several years, there was even a three-way division after a local council of bishops in Pisa, thinking it had the authority to depose both the sitting Pope and the antipope, elected an antipope of its own.)

This series of events from 1378 to 1414 is called the *Western Schism*. The Ecumenical Council of Constance, convened in 1414, finally resolved the controversy by convincing the true Pope to resign and deposing the two antipopes. It then elected a new Pope, Martin V. The Avignon Papacy followed by the Western Schism diminished respect for the papal office and its authority throughout Western Europe.

Corruption

Although the Western Schism had ended, corruption surrounding the papacy and other high Church offices did not. Powerful noble families had gained control over the appointment of some bishops and cardinals, which in turn influenced papal elections. As a result, some of the men who held the papal office were far from the examples of virtue and holiness we would hope to see in a Pope.

A case in point was Pope Alexander VI, who reigned from 1492 to 1503. While his political skill made him a strong secular leader, his political involvement and his scandalous personal life (fathering nine illegitimate children) tarnished the moral authority of the Church and made many political enemies. Alexander divided the papal lands for his sons and formed many political marriages with his children. Much to the Pope's historical shame, Alexander's son Cesare was the model ruler for Machiavelli's famous treatise on political intrigue, *The Prince*.

Although the private lives of the Popes in this period were quite unbecoming for the successor of St. Peter, remarkably, they still fulfilled their religious duties as Popes. In a time of confusion and secularization, they upheld the teachings of the Church. Still, they failed to live good, moral lives and missed opportunities for much-needed reform. As a result, the authority of the Church was eroded and many people assumed that some Church officials were more interested in personal power than the salvation of souls.

THE REFORMATION BEGINS

While Martin Luther is usually the first name that comes to mind when the Protestant Reformation is mentioned because he represents the first major schism of the sixteenth century, Luther was not the only person advocating reform of the Church. Contemporaries of his, in particular John Calvin and Ulrich Zwingli, also preached reform in various parts of Europe and gained support for their points of view.

All of these reformers recognized some legitimate need for the reform of some practices in the Church. However, they went further to reject points of doctrine and even the very teaching authority of the Church. Before long, there emerged doctrinal differences even among the reformers. Various efforts were made to unite these parallel reform movements, but their own disagreements proved too considerable to be reconciled. In the end, they formed distinct ecclesial communities, united only in their disagreement with and rejection of the Catholic Church.

We will look first at Luther, the key concepts that inspired the Reformation, and then at Calvin and Zwingli.

MARTIN LUTHER (1483-1546)

Martin Luther was born in present-day Germany in 1483. He entered an Augustinian monastery in 1505 and was ordained to the priesthood in 1507.

Martin Luther by Cranach.
This portrait shows Luther
in the habit of the Augustinian Order.

During his time in the monastery, Luther began to focus on his own sinfulness and found that he could not rid himself of his guilt, no matter how much he prayed, did penance, gave alms, or performed good works. Not experiencing the mercy of God, he could find no forgiveness in his heart or peace in his soul. He desperately wanted to "feel" his *justification*, a state of being in a right relationship with God.

Reading St. Paul's Letter to the Romans upon the advice of his confessor, Luther was struck by the words: "Man is justified by faith apart from works of law." This revelation led Luther to swing to the opposite extreme of what he had formerly believed: Instead of seeing justification as something we work for, he decided that it must be received by "faith alone." He came to see all religious works as having no merit at all. Only by faith, he concluded, does one receive justification from Christ.

Furthermore, Luther believed, this justification does not fundamentally change a person; instead, it just clothes his unrighteousness with the righteousness of Christ. This life-changing transformation in Luther's thinking felt like an epiphany, and his new idea would set the direction of the rest of his life.

Martin Luther and the *Ninety-five Theses*

At the same time that Luther was formulating his new thinking on justification, a Dominican friar named Johann Tetzel came to the towns surrounding Wittenberg, where Luther was residing, and began to preach about indulgences. An *indulgence*, the remission of the temporal punishment due to sins that already have been forgiven, is granted by the Church after a penitent follows a prescribed set of conditions.

CATHOLICS, LUTHER, AND THE BIBLE

atholics and Protestants share a belief in the inspiration and inerrancy of the Sacred Scriptures, and this common authority allows for a shared language on theological topics between the two groups. However, one roadblock to unity when it comes to the Bible is that Catholics and most Protestants do not agree about which books should be included in the Bible.

The 1522 *Luther New Testament* open at the "Vision of the Seven Candlesticks." The workshop of Lucas Cranach the Elder produced 21 full-page woodcuts for the Book of the Apocalypse. The first 3,000 copies sold out within a few weeks.

The Catholic Bible has seven books not included in the Protestant Bible, all of them found in the Old Testament. In addition, a few other Old Testament books in the Catholic Bible are longer than the same books in the Protestant Bible.

To understand the differences, we need to look at the development of the Scriptures. The Old Testament books were not written all at once in a complete and final form but rather over a period of more than 1000 years.

They were originally written in Hebrew, and they remained in that language for centuries. However, by the third century before Christ, many Jews—especially those living outside the Promised Land, who were descendants of those who had been exiled—could not read Hebrew, so the Old Testament books were translated into Greek. This translation is known as the *Septuagint* (from the Latin for "seventy," which is the number of translators tradition ascribes to the task of translation). The Septuagint also included some books that were written in Greek such as Tobit, 1 and 2 Maccabees, and Sirach.

The Septuagint translation soon became popular among Jews. With the advent of Christianity, Christians, including the Apostles, used the Septuagint. This version of the Old Testament became even more important due to the influx of Greek-speaking Gentiles who were not familiar with the Hebrew language. Eventually, these forty-six books of the Old Testament were included in the canon of Christian Scripture, which was fixed by Catholic bishops meeting in council during the fourth and fifth centuries.

The Church's acceptance of this canon of Old Testament Scripture was unchallenged until the time of Martin Luther. Luther questioned the legitimacy of several books of the Bible that he believed contradicted the true Christian Gospel. For example, he wanted to remove the Epistle of St. James from the New Testament, which teaches against his doctrine of salvation by faith alone.

Because of instances in which they contradicted his personal beliefs, Luther rejected the Greek books of the Old Testament. For example, the Book of Tobit states, "Almsgiving delivers from death, and it will purge away every sin" (12: 9). This contradicted Luther's views on the value of works. The Second Book of Maccabees shows Jews praying for those who had died, and that went against Luther's rejection of the existence of purgatory.

Because of these and other teachings with which he disagreed, Luther removed from the Bible the Greek books that originated with the Septuagint. Most Protestant denominations have done likewise, resulting in the discrepancy between Catholic and Protestant Bibles. Some Protestant Bibles today do include some or all of the seven books of the Catholic Bible but place them in a separate section from the Old and New Testaments and label them the *apocrypha*, Greek for "hidden," which refers to their "questionable authenticity."

Unfortunately, Tetzel made it sound as though, by giving money to "buy" an indulgence, people could "buy" salvation for their deceased loved ones in *purgatory*—a grave misrepresentation of what indulgences really are.

Luther was angered: Salvation was a gift from God, not a commodity to be bought. This led Luther to post *Ninety-five Theses* on the door of his parish church in Wittenberg on October 31, 1517. These statements challenged Catholic teaching directly on a range of subjects including indulgences, penances, and the Church's teaching authority.

Luther did not initially intend to break away from the Catholic Church but only to reform her from within. But his stubbornness, the popular sense of the need for reform, and the mishandling of the controversy by some Church authorities all contributed to an eventual schism. Within a few years, his movement was spreading rapidly. The Reformation had begun.

Martin Luther at the Diet of Worms by Werner.
The Diet of Worms of 1521 was a formal imperial assembly of the Holy Roman Empire called by Emperor Charles V to ask Martin Luther to retract his writings against the Church. He refused. "I cannot and will not retract..."

FOUNDATIONS OF THE PROTESTANT REFORMATION

We will now look at each of these three fundamental tenets of the Protestant Reformation in turn and provide a brief evaluation from a Catholic perspective.

Sola Scriptura

Beginning with Luther, one of the key rallying cries of the Protestant Reformation was the phrase *sola Scriptura* ("Scripture alone"). The statement means that the Bible is the sole authority for Christians and alone provides the rule of faith and practice for the Church.

Luther and other reformers thought that the Catholic reliance on Sacred Tradition and the Magisterium of the Church was unwarranted and led to the corruption of what God has revealed in Christ. They taught that Christ did not leave behind an infallible teaching authority to guide the Church through all time. Rather, only the Bible itself is infallible, and the interpretation of what the Bible says is ultimately up to each individual Christian conscience.

Following Luther, Protestants believe in the *perspicuity* of Scripture, meaning that it is so clear that any believer can understand it. Catholics, on the other hand, believe that Christ established the Church on St. Peter and the Apostles and gave them the mission to teach faithfully the Deposit of Faith, which includes both Scripture and Tradition. This fundamental difference is a primary cause of the division between the Catholic and Protestant teaching.

Sola Fide

Another of Luther's ideas that became an accepted belief among all Protestant reformers was the idea of *sola fide* ("faith alone"), the full meaning of which is "justification by faith alone." In Luther's thinking, there can be no cooperation between human freedom and God's grace.

Sola fide was in large part a rejection of what Luther falsely perceived to be the Catholic and Orthodox teaching: That we can gain salvation and receive God's grace through our actions *apart* from faith, particularly by receiving the Sacraments, through prayer, through works of charity, and through other acts such as gaining indulgences.

St. James by El Greco.
Faith and works are both necessary for salvation.

While isolated passages in St. Paul's writings might seem to suggest works are unnecessary—as when St. Paul writes to the Romans that "a man is justified by faith apart from works of law"[1]—Scripture also strongly affirms the necessity of works, as in the Epistle of St. James: "So faith by itself, if it has no works, is dead."[2] Another example comes in the Parable of the Last Judgment in the Gospel of St. Matthew; Christ described the fate of souls as being determined by the good works they performed—or failed to perform—in their lifetime without mention of their faith.[3] But Luther was so insistent of *sola fide* that, when he wrote his own translation of the Bible, he added the word "alone" to St. Paul's letter so that it would read, "A man is justified by faith *alone* apart from works of law."

According to Luther and most Protestants, justification produces no change in the individual. Rather, if a person has faith, God simply *declares* him or her justified.

The Catholic Church teaches that justification and salvation come by way of grace, which is a gift from God. Through actual grace we are led to believe in God, to love him, and to trust in him, and through sanctifying grace we are given the divine life of God in our souls. Yet, God asks us to respond to this gift of grace. This response involves our whole cooperation with God in all aspects of our being.

Good works—for example, prayers, moral living, acts of charity, and compassion toward others—are part of our response to God's grace. In fact, it is through our actions that our faith in God and our love for him is manifested. They also help to strengthen our union with God.

Faith and works are integrally linked by love. We indeed are justified and saved by grace through faith, but our faith must be a living faith, evidenced by our actions. Faith and works indeed are both necessary for salvation, but it would take more than four centuries before Lutheran and Catholic leaders would jointly and formally recognize this truth.[4]

Common Priesthood of the Faithful

Luther never used the phrase "common priesthood of the faithful," but he did express the concept based on his reading of the First Epistle of St. Peter: "You are a chosen race, a royal priesthood, a holy nation."[5] While this affirmation of Luther regarding the priesthood of all believers was correct, it was misunderstood and distorted by other reformers and their followers. His idea turned into essentially an anti-clerical campaign, one that meshed well with the anti-authoritarian implications of *sola Scriptura* and *sola fide*. If only Scripture or only faith is necessary, then nobody really needs bishops or priests or even the Sacraments in order to live our faith.

The Second Ecumenical Council of the Vatican articulated the Catholic teaching on the common priesthood of the faithful: All the baptized share in the priesthood of Christ. This, however, differs in essence from the *ministerial priesthood* by which some men are called to serve the faithful and provide sacramental ministry by receiving Holy Orders.

CATHOLIC REFORMERS: DESIDERIUS ERASMUS

ot all reformers dissented from Catholic doctrine or ended up separating from the Church. Many advocated reform from within, remaining faithful Catholics all the while. One such faithful reformer was the Dutch priest Desiderius Erasmus.

Erasmus (1469-1536) recognized many problems that existed in the Church of his day. He was most concerned about the education and edification of the lay faithful. He criticized the lavish lifestyle of many clerics and even Popes. He called for priests to take more seriously their roles as teachers of the faith so the faithful might understand the reasons behind Church teachings and traditions. He encouraged the laity to read Scripture, to be attentive to personal prayer, and to develop a piety that involves more than just the reception of the Sacraments. He was an excellent preacher and skilled writer who used satire to great effect. He also undertook an ambitious project of composing fresh translations of the New Testament in both Greek and Latin.

As the Reformation began Erasmus and Martin Luther expressed a degree of admiration for one another's views, and Erasmus was encouraged by many to join the Reformation movement. However, Erasmus soon came to the conclusion that Luther had gone too far in his rejection of Church authority and doctrine.

One famous area of disagreement was over the idea of free will. Luther, reflecting on his concept of justification by faith alone apart from works, had written that sinful human beings do not have free will; sin corrupts so much that a person cannot choose freely to do good. Only God's grace can turn him or her around to compel him or her to do good. Either way, everyone is dominated, either by Satan or by God in the same way that a rider dominates and directs a horse.

Desiderius Erasmus by Holbein.
Erasmus had a deep desire for reform and progress through education and tolerance.

Erasmus opposed this with the Catholic view that every human person possesses the freedom to choose good or evil. Of course, the grace of God is always necessary to discern and choose good over evil. In other words, grace is a free gift from God, and we must use our free will to cooperate with grace and respond to God's gift of redemption.

Portrait of Young John Calvin by Flemish Master. Calvin wrote the seminal work of the Protestant Reformation, *The Institutes of Christian Religion.*

Looting of the Churches of Lyon by the Calvinists, 1562 by Caron. Calvin directed iconoclastic actions, destroying stained glass windows, statues, crucifixes, vestments, and altars.

JOHN CALVIN (1509-1564)

Around the same time that Luther was preaching his reforms in Germany, a theologian named John Calvin was developing his theological views in France. John Calvin is considered one of the leaders of the Protestant Reformation. He was methodical and precise in his theological writings. In fact, no one was more influential in developing the theology of Protestantism than Calvin.

Born in France in 1509, his training was primarily in law. By the early 1530s Calvin began to embrace the Protestant Reform. Due to uprisings against Protestants in France, he moved to Switzerland, eventually settling in Geneva, and it was there that his influence reached its apex.

Upon arriving in Switzerland Calvin began writing what would become the seminal work of the Protestant Reformation, *The Institutes of Christian Religion*. In these writings he worked out a systematic theology. Because of this, Protestantism became a more established religion. The first edition was released in 1536, but Calvin eventually produced five editions, with the last, published in 1559, running five times as long as the first edition.

Calvin agreed with Luther on the main tenets of Protestantism such as *sola fide* and *sola Scriptura*, but his theology differed from Luther's in some important areas. As their respective communities developed, their views diverged increasingly.

One particularly striking difference was in the two reformers' views of the Eucharist. Although Luther rejected the Catholic understanding of transubstantiation, which holds that the consecrated bread and wine truly become the Body and Blood of Christ, he did believe that Christ was somehow present in the bread and wine received in communion. Calvin taught, rather, that when one *receives* communion Christ becomes present to the communicant. He compared it to the presence of the Holy Spirit coming upon Christ at his baptism: The bread and the wine do not change in any way, but when they are received Christ enters into the soul of the believer.

Another Calvinist view is his understanding of predestination. If all things happen according to God's plan, then the fate of those who go to heaven or hell must have been predestined by God. This belief that the fates of both the saved and the condemned are predestined is called *double predestination*. (Although Calvin is more closely associated with predestination, Martin Luther taught a double predestination very similar to Calvin's.)

Calvin's great achievement, however, was to transform some of the key ideas of the Reformation into a systemized theology.

ULRICH ZWINGLI (1484-1531)

Another influential figure of the Reformation and early Protestantism was Ulrich Zwingli. Born in Switzerland in 1484, Zwingli received a well-rounded education, became a pastor, and was actually a strong supporter of the papacy early in life. He devoted himself zealously to the task of preaching, studying the Bible, and even learning Hebrew to understand the Scriptures more fully.

Ulrich Zwingli by Asper.
Zwingli taught that Holy Communion is a symbolic ritual in which Christ is not present.

Around the time that Luther posted his *Ninety-five Theses*, Zwingli was advocating reform in the Church. But Zwingli was not focused on doctrinal issues; rather, he was mostly concerned with how secular affairs impacted the Church.

However, it was not long before Zwingli turned his attention to theology and spirituality. In 1522 at a time when his prestige had greatly increased, he called into question the rules of fasting during Lent—a relatively minor disciplinary matter, but one that presented a direct challenge to Church authority nevertheless. Soon he found many more causes for complaint. He was something of an iconoclast, objecting to the use of images. He opposed the discipline of clerical celibacy. Most significantly, he questioned the Church's teaching authority and in time came to espouse Luther's teaching of *sola Scriptura*.

Zwingli went on to develop new doctrines. The most influential of these was his view that Sacraments, far from serving as visible signs that confer God's grace, were chiefly symbolic. He taught that Baptism does not wipe away sin but is chiefly a pledge made to God. Holy Communion is a symbolic ritual in which Christ is not present. This was a radical break not only from Catholic teaching but also from Luther, whose understanding was comparatively closer to the Catholic teaching.

It was Zwingli's teaching on the Sacraments and not Luther's that would most greatly influence the development of Reformation doctrine. The majority of Protestants today, especially those from an evangelical tradition, view Baptism and the Eucharist as primarily symbolic. (Indeed, without valid Apostolic Succession—and, therefore, a valid priesthood—communion in Protestant services cannot be anything *but* symbolic.) If Calvin can be said to have systemized Protestantism, Zwingli did much to sever it more completely from its Catholic origins by rejecting not only Church authority but also the entire sacramental economy that is so central to a Catholic understanding of salvation.

For all his significance in the Reformation, Zwingli is not claimed as the founder of any ecclesial community except for the Swiss Reformed Church. However, his thought and teachings strongly influenced the teachings and practices of the Reformed movement.

Heinrich Bullinger by Asper.
After Zwingli died in the Battle of Kappel in 1531, Heinrich Bullinger (1504-1575) succeeded him as the Zurich Antistes (head of the church in the Reformed Churches in Switzerland).

OTHER REFORMATION AND POST-REFORMATION FIGURES

Martin Luther, John Calvin, and Ulrich Zwingli were the leading agents of the Protestant Reformation, and King Henry VIII sparked the Anglican schism. However, there were many other reformers who played important roles in the fracturing of Christendom in the sixteenth century and beyond. These include the following:

John Knox, who was influenced by Calvin, spent several years in Geneva in the mid-1550s before leading his Reformed movement in Scotland and establishing a distinct governing structure. His followers became known as Presbyterians, and the ecclesial community he founded spread to England, Ireland, and North America.

Philip Melanchton was an influential colleague of Luther's who helped systematize his theology.

Menno Simons was a sixteenth-century Catholic priest who came to doubt the Real Presence of Christ in the Eucharist and the validity of infant Baptism. He joined the Anabaptist movement but later broke off and founded the Mennonites.

William Tyndale was an Englishman best known for his error-filled translation of the Bible into English. He opposed papal authority and embraced Luther's idea of justification by faith alone. After he opposed King Henry VIII's divorce, the king had him executed in 1536.

Thomas Cranmer and Thomas Cromwell were collaborators with Henry VIII in the Anglican schism.

George Fox founded the Society of Friends, or Quakers, one of a number of movements that broke away from the Church of England in the seventeenth century.

John Wesley was an eighteenth-century minister who started a reform movement within the Church of England but later broke away to found the Methodists.

Thomas Cranmer (1489-1556).
Cranmer wrote and compiled the first two editions of the *Book of Common Prayer,* a complete liturgy for the Church of England.

John Wesley (1703-1791).
Wesley founded the Methodist movement in Great Britain. Wesley opposed Calvinism, notably the doctrine of predestination.

THE ANGLICAN SCHISM

Luther, Calvin, and Zwingli were all theologians who disputed Catholic doctrine on various points. In the case of King Henry VIII of England, we have a political ruler who supported the theology of the Catholic Church—so much so that he once was proclaimed "Defender of the Faith" by the Pope—but ultimately rejected the Pope's authority.

Strictly speaking, the English break from the Church was not part of the Protestant Reformation because it did not begin as a controversy over doctrine. Nor did Henry VIII deny the need for a teaching authority: He simply decided to make the Church of England an autonomous national church with himself as its head on the model of some of the Reformed communities, assuming authority over existing bishops, clergy, and Church institutions within his domain. The Anglican Communion that developed from Henry's break, however, eventually and increasingly did ally itself with Protestantism.

St. Thomas More by Holbein.
St. Thomas More (1478-1535) opposed King Henry VIII's separation from the Roman Catholic Church and refused to accept him as Supreme Head of the Church of England.

The reign of King Henry VIII is credited with increasing England's power and its influence in European affairs. Many men, including the future martyr St. Thomas More, believed that he would bring about a great English renaissance of learning, piety, and peace. In fact, at the beginning of the crisis initiated by Luther, Henry VIII defended the Catholic faith against the attacks of the Protestant reformers.

By around 1525 Henry became convinced that his wife, Catherine of Aragon, would never be able to conceive a male heir. Furthermore, he had developed an infatuation with Anne Boleyn, the sister of one of his mistresses. Anne initially resisted the King's efforts to seduce her but then determined only to yield to Henry's advances if she became the Queen. King Henry became obsessed with obtaining an annulment of his marriage to Catherine of Aragon.

For this reason, Henry devoted himself to convincing Pope Clement VII that his first marriage was not valid and that an annulment should be granted. His efforts failed: The Church declared that there were no grounds for an annulment. Henry then declared royal supremacy over the Church in England, had his marriage to Catherine declared null by the Archbishop of Canterbury Thomas Cranmer, who held the highest bishopric in the Catholic Church in England, and married Anne Boleyn.

Archbishop Cranmer and Henry's chief minister, Thomas Cromwell, were supporters of the Reformation going on in Europe at this time, and the doctrines and practices of the Reformers were introduced under Henry VIII and his successor, King Edward VI. Eventually, Catholicism was declared illegal, and those who refused to accept Henry as the head of the English Church were persecuted. Many were martyred. This ecclesial community, under the English monarch, came to be known as the Church of England.

As the Anglican Schism continued, some in the Church of England saw it as a "middle way" between Catholicism and Protestantism. It did not reject the sacramental economy completely, but it did teach that the only "Sacraments of the Gospel" are Baptism and "the Lord's Supper." It did not reject the idea of a church hierarchy—their hierarchy replaced the authority of the Pope with the authority of the English monarch—but it did forfeit Apostolic Succession by adopting invalid rites of ordination. Over the centuries, many different theologies developed within this communion, some leaning closer to their Catholic roots and others stepping completely over to a Protestant perspective. Even today, individual Anglican and Episcopal parishes, dioceses, and national entities can be found aligned all along the ideological spectrum.

DIVORCE AND ANNULMENT

One of the most prominent differences between the moral teachings of the Catholic Church and Protestant denominations regards marriage and divorce. The Catholic Church does not recognize divorce, basing her teaching on Christ:

> "From the beginning of creation, 'God made them male and female.' 'For this reason a man shall leave his father and mother and be joined to his wife, and the two shall become one flesh.' So they are no longer two but one flesh. What therefore God has joined together, let not man put asunder." And in the house the disciples asked him again about this matter. And he said to them, "Whoever divorces his wife and marries another, commits adultery against her; and if she divorces her husband and marries another, she commits adultery."
> (Mk 10: 6-12)

Marriage reflects the relationship of Christ and the Church (cf. Eph 5: 32), which means it is faithful, permanent, loving, and life-giving. Divorce, according to Christ, only came to be allowed due to the Israelites' hardness of heart. But with the sacramental grace now available through the coming of Christ, which gives us strength for a lifelong marriage, it is no longer allowed. Most Protestant denominations today, however, do permit divorce. Most of these denominations understand divorce to be a failure of some sort but do not forbid its practice.

What about annulments? An annulment is the recognition that a marriage never occurred because one or both parties were impeded from being validly married. This is distinct from a divorce, which attempts to dissolve the bonds of an existing marriage.

Every Sacrament must have a proper recipient in order to dispense sacramental grace. For example, a person who is not baptized cannot receive the grace of Confirmation. Likewise, a person who has already been validly baptized cannot be baptized again. The Sacrament of Matrimony is no different. In order for it to dispense sacramental grace, there must be no impediments; otherwise the Sacrament is not received.

Instances that would constitute an impediment to marriage would include situations where consent was not deliberate, fully voluntary, or freely given such as a person who acted under constraint, that is, acquiesced to marriage under pressure, lacked sufficient use of reason, or suffered from psychological illness. Other impediments to marriage would include lack of the required age, being too closely related, or if one of the parties had no intention of ever having children. In these cases, and many more like them as defined in canon law, the Church can grant an annulment, that is, a declaration that a valid marriage never took place. Each party is then free to enter into a sacramental marriage.

The Catholic Church does not recognize divorce, basing her teaching on Christ.

COUNTER REFORMATION

In the early sixteenth century, the Catholic Church needed reform. All levels of the Church hierarchy harbored corruption. Many of the faithful did not really understand the faith. The zealous preaching of the Gospel, necessary in every age, was greatly diminished. The initial impulses of Luther and some of the other reformers were noble to the extent that they wanted to ensure that the Church modeled Christ in her life and teachings. Yet, the Protestant reformers came to reject the authority of the Church and denied the truth of some of her magisterial teachings.

However, the Church's initial handling of the challenges posed by the Reformation succeeded neither in preventing schism nor in effecting positive reform from within. Catholic reforms were already underway, and reforms always take time to legislate and implement. In time, such a reformation did occur, and it is known in history as the *Counter*, or *Catholic*, *Reformation*.

The Catholic Reformation extended over a period lasting approximately from the mid-sixteenth century to the mid-seventeenth century. During this time, the Catholic Church took dramatic steps to correct abuses within her ranks and to reenergize both the clergy and the laity with the power of the Gospel.

Pope Paul III by Titian. During his pontificate new religious orders like the Jesuits were instrumental in advancing the Catholic Reformation.

One key event that jump-started the Catholic Reformation and gave it direction was the Ecumenical Council of Trent (1545-1563). Called by Pope Paul III, this council had as its purpose the reform of ecclesial structures and practices and the more clear definition of Catholic doctrine in light of Protestant challenges. On both fronts, the council was a resounding success, setting the course for the Catholic Church for the next 400 years.

What is remarkable about the Council of Trent is that Protestant representatives were invited to some of the sessions as full participants, "in all liberty to confer, make proposals, and treat on those things which are to be treated of in the said Synod;... and propose therein, as well in writing as by word of mouth, as many articles as to them shall seem good, and to confer and dispute..."[6] The council, which was so protracted mainly because of interruptions due to war and an outbreak of the plague, even held off on voting on key reforms until the Protestant delegates could be present. This invitation was a very early and magnanimous opening to ecumenical dialogue, one which, sadly, did not bear fruit in reconciliation.

Some of the key advocates of the Catholic Reformation came from the religious orders in the Church. The Capuchins, Ursulines, Carmelites, the Society of Jesus, and many others were instrumental in promoting and implementing the directives of the Ecumenical Council of Trent and advancing the Catholic Reformation.

Likewise, major spiritual movements flourished within the Church, especially within the religious orders, resulting in a renewal of focus on the interior life. Contemplative prayer and spiritual exercises became popular means for the faithful to draw closer to Christ. The teachings of Sts. Teresa of Avila, John of the Cross, and Ignatius of Loyola were particularly influential in these developments.

One of the most significant figures of the Counter Reformation was St. Charles Borromeo, Cardinal Archbishop of Milan. St. Charles embraced the cause of reform within the Church and devoted himself completely to eradicating abuses in his diocese and in the universal Church. He soon became a model of the devout Catholic bishop.

Though the Catholic Reformation did not result directly from the Protestant Reformation, it was not unrelated. The need for reform was obvious to all who cared deeply for the Church in the sixteenth century. Unfortunately, when that reform occurred it took two distinct directions—schism through the Protestant Reformation and renewal through the Catholic Reformation—enshrining divisions in Western Christendom that remain to this day.

CATHOLIC REFORMERS: ST. IGNATIUS OF LOYOLA AND THE JESUITS

very age faces a crisis. This is true at any time, including the sixteenth century, when too few people were responding to the universal call to holiness. If the Pope, the clergy, and the laity were living saintly lives, would Martin Luther have felt a need to leave the Church? Even if he had, would anyone have followed him if they saw men and women living lives of holiness within her?

St. Ignatius of Loyola by Rubens.
St. Ignatius wanted to emulate the saints of the Church, especially St. Francis of Assisi.

Fortunately for the Catholic Church, it was not long after the Protestant Reformation began that many saints responded to God's call. One in particular represented the new zeal within the Church to convert souls to Christ and to reform the Church internally: St. Ignatius of Loyola, the founder of the Jesuits.

St. Ignatius (1491-1556) was a contemporary of Martin Luther. His early life was spent as a Spanish military officer; in fact, he had no desire for the religious life. However, in 1521 (just four years after Luther's *Ninety-five Theses* were posted) he was injured in battle. During his long recuperation he contemplated his life and the life to come and realized his need for Christ. Transformed by this experience, he resolved to dedicate his life completely to Christ.

St. Ignatius had his most profound influence on the Church through the religious order he founded: the Society of Jesus, more commonly known as the Jesuits. In addition to vows of poverty, chastity, and obedience, the Jesuits added a special vow of obedience to the Pope, pledging to go wherever he sent them.

St. Ignatius's military background influenced his organization and rule of the Society, and the Jesuits became a disciplined order whose mission is to go anywhere in the world the Pope desires. Becoming front-line warriors in the Catholic Reformation, Jesuits spread Catholic teachings throughout Europe and the whole world. They were missionaries in many foreign lands, including the Far East and the New World, and influential members of the Church hierarchy. The vision of St. Ignatius—a religious order devoted to preaching the Gospel of Christ and obedient to his vicar on earth—became a reality through the grace of God and brought much needed reform to the Church.

LATER PROTESTANTISM

Protestantism grew rapidly in Europe. Before the century was over, about half the continent—including about half of modern-day Germany as well as the Netherlands, Denmark, Norway, Finland, Sweden, and much of Switzerland—had left the Catholic Church. However, as the differences among the founding fathers of the Reformation illustrate, the splinters in this new movement were never unified in doctrine. Protestantism was, one could say, born already in a state of schism. Once the Pandora's box of defiance to Church authority was opened, more and more dissension and division resulted.

The myriad distinct ecclesial communities within Protestantism are often called *denominations.* A denomination is a subgroup of Protestant Christians who have a common tradition and identity. Denominations form when a group within Protestantism decides to leave an existing denomination and form a new ecclesial community. There are now tens of thousands of such denominations. Sometimes, groups of denominations manage or merge or affiliate with one another in an umbrella organization, such as the World Lutheran Federation or the World Evangelical Fellowship.

Some of the differences between denominations even within a family can be significant, and sometimes a denomination might be closer in practice and theology to a denomination of another family than the denominations of its own family. In modern times the rate at which new denominations are forming has accelerated. Many of the newer denominations are independent of the major denominational families with no attachment to any other denomination. This type of denomination is usually just one or a few local churches administered by one pastor who determines the practices and theology of the group.

DENOMINATIONS IN PROTESTANTISM

The division in the Church wrought by the first phases of the Protestant Reformation and the Anglican separation from the Catholic Church led to more divisions within these breakaway ecclesial communities as they splintered into still smaller ecclesial communities. Without Apostolic Succession and an authentic teaching authority, the doctrine of *sola Scriptura* invited such division as a natural result of individual interpretation of the Bible.

The Savior by Juanes.
Luther met with Zwingli at the Marburg Colloquy in 1529, which was called to forge a Protestant coalition and debate the differences they had about the presence of Christ in the Eucharist.

The independent ecclesial communities started by Luther, Calvin, and Zwingli represented schisms not only from the Catholic Church but also from one another. These men knew of one another's efforts and championed one another's causes, yet they found themselves divided on key issues. Luther never met Calvin, but he did meet with Zwingli and several other reformers in 1529 in an effort to forge a common understanding of the idea of the presence of Christ in the Eucharist. They failed, and their reform movements took separate paths, even to the point of becoming bitter rivals for the loyalties of the people.

Later movements in Christianity sparked reform movements within Protestant denominations as well as within the Anglican Communion. In the seventeenth century there arose in Europe the Evangelical movement and the Pietist movement, both of which led directly to the formation of new denominations. The so-called periods of Great Awakening that took place in eighteenth-century Western Europe and the United States likewise impacted the direction of existing ecclesial communities but also gave rise to new ones.

While it would be difficult to examine all of the reasons, conflicts, and variant beliefs that led to each of these fractures, the following is a brief summary of how post-Reformation Protestantism developed with particular attention given to the contemporary situation in the United States.

As **Lutheranism** spread through Europe, its communities were governed generally along national boundaries that were more or less autonomous. In some nations Lutheranism was adopted as the state religion, and the civil leader of the country was recognized as the doctrinal head of Lutherans in that state. Although there was internal strife among Lutherans over matters of belief in practice, these divisions did not become apparent until Europeans began immigrating in large numbers to North America. Once there, Lutheran communities organized themselves into larger associations called *synods* based mainly upon their language groups and national origin. Similar rifts have occurred in many other nations as well.

Pope Benedict XVI Baptizing an Infant.
The main Radical Reformation movement, the Anabaptists, rejected infant baptism.

The various synods of the United States have gone through a series of divisions and mergers over issues of doctrine, governance, and practice and continue to be divided today. For example, the largest Lutheran body, the Evangelical Lutheran Church of America (ELCA), was formed in 1988 through a merger of two smaller Lutheran associations with another Lutheran group that had broken away from another synod. The ELCA expresses no official opinion as to the presence of Christ in the Eucharist and allows its members to hold various opinions. The next two largest bodies, the Lutheran Church-Missouri Synod and the Wisconsin Evangelical Lutheran Synod, do not ordain women and teach that Christ is somehow mysteriously present in Holy Communion, although like Luther they reject the Catholic teaching of transubstantiation.

Reformed ecclesial communities originating from the Calvinist and Zwinglian traditions likewise took different forms in different regions where they were initially established, sometimes as a state church. The two main branches of this movement are the Reformed communities and the Presbyterians. Similar to the Lutheran bodies, the Reformed and Presbyterian communities in the United States have experienced a number of divisions and mergers, often with new communities gathering disgruntled former members of other Protestant associations.

Today there are numerous separated ecclesial communities that can trace their origins to John Calvin. Among mainline Presbyterians of the United States, the largest denominations are the Presbyterian Church (USA) (PC [USA]) and the Presbyterian Church in America. In recent years more groups have been breaking away from PC (USA) because of its increasingly permissive positions on issues such as the ordination of women and homosexual acts.

The so-called **Radical Reformation** led by other reformers who were rejected by Luther, Calvin, and Zwingli also gave rise to multiple ecclesial communities. The main Radical Reformation movement, the Anabaptists, began largely as a splinter group from the Reformed movement of Zwingli, parting ways because they rejected infant baptism and insisted that converts be rebaptized as adults. Offshoots of the Anabaptist movement active in the United States include the Mennonites, the Hutterites, and the Amish, each of which is split into several smaller denominations.

The **Anglican** schism led to the establishment of autonomous national Episcopal associations that were united under what came to be known in the nineteenth century as the Anglican Communion. The Archbishop of Canterbury is the symbolic head of the Communion but has no doctrinal authority or jurisdiction over the Episcopal communities outside of England. Recent permissive trends in belief and practice within some national communions over issues such as the ordination of women and homosexual acts have created schisms and threats of schism along ideological lines.

Evangelicalism was a renewal movement that began across Protestant denominations in the seventeenth century. It emphasized personal conversion and piety over the role of ritual worship and stressed the urgency of the "born again" experience and making a firm commitment to Christ. It also moved away from Luther by recognizing the importance of works as a lived expression of the faith. Evangelicalism also placed great value on biblical study and in its preaching stressed the centrality of the Cross and the atoning Death of Jesus Christ. Evangelicalism helped spark the Methodist and Pietist movements and led both to new denominations and to ideological divergence within denominations.

The Crucifixion by Tiepolo. Evangelicalism stressed the centrality of the Cross and the atoning Death of Jesus Christ.

Pietism was a seventeenth- and eighteenth-century movement that began within Lutheranism. Like the Evangelical movement from which it sprang, it emphasized the individual's relationship with God and the living out of the Christian life—that is, faith translated into action. It, too, influenced John Wesley's Methodist movement and inspired the start of the Brethren movement, which saw itself as a recovery of the structure of the first Church communities.

Congregationalists began as a movement of "separatists" from the Anglican and Reformed/Presbyterian communities. They believed that each individual local congregation constituted the visible Body of Christ in itself. Their distinguishing commitment was to the complete autonomy of the local congregation. These congregations may affiliate with one another loosely; in the United States today, the United Church of Christ is made up almost entirely of autonomous Congregationalist groups. Several of the English colonies in North America colonies were founded with Congregationalism as an official religion.

The **Methodist** communities began as an Evangelical reform movement within Anglicanism led by John Wesley but split into a separate denomination in the late eighteenth century. Their name derives from their "methodical" approach to Bible study and Christian living. They are represented today by a number of splinter organizations, including the Methodist Episcopal, United Methodists, and dozens of others.

Baptists likely owe their origins largely to the influence of English separatist groups, such as the Puritans and Congregationalists, as well as disaffected Dutch Calvinists and Anabaptists. In the United States today, home to seventy percent of the world's Baptists, they are divided into several autonomous groups, the largest of which are the Southern Baptist Convention; the National Baptist Convention, a largely African-American association of communities that traces its formation to a division with the main Baptist body over the issue of slavery; and the Progressive National Baptist Convention.

Seventh-day Adventists emerged from the Baptist community in the early nineteenth century when a preacher named William Miller predicted that the Second Coming of Christ would take place during a certain time period in 1844. When Christ failed to appear, Miller predicted a later date that same year, which also was not fulfilled. This failure factionalized this early movement of Adventists. One leader decided they should worship on the Jewish Sabbath rather than Sunday, and another decided that Miller's prediction had to do with Christ entering the heavenly sanctuary. Ellen White, a claimed visionary, appropriated these two ideas and added anti-Catholic views to form the Seventh-day Adventists that we know today.

The **Holiness** movement split away from the Methodists in the late nineteenth century, which in turn led to the formation of several dozen more denominations, with names like Evangelical Christians, Church of God, Free Methodists, Church of the Nazarene, and Wesleyans. Adherents believe not only in justification by faith but also that one later must experience a "second work of grace" through the Holy Spirit in order to overcome concupiscence.

Pentecostalism grew out of the Holiness movement and began in the early twentieth century in the United States. It stresses direct personal experience of God through the "baptism of the Holy Spirit" by which a person would receive extraordinary gifts, particularly "praying in tongues" and healing. (In the 1960s Pentecostalism inspired the birth of the Charismatic Renewal movement within the Catholic Church.) Today there are more than 700 Pentecostal denominations and hundreds of independent Pentecostal congregations. Not all of these are Christian ecclesial communities, however, as some—such as the Oneness Pentecostals—believe the Father, Son, and Holy Spirit are not three divine Persons but merely three manifestations of God and thus do not baptize with the Trinitarian formula.

A number of **other ecclesial communities** were formed after the Reformation and also drew away members from various existing Protestant denominations. These largely involve congregationalist communities, but they generally do not identify with the Congregationalist movement or the United Church of Christ. The three main associations within this tradition in the United States today are somewhat confusingly named the "Christian Church (Disciples of Christ)," the "Churches of Christ," and the "Christian churches and churches of Christ."

SIMILARITIES AND DIFFERENCES AMONG CATHOLICS, PROTESTANTS, ANGLICANS, AND LATER PROTESTANT GROUPS

It is difficult to compare Catholicism and Protestantism in broad strokes because of the great diversity of belief and practice that exists among the numerous ecclesial communities that have emerged since the Reformation. The defining traits of all Protestantism, however, include a rejection of the Catholic Church and her authority and an acceptance of the concepts of *sola Scriptura* and *sola fide*.

For its part, Anglicanism began as a middle road between Catholicism and the Reformation movements, but today the various national communities within the Anglican Communion vary widely in doctrine and practice. We will compare selected elements—the Catholic, Protestant, and Anglican traditions—both in how the agree and how they disagree.

The Blessed Trinity and the Person of Christ. The early Protestant reformers accepted the doctrinal declarations of the first four Ecumenical Councils, which were instrumental in defining the Christian belief in the Blessed Trinity and the Person of Christ. They and the Christian ecclesial communities spawned by the Reformation, therefore, believe with the Catholic Church that there is one God in three Persons (Father, Son, and Holy Spirit) and that Jesus Christ is a divine Person with a human nature and a divine nature. The Catholic Church, the Anglican Communion, the Eastern Orthodox Churches, and the Oriental Orthodox Churches share these fundamental Christian tenets.

The Holy Trinity by El Greco.
The Catholic Church, the Anglican Communion, the Eastern Orthodox Churches, the Oriental Orthodox Churches, and many Protestant denominations believe in the Blessed Trinity.

The first Reformers, and the Protestants who followed immediately after, believed that the declarations of the early Ecumenical Councils were legitimate interpretations of Scripture and thus should be held by all Christians. In fact, the adherence to these teachings by mainline Protestant communities has been remarkable. Over the centuries many traditional teachings have been questioned, but mainline belief in the Blessed Trinity and the dual natures of Christ has remained consistent.

The same cannot be said of all religious groups that descended from the Reformation movement and its subsequent divisions. Some splinter denominations adopted views of God and Christ that do not affirm the Blessed Trinity professed by the original reformers. So it can be said that not all Protestant groups accept the Blessed Trinity. In moving away from a belief in the Blessed Trinity, of course, these denominations cease to be truly Christian.

Baptism. As with the doctrine of the Blessed Trinity and the belief in the unique dual nature of Christ (fully God and fully human), the early Protestant reformers and mainline Protestant communities have maintained a valid Baptism, which is a requirement for being Christian. A valid Baptism is what keeps Protestant ecclesial communities as well as Anglicans in communion—although an imperfect communion—with the Catholic Church. Because the use of the Trinitarian formula ("in the name of the Father, and of the Son, and of the Holy Spirit") is required for Baptism to be valid, the Protestant community administering the Baptism must also agree with the Catholic doctrine of the Blessed Trinity.

There exist variations in practice: Some Protestant denominations do not baptize children until they reach the age of reason, and some of these offer a "dedication" service for infants instead. Some believe immersion (rather than affusion, that is, pouring of the water on the individual's forehead) is the only proper method for baptizing. Such preferences in themselves do not affect the validity of Baptism.

Other Sacraments. Most Protestants reject the sacramental economy of salvation history as taught by the Catholic Church: the belief that God works through the Sacraments to bestow grace upon his followers and to bring them to union with him.

In Catholic theology as well as practice, the Sacraments are central to the life of the faithful. We enter into the life of the Church at Baptism, becoming adopted sons and daughters of God. We receive the fullness of the Holy Spirit at Confirmation and receive the very Body and Blood of Christ as our spiritual nourishment in Holy Communion. The Eucharist, in fact, is the root and center of all the sacraments and of the life of the Church. We are forgiven our sins through the Sacrament of Reconciliation. We are given the power to offer up our sickness and pain through the Anointing of the Sick. Matrimony and Holy Orders are Sacraments whose recipients are given particular missions in the Church.

The Last Supper (detail) by Bouts.
In Catholic theology as well as practice, the Sacraments are central to the life of the faithful.

Furthermore, Catholics believe that the Sacraments are efficacious signs: they are signs of what they actually effect in the life of the recipient. Baptism is performed by immersion or the pouring of water over the recipient. Water, in the natural world, signifies cleansing and life as well as death, and in Baptism, we are cleansed of sin and are born into a new life as adopted children of God. Through Baptism, God makes these things happen by grace.

This is not, however, what most Protestants believe about the Sacraments. In fact, most today would reject any sacramental system, viewing actions such as Baptism and the Eucharist as good insofar as they are merely symbolic but in no way necessary or efficacious signs of grace. Again, we need to remember the diversity of Protestant theology.

Luther reduced the number of Sacraments effectively to two or three. He believed that Christ instituted Sacraments as means of grace, but he did not see them as efficacious signs, probably because of his teaching on works. The performing of the rite cannot automatically confer God's grace, he figured; rather, God simply attaches his promise to the visible elements of the Sacrament. With that defined, he decided that Baptism and the Eucharist were Sacraments. He also wrote of "Confession and Absolution" as a "third Sacrament," although private confession is rarely used in Lutheran practice today.

The Elevation.
According to the Catholic teaching on transubstantiation, the Eucharistic species become Christ's Body and Blood but retain the appearance of bread and wine.

Luther held that Christ is truly present in the Eucharist, although the view he articulated about the change in the bread and wine was not in agreement with Catholic teaching. According to the Catholic view of transubstantiation, the Eucharistic species become Christ's Body and Blood but retain the appearance of bread and wine. Luther's explanation could better be described as *consubstantiation*, in which Christ mysteriously becomes present *along with* or *within* the visible bread and wine.

The Reformed movement also began by recognizing only Baptism and the Eucharist, considering them earthly signs and seals of God's grace. Most Protestant ecclesial communities followed suit and administer some kind of these two Sacraments. Keep in mind, however, that without Apostolic Succession and a valid priesthood, Protestants do not have a valid Eucharist. As we have seen, many Protestant denominations that celebrate Communion consider the sharing of the bread and wine to be only symbolic. The term "sacrament" itself is not used in some denominations; rather, the preferred term is "ordinance," that is, something Christ ordained, or prescribed.

The Anglican Communion is divided in its beliefs about the Sacraments. Those communities that are closer to the Catholic tradition acknowledge all seven Sacraments, while those communities that lean toward Reformation theology accept only Baptism and the Eucharist as Sacraments but consider the other five—Confession, Holy Matrimony, Holy Orders, Confirmation, and Anointing of the Sick—as "sacramental rites." This latter view is in keeping with *The Thirty-Nine Articles of Religion*, a statement of beliefs declared normative by the Church of England in the year 1563.

Inspiration and Inerrancy of Sacred Scripture. Most Protestants believe, as the Catholic Church teaches, that the Bible is inspired by God and is without error. This shared belief allows for a common language between Catholics and Protestants that does not exist between Catholics and adherents of non-Christian religions. The Catholic Church accepts the Bible as a true authority, and no teaching of the Church can ever be in contradiction with the words of Sacred Scripture, properly interpreted. The ecumenical value of this shared language should not be underestimated. It gives us a "family language" by which, as brothers and sisters in Christ, we can work together to resolve our divisions.

There are, however, nuances of difference between the Protestant belief in inspiration and inerrancy and the Catholic teaching on these subjects. Many Protestants view inspiration as akin to dictation, believing that God dictated the words of Scripture to the human author word for word. The Catholic Church, on the other hand, teaches that every book of the Bible was written by a human person in his own style but under the inspiration of the Holy Spirit. This is a mystery that cannot be resolved by simply removing the human author from the equation.

> For holy mother Church, relying on the belief of the Apostles (see John 20: 31; 2 Tim. 3: 16; 2 Peter 1: 19-20, 3: 15-16), holds that the books of both the Old and New Testaments in their entirety, with all their parts, are sacred and canonical because written under the inspiration of the Holy Spirit, they have God as their author and have been handed on as such to the Church herself. In composing the sacred books, God chose men and while employed by Him they made use of their powers and abilities, so that with Him acting in them and through them, they, as true authors, consigned to writing everything and only those things which He wanted. (*Dei Verbum*, 11)

St. Matthew and the Angel by Reni. There are nuances of difference between the Protestant belief in inspiration and inerrancy and the Catholic teaching on these subjects.

While the Catholic Church and most Protestants hold Sacred Scripture to be inerrant—it teaches only truth and never error—there are differences in how the text of Scripture is interpreted. The *Catechism* teaches, "To interpret Scripture correctly, the reader must be attentive to what the human authors truly wanted to affirm, and to what God wanted to reveal to us by their words"[7] (CCC 109). This requires sound exegesis in discovering the *literal sense* or the meaning intended to be conveyed by the words. Some Protestants, however, read the Bible literalistically, meaning they interpret the writings of the Scriptures as one would a news account or a history book instead of within the genre of the writing itself.

The human authors of Scripture, however, did not intend their writings to be read in such a way, and doing so has led to many misinterpretations. For example, some parts of Scripture are poetry such as Daniel and the Psalms and other parts are letters such as Romans and Jude. Neither of these genres should be read as a strictly historical record.

The Church, on the other hand, understanding the human element involved in the writing of the Bible, interprets the Scriptures bearing in mind the literary genre the writer used, and also considers the spiritual sense of the text. Due to the divine inspiration of the Bible, there are no errors. Still, we can discover the truth in it only when it is properly interpreted.

> Since everything asserted by the inspired authors or sacred writers must be held to be asserted by the Holy Spirit, it follows that the books of Scripture must be acknowledged as teaching solidly, faithfully and without error that truth which God wanted put into sacred writings for the sake of salvation. (*Dei Verbum*, 11)

Moral Teachings. Historically, Protestants and Catholics shared similar moral teachings, and still today some Protestants are in agreement with many Catholic moral teachings. However, in the twentieth century many Protestant denominations drifted from traditional Christian teaching on various moral topics such as abortion, divorce, homosexual acts, and contraception.

Until the twentieth century Christians had all rejected as sinful the practice of using means to prevent the conception of new human life. Many of the earliest Reformers, including Luther, condemned this practice vigorously. However, in the 1930s the Anglican Communion accepted the use of contraception in very limited circumstances.

This action, which seemed minor to many people at the time, opened the floodgates. Within forty years every major Protestant denomination accepted contraception for almost any reason. While it is true that many Catholics also began to use contraception, the Magisterium of the Church, guided by the Holy Spirit, continued and still continues to hold the moral teaching as Christians have handed it on throughout history. The Church also teaches that, for just reasons, spouses may use methods known as "Natural Family Planning" to space the births of their children.

Rest on the Flight into Egypt (detail) by Caravaggio.
The prolife movement is an example of ecumenical cooperation against a common foe.

After the acceptance of contraception, some Protestant denominations then accepted other practices such as abortion, which was permitted by some denominations starting in the 1970s. Homosexual activity was permitted by some Protestant groups soon afterward, and today some Protestant denominations bless homosexual "marriages" and others have vocal advocates to begin blessing them. Others allow people to serve as ordained ministers who engage in homosexual activity or who enter into unchaste homosexual relationships. Positions such as these, which are contrary to the teachings of the Catholic Church, present obstacles to full communion with many of the ecclesial communities. Despite this, however, some Protestant denominations remain strong defenders of unborn human life and the sanctity of marriage, positions that resonate strongly with Catholic teaching.

The Anglican Communion represents a wider spectrum of moral positions. While some Anglican bodies agree with the Catholic moral perspective, there has been a considerable softening among others in their positions. For example, the Episcopal Church in the United States, part of the worldwide Anglican Communion, officially opposes abortion except in cases of rape, incest, fetal deformity or when the mother's physical or mental health is at risk but recognizes the woman's "right" to abort her child in any instance.

In today's secular world, however, which promotes many practices contrary to traditional Christian moral teaching, many Catholics and Protestants have cooperated in combating the spread of moral evils. The prolife movement in the United States is an example of ecumenical cooperation against a common foe. Whether in setting up and running crisis pregnancy centers, lobbying political leaders, or praying in front of abortion clinics, Catholics and prolife Protestants have worked side by side for decades to end the scourge of legalized abortion.

Liturgical Practices. One common way of distinguishing the various liturgical practices of Christians, especially in the Anglican Communion, is to describe them as *low church* and *high church*. The terms refer to the degree of formal structure and ritual within the liturgy of a particular ecclesial community: Low-church communities have a rather informal rite of worship, while the liturgy of high-church communities has a richly structured format marked by many standard prayers, rituals, processions, and other such features.

Most modern Protestant denominations today are low church, although some churches in the Anglican Communion and in the Lutheran denominations celebrate high-church liturgies. Catholics, of course (not to mention Orthodox Christians), have a highly ritualized liturgical tradition. Even so, there are some commonalities between the Catholic and the mostly low-church Protestant liturgical practices.

For example, almost every Protestant service has a form of the Liturgy of the Word as celebrated in every Catholic Mass. The minister reads from the Sacred Scriptures and gives a sermon to interpret the text. In the Protestant tradition, the sermon is typically the central focus of the service, even if the service includes communion. This reflects the importance that the Protestant tradition places on the written Word of God and its exposition.

Ordination of Deacons to the Priesthood, St. Peter's Basilica.
The hierarchy of the Church was established by Christ through the Apostles. It is through the Sacrament of Holy Orders that the ministerial authority of Christ is passed down to the bishops, priests, and deacons of the Church.

While no Protestant service would be complete without a sermon, communion for most denominations is not a weekly occurrence. This, too, reflects the underlying Protestant theology that sees communion as a symbolic event with no real sacramental value.

Some Protestant denominations have adopted the same lectionary, or Scripture cycle, as the Catholic Church, reading the same biblical passages as Catholics each Sunday. This common practice has the effect of being a small sign of unity in our shared love and veneration of the Scriptures.

Ecclesiology. *Ecclesiology* is the branch of theology concerning the nature and constitution of the Church. We have studied already how Christ established his Church as a hierarchy, a visible structure with a visible head (St. Peter and his successors), made up of human members that together comprise the Body of Christ, who are nourished in the Sacraments and unified especially through the Eucharist.

On nearly every one of these points, the majority of Protestant denominations would disagree. In most Protestant theologies, the Church is an invisible institution that consists of all who believe in Christ. It is not visible, nor hierarchical, nor sacramental, nor united by the Eucharist. No one here on earth knows the complete membership of the Church; only Christ knows. Additionally, those ecclesial communities that do have a hierarchical structure do not accept the authority of the Pope.

This view of the Church has vast implications for Protestant life. It is one reason there are so many Protestant denominations—for if the Church is simply the collection of believers here on earth, then one who leaves his denomination does not leave the Body of Christ. A person who breaks from one denomination and joins—or forms—another is simply trying to practice the Christian faith more purely. What to Catholics may look like continual schisms in the Protestant communion has, according to Protestant ecclesiology, no effect on the unity of the "church."

Another significant implication of this ecclesiology is the emphasis on the local church over the universal Church. For most Catholics, when one speaks of "the Church," it is generally understood as the universal Catholic Church. Yet, because Protestant theology regards the universal Church as invisible, a Protestant does not generally look beyond his local church to a worldwide organization. Rather, the local church is the essence of the Protestant Christian's conception of the "Church."

The typical Protestant view of ecclesiology also impacts church government. Since, to most Protestants, the Church is an invisible institution, the manner in which it is governed here on earth is purely a human decision—that is, there is no divinely instituted form of government for the Church. This has led to a vast diversity of "governments" among Protestant denominations from hierarchical to completely localized, democratic control.

Some local communities might have a council of elders making decisions. For others, the pastor is the sole authority. Still others may give a vote to each member of the congregation. Some denominations have levels of government above the local congregation, and sometimes a local congregation is completely autonomous. Because there is no divinely instituted form of "government," there exists almost as many forms of church government as there are denominations.

Other Catholic Beliefs. The differences listed above represent the major points of contention between the Catholic Church and most Protestant denominations, but they do not represent a comprehensive list of all the many differences between the two.

Protestants, on the whole, reject the doctrine of purgatory, that souls who die in a state of grace but are not completely purified must undergo purification before entering into heaven. This teaching, in fact, was a key cause of Martin Luther's break from the Church and is related to many of his *Ninety-five Theses*. However, the Methodist reformer John Wesley believed in some sort of "intermediate state" as purgatory, and some of the more conservative Anglicans and Lutherans also hold to a concept of purgatory close to the Catholic belief.

Virgin and Child in Glory with Saints by Carlone. Some Protestants falsely think that Catholics worship the Blessed Virgin Mary and the saints.

Most Protestants do not accept the intercession of the angels and saints. They believe it is "unbiblical" to ask those who have gone before us and are now in heaven to pray for us. Protestants commonly say that Christ is our only intercessor or mediator, so we should pray directly to Christ rather than ask the saints to pray for us. Some Protestant denominations believe the dead are not raised until the end of time, so to pray for the intercession of the dead is pointless for that reason alone.

Many Protestants are iconoclasts, uncomfortable with statues or other visual representations of the saints, believing them to be violations of the Commandment against graven images. Some charge that Catholics worship the Blessed Virgin Mary and the saints. This is obviously false: Catholics venerate or honor her and all the saints—admiring their example and seeking their intercession—but worship God alone.

In the arena of the spiritual life there are also many differences. The Protestant spiritual life, on the whole, revolves around the Bible and the local church. If spiritual writings are used, they are usually commentaries on the Scriptures, probably limited to ones recommended by the local church. Although a love for Scripture is praiseworthy, Protestant spirituality is generally devoid of devotion to Our Lady and the saints and the many other spiritual practices developed by Catholics over the centuries.

Pope Benedict XVI and the Archbishop of Canterbury Dr. Rowan Williams along with church leaders from England, Scotland, Ireland, and Wales attended a Service of Evening Prayer at Westminster Abbey on September 17, 2010. Pope Benedict XVI: "I thank the Lord for this opportunity to join you, the representatives of the Christian confessions present in Great Britain, in this magnificent abbey church dedicated to St. Peter, whose architecture and history speak so eloquently of our common heritage of faith. Here we cannot help but be reminded of how greatly the Christian faith shaped the unity and culture of Europe and the heart and spirit of the English people. Here too, we are forcibly reminded that what we share, in Christ, is greater than what continues to divide us."

CONCLUSION

Before the sixteenth century, the Christian community spoke with a single voice in the West, but after the Reformation that voice fragmented. Blame for the destruction of unity cannot be placed on any person or group of people. The Catholic Church suffered from scandals and abuses, and the Protestant Reformation was a natural reaction to such sins. However, the Reformers confused the use of legitimate beliefs and practices with the *misuse* of them. Instead of working to reform the Church from *within*, the early Protestants removed themselves from the communion of the Church, thus making their desire for true reformation impracticable.

The Church teaches that Christians born in separated Churches or communities are not guilty of the sin of separation. They are perceived not as opposing or moving away from the Catholic Church, but as being raised in a state of imperfect communion they did not create, and thus they are regarded positively as separated brethren. The basis for this positive regard is their faith in Christ and true Baptism. As Christ's Body is the Church, the only concrete relation of which is the Catholic Church, all baptized Christians are in some way in communion with the Catholic Church, albeit an "imperfect communion."

Today, we must work tirelessly to restore the unity among Western Christians that once existed. Interestingly, the rejection of Christian morals by the modern world has led to many opportunities for Christians who a century ago would have avoided each other to work together for the common good. As a consequence, Catholics and Protestants have witnessed the beauty and truth that exists in each community. Obstacles continue to arise in both doctrine and practice among Protestant communities, but we can pray that our closer connections will help lead us again one day to full communion.

CHALLENGES:

What caused the Protestant Reformation and the Anglican schism?

The Protestant Reformation of the sixteenth century can be said fairly to have resulted, at least indirectly, from the political entanglements and corruption that had crept into the Church during the late Middle Ages.

The relationship between the Church and the secular rulers of Western Europe led to power struggles and even wars. The Pope exercised a significant degree of temporal authority as well as religious authority, and kings sometimes asserted themselves in order to retain control over their own domain against the power of the Church. Such struggles led to the Avignon Papacy, when the Popes moved the seat of the papacy to France in order to please the powerful French monarchy, and the subsequent Great Western Schism, a series of antipopes that continued to claim papal authority from Avignon even after the legitimate Pope Gregory XI had returned the papacy to Rome. This entire controversy resulted in a loss of respect for Church authority and for the office of the Pope.

Luther Nailing His Ninety-five Theses to the Door of Wittenberg Church by Vogel.

Respect was further eroded by the scandalous lives led by many priests, bishops, cardinals, and Popes, though their personal hypocrisy did not pervert the purity of the Church's magisterial teaching. Some clerics lived like royalty, and others were publicly unfaithful to their priestly vows. Some bishops received their positions through nepotism, simony, bribery, or pressure exerted by secular authorities. Such infidelity to the faith, at least in moral terms, led many to question the Church's authority and leadership. And once her teaching authority itself came into question, it was a short step to questioning the content of what that authority was teaching.

One of the final straws that contributed to the Reformation was the selling of indulgences. A priest named Johann Tetzel promoted the sale of indulgences in an erroneous and offensive way—as though contributing money itself would free the souls of loved ones from purgatory—and Martin Luther was rightly outraged and scandalized by this.

Luther posted his *Ninety-five Theses*, challenging not only indulgences but also other matters pertaining to Church doctrine, practice, and authority. In the following years, he developed his theology of justification by faith alone and Scripture as a sole authority.

Although Luther did not intend initially to leave the Church, his views found a receptive audience, and the Reformation soon was underway. Other reformers in other parts of Europe felt empowered to speak out, and further objections were raised on matters such as the Eucharist and the Sacraments. Because these reformers could not agree among themselves, the Reformation began as several parallel movements away from the Catholic Church and continued to split again and again as time went on.

The Anglican schism occurred later in the same century, no doubt taking inspiration from the Protestant Reformation already under way. King Henry VIII of England wanted to obtain an annulment so he could marry a different woman, but the Church would not grant it. So Henry decided to nationalize the Church, taking over its institutions and clergy with himself as the head of the Church instead of the Pope. Like Luther, perhaps he did not really see himself as breaking away from the Catholic Church, but by usurping papal authority he did just that.

PILLARS OF THE FAITH

ST. PAUL VI

While his predecessors opened the door cautiously to ecumenical dialogue, St. Paul VI swung it wide open, ushering in the most dramatic progress toward achieving Christian unity since the Great Schism.

St. Paul VI shepherded the Catholic Church during most of the 1960s and 1970s, a challenging era of immense change and reform following the Second Vatican Council. Born Giovanni Battista Montini in Concesio, Italy, in 1897 to staunchly Catholic parents, he was ordained a priest in 1920 and soon undertook graduate studies and foreign-service training. Soon afterward he was given a position in the Vatican Secretariat of State, where he climbed the ladder of responsibility for the next thirty-one years.

Cardinal Eugenio Pacelli became papal secretary of state in 1930 and appointed Montini to his personal staff. Pacelli was elected Pope Pius XII in 1939, and in 1944 he appointed Montini to a Vatican position from which he directed the Church's war-relief efforts—rescuing and protecting Jews and political refugees from Nazi and Fascist forces and helping to resettle families displaced by the horror of World War II. Later, he served as Archbishop of Milan and was named a cardinal by St. John XXIII.

St. John XXIII surprised everyone by calling an Ecumenical Council, as he said, to "throw open the windows of the Church" and consider ways it ought to be reformed. He died in 1963, with only one session of the Second Vatican Council having been convened. Elected as his successor, Montini—St. Paul VI—chose to continue the Council and see it through to its completion. Over the course of the next three years, he oversaw the Council proceedings as the assembled bishops produced sixteen key documents, including three pertaining to ecumenism and interreligious dialogue: *Orientalium Ecclesiarum* (Decree On the Catholic Churches of the Eastern Rite); *Unitatis Redintegratio* (Decree on Ecumenism); and *Nostra Ætate* (Declaration On the Relation of the Church to Non-Christian Religions).

St. Paul VI (1897-1978).
St. Paul VI succeeded St. John XXIII, continued the Second Vatican Council , and worked for improved ecumenical relations with Orthodox and Protestants throughout his pontificate.

Before the Council had adjourned its final session in 1965, St. Paul VI was already busy in the important work of Christian unity. He made a habit of referring to other

Continued

ST. PAUL VI

Continued

Christians as "our separated brothers and sisters" and invited many to attend the Council as observers. In 1964 he visited the Orthodox Ecumenical Patriarch Athenagoras I in Jerusalem, where the two leaders rescinded the mutual excommunications of 1054. A year later, dialogue with Orthodox leaders in Constantinople resulted in a joint declaration which, while not ending the schism, expressed desire for reconciliation. More dialogue and visits with other Orthodox leaders have followed.

Early in his pontificate, St. Paul VI received at the Vatican the Anglican Archbishop of Canterbury, Michael Ramsey, telling him that "by entering into our house, you are entering your own house; we are happy to open our door and heart to you." They, too, signed an ecumenical declaration pledging to work toward unity.

Formal dialogues were instituted between Catholics and several Protestant communions, including the Lutherans, Methodists, and Reformed denominations (Presbyterians and Congregationalists). St. Paul VI authorized levels of cooperation with the World Council of Churches and a joint observance in the Week of Prayer for Christian Unity. He also gave his support to the development of joint Catholic-Protestant translations of the Bible in cooperation with various Bible societies.

He was the first Pope, perhaps since apostolic times, to travel extensively and the first since 1809 to venture outside Italy. He visited twenty countries on six continents—earning the nickname "the Pilgrim Pope"—and incorporated ecumenical gestures and meetings into his itinerary often. With his openness and determination to advance the cause of ecumenism and interfaith understanding, St. Paul VI set the Church on a relentless course toward the unity of all Christians as Christ himself intends.

He died in 1978, and after the thirty-four-day reign of his immediate successor, John Paul I, the cardinals elected another pontiff who continued his ecumenical outreach: St. John Paul II.

The Second Vatican Council took place in four sessions from October 1962 to December 1965 and is embodied in sixteen documents.

SUPPLEMENTARY READING

A Close Affinity Exists Between the Catholic Church and the Ecclesial Communities

In the great upheaval which began in the West toward the end of the Middle Ages, and in later times too, Churches and ecclesial Communities came to be separated from the Apostolic See of Rome. Yet they have retained a particularly close affinity with the Catholic Church as a result of the long centuries in which all Christendom lived together in ecclesiastical communion.

However, since these Churches and ecclesial Communities, on account of their different origins, and different teachings in matters of doctrine on the spiritual life, vary considerably not only with us, but also among themselves, the task of describing them at all adequately is extremely difficult; and we have no intention of making such an attempt here.

Although the ecumenical movement and the desire for peace with the Catholic Church have not yet taken hold everywhere, it is our hope that ecumenical feeling and mutual esteem may gradually increase among all men.

It must however be admitted that in these Churches and ecclesial Communities there exist important differences from the Catholic Church, not only of an historical, sociological, psychological and cultural character, but especially in the interpretation of revealed truth. To make easier the ecumenical dialogue in spite of these differences, we wish to set down some considerations which can, and indeed should, serve as a basis and encouragement for such dialogue.

— Second Ecumenical Council of the Vatican, Decree on Ecumenism *Unitatis Redintegratio*, no. 19

The Fruits of Justification, That Is, the Merit of Good Works, and the Nature of That Merit

Therefore, to men justified in this manner, whether they have preserved uninterruptedly the grace received or recovered it when lost, are to be pointed out the words of the Apostle: Abound in every good work, knowing that your labor is not in vain in the Lord.[8]

For God is not unjust, that he should forget your work, and the love which you have shown in his name;[9] and, Do not lose your confidence, which hath a great reward.[10]

Hence, to those who work well unto the end[11] and trust in God, eternal life is to be offered, both as a grace mercifully promised to the sons of God through Christ Jesus, and as a reward promised by God himself, to be faithfully given to their good works and merits.[12]

For this is the crown of justice which after his fight and course the Apostle declared was laid up for him, to be rendered to him by the just judge, and not only to him, but also to all that love his coming.[13]

For since Christ Jesus Himself, as the head into the members and the vine into the branches,[14] continually infuses strength into those justified, which strength always precedes, accompanies and follows their good works, and without which they could not in any manner be pleasing and meritorious before God, we must believe that nothing further is wanting to those justified to prevent them from being considered to have, by those very works which have been done in God, fully satisfied the divine law according to the state of this life and to have truly merited eternal life, to be obtained in its [due] time, provided they depart [this life] in grace,[15] since Christ our Savior says:

If anyone shall drink of the water that I will give him, he shall not thirst forever; but it shall become in him a fountain of water springing up into life everlasting.[16]

SUPPLEMENTARY READING Continued

Thus, neither is our own justice established as our own from ourselves,[17] nor is the justice of God ignored or repudiated, for that justice which is called ours, because we are justified by its inherence in us, that same is [the justice] of God, because it is infused into us by God through the merit of Christ.

Nor must this be omitted, that although in the sacred writings so much is attributed to good works, that even he that shall give a drink of cold water to one of his least ones, Christ promises, shall not lose his reward;[18] and the Apostle testifies that, That which is at present momentary and light of our tribulation, worketh for us above measure exceedingly an eternal weight of glory;[19] nevertheless, far be it that a Christian should either trust or glory in himself and not in the Lord,[20] whose bounty toward all men is so great that He wishes the things that are His gifts to be their merits. And since in many things we all offend,[21] each one ought to have before his eyes not only the mercy and goodness but also the severity and judgment [of God]; neither ought anyone to judge himself, even though he be not conscious to himself of anything;[22] because the whole life of man is to be examined and judged not by the judgment of man but of God, who will bring to light the hidden things of darkness, and will make manifest the counsels of the hearts, and then shall every man have praise from God,[23] who, as it is written, will render to every man according to his works.[24]

After this Catholic doctrine on justification, which whosoever does not faithfully and firmly accept cannot be justified, it seemed good to the holy council to add to these canons, that all may know not only what they must hold and follow, but also what to avoid and shun.

—Ecumenical Council of Trent, Session 6, *Decree on Justification*, Chapter 16

St. Peter Enthroned and Four Saints by Basaiti.
Through Apostolic Succession, the Pope is the Vicar of Christ.
The role of the papacy has evolved through the centuries, but what has remained constant is that the papacy is the Church's highest moral and doctrinal authority.

VOCABULARY

ABORTION
The destruction of a child after conception but before birth. Direct abortion or cooperation in it is forbidden by the Fifth Commandment. Attached to this sin is the penalty of excommunication because, from the moment of conception, every human being must be absolutely respected and protected in his integrity.

ANNULMENT
More properly called a "decree of nullity," a declaration by an ecclesiastical court that a presumed marriage was never valid.

ANTIPOPE
Any of a number of false claimants to the papacy over the course of Church history who were elected by a renegade minority of papal electors.

BLACK DEATH
Also known as the Black Plague, this deadly epidemic broke out in Europe around the year 1347, decimating the population. The disease took on three forms: The bubonic plague, carried by fleas that had bitten infested rats, was characterized by swelling lymph glands and black patches on the skin; the pneumonic plague spread quickly through coughing and sneezing and was more deadly than the bubonic; the septicemic plague was the deadliest form, infecting the blood stream and killing its victims the most quickly.

COMMON PRIESTHOOD OF THE FAITHFUL
The participation in the priesthood of Christ, which all of the faithful share through Baptism.

CONSUBSTANTIATION
A term describing Christ's substantial coexistence in the Eucharistic bread and wine. Luther used this term to describe how, in the Eucharist, Christ became present in it as heat is in a hot iron. This differs from the Catholic doctrine of transubstantiation that holds the entire substance of the bread is changed into the Lord's Body and the entire substance of the wine into his Blood.

CONTRACEPTION
The use of mechanical, chemical, or medical procedures to prevent conception from taking place as a result. This is a grave disorder against the openness to life required of marriage and the inner truth of conjugal love.

COUNTER REFORMATION
A reformation from within the Catholic Church that occurred in the sixteenth century. The Council of Trent was a pivotal event in this effort.

DENOMINATION
A group of Protestant Christians that share a common belief system and tradition. There are thousands of Protestant denominations, each with slightly different beliefs and practices.

ECCLESIOLOGY
The branch of theology that studies the nature and constitution of the Church. Ecclesiology is concerned with who has authority in the Church, how much authority they have, and what the origin of that authority is. Also, it expresses how a Church is organized and structured throughout the world.

GREAT WESTERN SCHISM
The time, spanning from 1378 to 1417, during which multiple men claimed to be Pope at the same time. This was a time of great scandal for the Church—the average Catholic did not know who the true Pope was. It led to a general decline in respect for the office of the papacy.

HIGH CHURCH
A type of denomination or ecclesial community that embraces a formalized, ritual liturgy.

INCARNATION
From the Latin for "to make flesh." The mystery of the hypostatic union of the divine and human natures in the one divine Person, the Word, Jesus Christ. To bring about man's salvation, the Son of God was made flesh (cf. John 1: 14) and became truly man.

VOCABULARY Continued

INDULGENCE
The remission of the temporal punishment due to sin that has already been forgiven.

INERRANCY
Being free of errors. The attribute of the books of Scripture whereby they faithfully and without error teach that truth which God intended and still intends to communicate to us, for the sake of our salvation (cf. CCC 107).

INSPIRATION
The gift of the Holy Spirit that assisted human authors to write the books of the Bible. God is the author of Scripture, and it teaches faithfully, without error, the saving truth that God has willed to be communicated to us.

INTERCESSION
The prayers and works of the saints that are offered for the salvation of souls on earth. Once in heaven, the saints constantly intercede for those on earth in order to help them obtain heavenly bliss.

JUSTIFICATION
Being made right (just or righteous) with God. It is a free and undeserved gift of God to a person through the sacrifice of Jesus Christ. It includes the remission of sins, and also the sanctification and renewal of the interior man.

LECTIONARY
A book that organizes specific biblical readings for specific days of the year. The Catholic Church uses a lectionary for the Mass readings, as do many other churches and denominations.

LITURGY OF THE WORD
The first part of the Mass. Within this, the Scriptures are read and expounded upon by the deacon or priest. It parallels the liturgy of the Jewish synagogue (cf. CCC 1031).

MIDDLE AGES
The period between the end of the Roman Empire and the beginning of the Renaissance in the West. The Church was frequently the only force that preserved order during this time.

MINISTERIAL PRIESTHOOD
The priesthood of men who are called to the Sacrament of Holy Orders so as to serve the faithful of the common priesthood and call forth their baptismal graces.

NEPOTISM
From the Latin for "grandson" or "nephew." The appointment to positions of authority based on family relation rather than qualification.

PERSPICUITY
The quality of being clear and easy to understand. Many Protestants believe that the Bible is perspicuous for each individual believer.

PURGATORY
A state of final purification after death but before entrance into heaven; this is for those who died in God's friendship but were only imperfectly purified.

SACRAMENTAL ECONOMY
The life of the Sacraments in which every Catholic participates. In God's plan of salvation, he chose specific physical objects—such as water, bread, and wine—to be means by which we receive grace and achieve salvation. It is "the communication (or 'dispensation') of the fruits of Christ's Paschal mystery in the celebration of the Church's 'sacramental' liturgy" (CCC 1076).

SEPTUAGINT
A third-century BC Greek translation of the Scriptures (Old Testament) made by seventy Jewish scholars. This translation was accepted by the early Christians as authoritative and inspired, and the writers of the New Testament quoted from it.

SOLA FIDE
Latin for "faith alone," this is the teaching that it is only by faith—and not by any works—that man is justified by God. Condemned by the Catholic Church, which recognizes the importance of works, love, and grace in being justified, it is the belief of nearly all Protestants.

VOCABULARY Continued

SOLA SCRIPTURA
"Scripture alone." This heretical idea makes the Bible the sole rule of faith, ignoring history and Tradition; this is a tenet of most of Protestantism.

SYSTEMATIC THEOLOGY
A discipline of Christian theology that seeks to create an organized system of faith and beliefs.

TRANSUBSTANTIATION
The scholastic term used to designate the unique change, in a true, real, and substantial manner, of the entire substance of the Eucharistic bread and wine into the Body and Blood of Christ, with his Soul and Divinity, leaving intact the "accidents" (the "forms" of bread and wine).

WORKS
Any actions, other than an act of faith, which a believer does in response to God's grace and to draw closer to him. Such actions could include devotions, acts of charity or attending Mass. According to Martin Luther, all such "works" are meaningless regarding one's salvation—it is faith alone that saves. Luther's position was condemned by the Catholic Church at the Council of Trent.

STUDY QUESTIONS

1. How did the Great Western Schism help pave the way for the Protestant Reformation?
2. What were the primary targets of Luther's *Ninety-five Theses*?
3. Why did Luther's protest spread throughout Europe so quickly?
4. What are the two bedrock beliefs of Protestantism?
5. Why is authority essential for discovering the truth?
6. What does the "perspicuity" of Scripture mean?
7. What passage of Scripture did Luther change and why?
8. Who was Desiderius Erasmus? Describe his position during the Reformation.
9. Who is considered the systematic theologian of the Protestant Reformation?
10. What was the teaching of Calvin regarding communion?
11. What was Zwingli's teaching on the Eucharist?
12. Name and describe the roles of some of the lesser-known reformers.
13. What was the initial cause of King Henry VIII's desire to break from the Church?
14. Why was the Anglican Communion for many years considered a "middle way" between Catholicism and Protestantism?
15. What efforts toward reform were already under way in the Catholic Church at the time of the Reformation?
16. How does a new Protestant denomination typically form?
17. Why do Protestants have such diverse beliefs?

STUDY QUESTIONS Continued

18. Which Ecumenical Councils do most Protestants accept as teaching truth, and what doctrines were these councils concerned with?
19. Why are Protestant Baptisms usually considered valid by the Catholic Church?
20. Why are most Protestants considered truly Christian by the Catholic Church?
21. What is the common "family language" of both Catholics and Protestants?
22. A Sacrament is a sign. In what important way is it different from other signs, such as traffic signs?
23. What are some different views of Protestants towards the Sacraments?
24. How does the belief in inspiration between Catholics and Protestants differ?
25. How does the belief in inerrancy between Catholics and Protestants differ?
26. When did the moral teachings of the Protestant denominations begin to differ from Catholics? What are some examples of differences?
27. Most Protestant services are like which part of the Mass?
28. What is the central focus of the Protestant service?
29. How does the view of Protestants about the Church lead to the proliferation of denominations?
30. Why are some Protestants uncomfortable with the Catholic use of statues? Thinking back to last chapter's discussion of icons, why is their use legitimate?

PRACTICAL EXERCISES

1. Before Martin Luther, others called for making Scripture the sole authority for Christians. Why did Luther's message ignite the Protestant Reformation?

2. We discussed the three major figures of the Protestant Reformation. Write a 500-word essay comparing and contrasting these three men.

3. Volunteer at an ecumenical outreach such as a pregnancy center, a soup kitchen, or a clothing drive.

4. Choose a Protestant mainline denomination to research. Who founded it and when? Why did it break off from the body to which it used to belong, whether the Catholic Church or one of the Reformation ecclesiastical communities?

FROM THE CATECHISM

120 It was by the apostolic Tradition that the Church discerned which writings are to be included in the list of the sacred books.[25] This complete list is called the canon of Scripture. It includes 46 books for the Old Testament (45 if we count Jeremiah and Lamentations as one) and 27 for the New.[26]

The Old Testament: Genesis, Exodus, Leviticus, Numbers, Deuteronomy, Joshua, Judges, Ruth, 1 *and* 2 Samuel, 1 *and* 2 Kings, 1 *and* 2 Chronicles, Ezra *and* Nehemiah, Tobit, Judith, Esther, 1 *and* 2 Maccabees, Job, Psalms, Proverbs, Ecclesiastes, *the* Song of Songs, *the* Wisdom of Solomon, Sirach (Ecclesiasticus), Isaiah, Jeremiah, Lamentations, Baruch, Ezekiel, Daniel, Hosea, Joel, Amos, Obadiah, Jonah, Micah, Nahum, Habakkuk, Zephaniah, Haggai, Zachariah *and* Malachi.

The New Testament: the Gospels according to Matthew, Mark, Luke *and* John, the Acts of the Apostles, *the* Letters of St. Paul to the Romans, 1 *and* 2 Corinthians, Galatians, Ephesians, Philippians, Colossians, 1 *and* 2 Thessalonians, 1 *and* 2 Timothy, Titus, Philemon, *the* Letter to the Hebrews, *the* Letters of James, 1 *and* 2 Peter, 1, 2 *and* 3 John, *and* Jude, *and* Revelation (the Apocalypse).

166 Faith is a personal act—the free response of the human person to the initiative of God who reveals himself. But faith is not an isolated act. No one can believe alone, just as no one can live alone. You have not given yourself faith as you have not given yourself life. The believer has received faith from others and should hand it on to others. Our love for Jesus and for our neighbor impels us to speak to others about our faith. Each believer is thus a link in the great chain of believers. I cannot believe without being carried by the faith of others, and by my faith I help support others in the faith.

406 The Church's teaching on the transmission of original sin was articulated more precisely in the fifth century, especially under the impulse of St. Augustine's reflections against Pelagianism, and in the sixteenth century, in opposition to the Protestant Reformation. Pelagius held that man could, by the natural power of free will and without the necessary help of God's grace, lead a morally good life; he thus reduced the influence of Adam's fault to bad example. The first Protestant reformers, on the contrary, taught that original sin has radically perverted man and destroyed his freedom; they identified the sin inherited by each man with the tendency to evil (*concupiscentia*), which would be insurmountable. The Church pronounced on the meaning of the data of Revelation on original sin especially at the second Council of Orange (529)[27] and at the Council of Trent (1546).[28]

817 In fact, "in this one and only Church of God from its very beginnings there arose certain rifts, which the Apostle strongly censures as damnable. But in subsequent centuries much more serious dissensions appeared and large communities became separated from full communion with the Catholic Church—for which, often enough, men of both sides were to blame."[29] The ruptures that wound the unity of Christ's Body—here we must distinguish heresy, apostasy, and schism[30]—do not occur without human sin:

> Where there are sins, there are also divisions, schisms, heresies, and disputes. Where there is virtue, however, there also are harmony and unity, from which arise the one heart and one soul of all believers.[31]

1268 The baptized have become "living stones" to be "built into a spiritual house, to be a holy priesthood."[32] By Baptism they share in the priesthood of Christ, in his prophetic and royal mission. They are "a chosen race, a royal priesthood, a holy nation, God's own people, that [they] may declare the wonderful deeds of him who called [them] out of darkness into his marvelous light."[33] *Baptism gives a share in the common priesthood of all believers.*

FROM THE CATECHISM Continued

1472 To understand this doctrine and practice of the Church, it is necessary to understand that sin has a *double consequence*. Grave sin deprives us of communion with God and therefore makes us incapable of eternal life, the privation of which is called the "eternal punishment" of sin. On the other hand every sin, even venial, entails an unhealthy attachment to creatures, which must be purified either here on earth, or after death in the state called Purgatory. This purification frees one from what is called the "temporal punishment" of sin. These two punishments must not be conceived of as a kind of vengeance inflicted by God from without, but as following from the very nature of sin. A conversion which proceeds from a fervent charity can attain the complete purification of the sinner in such a way that no punishment would remain.[34]

1987 The grace of the Holy Spirit has the power to justify us, that is, to cleanse us from our sins and to communicate to us "the righteousness of God through faith in Jesus Christ" and through Baptism:[35]

> But if we have died with Christ, we believe that we shall also live with him. For we know that Christ being raised from the dead will never die again; death no longer has dominion over him. The death he died he died to sin, once for all, but the life he lives he lives to God. So you also must consider yourselves as dead to sin and alive to God in Christ Jesus.[36]

1988 Through the power of the Holy Spirit we take part in Christ's Passion by dying to sin, and in his Resurrection by being born to a new life; we are members of his Body which is the Church, branches grafted onto the vine which is himself:[37]

> [God] gave himself to us through his Spirit. By the participation of the Spirit, we become communicants in the divine nature.... For this reason, those in whom the Spirit dwells are divinized.[38]

St. Peter's Square overflowing with the People of God.

The Throne of St. Peter in St. Peter's Basilica by Bernini.
The large bronze throne houses a precious relic, the *Cathedra Petri*, a chair often claimed to have been used by St. Peter. Because the chair was deteriorating and no longer usable, Pope Alexander VII had it enshrined in splendor. It is supported by four Doctors of the Church: Sts. Ambrose, Augustine, Athanasius, and John Chrysostom.

ENDNOTES – CHAPTER FIVE

1. Rom 3:28.
2. Jas 2:17.
3. Mt 25.
4. *Joint Declaration on the Doctrine of Justification*, 1999.
5. 1 Pt 2:9.
6. Council of Trent, thirteenth session.
7. Cf. *DV* 12 § 1.
8. See 1 Cor 15:58.
9. Heb 6:10.
10. Heb 10:35.
11. Mt 10:22.
12. Rom 6:22.
13. See 2 Tm 4:8.
14. Jn 15:1f.
15. Rev 14:13.
16. Jn 4:13f.
17. Rom 10:3; 2 Cor 3:5.
18. Mt 10:42; Mk 9:40.
19. See 2 Cor 4:17.
20. See 1 Cor 1:31; 2 Cor 10:17.
21. Jas 3:2.
22. See 1 Cor 4:3f.
23. Ibid., 4:5.
24. Mt 16:27; Rom 2:6; Rev 22:12.
25. Cf. *DV* 8 § 3.
26. Cf. DS 179; 1334-1336; 1501-1504.
27. DS 371-372.
28. Cf. DS 1510-1516.
29. *UR* 3 § 1.
30. Cf. CIC, can. 751.
31. Origen, *Hom. in Ezech.* 9, 1: PG 13, 732.
32. 1 Pt 2:5.
33. 1 Pt 2:9.
34. Cf. Council of Trent (1551): DS 1712-1713; (1563): 1820.
35. Rom 3:22; cf. 6:3-4.
36. Rom 6:8-11.
37. Cf. 1 Cor 12; Jn 15:1-4.
38. St. Athanasius, *Ep. Serap.* 1, 24: PG 26, 585 and 588.

CHAPTER 6

Ecumenical Efforts

The Church affirms the responsibility of all Christians to pray for the unity that Christ wills for the Church on earth. At times we may be able to pray in common with our separated brethren.

Ecumenism and Interreligious Dialogue

CHAPTER SIX

Ecumenical Efforts

INTRODUCTION

hen we consider how splintered and fragmented Christians are today, we cannot help but sense a very deep concern. Surely, this is not what Christ had in mind when he prayed to his heavenly Father that his followers "may be one, even as we are one."[1] And it seems that over the twenty centuries of Christianity—from the foundation of the Church, through the Eastern schisms, through the Reformation, to the present day—the divisions within the Church have gone without resolution.

Pope Benedict XVI and Archbishop of Canterbury Dr. Rowan Williams jointly led Vespers in the Chapel of St. Gregory the Great at the Church of San Gregorio Magno al Celio in Rome, March 10, 2012.

Yet, over the last century renewed efforts to restore Christian unity through ecumenical dialogue and cooperation have been undertaken and have begun to bear fruit. Although full unity of all Christians has yet to be achieved, the initial steps at building trust and understanding among the various churches and ecclesial communities lend a measure of hope. Ecumenical work remains a sacred commitment and mission of all Christians for the simple reason that it is the will of Christ.

In this chapter, we will survey:

- Early ecumenical efforts of the Popes over the past 200 years;
- Some movements toward unity in the early twentieth century;
- Progress in Catholic ecumenical efforts since the Second Vatican Council;
- Guiding principles for ecumenism set forth by the Church.
- Ecumenical prayer and Dialogue; and
- False forms of ecumenism.

TOWARD GREATER CHRISTIAN UNITY

The task of working toward Christian unity or reunification is called *ecumenism* (literally, *uniting the whole*). As members of the Church, we are called to engage in ecumenism.

In the writings of the Second Ecumenical Council of the Vatican, particularly *Unitatis Redintegratio* (Decree on Ecumenism), we are able to identify four principles for engaging in ecumenical work.

First, each of us is called to greater conversion of heart. Divisions are brought about because of sin, but the cultivation of virtue and holiness gives us unity of life and moves each of us toward greater Christian unity with others.

The Last Sermon of Our Lord by Tissot.
"And now I am no more in the world, but they are in the world, and I am coming to thee. Holy Father, keep them in thy name, which thou hast given me, that they may be one, even as we are one. While I was with them, I kept them in thy name, which thou hast given me; I have guarded them, and none of them is lost but the son of perdition, that the scripture might be fulfilled. But now I am coming to thee; and these things I speak in the world, that they may have my joy fulfilled in themselves." (Jn 17: 11-13)

Second, a deeper understanding between Catholics and our separated brethren is also encouraged both in terms of theological dialogue with and personal knowledge of one another. As has been the case in the past, simple misunderstandings between Catholics and non-Catholics have given rise to suspicion and greater division. Therefore, efforts should be made to understand the positions of our separated brethren and to look for areas of agreement.

Third, although we are to seek common ground with our separated brethren, it is essential that the truth of the Catholic faith be represented accurately and in its entirety. The Catholic Church is the pillar and foundation of truth,[2] and the infallible teaching authority given to her by Christ is essential for preserving the visible unity of the Pilgrim Church. "Nothing is so foreign to the spirit of ecumenism as a false conciliatory approach which harms the purity of Catholic doctrine and obscures its assured genuine meaning."[3] In other words, we cannot create genuine unity by watering down the truth.

Finally, the Church affirms the responsibility of all Christians to pray for the unity that Christ wills for the Church on earth. At times we may be able to pray in common with our separated brethren.

> Christ always gives his Church the gift of unity, but the Church must always pray and work to maintain, reinforce, and perfect the unity that Christ wills for her. This is why Jesus himself prayed at the hour of his Passion, and does not cease praying to his Father, for the unity of his disciples: "That they may all be one. As you, Father, are in me and I am in you, may they also be one in us,...so that the world may know that you have sent me."[4] (CCC 820)

CATHOLIC ECUMENICAL ADVANCES IN THE NINETEENTH CENTURY

The Catholic Church has always sought the unity of all Christians. There have been many historic efforts of Popes and Ecumenical Councils to unite the Church in doctrine and essential practice and to correct heresy while at the same time showing where legitimate diversity of belief or custom can exist. Even after the major divisions in Christendom—first with the Orthodox Churches and later with the Protestant and Anglican ecclesial communities—the Catholic Church continued to work toward healing and reversing these breaches of Christian unity.

There have been many points of success. Periodically, the Catholic Church has welcomed back portions of the Orthodox faithful and clergy who decided to return to full communion with Rome. The Church made increasing accommodations so these communities could retain their Eastern Christian traditions, including their liturgies and languages, which were not at variance with essential Catholic doctrine. These Eastern Catholic Churches were also led by their own patriarchs and bishops, united under the Pope.

This was the model for Catholic ecumenical efforts in the nineteenth and early twentieth centuries. The focus was on encouraging those churches not in full communion to "come home," as it were,

OTHER FIGURES OF CATHOLIC-ORTHODOX ECUMENISM

here are many great Church leaders whose work helped to pave the way for closer ties between the Orthodox and Catholic Churches. These are just a few:

St. Josaphat Kuntsevych was a monk and archbishop of the Ukrainian Greek Catholic Church in present-day Belarus (then part of the Polish-Lithuanian Commonwealth). He was just a boy in 1596 when the Union of Brest reunited what was then the Ruthenian Orthodox Church with the Catholic Church. Not all the Ruthenian faithful and leaders agreed, however, out of fear they would lose their Eastern Christian traditions through a forced "Latinization." There was still bitter division when he was appointed bishop in 1618, and he worked with great success to win over a large percentage of the people to the cause of reunion with the Catholic Church. In 1623 on a visit to Vitebsk where there was great opposition,
St. Josaphat was attacked and murdered by an Orthodox mob.

Fr. Ivan Gagarin was the son of a Russian prince and a diplomat who converted from Orthodoxy to Catholicism in 1842, thus sacrificing his inheritance. He became a Jesuit priest; took the name Jean-Xavier; and served in France, Belgium, and Switzerland. He wrote extensively urging the reunion of the Russian Orthodox Church with the Catholic Church, holding that such unification was necessary for the stability of the Russian state against the threats of revolution and communism. Fr. Ivan died in 1882 just as socialism was building strength in his homeland.

Dom Lambert Beauduin was a Benedictine monk who founded a monastery in Belgium in 1925 devoted entirely to promoting Christian unity through prayer, study, and dialogue. Today called Chevetogne Abbey, the community has monks of both the Western and Eastern traditions and celebrates liturgies in both the Roman Rite and the Byzantine Rite. They have built positive relationships and dialogues with Eastern Orthodox and Oriental Orthodox Churches as well as the Anglican Communion and some Protestant ecclesial communities.

to the Church instituted by Christ by recognizing the primacy and authority of the Pope and the teachings of the Catholic faith. In this era such attention was directed almost exclusively toward the Orthodox Churches, who, as we have seen, continue to be much closer to Catholicism in belief and practice than Protestant ecclesial communities.

In the mid-nineteenth century, Pope Bl. Pius IX took a particularly keen interest in Catholic-Orthodox reunion. He wrote a series of apostolic letters and encyclicals defining the terms and conditions for reunification. The first of these, popularly called "The Epistle to the Easterns," addressed the Orthodox as "venerable brothers," whom he invited to full communion with these words:

> We ask of you only those things that are strictly necessary: return to unity; agree with us in the profession of the true faith that the Catholic Church holds and teaches; and, along with that of the whole Church itself, maintain communion with the supreme see of Peter. With respect to your sacred rites, only those things found in them contrary to catholic faith and unity are subject to correction. Once remedied in this regard, your ancient Eastern liturgies will remain unchanged. (*On the Supreme Throne of Peter the Apostle*, 1848)

Pope Leo XIII (1810-1903) asked all Catholics to pray for Christian unity. In 1896 Pope Leo set aside Ascension Day to Pentecost as a Novena of Prayer for Christian unity on a permanent basis.

That invitation was answered later that year by the world's Orthodox patriarchs. Calling the papacy a "heresy," they reiterated their opposition to papal primacy and the insertion of *Filioque* into the Creed.

In his 1862 encyclical *Amantissimus* ("On the Care of the Churches"), Bl. Pius IX stated again the grounds for papal primacy; invited the Orthodox to reunion, assuring them that they would be able to retain their liturgical rites after reunion; and offered resources to help the Orthodox leaders guide their clergy and faithful in the transition to Catholic unity.

In 1894 Pope Leo XIII's encyclical *Præclara Gratulationis Publicæ* ("The Reunion of Christendom") also invited a Catholic-Orthodox reconciliation. It read, in part:

> Suffer that we should invite you to the Unity which has ever existed in the Catholic Church and can never fail; suffer that We should lovingly hold out Our hand to you. The Church, as the common mother of all, has long been calling you back to her.

Neither was this letter well received by the Orthodox patriarchs, who the following year wrote a letter again disputing papal primacy.

The approach of the Catholic Church to restoring unity at this time was perhaps more about capitulation rather than dialogue and collaboration. Ecumenism was seen not as a mutual process but as a movement toward Rome. The desire for unity was there, but the method was not making much progress toward the intended result.

Yet, Pope Leo XIII did one other thing in the name of ecumenism: He asked all Catholics to pray for Christian unity, and for this purpose composed a *novena*—a series of devotional prayers to be recited over a period of nine days—to be prayed between the feasts of the Ascension and Pentecost each year.

Pope Benedict XVI beatified Cardinal John Henry Newman in a historic Mass at Cofton Park, Birmingham, on September 19, 2010. This was the first beatification ever to take place on British soil. 55,000 people attended the open-air ceremony. The music for the ceremony began with Newman's hymn, "Praise to the holiest in the heights and in the depth be praise. In all his words most wonderful, Most sure in all his ways."

OXFORD MOVEMENT

One of the major movements among other Christian communities toward Catholicism during the nineteenth century originated among Anglican clergymen in England. There are Anglicans, as we read earlier, who mistakenly believe the Anglican Church to have retained valid apostolic succession and see it as part of the one, holy, catholic, and apostolic Church, a kind of alternative to either Eastern Orthodoxy or to the Catholic Church as governed by the papacy. On this and similar views, the Anglican Church would also be a kind of middle ground between the Catholic Church and Protestantism. In the years since the schism with Rome, however, there had been a palpable drift from some of the teachings they once shared in common.

In 1833 a group of young clerics at the University of Oxford led by John Keble sought to bring about a revival within Anglicanism. They saw Anglicanism as one of three "branches," along with the Roman Catholic and Orthodox Churches, of the original Catholic Church, a claim that was known as the *Branch Theory*. Therefore, they reasoned, Anglicans should identify more closely with its Catholic rather than Protestant roots. They began to preach and publish tracts—directed mainly to the clergy—calling for a renewed emphasis on Catholic doctrines and greater attention to beauty in liturgy and church architecture. Because of this, they were called Tractarians in their day, and their cause later became known as the *Oxford Movement*.

The tracts met with great initial success but also attracted opposition. Some Anglicans were resistant to reform, or preferred to seek greater unity with other Christian communities rather than the Catholic Church. Those who believed that the Oxford Movement intended to unite the Anglicans to the Catholic Church called them "Romanists" derisively. British elected officials also objected because the Tractarians called for less government intrusion into religious affairs. As a result of the backlash, several Oxford Movement leaders were periodically barred from preaching in public.

In 1845 one of the leading Tractarians, John Henry Newman, who had been strongly anti-Catholic, converted to Catholicism. The Oxford Movement then took on a new phase: For its detractors Newman's defection was proof of its Romanizing tendencies, and a crackdown on its leaders grew stronger.

ST. JOHN HENRY NEWMAN

St. John Henry Newman is perhaps the most famous Anglican convert to the Catholic faith. Newman was born in London in 1801, the eldest of six children. As a youth, he was an avid reader, drawn first to great novels and then to the popular enlightenment writings of philosophers such as David Hume and Voltaire.

Although he was exposed to the Bible at an early age and always believed in God, he had no particular religious convictions until he was fifteen, when he had a profound conversion. He became an enthusiastic evangelical Calvinist. He thought God might be calling him to become a missionary and to a life of celibacy, and he was open to both.

At Oxford University Newman first studied law but later decided that God was calling him to the clergy. In 1825 he was ordained an Anglican priest. For two years he served St. Clement Parish in Oxford but slowly became disillusioned with Calvinistic theology as too individualistic and unable to explain human nature.

In 1827 Newman returned to Oxford, where he continued his theological studies and became a highly influential voice in the Oxford Movement. He saw the Anglican Church as the *via media*, or middle way, between Protestant extremes and Catholic "errors." Many in England considered him the most brilliant religious scholar and writer of his day.

Newman's deep reading of the Church Fathers brought him into contact with Sacred Tradition. His extensive study of early Christianity drew him, against his wishes, closer to the Catholic Church. In 1842 he left Oxford and moved to the Oxford suburb of Littlemore, where he and several friends lived a monastic-style life devoted to prayer, study, and writing. After two years Newman saw clearly that the teachings of the early Church were preserved in their fullness only in the Catholic Church, so he made the highly unusual decision to convert.

St. John Henry Newman (1801-1890)

Many close friends, colleagues, and even family members abandoned him, and he was attacked publicly.

Newman left for Rome, where he was ordained an Oratorian priest, a congregation established by St. Philip Neri. Upon his return to London, he joined other English Oratorians and helped to establish the London Oratory.

Newman published numerous books, tracts, letters, and articles, the most famous of which is his *Apologia pro Vita Sua*. This autobiographical book follows the course of his religious thought from his youth through his entrance into the Catholic Church. Its publication did much to change the public opinion of Newman, his conversion, and the Catholic Church in England. Through this and other publications as well as his example he helped to reconcile many of the misunderstandings between Catholics and Protestants in England and paved the way for tens of thousands of people to become Catholic.

In 1879 Pope Leo XIII honored Newman by making him a cardinal, an event that was celebrated by both Catholics and Protestants alike. St. John Henry Newman died in 1890 and was canonized by Pope Francis in 2019. His Feast Day is October 9.

Although Newman was the only Tractarian leader to convert, many other Anglicans did become Catholic at least in part due to the influence of the Oxford Movement. In the latter half of the nineteenth century, the revival toward greater Catholic identity within Anglicanism became known as the Anglo-Catholic movement.

One of the initiatives of the Oxford Movement was to petition the Catholic Church to recognize the validity of Anglican orders—in other words, to accept that the Anglicans have maintained Apostolic Succession and therefore have valid priests and valid Sacraments. For centuries the Catholic Church had considered the Anglican orders invalid, for although at the time of the schism the bishops and priests of the breakaway ecclesial community had indeed been validly ordained, Anglican leaders had made changes in the ordination rite in the mid-sixteenth century, altering the prayers of ordination in such a way that they no longer invoked the Holy Spirit or stated with clarity the distinctive nature of the priesthood. Therefore, ordinations after the year 1552 were not valid. Although the Anglicans changed the wording again a century later, by then all the bishops who had been validly ordained prior to 1552 had passed away.

Pope Leo XIII called together a commission to discuss the matter. In 1896 the commission was unanimous and the Pope agreed. The official position of the Catholic Church reaffirmed that Anglican orders were not valid. With the demise of the Branch Theory came another influx of new converts to Catholicism.

ECUMENICAL PRAYER

Around the beginning of the twentieth century, recognition grew among Christians of the need to work toward the unity that Christ desired for his followers.

Part of what the Oxford Movement of the nineteenth century had advocated was the establishment of an Anglican monastic tradition: consecrated life of men and women such as is common in the Catholic Church. At the time of the Anglican schism, King Henry VIII had put an end to monastic life in England and had confiscated all the land and property owned by religious orders. Thanks to the Tractarians' influence, there began a small-scale revival of monastic communities within Anglicanism.

In 1898 an Anglican priest named Paul (Louis) Wattson and a young novice named Lurana White established the Society of the Atonement in Graymoor, New York, a community of friars and sisters in

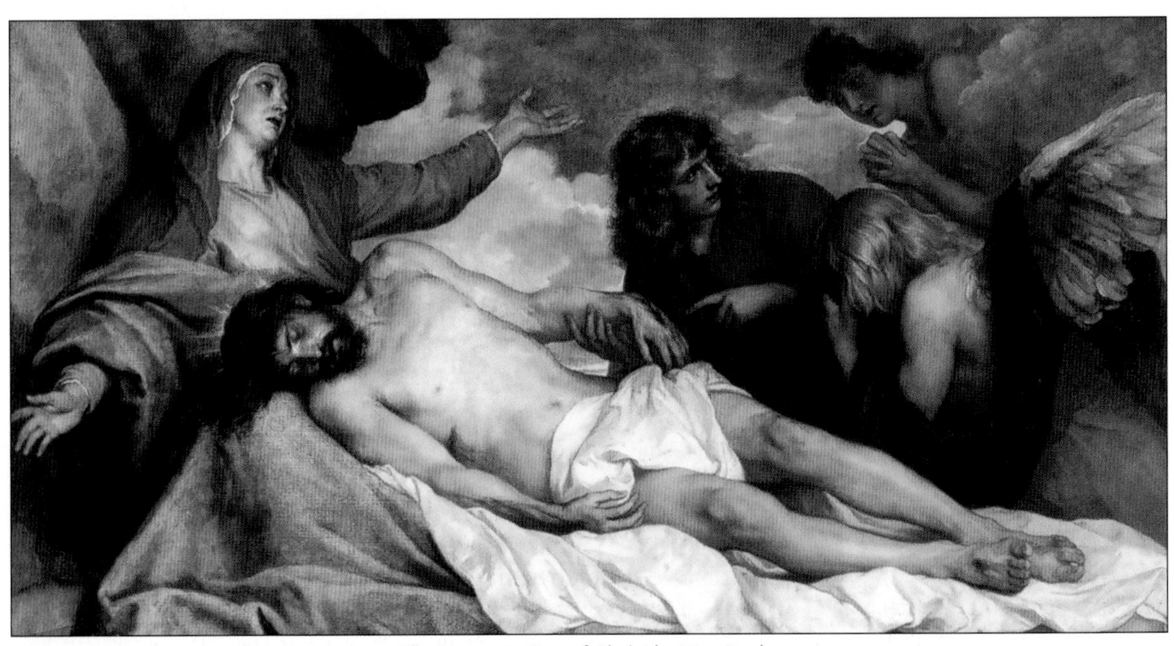

The Lamentation of Christ by Van Dyck.
Founder of the Society of Atonement Fr. Paul Wattson gave Mary, the Blessed Mother, the title *Our Lady of Atonement.* He saw Mary at the foot of the Cross as intimately associated with the Atonement.

the Franciscan tradition with a special commitment to fostering Christian unity. At first they worked to encourage Episcopalians (members of the Anglican Communion in the United States) to unite with the Catholic Church, which made them unpopular within their own ecclesial community, and they were often barred from speaking at Episcopal functions. For years they and their growing community struggled for this cause, living in poverty.

In 1908 Wattson and an Anglican priest, Spencer Jones, proposed eight days of prayer for Christian unity to be called the *Octave of Christian Unity*. The octave would begin on January 18, the Feast of the Confession of St. Peter in many places, and end on January 25, the Feast of the Conversion of St. Paul. The beginning date was selected because Wattson wanted this octave to emphasize the role of the Petrine ministry—the papacy—in the work of Christian unity. (For this reason the observance came to be known in the 1930s as the Chair of Unity Octave, referring to the papal office as the Chair of St. Peter.)

Our Lady of the Atonement, Mother of the Christian Unity Octave.
"...the atonement—the wonderful at-one-ment which was achieved by our Lord Jesus Christ as He shed His Most Precious Blood upon the Cross at Calvary, through which came the reconciliation of man with God, and of man with man, making us 'at one' in His Sacred Heart."
—Fr. Paul Wattson

St. Pius X gave his blessing to this initiative, and several years later Pope Benedict XV encouraged its practice throughout the entire Catholic Church. Although the octave was instituted by two Anglican priests, it was observed almost exclusively by Catholics.

In the meantime, in 1909 Wattson, White, and their communities, sixteen members strong, converted to Catholicism, and Wattson was ordained a Catholic priest. Their communities, which still work for ecumenism today, are known as the Franciscan Friars (Sisters) of the Atonement, or simply the Graymoor Friars (Sisters).

In 1910 the Episcopal leaders in the United States proposed that Christian leaders gather to begin planning a major ecumenical event to be called the World Conference on Faith and Order. Sixteen years later, a year before the inaugural conference, the Faith and Order leadership proposed an octave for Christian unity as well but on a different timetable. Their version disengaged the observance from any connection to St. Peter or the papacy and instead planned it for the eight days leading up to Pentecost Sunday.

That same year there was a large gathering of Protestant representatives from various ecclesial communities at a World Missionary Conference in Edinburgh, Scotland. Its purpose was to discuss a strategy for cooperation in Christian missionary efforts worldwide. Although no Catholic or Orthodox delegates were present, the meeting was the first large-scale gathering of Christian denominations to date. It is often regarded as the formal beginning of the Protestant ecumenical movement.

In 1935 a French Catholic priest, Fr. Paul Couturier, wanted to broaden the outreach of the Octave for Unity as observed by Catholics, and proposed renaming the Octave the "Universal Week of Prayer for Christian Unity." In addition, he wanted to make the intention of the prayer for "unity as Christ wills it," thus making it more palatable to non-Catholics. In 1941 the World Conference on Faith and Order changed their Octave to coincide with the January dates observed by the Catholic Church.

The Catholic Church accepted the broader outreach promoted by Fr. Couturier in 1966. The first official joint observation of the Week of Prayer for Christian Unity by the Catholic Church and Protestant communities took place in 1968. By focusing on prayer the organizers of the Week recognized that the reunion of Christians is impossible without God. As we set aside a week each year to pray for unity, we are reminded that each one of us must work for Christian unity, and our work must begin and end in prayer.

FROM PRAYER TO DIALOGUE

The history of the past two centuries shows a certain development in the ecumenical philosophy of the Catholic Church. Through the end of the nineteenth century, as we read earlier, the Church simply invited the Orthodox Churches and other ecclesial communities back into the Catholic fold, assuring them of a warm welcome. Around the turn of the twentieth century, the Church increasingly encouraged everyone to pray for Christian unity and to participate in such prayer with other Christians.

Yet, when the World Conference on Faith and Order, the World Council of Churches, and the National Council of Churches were formed for the purpose of ecumenical dialogue, Church leaders were quite reticent to participate. They were concerned that such talks would be unproductive or that Catholic participation in them would imply that compromise in essential teachings or positions would be expected in order to achieve some kind of unity. Further, a Christian "union" that did not include a true full communion would be a false union, the reasoning went, and thus participation in such talks might encourage a deformed view of Christianity.

Writing on the subject in 1928, Pope Pius XI stated:

> It is clear that the Apostolic See cannot on any terms take part in their assemblies, nor is it anyway lawful for Catholics either to support or to work for such enterprises; for if they do so they will be giving countenance to a false Christianity, quite alien to the one Church of Christ. (*Mortalium Animos*, 8)

Over time, however, Church leaders became more interested in the ecumenical movement and acknowledged the possible benefits of working with it. In 1949 the Vatican's doctrinal office issued a decree, which stated in part:

> [Bishops] should therefore not only carefully and efficaciously keep this movement under vigilant observation, but also prudently foster and guide it unto the twofold end of assisting those who are in search of the truth and the true Church. (*Ecclesia Catholica*)

When St. John XXIII was elected in 1958, he was seventy-seven years of age, and little if anything was expected of him, perhaps least of all in terms of ecumenism. Yet, a few months after his election, he announced to the world his intention to call an Ecumenical Council. The date of this announcement was January 25, and the occasion—not by coincidence—was the close of the Octave of Christian Unity.

That summer St. John XXIII issued his first encyclical, *Ad Petri Cathedram*, which dealt in part with Christian unity. In it he praised the ecumenical progress that had been made and affirmed that unity was only possible with the Catholic Church:

> We have taken note that almost all those who are adorned with the name of Christian even though separated from Us and from one another have sought to forge bonds of unity by means of many congresses and by establishing councils. This is evidence that they are moved by an intense desire for unity of some kind.
>
> When the Divine Redeemer founded His Church, there is no doubt that He made firm unity its cornerstone and one of its essential attributes.... But this unity, Venerable Brethren and beloved sons, must be solid, firm and sure, not transient, uncertain, or unstable.[5] Though there is no such unity in other Christian communities, all who look carefully can see that it is present in the Catholic Church. (*Ad Petri Cathedram*, 64-66)

St. John XXIII
(1881-1963)

St. John XXIII was serious in his commitment to ecumenism. Early in his brief papacy, he established the Secretariat for Promoting Christian Unity for this purpose. He sent observers to the World Council of Churches assembly held in New Delhi in 1961, marking the first official Catholic involvement in that ecumenical body. He also announced that he would invite Orthodox, Anglican, and Protestant observers to the council proceedings. According to his vision, the Council would serve, at least in part, as a model for a new approach to ecumenical relations.

CATHOLIC SCHISMS SINCE THE PROTESTANT REFORMATION

ince the Protestant Reformation, the Catholic Church has experienced the loss of a few additional small breakaway groups:

Old Catholics is a name meant to refer to "old (or original) Catholicism," the collective name for a group of national churches which at various times have separated from Rome. The Diocese of Utrecht in the Netherlands separated from Rome in 1724 when it insisted on electing its own archbishop. In 1870 several Old Catholic groups formed in Germany, Austria, and Switzerland in rejection of the definition of papal infallibility at the First Ecumenical Council of the Vatican, and a few smaller groups followed at various points in the 1900s.

The Old Catholic churches have valid Apostolic Succession and valid Sacraments, maintained through the Diocese of Utrecht. However, they have begun to ordain women as priests, and these ordinations are invalid. They believe in the Real Presence of Christ in the Eucharist but do not consider it a matter of transubstantiation.

The Polish National Catholic Church in the United States broke communion with Rome in 1897 over pastoral and property disputes. Their first bishops were ordained through the Old Catholic line, so they have Apostolic Succession and valid Sacraments. However, the Polish church broke ranks with the Old Catholics when the latter decided to allow women priests. A Croatian Old Catholic church that formed in 1924 also broke with the Old Catholics for a similar reason.

The Society of St. Pius X (SSPX), also called the Lefebvrites or Tridentines, was founded as a breakaway sect by French Archbishop Marcel Lefebvre in 1970 in objection to the Second Ecumenical Council of the Vatican, the liturgical reforms that followed, and its support for ecumenical and interfaith dialogue. The Church made many overtures to reconcile with the movement. When Lefebvre ordained four bishops in 1988 over objections from St. John Paul II, Lefebvre and the four bishops were excommunicated.

In the same document publicizing their bishops' excommunication, the Pope appealed to SSPX members to return to the Catholic Church and strongly encouraged local bishops to allow the celebration of the older liturgies—popularly called the Tridentine Rite, Traditional Latin Mass, or extraordinary form of the Latin Rite—in dioceses where a significant number of the faithful earnestly desired it. He formed a pontifical commission to help facilitate the return of SSPX members and others who had separated from the Church over similar issues, establishing the Priestly Fraternity of St. Peter as a society of priests to provide pastoral care for Catholics according to these rites. Since that time, many former SSPX members and some SSPX communities have returned to full communion with the Catholic Church.

Elevation of the chalice during a Traditional Latin Mass celebrated by the Priestly Fraternity of St. Peter.

In 2009 Pope Benedict XVI lifted the excommunications of the four surviving bishops to begin a dialogue in hopes of encouraging the SSPX to reconcile with the Catholic Church. In 2011 as a result of these dialogues, the Pope offered a "doctrinal preamble," which, if accepted, would restore the Society to full communion with the Catholic Church and give it a special canonical status, but the SSPX did not give an official answer to that offer by the time of Pope Benedict's resignation in 2013. As of this writing, the SSPX remains in imperfect communion with the Catholic Church.

Second Vatican Council Opening Procession in St. Peter's Basilica. One of sixteen Council documents, *Unitatis Redintegratio* ("The Restoration of Unity"), signaled the Church's full embrace of ecumenical dialogue.

THE SECOND VATICAN COUNCIL AND NON-CATHOLIC CHURCHES

The Second Ecumenical Council of the Vatican had a monumental impact on the Catholic Church in the twentieth century. Many of the Church's teachings and practices were seen in a new light, and many changes were made that affected the daily life of Catholics. One of the most significant was the Church's new articulation on ecumenical dialogue and cooperation.

When the Second Vatican Council began in 1962, thirty-nine invited observers from non-Catholic Christian Churches and ecclesial communities were there, seated together. In a special audience held for them two days later, St. John XXIII told them of his own reaction at seeing them there in the assembly: "Every now and then my eyes turned to all my sons and brothers. And when my glance fell on your group, on each one of you, I found that your presence gave me joy."

St. John XXIII died the following year as the council he convoked was barely underway. His successor, St. Paul VI, saw the council through to its 1965 completion. While most of the resulting sixteen documents of the council reflected an ecumenical and interfaith spirit to some degree, one document in particular, *Unitatis Redintegratio* ("The Restoration of Unity"), signaled the Church's full embrace of ecumenical dialogue and outlined Catholic involvement in the ecumenical movement.

Unitatis Redintegratio did not change the Church's traditional teaching, but it did adjust the tone with which the Church engaged ecumenical issues. Instead of emphasizing areas of disagreement, the Church began to focus on those beliefs held in common between Catholics and non-Catholics.

Whereas official Church documents sometimes referred to non-Catholic Christians as heretics or schismatics, *Unitatis Redintegratio* called them "separated brethren," thus emphasizing the common status of all Christians as children of God through the grace of Baptism. Furthermore, instead of focusing on how these separated brethren would benefit by reunion, the Church acknowledged that Catholics also would be enriched:

> Nor should we forget that anything wrought by the grace of the Holy Spirit in the hearts of our separated brethren can contribute to our own edification. Whatever is truly Christian is never contrary to what genuinely belongs to the faith; indeed, it can always bring a more perfect realization of the very mystery of Christ and the Church. (*Unitatis Redintegratio*, 4)

Unitatis Redintegratio distinguished between the "two principal types of division"[6] that plague Christendom: the division between East and West and the divisions within the West (Protestantism). Because of the diverse history of these two primary types of divisions, the approach taken toward reunion with the East will necessarily be very different from that taken with the Protestant denominations of the West. The separation between the Catholic and Orthodox Churches is more ancient, but it does not entail nearly as many doctrinal obstacles as does the separation between the Catholic Church and the Protestant ecclesial communities.

The Church, therefore, holds out greater hope for restoring full communion with the Orthodox Churches, which after all are true churches because they maintain Apostolic Succession, valid Sacraments, and a shared understanding of interpreting revealed truth, i.e., that the Deposit of Faith is contained in Sacred Tradition and Sacred Scripture. Furthermore, because of the evolution of Protestant beliefs and practices over the centuries—and especially in recent years—greater obstacles exist to union with those communities. Protestant bodies are far more diverse in their beliefs and have many divisions among themselves, so Protestant-Catholic ecumenism often involves separate initiatives on many different fronts. Whereas the patriarchs of the Eastern Orthodox Churches are in substantial doctrinal agreement, the myriad Protestant denominations have no such official unity. Dialogue with Protestant and Anglican bodies, then, must be done on a denominational or affiliation basis with variations in the important dividing issues in each instance. For example, the ongoing Catholic-Lutheran World Federation dialogue does not include the participation of the Lutheran Church-Missouri Synod, the second-largest Lutheran synod in the United States.

We will examine *Unitatis Redintegratio* and the principles it sets forth in more detail later in the chapter.

ECUMENISM AFTER THE COUNCIL

Buoyed by *Unitatis Redintegratio* and the ecumenical spirit of the Second Vatican Council, the Catholic Church and her leadership began to pursue ecumenical dialogue at an unprecedented pace. And because many other Christian leaders were willing to engage with the Church, these efforts began to bear fruit.

Statue in the Arcade of the Church of the Annunciation, Nazareth, Israel commemorates the Ecumenical meeting of St. Paul VI and Ecumenical Patriarch Athenagoras I on January 5, 1964.

The story of this progress is perhaps best told with regard to the papacies that followed the council, as each Pope had his own ecumenical interests and initiatives that gave inertia to the mission of restoring Christian unity. While each Pope made significant strides on multiple ecumenical fronts, we will focus here on just a few of the highlights.

St. Paul VI began his ecumenical initiatives while the Council was still in session. During a visit to Jerusalem in 1964, he met with Ecumenical Patriarch Athenagoras I of Constantinople. The two leaders afterward released a joint declaration calling for renewal within the churches, a "dialogue of charity" with "regular and profound contacts" between church leaders, and cooperation in theological studies, resolution of pastoral problems, and initiatives toward peace and justice. A year later they mutually rescinded the excommunications of 1054 that had been directed against one another's delegates. While this effort did not heal the centuries-old schism, it was an important symbolic gesture of immense ecumenical significance. The patriarch reciprocated with a visit to Rome in 1967.

St. Paul VI also met with the Archbishop of Canterbury, Michael Ramsey, in 1967. Afterward they announced the start of a "serious dialogue" between the Catholic Church and the Anglican Communion. "After four hundred years of separation between the Roman Catholic and Anglican Churches, official representatives from both have taken the first step towards restoring full unity," they said in a joint statement afterward. That marked the establishment of the Anglican-Roman Catholic International Commission (ARCIC).

During St. Paul VI's papacy, the Catholic Church began dialogues with several different Protestant denominations, including the World Lutheran Federation (which includes the Evangelical Lutheran Church of America), the Methodists, and the Reformed communities. He also appointed a consultative group to work with the World Council of Churches in order to find avenues for dialogue and cooperative efforts in social justice and issues affecting the developing nations.

St. John Paul II and Patriarch Teoctist of Romania celebrating together in Bucharest in 1999.

St. John Paul II, over the course of his twenty-six-year papacy, built upon the ecumenical efforts made by his predecessors. With regard to the Orthodox Churches, he became the first Pope to visit a predominantly Orthodox country when, at the invitation of Patriarch Teoctist, he traveled to Romania in 1999. While there, he and the patriarch attended one another's liturgies, which was also an ecumenical first. Two years later during a meeting in Greece, St. John Paul II asked God's forgiveness publicly for past offenses of Catholics against Orthodox Christians, prompting applause from Archbishop Christodoulos of Athens, and he enjoyed close friendships with the Ecumenical Patriarchs and together with them encouraged the advancement of Catholic-Orthodox dialogue. Early in his papacy, the joint Catholic-Orthodox theological commission proposed under St. Paul VI began to formulate a strategy for reconciliation of the two Churches.

A number of significant developments in ecumenical dialogue with Christian ecclesial communities took place during his pontificate. From the Catholic-World Lutheran Federation dialogue, which had produced a number of statements on doctrinal issues, emerged a *Joint Declaration on the Doctrine of Justification,* one of the key points of disagreement dating to the Reformation. The declaration explains how the traditional stated positions of Catholics and Lutherans emphasize different aspects of the same truths regarding the relation of works to grace and salvation but are in essential agreement:

> Together we confess: By grace alone, in faith in Christ's saving work and not because of any merit on our part, we are accepted by God and receive the Holy Spirit, who renews our hearts while equipping and calling us to good works. (*Joint Declaration on the Doctrine of Justification*, 15)

In 1998 the ARCIC produced a statement, *The Gift of Authority*, discussing how Anglicans might be reunited with Catholics under the Pope. While it was groundbreaking in theory, the worldwide Anglican Communion was by then experiencing further deterioration in its own unity, with changes in theology and practice that separated it even further from full communion with the Church. However, the ensuing divisions in the Anglican Communion, which were caused by these theological developments, resulted in a renewed interest in the Catholic faith among many of the Anglican faithful and clergy.

In 1995 St. John Paul II issued the encyclical *Ut Unum Sint* ("That They May Be One"). With the second millennium of Christianity fast approaching, the Pope earnestly desired that all Christians redouble their efforts to restore the unity that had been compromised by divisions. Reiterating the essential nature of the Church and the importance of the papacy as a sign of unity, he emphasized the importance of prayer, dialogue, and ecumenical cooperation.

> It is absolutely clear that ecumenism, the movement promoting Christian unity, is not just some sort of "appendix" which is added to the Church's traditional activity. Rather, ecumenism is an organic part of her life and work, and consequently must pervade all that she is and does. (*Ut Unum Sint*, 20)

We will examine this encyclical more thoroughly in Chapter 9.

Pope Benedict XVI continued to foster the good relationships that his predecessors had developed with representatives of the Orthodox Churches and Protestant ecclesial communities. But some of his most significant initiatives have involved efforts to restore full communion with members of the Anglican Communion and the traditionalist Catholic movements.

As the threat of schism within the Anglican Communion became more severe, particularly within the Episcopal Church in the United States, many Anglicans looked to the Catholic Church as their new home. Increasingly, entire Episcopal parishes, some of which identify themselves as Anglo-Catholic, petitioned to be received into the Church corporately, hoping to retain their parish status and their Anglican traditions while fully incorporating themselves into the Catholic faith.

This was not an unforeseen circumstance. As early as 1970 as hopes for full Catholic-Anglican reunion were being kindled, St. Paul VI indicated that such a restoration of communion would include accommodation of Anglican liturgical tradition:

> There will be no seeking to lessen the legitimate prestige and the worthy patrimony of piety and usage proper to the Anglican Church when the Roman Catholic Church—this humble "Servant of the Servants of God"—is able to embrace her ever beloved Sister in the one authentic communion of the family of Christ. (*Homily at the Canonization of the Forty Martyrs of England and Wales*, Oct. 25, 1970)

Pope Benedict XVI and Archbishop of Canterbury Dr. Rowan Williams met for the first time at the Vatican in November 2009.

Ten years later St. John Paul II had allowed a "pastoral provision" by which former Episcopal priests, whether celibate or married, who converted to Catholicism could receive Holy Orders on a case-by-case basis. The same pastoral provision allowed for the establishment of "personal worship communities" that would retain certain Anglican elements in celebrating the Catholic liturgy.

In 2009 to answer this need, Benedict XVI provided that *personal ordinariates* could be established to allow Anglicans to enter into full communion with the Catholic Church while retaining many elements of their Anglican spirituality and liturgical tradition. A personal ordinariate functions like a diocese with its own clergy and administrator but serves the pastoral needs of Anglican converts within its jurisdiction. The first of these Anglican ordinariates was established in 2011, covering the territory of England and Wales; ordinariates have since been established in Australia and North America.

> In recent times the Holy Spirit has moved groups of Anglicans to petition repeatedly and insistently to be received into full Catholic communion individually as well as corporately. The Apostolic See has responded favourably to such petitions. Indeed, the successor of Peter, mandated by the Lord Jesus to guarantee the unity of the episcopate and to preside over and safeguard the universal communion of all the Churches,[7] could not fail to make available the means necessary to bring this holy desire to realization. (Pope Benedict XVI, *Anglicanorum Cœtibus*)

Pope Francis met with Archbishop of Canterbury Justin Welby for the first time at the Vatican on June 14, 2013.
"Today's meeting is an opportunity to remind ourselves that the search for unity among Christians is prompted not by practical considerations, but by the will of the Lord Jesus Christ himself, who made us his brothers and sisters, children of the One Father." —Pope Francis

ESSENTIAL GUIDELINES FOR ECUMENISM

Recall for a moment that the word "ecumenism" is rooted in the Greek word *oikoumene*, which means "the whole (inhabited) world." This definition ought to remind us of the Great Commission given to the Apostles by Jesus Christ to "go, therefore, and make disciples of all nations,"[8] and his assurance that the Gospel would be "preached throughout the whole world, as a testimony to all nations."[9] This etymology underlines the fundamental purpose of ecumenism, that of fostering unity between the Catholic Church and other churches and Christian ecclesial communities.

But how does this ecumenism take place? What is involved in ecumenical work? Theological and pastoral reflection on centuries of Christian history—both the good and the bad—has helped the teaching authority of the Church to develop the necessary goals and principles governing the quest for Church unity.

The *Catechism of the Catholic Church* lists seven key requirements for effective ecumenism:

> —a permanent *renewal* of the Church in greater fidelity to her vocation; such renewal is the driving-force of the movement toward unity;[10]
>
> —*conversion of heart* as the faithful "try to live holier lives according to the Gospel"[11]; for it is the unfaithfulness of the members to Christ's gift which causes divisions;
>
> —*prayer in common*, because "change of heart and holiness of life, along with public and private prayer for the unity of Christians, should be regarded as the soul of the whole ecumenical movement, and merits the name 'spiritual ecumenism;'"[12]
>
> —*fraternal knowledge of each other*;[13]
>
> —*ecumenical formation* of the faithful and especially of priests;[14]
>
> —*dialogue* among theologians and meetings among Christians of the different churches and communities;[15]
>
> —*collaboration* among Christians in various areas of service to mankind.[16] "Human service" is the idiomatic phrase. (CCC 821)

These are the fundamental aims that animate Catholic ecumenical initiatives. Let us look at each of these in turn in light of key passages from *Unitatis Redintegratio*.

Renewal of the Church in Fidelity to Her Vocation

One of the remarkable lessons of the Protestant Reformation is capsulated in a motto that came out of some of the Reformed movements of the seventeenth century: *Ecclesia semper reformanda est* ("The Church is always in need of reform"). The Fathers of the Second Vatican Council echoed this idea, affirming that the Church is "at once holy and always in need of purification, follow[ing] constantly the path of penance and renewal."[17]

The Church is holy and perfect because she is the Body of Christ, yet her members, all sinners, do not always live up to this holiness. She teaches truth in the name of Christ, which is kept free from error by the Holy Spirit, but her faithful—even those in leadership positions—fail to live by that truth, which causes scandal and offense to others. Thus is the Church, which is always in need of reform and renewal, called to a continual examination of conscience to ensure that she reflects within herself the unity and commitment to truth according to the will and example of Christ.

Since real unity is based on the truth, it is not simply a matter of compromise on both sides until agreement is reached. Mutual union with Jesus Christ, who is the Truth, brings unity. For this to happen, the Catholic Church must first be true to her calling to follow the Lord faithfully.

In every age, however, the followers of Christ have failed to live up to their calling as his disciples. In every age, therefore, there must be renewal of the Church.

> Christ summons the Church to continual reformation as she sojourns here on earth. The Church is always in need of this, in so far as she is an institution of men here on earth. Thus if, in various times and circumstances, there have been deficiencies in moral conduct or in church discipline, or even in the way that church teaching has been formulated—to be carefully distinguished from the deposit of faith itself—these can and should be set right at the opportune moment. Church renewal has therefore notable ecumenical importance. (*Unitatis Redintegratio*, 6)

Sermon on the Mount (detail) by Bloch. Mutual union with Jesus Christ, who is the Truth, brings unity.

Conversion of Heart

Christ, from the beginning of his public ministry, called on people to repent of their sins. This repentance is a change of heart—a turning from sinful desires and practices to a holy life, one that has its foundation in the life and teachings of Christ. This means living a life of humility and love for others.

Conversion of heart is necessary for ecumenism as well, for without humility and love, efforts at unity will always fall short. Humility allows a person to recognize the faults of his or her own faith community, and love generates the desire to be united with all separated brothers and sisters. Christ calls every person to a conversion of heart, a conversion that leads to a flowering of his will here on earth.

> There can be no ecumenism worthy of the name without a change of heart. For it is from renewal of the inner life of our minds,[18] from self-denial and an unstinted love that desires of unity take their rise and develop in a mature way. We should therefore pray to the Holy Spirit for the grace to be genuinely self-denying, humble, gentle in the service of others, and to have an attitude of brotherly generosity towards them. (*Unitatis Redintegratio*, 7)

Prayer in Common

With prayer nothing is impossible, for nothing is impossible for God. Working for unity among Christians can seem like an incredibly difficult task. Christians have been divided for over a thousand years; how can we ever repair the damage?

In short, we cannot. To restore such unity is beyond human ability. It is, however, possible in Christ. This is why prayer in common among divided Christians is encouraged when appropriate. Common services among separated brethren should include prayers for unity.

However, due to the divisions that have arisen among Christians, there are limits to our ability to pray as one. Without full communion, shared sacramental worship is not yet possible, for it would signify a union that does not yet exist. This lack of full communion should encourage the Church to pray more fervently and earnestly for the reunion of all Christians.

> In certain special circumstances, such as the prescribed prayers "for unity," and during ecumenical gatherings, it is allowable, indeed desirable that Catholics should join in prayer with their separated brethren. Such prayers in common are certainly an effective means of obtaining the grace of unity, and they are a true expression of the ties which still bind Catholics to their separated brethren. "For where two or three are gathered together in my name, there am I in the midst of them."[19] (*Unitatis Redintegratio*, 8)

Fraternal Knowledge

Think about the friends about whom you care the most. Now think about the time you spend getting to know these friends: the hours spent together playing sports, studying together, or just hanging out. Your love for your friends grows as you know them better. This is true of all human relationships: We need to know someone deeply in order to love him or her deeply. Yet, for centuries, Christians of different faith traditions have spent little or no time together trying to understand each other. How are love and unity to come about in such a scenario? For ecumenism to bear any fruit, Catholics and other Christians must work together to grow in knowledge of one another: our different beliefs, practices, and presuppositions.

Pentecost by Tristan.
For ecumenism to bear any fruit, Catholics and other Christians must work together to grow in knowledge of one another.

Misunderstanding and distrust are common between groups that do not interact often; therefore, the ecumenical movement calls on all Christians to learn more about other faith traditions' ways of following Christ. This mutual exchange of ideas, carried out in love, brings each party to a deeper appreciation of the other.

> We must get to know the outlook of our separated brethren. To achieve this purpose, study is of necessity required, and this must be pursued with a sense of realism and good will. Catholics, who already have a proper grounding, need to acquire a more adequate understanding of the respective doctrines of our separated brethren, their history, their spiritual and liturgical life, their religious psychology and general background.... From such dialogue will emerge still more clearly what the situation of the Catholic Church really is. In this way too the outlook of our separated brethren will be better understood, and our own belief more aptly explained. (*Unitatis Redintegratio*, 9)

The Way to Calvary by Domenichino.
To restore Christian unity is beyond human ability. It is, however, possible in Christ.

Ecumenical Formation of Clergy and Laity

All Christians should be involved in ecumenism, but naturally there must be leaders who will work with other Christian church leaders to achieve full communion. Therefore, certain individuals, both lay and clerical, must be trained in the Church's teachings on ecumenism. For example, a student of the Catholic liturgy may study the liturgies of the Oriental Orthodox in order to discover commonalities and differences. These trained men and women can work directly with leaders of other Christian groups to further ecumenical relations.

> Sacred theology and other branches of knowledge, especially of an historical nature, must be taught with due regard for the ecumenical point of view, so that they may correspond more exactly with the facts. (*Unitatis Redintegratio*, 10)

Dialogue Among Theologians

Theologians are tasked with the sacred duty of studying the things of God: who he is, how he works, how we follow him. Due to the divisions that have arisen among Christians, these questions have been answered in differing ways through the centuries by theologians of different faith traditions. Catholic theologians can engage in dialogue with theologians of other Christian churches and communities to determine exactly where we agree and where we disagree on the important questions of theology.

> In ecumenical dialogue, Catholic theologians standing fast by the teaching of the Church and investigating the divine mysteries with the separated brethren must proceed with love for the truth, with charity, and with humility. When comparing doctrines with one another, they should remember that in Catholic doctrine there exists a "hierarchy" of truths, since they vary in their relation to the fundamental Christian faith. Thus the way will be opened by which through fraternal rivalry all will be stirred to a deeper understanding and a clearer presentation of the unfathomable riches of Christ.[20] (*Unitatis Redintegratio*, 11)

Collaboration Among Christians

Our world has become increasingly hostile to Christian faith and values in recent years. Decreased respect for the dignity of life, attacks on the sanctity of marriage, and discrimination against religious institutions are just a few examples of how our world has become "post-Christian." Because of this state of affairs, however, Christians have marvelous opportunities to join forces in their efforts to overcome the anti-Christian movement. Through working to better our world, Christians who are divided on many matters can come together and, in doing so, to grow in mutual love and respect for each other. Such efforts are instrumental in building "grassroots" support for ecumenism.

> **In these days when cooperation in social matters is so widespread, all men without exception are called to work together, with much greater reason all those who believe in God, but most of all, all Christians in that they bear the name of Christ. Cooperation among Christians vividly expresses the relationship which in fact already unites them, and it sets in clearer relief the features of Christ the Servant....All believers in Christ can, through this cooperation, be led to acquire a better knowledge and appreciation of one another, and so pave the way to Christian unity.** (*Unitatis Redintegratio*, 12)

FALSE IDEAS ABOUT ECUMENISM

Ecumenism is a sacred obligation for Catholics, a call of Christ himself. We must work toward Christian unity and celebrate whatever progress we are able to achieve. We must act always with respect for the truth, for we cannot achieve authentic unity apart from truth. Most Christians, in one way or another, embrace the idea that all Christ's followers should be united as one Body.

Unfortunately, not everyone embraces the true nature and aims of ecumenism. The extremes can be identified in two camps: Those who wish to claim Christian unity by ignoring the very deep and real divisions that exist by "agreeing to disagree" even on key doctrinal issues and those who believe ecumenism is a waste of time that threatens only to compromise Church teaching in the name of Christian unity. We will look at each of these extremes in turn.

"Too-Easy" Ecumenism: The Truth Cannot Be Comprised

Before he was elected Pope Benedict XVI, Joseph Cardinal Ratzinger warned about "too-easy ecumenism." The essential teachings of the Church cannot be diluted or compromised for the sake of "unity."

Some Christians seem to be looking for a shortcut to reunion. They want to remove any obstacles that exist—even if those "obstacles" are necessary elements of true Christian unity. In their enthusiasm for achieving union, such advocates want to set aside any doctrinal differences as unessential. So a community's belief regarding the Blessed Trinity, the Eucharist, or moral issues might be ignored and serious doctrinal divisions glossed over as long as on some level there was a basic desire to follow Christ, however he may be perceived. The problem with this is that it attempts to lay the foundation of unity on a falsehood.

Serving as the prefect of the Congregation for the Doctrine of the Faith, Joseph Cardinal Ratzinger—long before he was elected Pope Benedict XVI—expressed caution against thinking or acting as though full Christian unity had been achieved on the basis of shared ecumenical prayer and cooperation:

> **We must beware of a too-easy ecumenism which can lead Catholic charismatic groups to lose their**

> identity and, in the name of the "Spirit" (seen as the antithesis of the institution), uncritically associate with forms of Pentecostalism of non-Catholic origin. [Catholic renewal groups must therefore] think with the Church—*sentire cum ecclesia*—more than ever. They must always act in unity with the bishop, not least so that they will avoid the consequences that always arise when Holy Scripture is taken out of its context in the fellowship of the Church, which results in fundamentalism and the marks of the esoteric group and the sect.[21]

Ratzinger's concern was not limited to only charismatic groups, nor did it imply that all charismatic groups fall into such errors. However, his exhortation—always to "think with the Church" and "act in unity with the bishop"—is an indispensable element of Catholic ecumenism. Our Lord entrusted the Apostles with certain teachings and established his Church to preserve and transmit those teachings until the end of time. The essential teachings of the Church, therefore, cannot be diluted or compromised for the sake of "unity," for if we are not united in the truth—that is to say, united in the truth of Christ in its fullness—then we are not united at all. We cannot achieve unity by sacrificing truth.

> This Sacred Council exhorts the faithful to refrain from superficiality and imprudent zeal, which can hinder real progress toward unity. Their ecumenical action must be fully and sincerely Catholic, that is to say, faithful to the truth which we have received from the apostles and Fathers of the Church, in harmony with the faith which the Catholic Church has always professed, and at the same time directed toward that fullness to which Our Lord wills His Body to grow in the course of time. (*Unitatis Redintegratio*, 24)

Some Groups Have Rejected Ecumenical Dialogue

Some entire ecclesial communities, as a matter of policy, reject the very notion of ecumenism. Some Christians across all denominational lines often fail to see the point or the urgency of ecumenical dialogue.

This is an attitude that is seen even among some Catholics. They would say that since the fullness of truth is found in the Catholic Church, all non-Catholics must simply renounce their errors and become Catholic. Refusing to see any elements of truth in other churches and communions, they do not perceive any benefit to the Catholic Church from a potential reunion of estranged communities.

Yet, dating back to the first Christians, the Church has always recognized elements of truth in other belief systems and philosophies. The early Church Fathers spoke about "seeds of the Word" found in Greek philosophy, recognizing and praising truth no matter where it was found. Furthermore, in some cases other Christian communities might embrace certain truths more vigorously than Catholics typically do. For example, many Protestant Christians take seriously their duty to evangelize non-Christians—an outlook many modern-day Catholics would benefit from emulating.

The Repentant Peter by El Greco.
"Seeds of the Word"—recognizing and praising truth no matter where it was found.

> Some and even very many of the significant elements and endowments which together go to build up and give life to the Church itself, can exist outside the visible boundaries of the Catholic Church: the written word of God; the life of grace; faith, hope and charity, with the other interior gifts of the Holy Spirit, and visible elements too. All of these, which come from Christ and lead back to Christ, belong by right to the one Church of Christ. (*Unitatis Redintegratio*, 3)

In addition, many who reject the ecumenical movement hesitate to admit any failings in the members of the Catholic Church in her long history. They place all blame for any disunion with non-Catholics who knowingly and willfully broke communion with the Church founded by Christ. However, as we have learned from our survey of Christian history in this textbook, Catholics must accept that the actions and missteps of Catholics throughout history have led many times to divisions within Christianity and sometimes have continued to keep those divisions alive.

As the Fathers of the Second Vatican Council stated:

> **Although the Catholic Church has been endowed with all divinely revealed truth and with all means of grace, yet its members fail to live by them with all the fervor that they should, so that the radiance of the Church's image is less clear in the eyes of our separated brethren and of the world at large, and the growth of God's kingdom is delayed.** (*Unitatis Redintegratio*, 4)

Catholics are called to embrace the ecumenical movement in the same manner that the Church has: with a deep desire for the visible union of all Christians and a firm commitment to preserving the teachings handed on to us by Christ.

CONCLUSION

Ecumenism is working toward Christian unity or reunification, and, as members of the Church, we are called to engage in ecumenism. As we follow the history of Christian division and ecumenism up to the present age, we can survey the landscape with a measure of hope. Yes, the schisms and disagreements, sometimes demonstrated with acrimonious words and even violence, have severely wounded the unity of Christendom. There is much to forgive and much blame to be shared on all sides of these conflicts.

At the same time, Christianity has survived. Although divided, there remains abundant faith in the world in the name of Jesus Christ. Most importantly, the Catholic Church, despite the shortcomings of her faithful over the centuries, remains standing and strong, imbued as she is with the guidance and truth of the Holy Spirit and the assurance from Christ that "the powers of death shall not prevail against" his Church.[22]

In addition, today there is broad recognition among Christians that unity is important, something that we have an obligation to seek through prayer, lived testimony, charity, dialogue, and the renewal of our personal faith and faith communities. Christians everywhere are learning to work and pray together in hopes of arriving at true unity someday. While truth cannot be comprised, there is much to gain in knowing our separated brothers and sisters. We do not know exactly how reunification will happen or when, but in faith we do know one thing: We have Christ on our side, who wills that "all may be one." Ecumenism, at its heart, is an act of faith.

Sts. Peter and Paul Present God's Temple, Byzantine icon. The Catholic Church, despite the shortcomings of her faithful over the centuries, remains standing and strong.

CHALLENGES:

It seems as though Christianity is divided beyond repair. Is there any hope for unity?

Christianity has splintered on so many levels that it can indeed seem divided beyond any hope of reconciliation. There are so many issues, so many disagreements, and such divergent teachings and practices that one can easily despair of ever seeing a united Christendom again. It is seemingly impossible enough to get even one ecclesial community to return to full communion with the Catholic Church; how much tougher will it be for tens of thousands of Orthodox churches, Protestant denominations, and independent Christian communities to come together as one?

Although a number of groups have returned to full communion with the Church sporadically over the intervening centuries after the historic schisms in Christendom, a comprehensive and widespread movement toward Christian unity did not really develop until the twentieth century. From within the Catholic Church came the idea for an Octave of Prayer for Christian Unity in 1908, and Protestant representatives in 1910 organized a World Missionary Conference; in 1948 they formed the World Council of Churches as a way of seeking a degree of unity and cooperation among themselves.

The Second Ecumenical Council of the Vatican (1962-1965) inaugurated the Catholic Church's full embrace of the ecumenical movement. Since then Popes have reached out in conciliatory gestures to Anglican, Orthodox, and Protestant leaders, and entire Vatican offices are devoted to ecumenical and interreligious relations. In the intervening decades the Church has initiated and sponsored numerous dialogues and meetings with representatives and theologians of Orthodox churches and Protestant ecclesial communities in an effort to begin the journey toward full unity. These encounters have included face-to-face discussions of dividing issues and commonalities, shared prayer, and collaborations in human service and charitable causes wherever possible.

Pope Benedict XVI and Lutheran World Federation Bishop Dr. Munib Younan met in December 2010. "We felt encouraged by the way you have been promoting the value of profound and honest theological discernment in ecumenical dialogues,..." (LWT letter to Pope Benedict, February 28, 2013)

Although full unity has yet to be achieved, we are moving in the right direction. Major breakthroughs have also been seen as the fruit of theological dialogue.

In 1999 after years of dialogue, the Catholic Church and the Lutheran World Federation—an organization representing many, but not all, branches of Lutheranism—together issued the *Joint Declaration on the Doctrine of Justification*, which stated that Catholics and Lutherans share "a common understanding of our justification by God's grace through faith in Christ." Justification by faith, of course, was one of the major doctrinal foundations of the Reformation under Martin Luther, and this declaration described how both the Catholic and Lutheran position are in essential agreement but emphasize particular aspects of the same truth. As always, divisions remain: Even some members of the Lutheran World Federation itself rejected the statement. However, the document later was accepted by the World Methodist Conference in 2006.

Meanwhile, the Anglican-Roman Catholic Interfaith Commission (ARCIC), in regular dialogue since 1970, has released several joint statements on subjects including the Eucharist, salvation, authority in the Church, and morality. The most recent statement, *Mary: Grace and Hope in Christ*, was promulgated in 2004. While these statements are not magisterial statements and do not necessarily draw Catholics and Anglicans into closer communion, they do constitute progress in developing common understandings of theological issues that may lay the foundation for future Christian unity.

All this may sound like very little has been accomplished. Yet, as is the case with evangelization, although we are the ones who engage in dialogue and witness with other Christians and persons of other faiths, we are not the ones who can change their hearts. That is the work of the Holy Spirit. We must do all we can, as individual believers and as a Church, to seek and achieve true Christian unity, but the rest is up to the Holy Spirit. And since we know we have the Holy Spirit behind us and we know that with God all things are possible, we can move forward certainly with great ecumenical hope.

PILLARS OF THE FAITH

BL. MARIA GABRIELLA SAGHEDDU

It was not until the second half of the twentieth century that Catholics by and large embraced ecumenism. But that does not mean that no Catholic understood the importance of unity among Christians before that time. For example, in 1908 the Catholic Church promoted an Octave for Prayer for Christian Unity. At that time Catholics also began to become more involved in ecumenical work within the boundaries set by Rome, and many more began to pray earnestly for Christian unity. One such soul was Sister Maria Gabriella Sagheddu.

Bl. Maria Gabriella was born in 1914 in Sardinia, the fifth of eight children, and was by all accounts a normal child: not overly pious or exceptionally well behaved. But after the death of her older sister when Bl. Maria Gabriella was sixteen, she reexamined her life. She became more serious about prayer and helping those in need. Eventually she felt that God was calling her to the religious life, and she became a Trappist nun.

One day a booklet arrived at the convent promoting the Week of Christian Unity. Bl. Maria Gabriella was moved by the mission of Christian Unity and began to pray fervently for the reunion of all Christians. Eventually, she went to her superior and asked that she be allowed to offer her life formally for Christian Unity. After some discussion, her superior and the chaplain agreed.

Shortly after her offering, she felt a pain in her shoulder. Her health quickly deteriorated and she was diagnosed with tuberculosis, which was fatal in her era.

Bl. Maria Gabriella Sagheddu
(1914-1939)

For months Bl. Maria Gabriella suffered tremendously at the hands of this dreaded affliction. But throughout her struggles she offered herself, like Christ offered himself, that all might be one. Finally, on April 23, 1939, she died with a smile on her face, content that she had offered her life to God.

On January 25, 1983—at the end of that year's Week of Prayer for Christian Unity—St. John Paul II beatified Bl. Maria Gabriella. Twelve years later in his great encyclical on ecumenism, he wrote:

Continued

BL. MARIA GABRIELLA SAGHEDDU

Continued

Praying for unity is not a matter reserved only to those who actually experience the lack of unity among Christians. It was in order to reaffirm this duty that I set before the faithful of the Catholic Church a model which I consider exemplary, the model of a Trappistine Sister, Blessed Maria Gabriella of Unity, whom I beatified on 25 January 1983.[23] Sister Maria Gabriella, called by her vocation to be apart from the world, devoted her life to meditation and prayer centered on chapter seventeen of Saint John's Gospel, and offered her life for Christian unity. This is truly the cornerstone of all prayer: the total and unconditional offering of one's life to the Father, through the Son, in the Holy Spirit. The example of Sister Maria Gabriella is instructive; it helps us to understand that there are no special times, situations or places of prayer for unity. Christ's prayer to the Father is offered as a model for everyone, always and everywhere. (*Ut Unum Sint*, 27)

Christ Taking Leave of the Apostles by Duccio.
After the death of Bl. Maria Gabriella, it was noted that in her Bible, Chapter 17 of St. John's Gospel had become yellowed and worn from being read often.
"I do not pray for these only, but also for those who believe in me through their word, that they may all be one; even as thou, Father, art in me, and I in thee, that they also may be in us, so that the world may believe that thou hast sent me." (Jn 17: 20-21)

SUPPLEMENTARY READING

Elements of Truth Exist Outside the Boundaries of the Catholic Church

Even in the beginnings of this one and only Church of God there arose certain rifts,[24] which the Apostle strongly condemned.[25] But in subsequent centuries much more serious dissensions made their appearance and quite large communities came to be separated from full communion with the Catholic Church—for which, often enough, men of both sides were to blame. The children who are born into these Communities and who grow up believing in Christ cannot be accused of the sin involved in the separation, and the Catholic Church embraces upon them as brothers, with respect and affection. For men who believe in Christ and have been truly baptized are in communion with the Catholic Church even though this communion is imperfect. The differences that exist in varying degrees between them and the Catholic Church—whether in doctrine and sometimes in discipline, or concerning the structure of the Church—do indeed create many obstacles, sometimes serious ones, to full ecclesiastical communion. The ecumenical movement is striving to overcome these obstacles. But even in spite of them it remains true that all who have been justified by faith in Baptism are members of Christ's body,[26] and have a right to be called Christian, and so are correctly accepted as brothers by the children of the Catholic Church.[27]

Moreover, some and even very many of the significant elements and endowments which together go to build up and give life to the Church itself, can exist outside the visible boundaries of the Catholic Church: the written word of God; the life of grace; faith, hope and charity, with the other interior gifts of the Holy Spirit, and visible elements too. All of these, which come from Christ and lead back to Christ, belong by right to the one Church of Christ.

The brethren divided from us also use many liturgical actions of the Christian religion. These most certainly can truly engender a life of grace in ways that vary according to the condition of each Church or Community. These liturgical actions must be regarded as capable of giving access to the community of salvation.

It follows that the separated Churches[28] and Communities as such, though we believe them to be deficient in some respects, have been by no means deprived of significance and importance in the mystery of salvation. For the Spirit of Christ has not refrained from using them as means of salvation which derive their efficacy from the very fullness of grace and truth entrusted to the Church.

Nevertheless, our separated brethren, whether considered as individuals or as Communities and Churches, are not blessed with that unity which Jesus Christ wished to bestow on all those who through Him were born again into one body, and with Him quickened to newness of life—that unity which the Holy Scriptures and the ancient Tradition of the Church proclaim. For it is only through Christ's Catholic Church, which is "the all-embracing means of salvation," that they can benefit fully from the means of salvation. We believe that Our Lord entrusted all the blessings of the New Covenant to the apostolic college alone, of which Peter is the head, in order to establish the one Body of Christ on earth to which all should be fully incorporated who belong in any way to the people of God. This people of God, though still in its members liable to sin, is ever growing in Christ during its pilgrimage on earth, and is guided by God's gentle wisdom, according to His hidden designs, until it shall happily arrive at the fullness of eternal glory in the heavenly Jerusalem.

— Second Ecumenical Council of the Vatican, Decree on Ecumenism *Unitatis Redintegratio*, 3

VOCABULARY

ANGLO-CATHOLIC
Term to describe persons, beliefs, and practices within the Anglican Communion that embrace Catholic heritage and identity to a significant degree.

BRANCH THEORY
A concept held by some Anglicans that the Catholic Church, the Orthodox Churches, and Anglican Communion form three branches of the one, holy, catholic, and apostolic Church.

NOVENA
A private or public devotion, usually lasting nine days, in order to obtain special graces.

OCTAVE OF CHRISTIAN UNITY
Also called the Week of Prayer for Christian Unity. An eight-day period, extending from January 18 (St. Peter's Chair at Rome in the Extraordinary Form; also referred to as the Feast of St. Peter's Confession by Anglicans and Lutherans) to January 25 (Feast of the Conversion of St. Paul the Apostle), designated especially for ecumenical prayer among all Christians.

OXFORD MOVEMENT
A nineteenth-century movement among faculty at Oxford University advocating the Branch Theory and calling for the Anglican Communion to move closer to its Catholic roots in liturgy and practice. It led directly to the rise of Anglo-Catholicism.

PERSONAL ORDINARIATE
A canonical structure in the Catholic Church that allows Anglicans to enter full communion with the Church while retaining elements of their Anglican spirituality and liturgical tradition.

Archbishop Christodoulos (1939-2008) consented to the Greek government's decision to allow St. Pope John Paul II to visit Greece in 2001. He commented that he would not "close the door" on the Pope, because he was coming to the country as a pilgrim.

STUDY QUESTIONS

1. What was the Oxford Movement? What were its aims? What effect did it have on the Anglican Communion?
2. Describe "Branch Theory."
3. Name several groups or initiatives that foster positive ecumenical relations through prayer.
4. Why does the Catholic Church hold greater hope for reunion with Orthodox than Protestants?
5. What is an Anglican Ordinariate?
6. What are seven key requirements for effective ecumenical work?
7. Why is conversion of the heart necessary for ecumenism?
8. What is the role of shared prayer in the ecumenical movement?
9. What would constitute a "false ecumenism"? Give examples.
10. How have anti-Christian activities in recent years helped the ecumenical movement?
11. What is *Unitatis Redintegratio*?
12. What are the two principal types of division according to *Unitatis Redintegratio*?

PRACTICAL EXERCISES

1. Prayer services in which Catholics and non-Catholic Christians pray together are not uncommon today. Explain the potential benefits and potential problems of this type of prayer service.

2. Read one of the magisterial documents on ecumenism mentioned in this chapter written before the Second Vatican Council. How does the language of *Unitatis Redintegratio* differ from this older document?

Archbishop of Canterbury Dr. Rowan Williams and Pope Benedict XVI during the Pope's Apostolic Journey to Great Britain in 2010.

FROM THE CATECHISM

822 Concern for achieving unity "involves the whole Church, faithful and clergy alike."[29] But we must realize "that this holy objective—the reconciliation of all Christians in the unity of the one and only Church of Christ—transcends human powers and gifts." That is why we place all our hope "in the prayer of Christ for the Church, in the love of the Father for us, and in the power of the Holy Spirit."[30]

1127 Celebrated worthily in faith, the sacraments confer the grace that they signify.[31] They are *efficacious* because in them Christ himself is at work: it is he who baptizes, he who acts in his sacraments in order to communicate the grace that each sacrament signifies. The Father always hears the prayer of his Son's Church which, in the epiclesis of each sacrament, expresses her faith in the power of the Spirit. As fire transforms into itself everything it touches, so the Holy Spirit transforms into the divine life whatever is subjected to his power.

1128 This is the meaning of the Church's affirmation[32] that the sacraments act *ex opere operato* (literally: "by the very fact of the action's being performed"), i.e., by virtue of the saving work of Christ, accomplished once for all. It follows that "the sacrament is not wrought by the righteousness of either the celebrant or the recipient, but by the power of God."[33] From the moment that a sacrament is celebrated in accordance with the intention of the Church, the power of Christ and his Spirit acts in and through it, independently of the personal holiness of the minister. Nevertheless, the fruits of the sacraments also depend on the disposition of the one who receives them.

2790 Grammatically, "our" qualifies a reality common to more than one person. There is only one God, and he is recognized as Father by those who, through faith in his only Son, are reborn of him by water and the Spirit.[34] The *Church* is this new communion of God and men. United with the only Son, who has become "the firstborn among many brethren," she is in communion with one and the same Father in one and the same Holy Spirit.[35] In praying "our" Father, each of the baptized is praying in this communion: "The company of those who believed were of one heart and soul."[36]

2791 For this reason, in spite of the divisions among Christians, this prayer to "our" Father remains our common patrimony and an urgent summons for all the baptized. In communion by faith in Christ and by Baptism, they ought to join in Jesus' prayer for the unity of his disciples.[37]

2792 Finally, if we pray the Our Father sincerely, we leave individualism behind, because the love that we receive frees us from it. The "our" at the beginning of the Lord's Prayer, like the "us" of the last four petitions, excludes no one. If we are to say it truthfully, our divisions and oppositions have to be overcome.[38]

2793 The baptized cannot pray to "our" Father without bringing before him all those for whom he gave his beloved Son. God's love has no bounds, neither should our prayer.[39] Praying "our" Father opens to us the dimensions of his love revealed in Christ: praying with and for all who do not yet know him, so that Christ may "gather into one the children of God."[40] God's care for all men and for the whole of creation has inspired all the great practitioners of prayer; it should extend our prayer to the full breadth of love whenever we dare to say "our" Father.

Christ Handing the Keys to St. Peter (detail) by Perugino.
Because we know we have the Holy Spirit behind us, and we know that with God all things are possible, we can move forward with great ecumenical hope.

ENDNOTES – CHAPTER SIX

1. Jn 17:11.
2. Cf. 1 Tm 3:15.
3. *UR* 11.
4. Jn 17:21; cf. Heb 7:25.
5. Cf. the encyclical letter of Pope Pius XI fostering true religious unity, *Mortalium Animos*: AAS 20 (1928) 5 ff.
6. *UR* 13.
7. Cf. *LG* 23; Congregation for the Doctrine of the Faith, Letter *Communionis Notio*, 12; 13.
8. Mt 28:19.
9. Mt 24:14.
10. Cf. *UR* 6.
11. *UR* 7 § 3.
12. *UR* 8 § 1.
13. Cf. *UR* 9.
14. Cf. *UR* 10.
15. Cf. *UR* 4; 9; 11.
16. Cf. *UR* 12.
17. *LG* 8 § 3.
18. Cf. Eph 4:24.
19. Mt 18:20.
20. Cf. Eph 3:8.
21. Messori, Vittorio. *The Ratzinger Report: An Exclusive Interview on the State of the Church.* (San Francisco: Ignatius Press) 1985.
22. Mt 16:18.
23. Maria Sagheddu was born at Dorgali (Sardinia) in 1914. At twenty-one years of age she entered the Trappistine Monastery in Grottaferrata. Through the apostolic labors of Abbé Paul Couturier, she came to understand the need for prayers and spiritual sacrifices for the unity of Christians. In 1936, at the time of an *Octave for Unity*, she chose to offer her life for the unity of the Church. Following a grave illness, Sister Maria Gabriella died on April 23, 1939.
24. Cf. 1 Cor 11:18-19; Gal 1:6-9; 1 Jn. 2:18-19.
25. Cf. 1 Cor 1:11 sqq; 11:22.
26. Cf. Conc. Florentinum, Sess. VIII (1439), *Decretum Exultate Deo*: Mansi 31, 1055 A.
27. Cf. S. Augustinus, In Ps. 32, *Enarr.* 11, 29: PL 36, 299.
28. Cf. Conc. Lateranense IV (1215) Constitutio IV: Mansi 22, 990; Conc. Lugdunense II (1274), *Professio fidei Michaelis Palaeologi*: Mansi 24, 71 E; Conc. Florentinum, Sess. VI (1439), *Definitio Laetentur Caeli*: Mansi 31, 1026 E.
29. *UR* 5.
30. *UR* 24 § 2.
31. Cf. Council of Trent (1547): DS 1605; DS 1606.
32. Cf. Council of Trent (1547): DS 1608.
33. St. Thomas Aquinas, *STh* III, 68, 8.
34. Cf. 1 Jn 5:1; Jn 3:5.
35. Rom 8:29; cf. Eph 4:4-6.
36. Acts 4:32.
37. Cf. *UR* 8; 22.
38. Cf. Mt 5:23-24; 6:14-15.
39. Cf. *NA* 5.
40. Jn 11:52.

CHAPTER 7

Relations Between the Catholic Church and the Jewish People

The Jewish people are the original People of God, while Christians are the new People of God.

Ecumenism and Interreligious Dialogue

CHAPTER SEVEN

Relations Between the Catholic Church and the Jewish People

INTRODUCTION

ntil now, we have been concerned with the relationship of the Catholic Church with other Christian churches and ecclesial communities. Over the previous two chapters, we have explored the two main divisions that occurred within Christendom: the Eastern schisms and the Protestant Reformation. These discussions concern the relationship and dialogue among Christians.

But Christians make up only about one-third of the world's population. What about the rest of the world? What about the relationship between the Catholic Church and non-Christians? Strictly speaking, such relationships do not fall under the umbrella of ecumenism but to what is referred to as interfaith relations or *interreligious dialogue*. This will be the topic of the next two chapters.

In this chapter, we will explore in particular the relationship of the Church with the Jewish religion, formally called Judaism. We will discuss:

- What is interreligious dialogue, and why is it important?
- What is unique about the relationship between the Catholic Church and the Jewish people?
- What are some commonalities and differences between Catholicism and Judaism?
- What has been done in recent decades to improve Catholic-Jewish relations and heal the regrettable anti-Semitism perpetuated by some Catholics in centuries past?
- What is the nature and purpose of Catholic-Jewish dialogue moving forward?

The Presentation of Jesus in the Temple by Lorenzetti. "And when the time came for their purification according to the law of Moses, they brought him up to Jerusalem to present him to the Lord." (Lk 2:22)

Pope John Paul II's World Day of Prayer for Peace in Assisi, Italy, October 27, 1986.
St. John Paul II brought together 160 religious leaders from all over the world: Catholic, Protestant, and Orthodox Christians, representatives of Hinduism, Sikhism, Buddhism, Judaism, Islam, African and North American animists, Shintoism, Zoroastrianism, and Baha'i. "For the first time in history, we have come together from every where,...in this sacred place dedicated to Saint Francis, to witness before the world, each according to his own conviction, about the transcendent quality of peace." —St. John Paul II

WHY INTERRELIGIOUS DIALOGUE?

Interreligious dialogue is the name given to the dialogue between the Catholic Church and non-Catholic religions. Although interreligious dialogue is distinct from ecumenism, the two initiatives bear much in common. Both involve building bridges of understanding and working together toward shared goals; both often seek in part to overcome old wounds and stereotypes.

Both initiatives also are linked to the mission Christ gave to his Church, for Christ desired unity not only for all Christians but also for all people. Scripture tells us that God "desires all men to be saved and to come to the knowledge of the truth,"[1] which is why Christ directed his Apostles to "make disciples of all nations, baptizing them in the name of the Father and of the Son and of the Holy Spirit, teaching them to observe all that I have commanded you."[2]

Interreligious dialogue, therefore, is related to *evangelization* as well. In his 1990 encyclical *Redemptoris Missio*, St. John Paul II stated plainly:

> Inter-religious dialogue is a part of the Church's evangelizing mission. Understood as a method and means of mutual knowledge and enrichment, dialogue is not in opposition to the mission *ad gentes*;[3] indeed, it has special links with that mission and is one of its expressions. This mission, in fact, is addressed to those who do not know Christ and his Gospel, and who belong for the most part to other religions. (*Redemptoris Missio*, 55)

Yet, the saintly Pope went on to state that interreligious dialogue and evangelization, although intimately connected, are not one and the same: They "should not be confused, manipulated or regarded as identical, as though they were interchangeable."[4] So while it may sound like a contradiction in terms, the Church's purpose in interreligious dialogue is to proclaim the truths of the Catholic faith while respecting the dignity of those who do not hold to that faith. This is done in the hope that the Holy Spirit might lead them toward the one true Church. A greater familiarity with the faith of others can also enrich our own faith. Thus, our relations with different types of non-Christians—Jews, Muslims, Hindus, Buddhists, atheists, and a host of other groups—can help us examine our common beliefs and practices truthfully in order for all to advance toward the Truth.

> Men expect from the various religions answers to the unsolved riddles of the human condition, which today, even as in former times, deeply stir the hearts of men: What is man? What is the meaning, the aim of our life? What is moral good, what sin? Whence suffering and what purpose does it serve? Which is the road to true happiness? What are death, judgment and retribution after death? What, finally, is that ultimate inexpressible mystery which encompasses our existence: whence do we come, and where are we going? (*Nostra Ætate*, 1)

Because of the diversity of answers that the different religions of the world give to these questions, the Catholic Church approaches each group differently, but all these discussions come under the heading of interreligious dialogue.

Christianity has a long history of recognizing truth no matter where it is found. If something is true, it is true no matter who believes it. In the second century St. Justin Martyr, the first great apologist of the Church, noted that "seeds of the Word" had been planted throughout the world. St. Justin had been a philosopher, and he recognized that many of the great philosophers of the Greek tradition had discovered truths about man and the world long before the advent of Christ. These truths are "seeds" planted by God throughout the world in various cultures throughout the centuries. Yet, the fullness of truth can only be found in the Word of God, Jesus Christ. To interreligious dialogue falls the task of discovering these seeds of truth and understanding them better.

> **The Catholic Church rejects nothing that is true and holy in these religions. She regards with sincere reverence those ways of conduct and of life, those precepts and teachings which, though differing in many aspects from the ones she holds and sets forth, nonetheless often reflect a ray of that Truth which enlightens all men. Indeed, she proclaims, and ever must proclaim Christ "the way, the truth, and the life" (Jn 14: 6), in whom men may find the fullness of religious life, in whom God has reconciled all things to Himself.[5] (*Nostra Ætate*, 2)**

As Christians we know of only one way to salvation: Baptism. We are unable to judge the eternal salvation of those who do not profess and follow Jesus Christ as the Risen Lord. God is not bound to the Sacraments.[6] We hope for all to be saved and leave judgment to the mercy of God.

> **Those also can attain to salvation who through no fault of their own do not know the Gospel of Christ or His Church, yet sincerely seek God and moved by grace strive by their deeds to do His will as it is known to them through the dictates of conscience.[7] Nor does Divine Providence deny the helps necessary for salvation to those who, without blame on their part, have not yet arrived at an explicit knowledge of God and with His grace strive to live a good life. Whatever good or truth is found amongst them is looked upon by the Church as a preparation for the Gospel.[8] (*Lumen Gentium*, 16)**

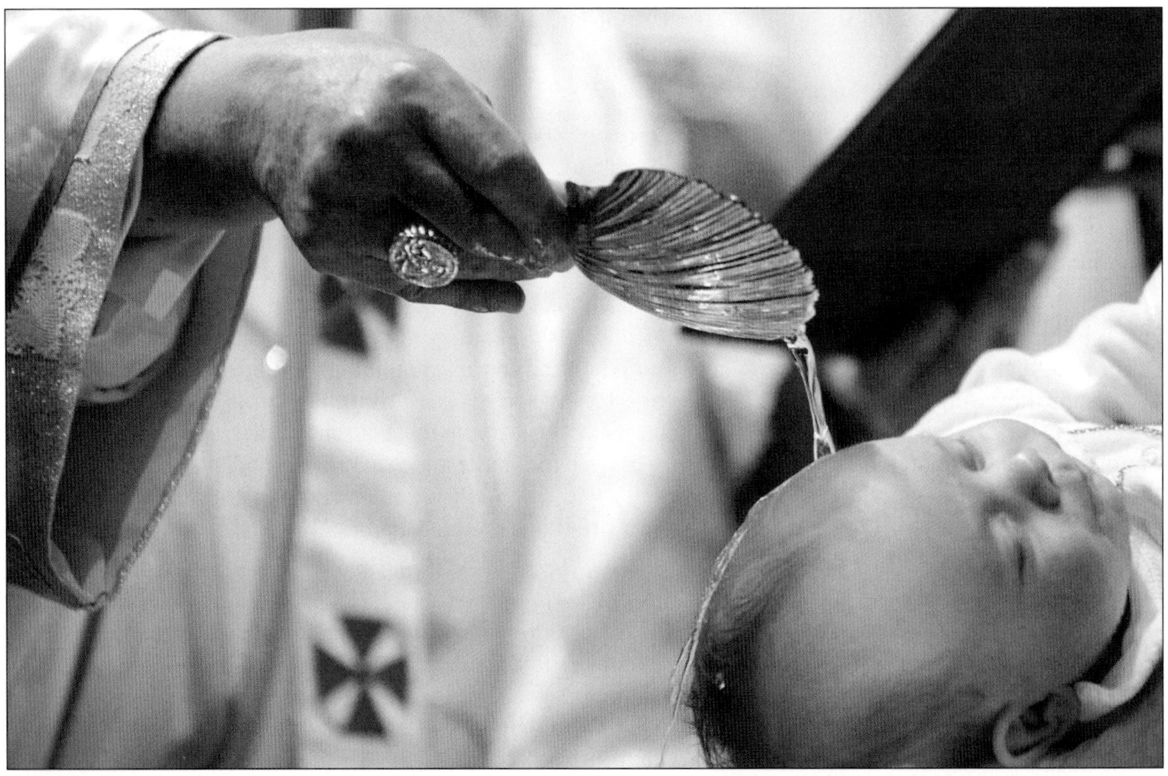

As Christians we know of only one way to salvation: Baptism.

Moses on Mount Sinai by Gerome.
In the history of salvation, God chose a people as his own and formed them into the nation of Israel. They were the first to hear the Word of God, the first to receive Divine Revelation.

THE JEWS, THE CHOSEN PEOPLE

Only one non-Christian religion received God's true Revelation, making it unique among all non-Christian creeds. That religion is the religion of the patriarchs Abraham, Isaac, and Jacob, and it is also the religion of the Blessed Virgin Mary, St. Joseph, and Jesus Christ. It became known eventually as Judaism.

In the history of salvation, God chose a people as his own and formed them into the nation of Israel. It was through this nation that he would fulfill his promise of redemption, and it was through Israel that he would bring salvation to the rest of the world. They were the first to hear the Word of God, the first to receive Divine Revelation. They were the special instruments used by God to further his plan of salvation in the world. This is a privilege unique among the nations.

After the reign of Solomon, the nation was divided. The Southern Kingdom of Judah was the only remnant of Israel that retained the knowledge of God and his laws and, henceforth, its people became known as the Jews. Even when conquered and carried away into captivity, they kept their identity as God's Chosen People and prayed for the coming of the Messiah, who indeed was born a Jew. This is what Christ meant when he declared, "Salvation is from the Jews."[9]

Because of this Judaism and Christianity are intricately linked. Christianity was formed in the womb of the Jewish faith and is firmly rooted in this tradition.

> When she delves into her own mystery, the Church, the People of God in the New Covenant, discovers her link with the Jewish People,[10] "the first to hear the Word of God."[11] The Jewish faith, unlike other non-Christian religions, is already a response to God's revelation in the Old Covenant. To the Jews "belong the sonship, the glory, the covenants, the giving of the law, the worship, and the promises; to them belong the patriarchs, and of their race, according to the flesh, is the Christ";[12] "for the gifts and the call of God are irrevocable."[13] (CCC 839)

Based on centuries of teachings uttered by the prophets, the Jews at the time of Christ eagerly awaited their promised Messiah. Many expected the Messiah to come as a great and powerful king or perhaps a military leader who would free the Jews from Roman occupation. Few if any thought that the Messiah would come as an infant born in poverty who would work as a carpenter before becoming an itinerant preacher in his adulthood. Few if any expected his message to highlight love, self-sacrifice, and forgiveness of enemies. Few thought he would reach out to the worst of sinners and be so critical of even the leading Jewish authorities of his time. No one expected their Messiah to die an ignominious death, crucified like a violent criminal.

Perhaps just as difficult for many Jews was the notion that the Messiah had come to save Gentiles as well as Jews, seemingly erasing the favored status long accorded by God to the people of Israel. Given such expectations, we can understand how many Jewish people of Christ's day might have been reluctant to accept him or his Gospel.

Most of the first Christians were Jews who recognized Jesus of Nazareth as the Messiah promised in the Scriptures. God became man as a Jew, and Christ lived faithfully as a Jew in his time. We share with the Jewish people the same ancestors in the faith: Abraham, Moses, David and all the great figures of the Old Testament whom God used to advance our salvation. The Jewish people are the original People of God, while Christians are the New People of God.

> When one considers the future, God's People of the Old Covenant and the new People of God tend towards similar goals: expectation of the coming (or the return) of the Messiah. But one awaits the return of the Messiah who died and rose from the dead and is recognized as Lord and Son of God; the other awaits the coming of a Messiah, whose features remain hidden till the end of time; and the latter waiting is accompanied by the drama of not knowing or of misunderstanding Christ Jesus. (CCC 840)

Jesus Among the Doctors by Ingres.
God became man as a Jew, and Christ lived faithfully as a Jew in his time.

Unlike some other faiths Christianity at its beginning did not proclaim itself a new religion but rather as the fulfillment of an existing religion. Christ said, "Think not that I have come to abolish the law and the prophets [of the Old Testament]; I have come not to abolish them but to fulfill them."[14]

Christianity, in fact, cannot be understood without some knowledge of the Jewish religion. The preaching of the first Christians was that Jesus is the promised Jewish Messiah who had come to save the world from sin. It is only in the context of the many centuries of God's preparation of the world through the Jewish people that the mission of Christ makes sense. The Sacrifice of Christ on the Cross, for example, can be fully understood only as the fulfillment of the Old Testament sacrifices, which were attempts to atone for the sins of the people.

The New Covenant with God was established by Christ with his Church, and Christianity has always participated in this covenant. But if Christianity is a New Covenant, that implies that there is an Old Covenant that preceded it. This Old Covenant consists of the promise of God to the Israelite people that they would be the means of salvation to the whole world. As we discussed in earlier chapters, it is this Old Covenant that Christians believe God fulfilled in the Person of Jesus Christ.

The Church recognizes the deep connection between Catholics and Jews. St. John Paul II, in the first visit by a Pope to a synagogue in modern times, noted:

> The Jewish religion is not "extrinsic" to us, but in a certain way is "intrinsic" to our own religion. With Judaism, therefore, we have a relationship that we do not have with any other religion. You are our dearly beloved brothers, and, in a certain way, it could be said that you are our elder brothers.

THE OLD TESTAMENT LAW AND CATHOLICS

he relationship of the Old Testament Law to Christians presented the most challenging controversy of the first century Church. Did new Gentile Christians have to be circumcised, as the Law prescribed for Jews? Did they have to follow the Jewish dietary laws? Did they have to observe all the rituals and ceremonies found in the Old Testament? These issues were debated hotly by the first Christians, and we can catch glimpses of these discussions in the pages of the New Testament, especially in the Acts of the Apostles and the Epistles of St. Paul.

The resolution to this controversy is found in Acts, which recounts the Council of Jerusalem, when the leaders of the Church gathered and determined that the ceremonial law of the Old Testament did not apply to Christians (cf. Acts 15). This decision eventually opened the door for missions to the Gentiles, for no longer did non-Jews have to abide by the Mosaic Law in order to become Christian.

Yet, some parts of the Old Law *are* still binding on Christians—the Ten Commandments, for instance. Yet, eating "unclean food" (such as pork) was an "abomination" (Lv 11:10), and this is something that the Church has permitted since the first century. Why must Christians obey some parts of the Old Testament Law while the observance of other parts have been abandoned?

The beginning of the answer lies in the authority of the Church. We must remember that Christ gave St. Peter and the Apostles the authority to "bind and loose," meaning that they had the authority to interpret the Scriptures properly as well as to determine properly what parts of the Law, if any, were still binding. The Church is guaranteed the guidance of the Holy Spirit to interpret the passages of the Bible.

Secondly, we must understand how the Law is organized in the Old Testament. Several different classifications of laws are found within these passages, but the Scriptures themselves do not distinguish between these different types. Based on Christian Tradition as well as biblical texts, St. Thomas Aquinas distinguished three types of Old Testament law: moral, ceremonial, and judicial. Deuteronomy states, "This is the commandment [moral], the statutes [ceremonial] and the ordinances [judicial] which the Lord your God commanded me to teach you, that you may do them in the land to which you are going over, to possess it" (Dt 6:1). And St. Paul says that the law is "holy [ceremonial] and just [judicial] and good [moral]" (Rom 7:12).

The moral laws are those that deal with human interactions and morality. Ceremonial laws deal with religious ceremonies and activities like the liturgy and ritual sacrifices. The judicial (or civil) laws determine political and legal rules and regulations for the nation of Israel. It makes sense that of these three, only the moral law is still binding on Christians. Liturgical worship was transformed by Christ's redemptive act, and the laws designed to protect God's Chosen People as a political nation are no longer relevant.

Furthermore, the moral law given in the Old Testament, unlike the ceremonial and judicial laws, is part of the natural law, meaning that law which is written on each person's heart at his or her creation. The Commandment against murder found in the Decalogue did not make that activity immoral; it had been immoral since the beginning of time (as can be seen from the story of Cain and Abel). In the same way, the moral commands found in the Law do not make certain activities immoral; they are immoral based on the very nature of our being and thus are binding for all time. The Church does not have the power to change them, for they are part of the way God created us.

BRANCHES OF MODERN JUDAISM

Modern Judaism is not a monolithic religion with a uniform set of beliefs and religious practices. Scripture attests to certain disagreements that existed even in the time of Christ among Jewish sects such as the Pharisees and the Sadducees. The biblical Samaritans, too, were originally an offshoot of the people of Israel that resulted from divergent traditions and practices that developed during the Babylonian and Assyrian exiles. A full-blown separation between Samaritans and Jews was in place by the fourth century BC and very much in evidence during Christ's earthy ministry.

A *Sefer Torah* is a special handwritten copy of the Torah or Pentateuch, the holiest book in Judaism. Orthodox Jews usually uphold traditional commentaries on the Torah and follow the ceremonial rituals closely.

In recent years Judaism has divided over doctrinal and practical matters into three main groups: Orthodox, Conservative, and Reform Judaism. The divisions occurred mostly in the nineteenth century when many Jews began to rethink the application of the Law in their lives. Thus, the major source of disagreement among these groups is their approach to the *Torah*, also called the *Pentateuch*, the first five books of the Bible.

Orthodox Judaism is the strictest of the three groups, maintaining that the Law is divine in origin and should be followed as perfectly as possible. Orthodox Jews usually uphold traditional commentaries on the Torah and follow the ceremonial rituals closely. Most every Orthodox Jew—rabbi or lay—follows the prescriptions of the Law. Because they adhere to traditional interpretations of the Jewish moral code, their teachings on moral issues align closely with Catholic teachings.

Conservative Jews, like their Orthodox counterparts, view the Torah as divinely given. However, unlike Orthodox Jews, Conservative Jews emphasize that the Torah came to us through the medium of human beings. Because of this certain parts of the Law are seen as more God-inspired than others, which engenders a hierarchy of laws. Some parts of the Law are followed more closely than others. While rabbis of the Conservative tradition abide closely by the prescriptions of the Law, most lay people do not.

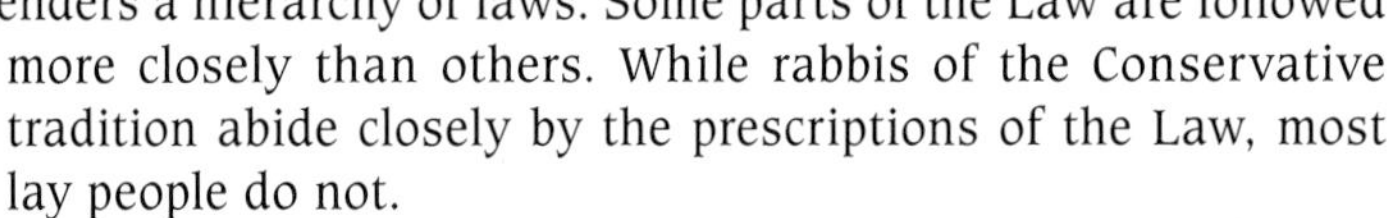

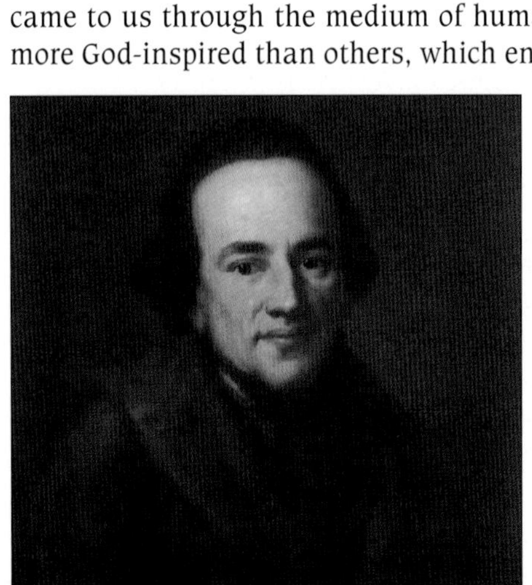

Moses Mendelssohn (1729-86). Considered a father of Reform Judaism, Mendelssohn was the leader of the *Jewish Enlightenment Movement* (or *Berlin Haskalah)* in 18th century Germany. This movement resulted in the division of Western Jews (outside of Israel) into three main groups.

Reform Judaism reinterprets the Law in response to the changes in the Western world. Reform Jews accept the Torah as inspired by God but place greater emphasis on the idea that it came to the world through the mediation of human beings. Because of this they are more likely to interpret the laws of the Torah as not binding on Jews today. Only the ethical laws are considered relevant, and many of these are interpreted in conformity to modern mores. Since the Torah is not considered binding, Reform Jews do not follow its prescriptions closely.

To this list we might add a fourth category, although they do not constitute a formal group. **Secular Jews** are people of Jewish heritage who still identify themselves as Jews but are not Jews in religious practice. Being a secular Jew is chiefly a cultural or familial identity.

In the United States, approximately eleven percent of Jews identify themselves as Orthodox, twenty-five percent as Conservative, and thirty-three percent as Reform Jews. Secular Jews comprise the remaining thirty percent.

Allegory of the Old and New Testaments by Holbein.
The story of God's salvation before the time of Christ—told through the Law, the prophets, and historical writings—is treasured in both the Jewish and Christian faiths.

CATHOLICS AND JEWS: SHARED ELEMENTS OF FAITH

Given the fact that the Church has her origins in the Jewish faith and tradition, it should not surprise us to learn that the two have many things in common. We present just a few of them.

The Scriptures. Christians and Jews share a mutual Scriptural heritage: the Old Testament, known in Hebrew as the *Tanakh*. The story of God's salvation before the time of Christ—told through the Law, the prophets, and historical writings—is treasured in both the Jewish and Christian faiths. This includes the *Torah*, or *Pentateuch*, which in its strictest meaning refers to the first five books of the *Tanakh* (Genesis, Exodus, Leviticus, Numbers, and Deuteronomy).

In the early centuries of Christianity there were movements that saw Christ's coming as a rejection of the Old Testament rather than its fulfillment. As we have seen, certain Gnostic heresies went so far as to believe in two rival gods—the god of the Jews and the god of Jesus. This was rejected vigorously by the Church, which proclaimed the continuity between the two faiths.

The Church has always valued the Old Testament highly in her liturgy, devotional life, and theological reflection. As the *Catechism* states:

> The Church, as early as apostolic times,[15] and then constantly in her Tradition, has illuminated the unity of the divine plan in the two Testaments through typology, which discerns in God's works of the Old Covenant prefigurations of what he accomplished in the fullness of time in the person of his incarnate Son. (CCC 128)
>
> Christians therefore read the Old Testament in the light of Christ crucified and risen. Such typological reading discloses the inexhaustible content of the Old Testament; but it must not make

us forget that the Old Testament retains its own intrinsic value as Revelation reaffirmed by our Lord himself.[16] Besides, the New Testament has to be read in the light of the Old. Early Christian catechesis made constant use of the Old Testament.[17] As an old saying put it, the New Testament lies hidden in the Old and the Old Testament is unveiled in the New.[18] (CCC 129)

It should be noted that within Christianity there is a measure of disagreement as to which books ought to be included in the Old Testament. The early Church adopted the collection of Old Testament books that came to be known as the *Septuagint*, so named because it was a Greek translation made by seventy (in Latin, *septuaginta*) Jewish scholars in the third to second centuries before Christ. This became, with slight variances, the accepted canon of Old Testament Scripture in the Catholic and Orthodox Churches and some Protestant ecclesial communities.

The Decalogue. Both Catholics and Jews respect the Decalogue, or Ten Commandments, as the basis of their moral codes. These Commandments, which simply reinforce the natural law present in the hearts of all men, are the origin of Jewish and Christian morality.

In ancient times, when many peoples and nations were living in ways diametrically opposed to God's Law, the Jewish people upheld the Decalogue as the ideal moral behavior that all men and women should strive to live faithfully. Christ ushered in his New Covenant, but explicitly reaffirmed the moral demands of the Decalogue: "If you would enter life, keep the commandments."[19] "If you keep my commandments, you will abide in my love."[20]

The Last Supper (detail) by Carducci. The Eucharist is sometimes called the New Passover because the Mass of the New Covenant is the fulfillment of the Passover of the Old Covenant.

Spiritual life. Christ's Sermon on the Mount,[21] in which he laid the foundations of Christian spiritual life, reveals the strong Jewish influences on Christianity.

As Christ said, he did not come to abolish the Law of Moses but to fulfill it. Thus, his teachings build on the foundation of existing Jewish Law. In his great sermon Christ addresses a number of Jewish laws found in the Old Testament, such as the prohibitions against adultery, divorce, and murder, and reinterprets them in light of his new Revelation.

In the Sermon on the Mount, Christ takes three pillars of Jewish spiritual life—prayer, fasting, and almsgiving—and gives them new meaning. Christ's teaching, "You, therefore, must be perfect, as your heavenly Father is perfect,"[22] is a reflection of God's command to the Israelites: "For I am the Lord your God; consecrate yourselves therefore, and be holy, for I am holy."[23]

The New Law given by Christ, although radical, was also a fulfillment of the existing Jewish Law.

Liturgical life. Liturgical worship is another shared element between the Jewish people and Catholics. The first Christians continued to worship at the Jewish Temple and at their local synagogues on the Sabbath. They also added a gathering on the Lord's Day (Sunday), during which they celebrated Christ's sacrificial Death and Resurrection as instituted by Christ at the Last Supper, that is, the Liturgy of the Eucharist. Over the next decades, there was a parting of the ways, with Christians no longer going to the synagogues on the Sabbath. Milestones along this parting include the expulsion of some apostolic preachers (some being recorded in the Acts of the Apostles), the aftermath of the destruction of the Temple AD 70, and the writings of second-century Fathers of the Church like St. Justin Martyr. Despite this, Christian worship retained many of the elements of the Jewish liturgy such as readings from the Scriptures and prayers of thanksgiving to God, which is preserved in the Liturgy of the Word.

The first Christians, who were predominantly Jewish converts to the faith, saw their liturgical services as a fulfillment of the Jewish liturgy. Instead of attending the Temple sacrifices in which the sacrifices by the priest would have to be repeated over and over to atone for the sins of the people, they gathered to be united to the one Sacrifice of Christ on Calvary, which atones for all sins for all time. The Eucharist is sometimes called the New Passover because the Mass of the New Covenant is the fulfillment of the Passover of the Old Covenant.

Belief in angels. Both Catholics and Jews acknowledge the existence of angels as messengers of God in this world. The Old Testament is full of accounts of angels who intervene on behalf of God in the lives of men, and this belief in angels was maintained in Christianity. In fact, Christ stated that each person has an angel watching over him or her, what we call *guardian angels*: "See that you do not despise one of these little ones; for I tell you that in heaven their angels always behold the face of my Father who is in heaven."[24] Angels are an important part of both the Jewish and Christian spiritual life since they protect us, guide us, and help us in times of trouble.

THE NEW TESTAMENT BOOKS WRITTEN FOR JEWISH CHRISTIANS

hough the first Christians were almost exclusively Jewish converts, most of the New Testament was written either by or for Gentiles. The Epistles of St. Paul are all geared toward a Gentile Christian audience; the Gospel of St. Luke and the Acts of the Apostles were written by the Gentile convert St. Luke; and the writings of St. John were written primarily after the Church had become predominantly Gentile in her composition. Three writings of the New Testament, however, do have heavy Jewish influences: the Gospel of St. Matthew, the Epistle to the Hebrews, and the Epistle of St. James.

Gospel of St. Matthew

The Gospel of St. Matthew was written by the Apostle St. Matthew. Like all the Apostles, St. Matthew was a Jew by birth although he was despised by his countrymen because he was a Roman tax collector. In a dramatic scene recounted in his own Gospel, he abruptly abandoned collecting taxes to follow Christ when the Lord called him. The Gospel that bears his name was written for new Jewish converts to Christianity. As a means of demonstrating that Jesus is the fulfillment of the Old Testament texts that promise a Messiah, St. Matthew weaves in many elements meaningful to Jews as he relates Christ's story.

St. Matthew wrote in this way to help his fellow Jewish converts. The first converts to Christ from Judaism had an incredible burden to bear. They may have faced estrangement from their families and battled challenges from many of their Jewish brethren regarding their newfound faith. Some were outright persecuted and suffered martyrdom such as St. Stephen.[25] St. Matthew's Gospel encourages them, showing them that Jesus of Nazareth really is the long-awaited Anointed One. For example, early in his Gospel St. Matthew describes various events surrounding the Birth of Christ and then follows each one with a quote from the Scriptures (Old Testament) that these events fulfill. And in the Sermon on the Mount, Christ is presented as a New Moses who brings with him a New Law. In these ways and many more St. Matthew demonstrates to his fellow Jews that Jesus is the Messiah.

Epistle to the Hebrews

The author of the Epistle to the Hebrews had a deep knowledge of the Jewish religion, and his letter demonstrates that Christ is the fulfillment of the Old Testament priesthood. The priesthood is an essential element of the Old Testament Jewish religion, and offering sacrifice to God for the people was the priest's most important task. The Levite priests who offered these sacrifices served as mediators between God and his people. The daily

Continued

THE NEW TESTAMENT BOOKS WRITTEN FOR JEWISH CHRISTIANS

Continued

sacrifice of bulls and goats was an offering made to God on behalf of the people, but these offerings could not take away sin.

The Epistle to the Hebrews reveals that Christ is the new High Priest. But he is not a priest only: He is also the victim of the Sacrifice. Unlike the sacrifice of bulls and goats, the Sacrifice of Christ on Calvary takes away our sins; there is no need for further sacrifice. The priesthood of Christ, therefore, is superior to that of the Levite priests.

The author of Hebrews also links Christ to the mysterious Old Testament figure Melchizedek, a pre-Levite priest who offered bread and wine in the presence of Abraham.[26] Christ is said to be a priest of the "order of Melchizedek,"[27] who comes before the Levites. His self-offering, re-presented now in the bread and wine offered in the Sacrifice of the Mass, truly forgives our sins.

Epistle of St. James

Tradition holds that this Epistle was written by St. James, the first Bishop of Jerusalem. He devotedly followed the Jewish Law his entire life even after becoming Christian. His adherence to the Law was so renowned that Josephus, a first century Jewish historian, in recounting St. James's martyrdom, notes that most Jews were unhappy about the death of a man so faithful to the Law.

The Epistle of St. James is a moral exhortation to live a godly life. The advice in the text is practical, engaging little in theological speculation. It is perhaps best known for its statement that faith must be accompanied by works.

> What does it profit, my brethren, if a man says he has faith but has not works? Can his faith save him? If a brother or sister is ill-clad and in lack of daily food, and one of you says to them, "Go in peace, be warmed and filled," without giving them the things needed for the body, what does it profit? So faith by itself, if it has no works, is dead." (Jas 2:14-17)

More than any other, these three writings—the Gospel of St. Matthew, the Epistle to the Hebrews, and the Epistle of St. James—highlight both the Jewish origins of Christianity as well as the intricate relationship between the two faiths.

CATHOLICS AND JEWS: DIFFERENCES IN BELIEFS AND RELIGIOUS PRACTICES

Catholics and Jews disagree significantly about the Person and mission of Jesus Christ. Catholics believe that he is the promised Messiah and the Son of God, whereas Jews believe him to be anything from an influential Jewish rabbi to a spiritual impostor. This rejection of Jesus as the Messiah and the Son of God is the wedge that divides the two religions. For this reason, Jews obviously do not accept the inspiration of the New Testament as the books therein relate to the Revelation of God in Jesus Christ.

There is, however, a movement that arose in the second half of the twentieth century among ethnic Jews who accepted that Jesus is the promised Messiah and hold to belief in the Blessed Trinity. Called *Messianic Judaism*, this movement claims to be a sect of Judaism much as the first Christians were considered by others as a Jewish sect before they were expelled from the synagogues. Jewish authorities consider the movement a Christian religion; Christians generally see it as a form of Evangelical Christianity.

The term *Hebrew Catholics* refers to a movement comprised of Jews who have converted to the Catholic Church. In full communion with the Catholic Church, they continue to keep various degrees of Jewish traditions that do not conflict with Catholic doctrine such as celebrating Jewish holidays while holding the beliefs and practices of Catholicism.

God, Jesus, and the Blessed Trinity. The Jewish people believe in one God, as Christians do, but reject belief in the Blessed Trinity and the divinity of Christ. Judaism was the first great religion to be *monotheistic*, and ardent *monotheism* has been a defining mark of Judaism since its inception. The Hebrew people maintained this belief in spite of intense pressure to accept the polytheistic practices of neighboring cultures.

When Christianity formed, it maintained this monotheism. But the first Christians were presented with a mystery: how could there be only one God if the Father is God, Jesus is God, and the Holy Spirit is God? This is the mystery of the Trinity, that there are three Persons in one God who share one divine nature. It is a mystery unique to Christianity.

Sacramental economy. The sacramental economy found in Catholicism is based on the Incarnation of the Son of God and is the means by which we live the Christian life. Judaism, on the other hand, relies on the ritual prescriptions found in the Old Testament, although they have been reinterpreted in light of the destruction of the Temple AD 70.

THE DESTRUCTION OF THE TEMPLE (AD 70)

The Temple was more than just a place to gather for the Jewish liturgy; it was the center of Jewish life. At the Temple sacrifices were offered, political leaders assembled, and financial decisions were made. For centuries the Temple *was* Jewish life, and it is unlikely that there was a Jew in the first century who could imagine life without it. This, in fact, was one of the struggles of Jewish converts to the Christian faith who tried to separate themselves from the life of the Temple. Behind much of the preaching of the first Christians was the proclamation that, with the Sacrifice of Christ, the Temple sacrifices were no longer necessary.

Following the destruction of the Temple, there were a few short-lived attempts to restore it, but it was never rebuilt. Eventually, the Jewish religion had to adapt to this new reality. How could the people follow the commands of the Law—many of which concerned the Temple or revolved around it—when there was no Temple? Yet, Judaism endured, developing into a faith centering on local synagogues that reinterpreted the prescriptions of the Law in a post-Temple existence.

Christians believe that the Sacrifice of Christ on the Cross superseded the Temple sacrifices, which were no longer needed. In fact, many Christians interpreted the destruction of the Temple about AD 70 as a sign that confirmed the end of the Old Covenant. Christ seems even to have foretold the destruction of the Temple.

> Jesus left the temple and was going away, when his disciples came to point out to him the buildings of the temple. But he answered them, "You see all these, do you not? Truly, I say to you, there will not be left here one stone upon another, that will not be thrown down." As he sat on the Mount of Olives, the disciples came to him privately, saying, "Tell us, when will this be, and what will be the sign of your coming and of the close of the age?"
> (Mt 24:1-3)

Following a litany of signs of the coming destruction, Christ said, "Truly, I say to you, this generation will not pass away till all these things take place" (Mt 24:34). In Jewish thought, a "generation" is forty years, and the destruction of the Temple occurred AD 70, about forty years after the Death of Christ.

In Catholic theology all the Sacraments originate with Christ, and it is only through Christ's redemptive work that the Sacraments are possible. The Sacraments are the primary means by which God dispenses his grace. Judaism does not have this concept of grace or sacrament. Although the Jews observed rituals that bear certain similarities to the Sacraments—among others, Passover, priestly sacrifices in atonement for the sins of the people, marriage ceremonies, prayers for the sick—these do not function according to the Catholic doctrine of Sacraments.

Concept of Original Sin. For Catholics, one of the fundamental lessons of the story of creation and the Garden of Eden is the doctrine of Original Sin. Because of man's initial rejection of God, all of the descendants of Adam and Eve are conceived lacking original holiness and justice and have the inclination to evil, which is called concupiscence. Almost all of Christian theology related to redemption and salvation is based on this doctrine of Original Sin, for if man is not in need of redemption, there is no need for a Redeemer. St. Paul, in his Epistle to the Romans, laid the foundations for the Christian teaching on Original Sin:

> **As sin came into the world through one man and death through sin, and so death spread to all men because all men sinned—sin indeed was in the world before the law was given, but sin is not counted where there is no law. Yet death reigned from Adam to Moses, even over those whose sins were not like the transgression of Adam, who was a type of the one who was to come. But the free gift is not like the trespass. For if many died through one man's trespass, much more have the grace of God and the free gift in the grace of that one man Jesus Christ abounded for many. And the free gift is not like the effect of that one man's sin. For the judgment following one trespass brought condemnation, but the free gift following many trespasses brings justification. If, because of one man's trespass, death reigned through that one man, much more will those who receive the abundance of grace and the free gift of righteousness reign in life through the one man Jesus Christ. Then as one man's trespass led to condemnation for all men, so one man's act of righteousness leads to acquittal and life for all men. For as by one man's disobedience many were made sinners, so by one man's obedience many will be made righteous.** (Rom 5:12-19)

Sermon on the Mount (detail) by Olrik. In his Sermon on the Mount, Christ gave a new and definitive interpretation of the moral law of the Decalogue.

It might be surprising, then, to learn that the Jewish religion does not accept the teaching on Original Sin. Although the Jews accept the biblical creation account as part of their Sacred Scriptures, they interpret it differently. Jews believe that a person enters the world pure and innocent, untainted by sin. The Jewish faith recognizes the presence of sin in life but believes this sin is due not to concupiscence but to the imperfection of human beings.

Moral teachings. Although both Jews and Catholics base their moral code on the Decalogue, the two faiths diverge significantly in the application of that code in their moral teachings. Christ, in his Sermon on the Mount, gave a new and definitive interpretation of the moral law, and this new interpretation is the foundation of Christian morality. Jews, of course, do not accept as definitive Christ's interpretations. The Law of Moses still forms the basis of their moral code.

Much of Jewish morality is consistent with Catholic teachings: an emphasis on justice and peace, compassion for those in need, and respect for the dignity of human life are all principles found in Judaism. Some forms of modern Judaism, however, have abandoned the traditional teachings on practices such as divorce, abortion, and contraception.

OBSTACLES TO DIALOGUE

Anti-Semitism

Anti-Semitism is discrimination against or hatred of Jews. The term *Semite* refers more broadly to the peoples of the Middle East, including Arabs and Shia Muslims, but anti-Semitism is used exclusively to refer to hatred of Jews. It is useful to distinguish anti-Semitism from anti-Judaism, which is the hatred of Jews for their religious beliefs. Both anti-Judaism and anti-Semitism represent sinful and unjust treatment of the Jewish people.

The history of anti-Semitism spans many peoples and cultures. In the centuries between the call of Abraham and the Birth of Christ, the people of Israel suffered war, enslavement, exile, conquest, and foreign occupation. Because their monotheistic faith led them to refuse to worship the pagan idols favored by their oppressors, they were subject often to persecution, discrimination, and even acts of genocide.[28]

In the early Christian era, evidence from Acts and the Epistles of St. Paul indicate that there were tensions between Jews and Christians in some places and harmonious relationships in others. During the period when the followers of Christ worshiped in the Temple and the synagogues alongside the Jews, the Jewish authorities sometimes regarded the Christians as heretics. Sometimes they conspired with the Romans to have Christians persecuted just as some Jewish leaders plotted against Christ.

The dispensation granted to the Gentile converts at the Council of Jerusalem and the destruction of the Temple by the Romans hastened the institutional separation between Jews and Christians. Scholars suggest that Christians were expelled from worship in the synagogues formally by the end of the first century. Nevertheless, Jews and Christians were both subject to oppression under Roman rule during the first few centuries after Christ and got along relatively well.

Destruction of the Temple in Jerusalem by Titus by Poussin. The destruction of the Temple in AD 70 is still mourned annually as the Jewish fast Tisha B'Av. The destruction of the Temple by the Romans hastened the institutional separation between Jews and Christians.

Increasingly, Jews found their civil rights and religious freedoms restricted in many places and in many ways. There were campaigns of forced conversions, attacks against synagogues, confiscation of property, and occasional massacres. Jews were accused of the ritual murder of Christian children (such accusations were called *blood libel*) and of conspiring with Muslim invaders against the Roman and Byzantine Empires. Some Christians blamed them for the Black Death, the spread of the bubonic plague that killed about one-third of Europe's population in the mid-fourteenth century. Crusaders who sought to liberate the Holy Land from the Muslims sometimes did violence to Jewish settlements along the way. Jews were sometimes expelled wholesale from cities and even entire nations, as in the case of England (1290), France (1394), and Spain (1492).

Few of these injustices had official Church support, and, in fact, numerous Popes and Church leaders did much to combat these abuses.

The Charge of "Deicide"

Because there were Jewish leaders involved in the Death of Christ, some Christians through the centuries have falsely labeled Jews as guilty of having killed God, or *deicide*.

Such corporate blame of the Jews for the Death of Christ has never been the teaching of the Church. The Church has condemned this attitude explicitly several times since at least the Council of Trent in the sixteenth century, which blamed the Crucifixion of Christ on Original Sin and the sins of all people:

> In this guilt are involved all those who fall frequently into sin; for, as our sins consigned Christ the Lord to the death of the cross, most certainly those who wallow in sin and iniquity crucify to themselves again the Son of God, as far as in them lies, and make a mockery of Him. This guilt seems more enormous in us than in the Jews, since according to the testimony of the same Apostle: If they had known it, they would never have crucified the Lord of glory; while we, on the contrary, professing to know Him, yet denying Him by our actions, seem in some sort to lay violent hands on him. (*Roman Catechsim*, "The Creed," Article 4)

THE GOSPEL OF ST. JOHN AND "THE JEWS"

serious charge against the Gospel of St. John is that it fosters anti-Semitism. This charge originates in the fact that St. John refers to the enemies of Christ often as "the Jews." Instead of singling out specific groups of Jews—such as the Pharisees or the Sanhedrin—as responsible for the hostilities against Christ, St. John simply puts these actions at the feet of "the Jews."

First, let us remember the protagonists of St. John's Gospel: Christ, the Apostles, and the Blessed Virgin Mary—all Jews. Almost everyone surrounding Christ was a Jew, and the only people considered on the outside would be the occupying Roman soldiers. Thus, at least *some* Jews were on the side of Christ during this conflict.

Second, the author of the Gospel is himself Jewish. He presents very clearly that Christ is the fulfillment of the promises made by God to the Jewish people. Christ is the New Passover Lamb "who takes away the sin of the world" (Jn 1: 29). St. John's themes are not anti-Jewish, for they presuppose that the Jews are God's Chosen People through whom God works to save the world.

Also, in many cases when St. John uses the term "Jews" he is actually referring only to some Jewish religious leaders, a fact that is clear from the context. For example, in John 1: 19, we read, "This is the testimony of John, when the Jews sent priests and Levites from Jerusalem to ask him, 'Who are you?'" The only meaning that makes sense in this passage is to mean Jewish religious leaders, for *all* Jews could not have sent priests and Levites to question St. John the Baptist. So, many passages that mention "the Jews" refer to just some Jewish leaders.

But not always, for there are passages in the Gospel when "Jews" does mean all Jews (cf. Jn 2: 6). That is why it is important to know the context of a passage in order to understand the meanings of the terms used.

However, throughout history these distinctions in St. John's Gospel have not always been properly understood. The most common mistake is to believe that the term "Jew" is applied to the whole Hebrew people in every instance. Because some passages claim that "the Jews" persecuted or killed Christ, this misinterpretation is used as a justification for the mistaken belief that all Jews, even those not yet born, are responsible for the Death of Christ. The Church has rejected this false interpretation, noting that only certain Jewish leaders advocated the Death of Christ (while others were his followers) and that his Death was ultimately due to our sins.

Christ Before Caiaphas (detail) by Giotto.
According to the Gospels, Joseph Caiaphas was the Jewish high priest (AD 18-36) involved in the plan to have the Romans find Jesus guilty of sedition which would result in execution. "being high priest that year he prophesied that Jesus should die for the nation, and not for the nation only, but to gather into one the children of God who are scattered abroad. So from that day on they took counsel how to put him to death." (Jn 11: 51-53)

Regarding this subject, the Fathers of the Second Ecumenical Council of the Vatican stated:

> True, the Jewish authorities and those who followed their lead pressed for the death of Christ;[29] still, what happened in His passion cannot be charged against all the Jews, without distinction, then alive, nor against the Jews of today. Although the Church is the new people of God, the Jews should not be presented as rejected or accursed by God, as if this followed from the Holy Scriptures. All should see to it, then, that in catechetical work or in the preaching of the word of God they do not teach anything that does not conform to the truth of the Gospel and the spirit of Christ.
>
> Furthermore, in her rejection of every persecution against any man, the Church, mindful of the patrimony she shares with the Jews and moved not by political reasons but by the Gospel's spiritual love, decries hatred, persecutions, displays of anti-Semitism, directed against Jews at any time and by anyone.
>
> Besides, as the Church has always held and holds now, Christ underwent His passion and death freely, because of the sins of men and out of infinite love, in order that all may reach salvation. It is, therefore, the burden of the Church's preaching to proclaim the cross of Christ as the sign of God's all-embracing love and as the fountain from which every grace flows. (*Nostra Ætate*, 4)

It is a fundamental teaching of the Church that the cause of Christ's Death was the sinfulness of humanity: Christ died for our sins in order to save us and redeem us. It is an historical fact that God became man as a Jew and that the first followers of Christ had been Jews. To think that all Jews, then and now, are somehow guilty of this crime is to ignore our own sharing of guilt through the transmission of Original Sin.

Unfortunately, anti-Semitism has persisted into modern times, and it has taken many forms: Jews have been persecuted for reasons political, economic, religious, and racial. The most horrific case of anti-Semitism is the *Holocaust* that took place during World War II (1939-1945), in which an estimated six million European Jews were killed in a genocide carried out as part of an official policy of the German government under Nazi chancellor Adolf Hitler. Although countless Catholic and Christian leaders and citizens throughout Europe went to heroic lengths to save and protect hundreds of thousands of Jews, there were many others who were complicit in the Holocaust.

During the rise of Nazism in Germany, Pope Pius XI condemned anti-Semitism, proclaiming: "Anti-Semitism is unacceptable. Spiritually, we are all Semites."[30]

St. Paul Preaching in Athens (detail) by Raphael.
"I ask, then, has God rejected his people? By no means! I myself am an Israelite, a descendant of Abraham, a member of the tribe of Benjamin. God has not rejected his people whom he foreknew." (Rom 11: 1-2)

CATHOLIC-JEWISH DIALOGUE

The dialogue the Church has with the Jewish people is unique. It is truly interreligious, for Jews and Catholics have fundamental differences of faith, spirituality, and practice. Yet, these two faiths are intrinsically linked by their common roots.

The primary aims of Catholic-Jewish dialogue are fourfold:

- To grow in mutual love and respect as sons and daughters of God. As the children of Abraham, Isaac, and Jacob, the Jews are our "elder brothers," and we should deepen our knowledge and respect for their august traditions.
- To give common witness on matters of peace and justice. As people of faith, Catholics and Jews can work together against violations of the dignity of the human person.
- To deepen mutual understanding of the one God and his plans for the world. We have seen that Christianity cannot be fully understood without reference to Judaism. By exploring the Jewish roots of the Catholic religion more carefully, Catholics can come to a deeper understanding of their own traditions. In turn, studying the Catholic faith can give Jews a different perspective on their own reading of the Scriptures.
- To bring all of humanity to faith in Christ and union with his Church. Finally, as we noted at the outset of this chapter, underlying all interreligious dialogue is the hope that the Gospel will be proclaimed and received by every human person, "to the ends of the earth,"[31] "to all nations."[32]

> The glorious Messiah's coming is suspended at every moment of history until his recognition by "all Israel," for "a hardening has come upon part of Israel" in their "unbelief" toward Jesus.[33] St. Peter says to the Jews of Jerusalem after Pentecost: "Repent therefore, and turn again, that your sins may be blotted out, that times of refreshing may come from the presence of the Lord, and that he may send the Christ appointed for you, Jesus, whom heaven must receive until the time for establishing all that God spoke by the mouth of his holy prophets from of old."[34] St. Paul echoes him: "For if their rejection means the reconciliation of the world, what will their acceptance mean but life from the dead?"[35] The "full inclusion" of the Jews in the Messiah's salvation, in the wake of "the full number of the Gentiles,"[36] will enable the People of God to achieve "the measure of the stature of the fullness of Christ," in which "God may be all in all."[37] (CCC 674)

Scriptural Model

Our model for dialogue with the Jewish religion comes from St. Paul's Epistle to the Romans. St. Paul, a Jewish religious leader who came to accept the risen Jesus as the Messiah, yearned for all Jews to do likewise.

> **I could wish that I myself were accursed and cut off from Christ for the sake of my brethren, my kinsmen by race. They are Israelites, and to them belong the sonship, the glory, the covenants, the giving of the law, the worship, and the promises; to them belong the patriarchs, and of their race, according to the flesh, is the Christ. God who is over all be blessed for ever. (Rom 9: 3-5)**

St. Paul understood that the Jews were God's Chosen People, and, using the metaphor of God's family as an olive tree, he taught that the Gentiles who accepted the Gospel were like wild olive branches grafted onto this tree, while the Jews are its natural branches:

> **If some of the branches were broken off, and you, a wild olive shoot, were grafted in their place to share the richness of the olive tree, do not boast over the branches. If you do boast, remember it is not you that support the root, but the root that supports you.... For if you have been cut from what is by nature a wild olive tree, and grafted, contrary to nature, into a cultivated olive tree, how much more will these natural branches be grafted back into their own olive tree. (Rom 11: 17-18, 24)**

St. Paul lamented over the rejection of Christ by most of his people, yet he had faith that all would one day be restored:

> **Lest you be wise in your own conceits, I want you to understand this mystery, brethren: a hardening has come upon part of Israel, until the full number of the Gentiles come in, and so all Israel will be saved; as it is written, "The Deliverer will come from Zion, he will banish ungodliness from Jacob"; "and this will be my covenant with them when I take away their sins."... [A]s regards election they are beloved for the sake of their forefathers. For the gifts and the call of God are irrevocable. (Rom 11: 25-29)**

Recent Advances in Dialogue

In modern times dramatic advances in Jewish-Catholic relations can be traced directly to Pope Pius XII himself. His 1943 encyclical *Divino Afflante Spiritu* ("Inspired by the Holy Spirit") encouraged broader and more vigorous biblical research methods, and Catholic scholars began to develop immediately a better understanding of what the New Testament—particularly St. John's Gospel and St. Paul's Epistle to the Romans (chapters 9 to 11, excerpted above)—has to say about the Jews. Pope Pius XII, who had built strong bonds of friendship with Jewish leaders due to his defense of the Jews during the war, began an informal dialogue with them over a series of meetings.

In his short reign as the successor of Pope Pius XII, St. John XXIII took Jewish-Catholic relations further. He had been a *nuncio*, or papal ambassador, under Pius XII and had also worked tirelessly to save Jews, shelter them from harm, and even to issue forged baptismal certificates and immigration documents to protect Hungarian Jews. As Pope he amended language in the Good Friday liturgy that had referred to "faithless" Jews. In receiving a Jewish delegation at a papal audience, he famously greeted them with the words, "I am Joseph, your brother"—an allusion to the biblical story of Joseph who was reunited with his brothers in Egypt.

St. John XXIII advanced Jewish-Catholic relations throughout his priestly life. "Forgive us for the curse we falsely attached to their name as Jews. Forgive us for crucifying Thee a second time in their flesh. For we know not what we did." (St. John XXIII quoted in the *Catholic Herald*, 1965)

POPE PIUS XII AND NAZISM

One of the greatest evils in history is the Nazi Holocaust, the genocide of millions of Jews led by Adolf Hitler. This horrific event, known also as the *Shoah* (Hebrew, "catastrophe"), was the culmination of millennia of anti-Semitism. "But how could it have happened; who is to blame?" Those questions have resounded for decades.

In an attempt to place blame, some people since the 1960s have gone so far as to claim that Pope Pius XII, pontiff during World War II, did nothing to help the Jews or was even complicit with the Nazis. Is this claim true? Does it correspond with the historical facts?

Before being elected Pope Pius XII in 1939, Eugenio Cardinal Pacelli served as *nuncio*, or papal ambassador, to Germany (1917-1929) and afterward as the Vatican Secretariat of State, the most powerful position in the Vatican after the Pope himself. In 1935, four years before becoming Pope and two years after the election of Hitler as chancellor of Germany, Cardinal Pacelli gave a forceful speech in Lourdes, France, condemning the Nazis. The speech became widely known. Because of it, as well as many diplomatic actions he initiated in protest of the Nazi Government, Pacelli was shown to be an enemy of the Nazi regime. When Pope Pius XI died, the Nazis worried that Cardinal Pacelli might become Pope, which is exactly what happened.

Soon after Pius XII was elected Pope, World War II broke out, and the Nazi campaign to exterminate the Jews accelerated dramatically. Although Pius XII was unable to do anything to politically stop the Nazis, he worked tirelessly to protect as many individual Jews as he could. Before the Nazis took control of Italy, he labored to find ways to allow Jews to escape. Afterwards, he devised hiding places for them, ordering monasteries (which ordinarily had rules against admitting outsiders) to give refuge to Jews. Thousands of Jews found refuge in the Vatican among various churches, basilicas, and other buildings owned by the Church.

Pope Pius XII (1876-1958)
Throughout the Nazi Holocaust, thousands of Jews were given refuge in the Vatican and other Church properties.

The Jews of his time noted Pius XII's work. The chief rabbi of Jerusalem, Isaac Herzog, declared: "The people of Israel will never forget what His Holiness and his illustrious delegates, inspired by the eternal principles of religion which form the very foundations of true civilization, are doing for us unfortunate brothers and sisters in the most tragic hour of our history, which is living proof of divine Providence in this world."[38] The chief rabbi of Rome, Israel Zolli, stated: "What the Vatican did will be indelibly and eternally engraved in our hearts.... Priests and even high prelates did things that will forever be an honor to Catholicism."[39] After the war, Zolli converted to Catholicism, and even took the baptismal name Eugenio in honor of the Pope, who had himself been baptized with that name. Some have estimated that the Catholic Church saved as many as 700,000 Jews during this time.

Continued

POPE PIUS XII AND NAZISM

Continued

So why is Pius XII accused of aiding the Nazis? The primary charge is that he was "silent" during the war, not making public speeches condemning the Nazis like he had done before the war. Did he change his mind about the Nazis after becoming Pope? No; what changed was the situation. The Nazis, now that war had broken out, acted more freely within their own borders to eliminate the Jews and reacted fiercely when prominent figures made pronouncements against them. For example, in 1942 Archbishop Johannes de Jong of Utrecht spoke out against the deportation of Dutch Jews. In retaliation the Nazis rounded up Catholic Jews (ethnic Jews who were practicing Catholics) in Holland and deported them to concentration camps where many died, including St. Teresa Benedicta of the Cross (born Edith Stein). The repercussions were too great—the threat of even more lives lost—for Pius XII to have spoken out publicly.

Nonetheless, today many condemn the Pope's silence as complicity. How did this come about? Ironically, the accusation originates from a 1963 German play titled "The Deputy." Lately discovered to have been backed by communists and perhaps even orchestrated by Soviet intelligence to discredit the Church—the Church being the main opponent of communism at the time—the play depicts Pius XII as too timid to resist the Nazis. The author acknowledged personally that the Pope had done much to help save Jews but criticized him for his not being more outspoken. Soon anti-Catholics latched on to the fictional work and accused Pius XII of complicity with the Nazis, ignoring his actions and equating his silence with support. Thus began the myth of Pius XII as "Hitler's Pope."

It is important to know the truth and an act of justice to defend people from false accusations. The myth of Pius XII's complicity with Nazism has turned people away from the Church and helped to pit Catholics against Jews. Yet, the truth of what happened can help to bring Catholics and Jews together, acknowledging the evil of the Holocaust while admiring those who worked against the Nazis during that dark time.

Jesus Wept by Tissot.
The truth of what happened can help to bring Catholics and Jews together, acknowledging the evil of the Holocaust while admiring those who worked against the Nazis during that dark time.

In 2000, St. John Paul II placed a prayer for brotherhood with the people of the Covenant at the Western Wall, a site of Jewish prayer and pilgrimage for centuries.

The Second Ecumenical Council of the Vatican, convened by St. John XXIII and continued by St. Paul VI, issued the declaration *Nostra Ætate* ("In Our Time"), which reinforced the bonds between Christianity and Judaism. St. Paul VI's own 1964 encyclical *Ecclesiam Suam* ("The Church Herself") praised the Jewish people for their great faith, stating that they are "worthy of our respect and love."

Under St. Paul VI, the Good Friday prayer for the Jews was rewritten in the 1970 revision of the Roman Missal to exclude references to the "blindness" of the Jews and petitions that God would remove the "veil from their hearts" so that they may be "delivered from their darkness." Instead, the new prayer asked that the Jewish people "may continue to grow in the love of his name and in faithfulness to his covenant" so that "the people you first made your own may arrive at the fullness of redemption."

St. John Paul II and Pope Benedict XVI continued to draw Jews and Catholics closer in friendship and dialogue. St. John Paul II was the first Pope to visit the Great Roman Synagogue, and in a trip to Israel he toured the Yad Vashem Holocaust Museum and prayed at the Western Wall, the only remaining part of the Temple, leaving in a niche a note with a prayer that reads in part:

> **We are deeply saddened by the behavior of those who in the course of history have caused these children of yours to suffer, and asking your forgiveness we wish to commit ourselves to genuine brotherhood with the people of the Covenant.**

After the death of St. John Paul II in 2005, the Jewish Anti-Defamation League issued a statement praising the pontiff for having made immense strides in Catholic-Jewish relations, noting that "more change for the better took place in his twenty-seven-year papacy than in the nearly 2,000 years before."

Even before he was elected to the papacy, Pope Benedict XVI had written extensively on Judaism and Christianity, particularly in regard to the continuity between the covenant that God made with Abraham and the covenant in Jesus Christ. As Pope he continued to meet with Jewish leaders and supported St. John Paul II's endorsement of the state of Israel's right to exist—a recognition opposed by many of Israel's neighbors.

CONCLUSION

No dialogue with non-Christians is as close to the heart of the Church as the one in which she engages with the Jewish people. Our "elder brothers" in the faith, it was the Jews who preserved monotheism in spite of tremendous pressures from pagan neighbors; it was the Jews whom God chose as his own people; and it has been observant Jews who have faithfully striven to follow the Commands of the Mosaic Covenant. And for Catholics it is most important to remember that it is from the Jews that Our Lord Jesus Christ sprang forth: "Salvation is from the Jews."[40] In so many different ways, the Catholic Church is rooted in the Jewish people.

Although there are differences between the religious beliefs of Christians and Jews, most notably concerning the Person of Jesus Christ, there is much that we share, including the sacred texts of the Old Testament. The Church has taught consistently that the Death of Jesus Christ was due to our sins and is not the responsibility of any particular group of people; thus, anti-Semitism is a grave sin that contradicts the teachings of Christ directly.

Before he was elected Pope Benedict XVI, Cardinal Ratzinger noted that Christians must come to a true appreciation of our Jewish brothers and sisters:

We also have to try to live our life together in Christ in such a way that it no longer stands in opposition to them or would be unacceptable to them but so that it facilitates their own approach to it....They are not excluded from salvation, but they serve salvation in a particular way, and thereby they stand within the patience of God, in which we, too, place our trust.[41]

CHALLENGES:

If the Church regards the Jewish people as our beloved "elder brothers," then why is there so much tension in Catholic-Jewish relations?

All Christians owe a great deal of respect to the Jewish people. It is the Jews who were the faithful remnant of those first called by God in a special way and were formed into his Chosen People. It is the Jews who remembered and held fast to God's promise to send the Messiah; it is the Jews who received his Law and covenants; it is the Jews whose faithfulness prepared the way for the Incarnation. The Son of God, Jesus Christ, was born a Jew, the son of Jewish parents, and an observant Jew himself. And it is to the Jews that Christ's Good News of salvation was first proclaimed. All the Apostles and most of the disciples of Christ were Jews, and for decades Christianity was originally considered by many as a sect within Judaism. Christianity, in fact, emerged out of Judaism, and it is upon the covenants and Scriptures (Old Testament) that Christianity is built.

Catholics have a great respect for Judaism because Jesus Christ is the fulfillment of the promises and covenants that God made with Israel. The Old Covenant is fulfilled in the New Covenant, sealed in the one Sacrifice of Christ and celebrated in the Sacrament of the Holy Eucharist, which is the New Passover. The Chosen People whom God gathered together in the Old Testament as Israel find their fulfillment in the Catholic Church, which has the divine mission of regathering all people into one body, the Body of Christ. Just as we saw earlier that the Church was in God's plan from the beginning, so we can say that the Church is the fulfillment of the Jewish faith itself.

Yad Vashem Hall of Remembrance in Jerusalem.
St. John Paul II and Pope Benedict XVI both came here to pray for victims of the Holocaust.

Tragically, however, Catholics and other Christians have not always regarded the Jewish people with the love and respect they deserve. Not all Jews, even those who witnessed Christ's earthly ministry and heard his and the Apostles' preaching with their own eyes and ears, accepted the Gospel. (The same also can be said of non-Jews who heard and rejected the Gospel.) Some Jewish leaders persecuted Christians, and eventually the Christians were expelled from the synagogues. Still, Jews and Christians, both persecuted under the Romans, lived in relative peace for several centuries.

With time, however, prejudices and animosities between Jews and Christians did develop, and unfortunately some Christians throughout the centuries have committed anti-Semitic acts. The Catholic Church unequivocally condemns anti-Semitism and any insinuation that the Jewish people share collective blame for the Death of Christ. However, lingering memories of these anti-Semitic acts inhibit the full healing of Catholic-Jewish relations despite the considerable efforts by leaders on both sides to restore full confidence and cooperation.

As we continue to build closer relations with our Jewish brothers and sisters, one of our firmest resolutions must be to eradicate every last bit of anti-Semitic prejudice from among our Christian brothers and sisters as well.

PILLARS OF THE FAITH

ST. TERESA BENEDICTA OF THE CROSS (Edith Stein)

During Yom Kippur in 1891—the Day of Atonement, the most important feast in the Jewish calendar—Edith Stein was born to a Jewish family in Germany, the youngest of eleven children. Her father died when she was very young, and although her mother worked hard to rear the large family by herself, the Jewish faith was not passed on, and Edith even lost her faith in God. Meanwhile, she received an excellent education and was a distinguished student. The subject of philosophy piqued her interest, and she studied under Max Scheler, a noted philosophy professor who introduced her to Catholicism. During World War I she worked as a field nurse and later received a doctorate with distinction. Although she wanted to become a professor, she found that as a woman and a Jew it was impossible.

One day as she was passing by a Catholic cathedral, she noticed a woman who slipped in to kneel and pray on her way back from the market. To Stein this was a novel idea: "In the synagogues and Protestant churches I had visited people simply went to the services. Here, however, I saw someone coming straight from the busy marketplace into this empty church, as if she was going to have an intimate conversation. It was something I never forgot."

In her studies Stein read a multitude of philosophical works, including the *Spiritual Exercises* of St. Ignatius of Loyola and the New Testament. She felt, however, that the latter works were not just to be read but practiced. One evening she became engrossed in the autobiography of St. Teresa of Avila. Reading through the night, Edith was transformed.

St. Teresa Benedicta of the Cross
(1891-1942)

In the morning she declared, "This is the truth." A few months later, on January 1, 1922, she was baptized a Catholic. January 1 was the Feast of the Circumcision of Jesus, celebrating the day that Our Lord's parents, following the covenant with Abraham, had their Son circumcised. It was a fitting day for the reception of this Jewish woman into the Church.

Continued

ST. TERESA BENEDICTA OF THE CROSS (Edith Stein)

Continued

Stein soon desired the religious life. She wanted to enter a Carmelite convent (the order of St. Teresa), but her spiritual directors prevented her from doing so. Instead, she spent several years teaching at Catholic schools, translating Catholic writings, and composing her own works. Eventually, Stein was allowed to enter a Carmelite convent, taking the name Teresa Benedicta of the Cross. Around the same time Hitler was elected chancellor of Germany.

As the anti-Semitism of Hitler's regime became increasingly apparent, St. Teresa was smuggled into the Netherlands to escape the Nazi threat. However, in 1942 the Gestapo arrested her because, although she was a Catholic nun, she was an ethnic Jew. She was sent to the concentration camp in Auschwitz where she was executed in the gas chambers along with many other Jews and Christians.

St. Teresa Benedicta of the Cross was beatified in 1987 and canonized in 1998 by St. John Paul II, and her feast day is August 9.

Elevation of the Cross by Rubens.
"In place of Solomon's temple, Christ has built a temple of living stones, the communion of saints. At its center, he stands as the eternal high priest; on its altar he is himself the perpetual sacrifice."
(*The Collected Works of Edith Stein, Vol. IV, Part I.2*)

SUPPLEMENTARY READING

The Great Spiritual Patrimony Common to Christians and Jews

As the sacred synod searches into the mystery of the Church, it remembers the bond that spiritually ties the people of the New Covenant to Abraham's stock.

Thus the Church of Christ acknowledges that, according to God's saving design, the beginnings of her faith and her election are found already among the patriarchs, Moses and the prophets. She professes that all who believe in Christ—Abraham's sons according to faith[42]—are included in the same patriarch's call, and likewise that the salvation of the Church is mysteriously foreshadowed by the chosen people's exodus from the land of bondage. The Church, therefore, cannot forget that she received the revelation of the Old Testament through the people with whom God in His inexpressible mercy concluded the Ancient Covenant. Nor can she forget that she draws sustenance from the root of that well-cultivated olive tree onto which have been grafted the wild shoots, the Gentiles.[43] Indeed, the Church believes that by His cross Christ, Our Peace, reconciled Jews and Gentiles, making both one in Himself.[44]

The Church keeps ever in mind the words of the Apostle about his kinsmen: "theirs is the sonship and the glory and the covenants and the law and the worship and the promises; theirs are the fathers and from them is the Christ according to the flesh" (Rom 9: 4-5), the Son of the Virgin Mary. She also recalls that the Apostles, the Church's main-stay and pillars, as well as most of the early disciples who proclaimed Christ's Gospel to the world, sprang from the Jewish people.

As Holy Scripture testifies, Jerusalem did not recognize the time of her visitation,[45] nor did the Jews in large number accept the Gospel; indeed not a few opposed its spreading.[46] Nevertheless, God holds the Jews most dear for the sake of their Fathers; He does not repent of the gifts He makes or of the calls He issues—such is the witness of the Apostle.[47] In company with the Prophets and the same Apostle, the Church awaits that day, known to God alone, on which all peoples will address the Lord in a single voice and "serve him shoulder to shoulder" (Zeph 3: 9).[48]

Since the spiritual patrimony common to Christians and Jews is thus so great, this sacred synod wants to foster and recommend that mutual understanding and respect which is the fruit, above all, of biblical and theological studies as well as of fraternal dialogues.

True, the Jewish authorities and those who followed their lead pressed for the death of Christ;[49] still, what happened in His passion cannot be charged against all the Jews, without distinction, then alive, nor against the Jews of today. Although the Church is the new people of God, the Jews should not be presented as rejected or accursed by God, as if this followed from the Holy Scriptures. All should see to it, then, that in catechetical work or in the preaching of the word of God they do not teach anything that does not conform to the truth of the Gospel and the spirit of Christ.

Furthermore, in her rejection of every persecution against any man, the Church, mindful of the patrimony she shares with the Jews and moved not by political reasons but by the Gospel's spiritual love, decries hatred, persecutions, displays of anti-Semitism, directed against Jews at any time and by anyone.

Besides, as the Church has always held and holds now, Christ underwent His passion and death freely, because of the sins of men and out of infinite love, in order that all may reach salvation. It is, therefore, the burden of the Church's preaching to proclaim the cross of Christ as the sign of God's all-embracing love and as the fountain from which every grace flows.

—Second Ecumenical Council of the Vatican, Declaration on the Relation of the Church to Non-Christian Religions, *Nostra Ætate*, no. 4

SUPPLEMENTARY READING Continued

St. John Paul II's Address at the Great Roman Synagogue

Today's visit is meant to make a decisive contribution to the consolidation of the good relations between our two communities, in imitation of the example of so many men and women who have worked and who are still working today, on both sides, to overcome old prejudices and to secure ever wider and fuller recognition of that "bond" and that "common spiritual patrimony" that exists between Jews and Christians.

This is the hope expressed in the fourth paragraph of the Council's Declaration *Nostra Ætate*, which I have just mentioned, on the relationship of the Church to non-Christian religions. The decisive turning-point in relations between the Catholic Church and Judaism, and with individual Jews, was occasioned by this brief but incisive paragraph.

We are all aware that, among the riches of this paragraph no. 4 of *Nostra Ætate*, three points are especially relevant. I would like to underline them here, before you, in this truly unique circumstance. The first is that the Church of Christ discovers her "bond" with Judaism by "searching into her own mystery" (cf. *Nostra Ætate*, ibid.). The Jewish religion is not "extrinsic" to us, but in a certain way is "intrinsic" to our own religion. With Judaism therefore we have a relationship that we do not have with any other religion. You are our dearly beloved brothers and, in a certain way, it could be said that you are our elder brothers.

The second point noted by the Council is that no ancestral or collective blame can be imputed to the Jews as a people for "what happened in Christ's passion" (cf. *Nostra Ætate*, ibid.). Not indiscriminately to the Jews of that time, nor to those who came afterwards, nor to those of today. So any alleged theological justification for discriminatory measures or, worse still, for acts of persecution is unfounded. The Lord will judge each one "according to his own works," Jews and Christians alike (cf. Rom 2: 6).

The third point that I would like to emphasize in the Council's Declaration is a consequence of the second. Notwithstanding the Church's awareness of her own identity, it is not lawful to say that the Jews are "repudiated or cursed," as if this were taught or could be deduced from the Sacred Scriptures of the Old or the New Testament (cf. *Nostra Ætate*, ibid.). Indeed, the Council had already said in this same text of *Nostra Ætate*, but also in the Dogmatic Constitution *Lumen Gentium*, no. 16, referring to Saint Paul in the Letter to the Romans (11: 28-29), that the Jews are beloved of God, who has called them with an irrevocable calling.

— St. John Paul II, *Address at the Great Roman Synagogue*, no. 4 (April 13, 1986)

St. John Paul II became the first Pope to make an official papal visit to a synagogue, when he visited the Great Roman Synagogue on April 13, 1986.

VOCABULARY

ALMSGIVING
The practice of Christian charity through the selfless donation of time, money, and other resources. Almsgiving, together with prayer and fasting, are traditionally recommended to foster interior penance.

ANGEL
From the Greek *angelos*, a translation of the Hebrew *malak*, meaning "messenger." A spiritual, personal, and immortal creature, possessing intelligence and free will, who glorifies God without ceasing and serves God as protector of and messenger to man. Demons are fallen angels, who exercised their free will to rebel against God for the glory of themselves. They actively seek to turn men away from God.

ANTI-SEMITISM
Discrimination, hatred, or persecution against Jews because of their Jewish heritage. The term comes from the word "Semite," which refers to the peoples of the Middle East, but in this case is restricted to Jews. Anti-Semitism has a long history in the world and persists to this day.

APOLOGIST
One who defends and explains the Christian faith. A group of Church Fathers who wrote during the second and third centuries in the Roman Empire frequently bear this title.

BLOOD LIBEL
A false allegation that Jews murder Christians, especially Christian children, to use their blood for ritual purposes.

DEICIDE
Literally, "God-killing." This charge has historically been laid on the Jewish people due to the role of some Jewish leaders in the Death of Jesus Christ. However, the Church has rejected this accusation, declaring that it is sinful to lay the Death of Christ at the feet of all Jews, both then and throughout history.

FASTING
Mortification by deprivation of food. This is an ancient religious practice that denies the desires of the flesh in order to strengthen the spirit.

GENOCIDE
The destruction of an entire nation or people.

GUARDIAN ANGEL
An angel personally assigned to protect and intercede for each human being.

HOLOCAUST
An Old Testament sacrifice wholly consumed by fire; a whole burnt offering. Also refers to the *Shoah*, the genocide against the Jews perpetrated by Nazi Germany during World War II.

INTERRELIGIOUS DIALOGUE
The interaction of people of different religions in a mutual search for truth. This dialogue can include discussions on such topics as doctrine, history, and religious practices. It is to be done in a prayerful, respectful atmosphere.

LORD'S DAY
Sunday; the principal day of the week for Christian worship. Each Sunday Mass commemorates the Resurrection of Christ on Easter Sunday and is a reminder of the first day of creation for those who have become a "new creation in Christ." Canon Law stipulates that Catholics are to attend Mass on Sunday and to abstain from any labors that impede Sunday worship or detract from the joy proper to the day.

MESSIANIC JUDAISM
A rather recent, syncretic religion that blends Jewish rites and rituals with the Christian belief that Jesus is the Messiah.

NUNCIO
A personal ambassador of the Pope.

PENTATEUCH
Greek for "of five books," it refers to the first five of the Old Testament: Genesis, Exodus, Leviticus, Numbers, and Deuteronomy.

PEOPLE OF GOD
Those born into the Church through faith in Christ and Baptism. The term is taken from the Old Testament in which God chose Israel to be his people. Christ instituted the new and eternal covenant by which a new priestly, prophetic, and royal People of God, the Church, participates in the mission and service of Christ.

VOCABULARY Continued

RABBI
Hebrew for "my master." This person is a teacher of the Jewish people and was the title disciples used for their teacher.

SHOAH
See Holocaust.

SYNAGOGUE
A Jewish house of prayer. Originally, the Temple was the only true gathering place for Jews, but due to the great distance many Jews had to travel to reach the Temple, synagogues arose to allow Jews to gather in prayer. After the destruction of the Temple AD 70, the local synagogue became the primary meeting place for Jews everywhere.

TANAKH
The Old Testament. It is the entirety of the Scriptures for the Jewish people.

TEMPLE
The house of God in Jerusalem that contained the Ark of the Covenant. When the Temple was dedicated, God's glory overshadowed it just as it had done in the tabernacle. The Temple became the center of worship for Israel and the unique site for offering sacrifice.

TORAH
The first five books of the Bible, also called the Pentateuch. Sometimes it refers to the entirety of Jewish law.

YOM KIPPUR
The Jewish Day of Atonement. It is the holiest day of the year for the Jewish people; its focus is on repentance for sins and God's atonement of his people.

Reconstruction of Jerusalem and the Temple of Herod [in the time of Jesus] by Tissot.

Modern-day Jews praying at the Western Wall, a remnant of the ancient wall that surrounded the Temple Mount courtyard.

STUDY QUESTIONS

1. What affectionate term did St. John Paul II use to refer to the Jewish people?
2. What is the goal of all ecumenism and interreligious dialogue?
3. What do people expect of the various religions?
4. What are the "seeds of the Word?"
5. Which non-Christian religion is the only one to receive God's true Revelation?
6. Whom did God originally choose to prepare the world for the coming of Christ?
7. What is expected by both God's people of the Old Covenant and his new people (the Church)?
8. Why is knowledge of Judaism necessary for a Christian?
9. What is the *Tanakh*?
10. What is the basis of both the Catholic and Jewish moral codes?
11. How is the Sermon on the Mount an example of the idea that Christ fulfilled rather than abolished the Law?
12. What are the three pillars of the Jewish spiritual life?
13. How is the Mass a fulfillment of the Jewish liturgy?
14. What is the most significant divide between Catholics and Jews in terms of belief?
15. How does the monotheism of Judaism differ from the monotheism of Christianity?
16. How do Catholics and Jews differ in their interpretation of Genesis 1-3?
17. What is anti-Semitism?
18. What is the primary reason for anti-Semitism used by supposed "Christians"?
19. What is the Church's teaching on this?
20. What are the aims of dialogue with the Jewish people?
21. What Scriptural passages are our models for dialogue with the Jewish people?

PRACTICAL EXERCISES

1. Visit a synagogue and talk to the rabbi. Is it a synagogue of Orthodox, Conservative, or Reform Judaism? What are the services like?

2. Write a paragraph explaining the unique relationship between Catholicism and Judaism. Include at least three of this relationship's unique aspects.

3. Give three historical examples of severe anti-Semitism. Why have the Jewish people suffered so much persecution?

4. Research the ongoing dialogue between Catholics and Jews. Give a recent example of a formal dialogue between the two faiths. What was discussed? What were the dialogue's conclusions?

FROM THE CATECHISM

201 To Israel, his chosen, God revealed himself as the only One: "Hear, O Israel: The LORD our God is one LORD; and you shall love the LORD your God with all your heart, and with all your soul, and with all your might."[50] Through the prophets, God calls Israel and all nations to turn to him, the one and only God: "Turn to me and be saved, all the ends of the earth! For I am God, and there is no other....To me every knee shall bow, every tongue shall swear. 'Only in the LORD, it shall be said of me, are righteousness and strength.'"[51]

578 Jesus, Israel's Messiah and therefore the greatest in the kingdom of heaven, was to fulfill the Law by keeping it in its all-embracing detail—according to his own words, down to "the least of these commandments."[52] He is in fact the only one who could keep it perfectly.[53] On their own admission the Jews were never able to observe the Law in its entirety without violating the least of its precepts.[54] This is why every year on the Day of Atonement the children of Israel ask God's forgiveness for their transgressions of the Law. The Law indeed makes up one inseparable whole, and St. James recalls, "Whoever keeps the whole law but fails in one point has become guilty of all of it."[55]

581 The Jewish people and their spiritual leaders viewed Jesus as a rabbi.[56] He often argued within the framework of rabbinical interpretation of the Law.[57] Yet Jesus could not help but offend the teachers of the Law, for he was not content to propose his interpretation alongside theirs but taught the people "as one who had authority, and not as their scribes."[58] In Jesus, the same Word of God that had resounded on Mount Sinai to give the written Law to Moses, made itself heard anew on the Mount of the Beatitudes.[59] Jesus did not abolish the Law but fulfilled it by giving its ultimate interpretation in a divine way: "You have heard that it was said to the men of old....But I say to you...."[60] With this same divine authority, he disavowed certain human traditions of the Pharisees that were "making void the word of God."[61]

582 Going even further, Jesus perfects the dietary law, so important in Jewish daily life, by revealing its pedagogical meaning through a divine interpretation: "Whatever goes into a man from outside cannot defile him....(Thus he declared all foods clean.). What comes out of a man is what defiles a man. For from within, out of the heart of man, come evil thoughts..."[62] In presenting with divine authority the definitive interpretation of the Law, Jesus found himself confronted by certain teachers of the Law who did not accept his interpretation of the Law, guaranteed though it was by the divine signs that accompanied it.[63] This was the case especially with the sabbath laws, for he recalls, often with rabbinical arguments, that the sabbath rest is not violated by serving God and neighbor,[64] which his own healings did.

592 Jesus did not abolish the Law of Sinai, but rather fulfilled it (cf. Mt 5:17-19) with such perfection (cf. Jn 8:46) that he revealed its ultimate meaning (cf. Mt 5:33) and redeemed the transgressions against it (cf. Heb 9:15).

593 Jesus venerated the Temple by going up to it for the Jewish feasts of pilgrimage, and with a jealous love he loved this dwelling of God among men. The Temple prefigures his own mystery. When he announces its destruction, it is as a manifestation of his own execution and of the entry into a new age in the history of salvation, when his Body would be the definitive Temple.

594 Jesus performed acts, such as pardoning sins, that manifested him to be the Savior God himself (cf. Jn 5:16-18). Certain Jews, who did not recognize God made man (cf. Jn 1:14), saw in him only a man who made himself God (Jn 10:33), and judged him as a blasphemer.

FROM THE CATECHISM Continued

1096 *Jewish liturgy and Christian liturgy.* A better knowledge of the Jewish people's faith and religious life as professed and lived even now can help our better understanding of certain aspects of Christian liturgy. For both Jews and Christians Sacred Scripture is an essential part of their respective liturgies: in the proclamation of the Word of God, the response to this word, prayer of praise and intercession for the living and the dead, invocation of God's mercy. In its characteristic structure the Liturgy of the Word originates in Jewish prayer. The Liturgy of the Hours and other liturgical texts and formularies, as well as those of our most venerable prayers, including the Lord's Prayer, have parallels in Jewish prayer. The Eucharistic Prayers also draw their inspiration from the Jewish tradition. The relationship between Jewish liturgy and Christian liturgy, but also their differences in content, are particularly evident in the great feasts of the liturgical year, such as Passover. Christians and Jews both celebrate the Passover. For Jews, it is the Passover of history, tending toward the future; for Christians, it is the Passover fulfilled in the Death and Resurrection of Christ, though always in expectation of its definitive consummation.

ENDNOTES – CHAPTER SEVEN

1. 1 Tm 2:4.
2. Mt 28:19-20.
3. Latin term meaning "to all peoples" or "to the world."
4. *RMiss* 55.
5. Cf. 2 Cor 5:18-19.
6. Cf. CCC 1257-1261.
7. Cfr. Epist. S.S.C.S. *Officii ad Archiep.* Boston.: Denz. 3869-72.
8. Cfr. Eusebius Caes., *Praeparatio Evangelica*, 1, 1: PG 2128 AB.
9. Jn 4:22.
10. Cf. *NA* 4.
11. *Roman Missal*, Good Friday 13: General Intercessions, VI.
12. Rom 9:4-5.
13. Rom 11:29.
14. Mt 5:17.
15. Cf. 1 Cor 10:6, 11; Heb 10:1; 1 Pt 3:21.
16. Cf. Mk 12:29-31
17. Cf. 1 Cor 5:6-8; 10:1-11.
18. Cf. St. Augustine, *Quaest. in Hept.* 2, 73: PL 34, 623; cf. *DV* 16.
19. Mt 19:17.
20. Jn 15:10.
21. Cf. Mt 5–7.
22. Mt 5:48.
23. Lv 11:44.
24. Mt 18:10.
25. Cf. Acts 6–7.
26. Cf. Gn 14:18-20.
27. Heb 6:20.
28. Cf. 2 Mc 5:11-16.
29. Cf. Jn 19:6.
30. Address to Belgian pilgrims, September 6, 1938.
31. Acts 1:8.
32. Mk 13:10; Lk 24:47; Rom 16: 25-27.
33. Rom 11:20-26; cf. Mt 23:39.
34. Acts 3:19-21.
35. Rom 11:15.
36. Rom 11:12, 25; cf. Lk 21:24.
37. Eph 4:13; 1 Cor 15:28.
38. Margherita Marchione, "Yours Is a Precious Witness: Memoirs of Jews and Catholics in Wartime Italy," p. 56.

38. *American Jewish Yearbook 1944-1945*, p. 233.
39. Jn 4:22.
40. Seewald, Peter. *God and the World: Believing and Living in Our Time.* (San Francisco: Ignatius Press) 2002.
41. Cf. Gal 3:7.
42. Cf. Rom 11:17-24.
43. Cf. Eph 2:14-16.
44. Cf. Lk 19:44.
45. Cf. Rom 11:28.
46. Cf. Rom 11:28-29; cf. dogmatic Constitution, *Lumen Gentium* (Light of nations) AAS, 57 (1965) p. 20
47. Cf. Is 66:23; Ps 65:4; Rom 11: 11-32.
48. Cf. Jn 19:6.
49. Dt 6:4-5.
50. Is 45:22-24; cf. Phil 2:10-11.
51. Mt 5:19.
52. Cf. Jn 8:46.
53. Cf. Jn 7:19; Acts 13:38-41; 15:10.
54. Jas 2:10; cf. Gal 3:10; 5:3.
55. Cf Jn 11:28; 3:2; Mt 22:23-24, 34-36.
56. Cf. Mt 12:5; 9:12; Mk 2:23-27; Lk 6:6-9; Jn 7:22-23.
57. Mt 7:28-29.
58. Cf. Mt 5:1.
59. Mt 5:33-34.
60. Mk 7:13; cf. 3:8.
61. Mk 7:18-21; cf. Gal 3:24.
62. Cf. Jn 5:36; 10:25, 37-38; 12:37.
63. Cf. Nm 28:9; Mt 12:5; Mk 2:25-27; Lk 13:15-16; 14:3-4; Jn 7:22-24.

CHAPTER 8

Islam and Other Non-Christian Religions

In an effort to draw closer as a human family and to promote the common good, the Church engages in dialogue with the major religions of the world.

Ecumenism and Interreligious Dialogue

CHAPTER EIGHT

Islam and Other Non-Christian Religions

INTRODUCTION

In the last chapter we studied Judaism, the "elder brother" of the Christian faith and the relationship and dialogue between the Church and the Jewish people. Outside of what is sometimes called the Judeo-Christian tradition, however, there are many other faith traditions arising from diverse cultures and peoples around the world. The human person is by nature a religious being, seeking answers for the fundamental questions that occur by virtue of the divine gift of reason. The human race, then, is inherently religious. Since the beginning of time, men and women have yearned to know more about the world beyond the senses and to be in accordance with that very real yet invisible world. All peoples and cultures have acknowledged that there exists something greater than what we see. As a result, countless religions have sprung up throughout the world.

The diversity of religious belief is vast, expressing itself in monotheism, polytheism, and pantheism. The Catholic Church teaches that, though there is only one true religion, still there can be elements of truth in other religions. God honors sincere attempts to know him that occur outside the visible confines of the Church. In an effort to draw closer as a human family and to promote the common good, the Church engages in dialogue with the major religions of the world, seeking a deeper knowledge of their beliefs and practices.

It would be impossible to discuss every non-Christian religion in existence today, but some of the most influential will be examined briefly in this chapter:

- Islam, including its history and key beliefs;
- Buddhism, Hinduism, and other major religions in the Far East and India;
- Mormonism, Jehovah's Witnesses, and other religions that are offshoots of Christianity;
- The nature of the relationship and interreligious dialogue between the Catholic Church and non-Christian religions in general.

Standing Buddha in Royal Attire, Bangkok, Thailand. The world's diversity of religious belief is vast, expressing itself in monotheism, polytheism, and pantheism.

Prayer in Cairo, 1865 by Gerome.
A detailed set of practices and regulations governs every aspect of life for a practicing Muslim, and at the center of these practices for a Sunni Muslim are the Five Pillars of Islam.

A BRIEF HISTORY OF ISLAM

After After Christianity, the second largest religion in the world is Islam. Those who follow the religion of Islam are known as Muslims. (The term "Muhammedan" is seen as archaic today since Muslims do not revere Muhammad as a god.) Islam, which means "submission [to God]," originated in the sixth century in the Arabian Peninsula (modern-day Saudi Arabia). This region was outside the Byzantine Empire and was populated by peoples of different religions, including polytheists as well as Nestorian and Monophysite Christians. While the teachings of Christianity and Judaism were known, the Catholic Church had little influence in the area.

The Rise of Muhammad

Around AD 570 a man named Muhammad was born in Mecca in modern-day Saudi Arabia. He was born to a well-to-do family, but both his parents died before he reached the age of seven. He was brought up by relatives and eventually joined his uncle on trading trips throughout the region, including some in predominantly Christian (though non-Catholic) lands.

The city of Mecca in Muhammad's time was thriving, but like many urban centers, it also included a large segment of the poor and destitute. According to Islamic tradition Muhammad was distressed by these social conditions and went often to a cave outside the city to pray. During one of these times of prayer, in the year 610 Muhammad claimed to have had a vision in which he saw the angel Gabriel commanding him to recite words that were given to him. Muhammad was initially frightened by the vision, but a Christian cousin instructed him to remember what he had been told. For the next twenty-two years until his death, Muhammad said he continued to have these visions.

Soon, Muhammad formed a small group of followers, mostly from those who believed in the local gods and goddesses. He then reached out to the Arabic-speaking people of Mecca, proclaiming himself to be a prophet like Abraham, Moses, and even Christ and teaching them to reject polytheism in favor of the teachings of his visions. At first, most people in Mecca rejected his message, so in 612 Muhammad decided to leave Mecca for a village to the north named Yathrib. Muslims mark this *hijra* (migration) as the founding of Islam. Yathrib later became known as Medina, or "the City of the Prophet."

It was in Medina that Muhammad's teachings flourished, and he gained political power. While there the visions he related included regulations on how to worship as well as the overall governance of the people. He used these visions as a basis for his rule over the people of Medina. It was also in Medina that Muhammad and his followers began to exercise military power, and soon they conquered surrounding towns. It was also during this time that Muhammad began to establish rules for relations with Jews and Christians who had submitted to Muslim rule. In one peace treaty a large Jewish tribe agreed to submit to Muhammad's political authority in exchange for being allowed to continue practicing their religion.

Eventually, the city of Mecca attacked Muhammad and his followers in retaliation for the raids that they had conducted. The Meccans, however, were defeated. Muhammad took this as a sign of divine assistance for his work. The Meccans continued to engage in skirmishes with the Medinans, but eventually Muhammad's forces conquered Mecca. Muhammad then defeated the surrounding towns and villages, and by his death in 632, he ruled the Arabian Peninsula. Muhammad was considered by his peers to be both a religious prophet and a powerful military and political leader.

Disagreement over Muhammad's Successor: Shiites and Sunnis

Muhammad's death came suddenly and at the height of his power. After his death his followers sought a successor (*caliph*). The customs of the time suggested that his closest male descendant, his son-in-law Ali, should be selected. However, Abu Bakr, the father of Muhammad's favorite of his twelve wives, was elected instead. He was head of the Muslim community for only two years and was followed by Umar (634-644), under whose leadership the Muslims conquered Jerusalem in 638. Then came Uthman (644-656) and finally Ali—the same son-in-law of Muhaammad—who reigned from 656 to 661. The majority of Muslims considers the Muslim community under these four men as ideal, the very basis for Islamic living.

However, the initial selection of Abu Bakr over Ali eventually resulted in a major schism within Islam. Although Ali later became the fourth caliph, even those who supported him initially were still dissatisfied. Tensions came to the forefront when Ali was assassinated and succeeded by Muawiya, who was rejected by Ali's followers. They broke away from the dominant Muslim group and became known as Shiites (from *shiya*, "party [of Ali]"), while the majority of Muslims are called Sunnis (*Sunni*, "[adherent of] Sunna"). Over the intervening centuries, the two groups have developed many differences in theology, politics, and law.

The Battle of Poitiers (detail) by Steuben. Triumphant Charles Martel (mounted) facing Abdul Rahman Al Ghafiqi (right) at the Battle of Tours.

This disagreement did not slow the growth of Islam, however. The caliphs continued to engage in aggressive, military-led expansions of Islam. Most of the conquered peoples who had polytheistic religions converted to Islam, choosing conversion instead of death, and many Jews and Christians also converted to avoid at best living as second-class citizens and at worst death. Before long, Muslims controlled almost all of the Middle East and Northern Africa.

Next, Islamic armies established control over much of the Iberian Peninsula (modern-day Spain and Portugal). Though they pushed on from there and gained territory briefly in modern-day France, ultimately they were unsuccessful. Christian forces led by Charles Martel stopped the progress of their invasion in north-central France at the Battle of Tours in 732, and by 759 the Muslims had retreated back into Iberia. They controlled much of the Iberian Peninsula for several more centuries until Christian armies gradually reclaimed the land. The last stronghold of Muslim control was defeated in 1492 by the forces of Queen Isabella and King Ferdinand of Spain.

The Taking of Jerusalem by the Crusaders, 15th July 1099 by Signol.
Christian control of the Holy Land did not last long; within a century Muslim forces drove the Christians out again.

Blocked from further expansion into Western Europe, Muslims began expanding eastward, conquering modern-day Iran, Pakistan, and parts of India within a few hundred years.

The Crusades

Because the early and rapid rise of Islam was abetted by military conquest, relations between Catholics and Muslims were difficult from the very beginning. When Christian lands were attacked and conquered by Muslims—including the cradle of Christianity itself, the Holy Land—Christians began to fight back, defending themselves from further incursions and recovering conquered territory. The Christian Eastern Roman (Byzantine) Empire herself was under constant attack and threat of attack, and there was a legitimate fear among Christians in Europe that Muslim armies would soon conquer the continent.

These two factors—the Islamic takeover of the Holy Land and the threat of European invasion—were primary motivators in the calling of the first of the Crusades. Although Muslims had controlled Jerusalem since 638, it was not an issue until access to Jerusalem was cut off to Christians seeking to travel there on pilgrimages. The crusaders' campaigns to liberate Jerusalem, fought between 1085 and 1291, impact Catholic-Muslim relations still today.

Although the Crusades were launched initially with the blessing of the Church, after the forces had departed for Jerusalem, the Church had little direct control over them. Just as crusader violence against Eastern Orthodox and Jewish settlements damaged relationships with those groups, so, too, did violent clashes with Islamic forces harden the minds and hearts of Muslims and Christians against each other. Even today, many Muslims consider the Crusades unforgiveable attempts to destroy their religion.

The First Crusade achieved its objective by retaking Jerusalem in 1099. The crusaders built many of the churches, shrines, and other infrastructure of the holy city, but, unfortunately, acts of violence were committed against Muslims and Jews living in Jerusalem. Christian control of the region did not last long; within a century Muslim forces drove the Christians out again.

ST. FRANCIS AND THE SULTAN

St. Francis of Assisi is one of the greatest and most beloved figures in the history of the Church. Because of his unrelenting desire to be conformed completely to the image of Our Lord, he has been called a "second Christ." God sealed this desire near the end of the saint's life when he received the stigmata, the wounds of Christ's Crucifixion. But St. Francis wanted not only to be like Christ himself but also to bring others to Christ so they, too, could find joy in the Christian life. He preached throughout Italy, converting many lukewarm Christians to ardent faith through his profound preaching and the witness of his life.

St. Francis lived at the time of the Crusades, when Europe was wracked with fear that Islamic forces would overrun the continent. Christians wished also to make pilgrimages to the Holy Land safe, which had been conquered by Muslims centuries before. This desire was given profound impetus by a change in the policy of Muslim rulers toward the presence of Christians in the Holy Land. While the Saracens had allowed Christian pilgrims safe passage to the Holy Land, in 1065 the conquering Turks massacred some 3,000 Christians in Jerusalem, causing others to flee the Holy Land and dissuading future pilgrims from visiting the holy sites of Christ's earthly life and ministry. The ensuing outrage in Europe fueled the demand for the First Crusade.

The means to recapture the Holy Land and to protect Europe, in the eyes of almost everyone, would be the force of arms. St. Francis thought differently; he desired to travel to the Middle East in order to preach to the Sultan of Egypt and to convert him and his people to Christianity.

Just obtaining a meeting with the Sultan would have been a miracle in itself, for the Sultan had offered a reward to anyone who brought him the head of a Christian. But St. Francis knew that conversion was the only true and permanent means of "conquering" the Islamic armies. So, though his first several attempts to reach the Holy Land failed, he finally arrived at the battlefields of the Crusades and was given an audience with the Sultan of Egypt.

When placed in front of the Sultan, St. Francis began to preach the Gospel and concluded with asking the Sultan to convert to Christianity. The poor, unarmed brother intrigued the Sultan, who listened to all that St. Francis had to say.

Trial by Fire Before the Sultan by Ghirlandaio. After this encounter St. Francis became a name respected in Islam.

The Sultan did not convert, but he was so impressed with St. Francis that he offered him many gifts and treasures. Being a man of poverty, St. Francis refused, but he did request—and was granted—safe passage for Christians through Muslim-controlled territory. After this encounter St. Francis became a name respected in Islam and an example to all Catholics of the boldness and trust in God each one of us should have in proclaiming the Gospel.

Battle of Lepanto by Cambiaso.
The turning point of Islamic expansion into Europe came in dramatic fashion. The Holy League fleet, which was greatly outnumbered, destroyed the Ottoman ships and prevented a Muslim conquest of the Mediterranean.

The Ottoman Empire and the Battle of Lepanto

As the Byzantine Empire continued to decline in power during the fourteenth and fifteenth centuries, Muslims began conquering ever more Christian lands. The Ottoman Empire, led by Turkish tribesmen who had converted to Islam, further shrank Byzantine holdings by advancing into southeastern Europe. When, after a long and bloody siege, the forces of Ottoman Sultan Mehmet II took the city of Constantinople in 1453, he renamed the city Istanbul and made it the capital of the Ottoman Empire.

By the mid-sixteenth century the Ottoman Empire comprised the Holy Land, much of the modern Middle East, North Africa, and western Asia; encompassed Greece, the Balkans; and reached nearly to the modern-day borders of Italy and Austria. Europe was under grave threat of further Muslim invasion. The primary emphasis of most histories of sixteenth-century Europe is the divisions caused by the Protestant Reformation, but often forgotten is their shared, gripping fear—the possibility that Western Europe would fall just as the Byzantine Empire had been defeated a century before. To prevent this, Pope St. Pius V organized a military alliance of nations called the Holy League to defend Europe against the Muslim threat.

The turning point of Islamic expansion into Europe came in dramatic fashion. In 1571 an enormous Muslim Turkish fleet sailed west from its port in Lepanto in western Greece. The Ottoman ships were met in battle by a fleet of ships from the Holy League. The situation was dire: Catholic forces were far outnumbered, and their defeat would make Italy a doorway to further incursions into Europe. So St. Pius V called on all of Europe to plead for the intercession of the Blessed Virgin Mary by praying the Holy Rosary. Miraculously, the Holy League destroyed much of the Muslim fleet on October 7, 1571, which prevented the Islamic forces from having free reign over the Mediterranean and its shipping lanes, effectively ending the threat to Europe.

St. Pius V needed no courier to tell him the good news. Even though he was hundreds of miles away from the site of the battle, at the moment of victory, he cried out, "The Christian fleet is victorious!" Our Lady had delivered.

The Battle of Lepanto came to be celebrated in the Church as the feast of Our Lady of Victory, crediting the Blessed Mother for the defeat of the invading fleet. Later, the name of the feast was changed to Our Lady of the Rosary, which is celebrated still on October 7.

Millions of Muslim pilgrims circle the Kaaba (also known as the Sacred House) during the start of Hajj at the Al-Masjid al-Haram Mosque in the center of Mecca. Multiple parts of the Hajj require pilgrims to walk seven times around the Kaaba in a counter-clockwise direction. Muslims are expected to face the Kaaba during prayers, no matter where they are in the world. One of the Five Pillars of Islam requires every Muslim to perform the Hajj pilgrimage at least once in his or her lifetime.

THE KORAN: THE MUSLIM HOLY BOOK

Muhammad recounted visions that he had received throughout his lifetime. Though he did not write them down, according to Islamic tradition his followers memorized them and recorded them in writing after his death. This collection of writings is known as the *Koran*, the holy book of Muslims.

Even though Allah (God) is considered the sole author of the Koran, there are a few verses, called *asbab al-nuzel* ("occasions of revelation"), which are believed to have come later and supersede previous revelations. The most significant are those related to Islamic relations with Jews and Christians. The first messages that Muhammad claimed to have received in Mecca speak strongly against polytheism but in a more conciliatory tone towards Jews and Christians. Later, after Muhammad was in Medina, his messages became more confrontational toward Jews and Christians. This is why there is some confusion today about the Islamic view of the other two major monotheistic religions. A significant number of Muslims resolve the issue by accepting the later revelation as superseding the former.

The Koran is the guiding book for the life of Muslims; Koran means "recitation," and it is considered the literal "word of God." Muslims also place importance on the traditions that surround the life and words of Muhammad, which have been collected into what are called *hadith* ("traditions").

In addition, Islamic scholars exert influence upon the beliefs and practices of Muslims. One set of standard interpretations of the Koran and the *hadith* that has existed since the eighth and ninth centuries is considered normative. But it is also important to remember that there is no one authority to which Muslims look for the proper understanding of the Koran or other Muslim teachings. Thus, individual interpretation of the holy texts is necessary.

ISLAMIC BELIEF AND PRACTICE

Islam, unlike Christianity, is not a creedal religion, that is, one governed by a formal profession of beliefs such as Christianity has in the Nicene Creed. Other than its basic declaration of faith, there are no detailed creeds in Islam. Furthermore, there is no normative catechism for Muslims such as those written to instruct Catholics. Other than its declaration of faith, probably the best summary of the Islam faith can be found in the Koran:

> O you who have believed, believe in Allah and His Messenger and the Book that He sent down upon His Messenger and the Scripture which He sent down before. And whoever disbelieves in Allah, His angels, His books, His messengers, and the Last Day has certainly gone far astray. (4:136)

A detailed set of practices and regulations governs every aspect of life for a practicing Muslim, and at the center of these practices for a Sunni Muslim are the Five Pillars of Islam. There are no sacraments in the Islamic religion, but these pillars form the basis of the Muslim spiritual life.

In Islam, five times each day are set aside for ritual prayer (*salah*).

- Declaration of Faith. This is the profession (*Shahada*) that all Muslims make: "There is no god but Allah, and Muhammad is his prophet."
- Prayer. Five times each day are set aside for ritual prayer (*salah*). The ritual is preceded by ablution (washing) and involves prescribed repetition of prayers recited while standing, bowing, and prostrating oneself. Various other prayers are also said depending on one's life situation and the time of year.
- Fasting. All Muslims who have reached puberty are required to fast (*sawm*) during the daylight hours of the month of Ramadan, which commemorates the time during which Muslims believe the Koran was given to Muhammad. In addition, there are other times individual Muslims choose to fast.
- Almsgiving. Muslims are required to contribute two-and-one-half percent of their income to charity; this is called *Zakah*.
- Pilgrimage. Once during his or her lifetime, a Muslim must make a pilgrimage (*Hajj*) to Mecca.

Shiites include these Five Pillars among their beliefs and obligatory religious practices.

ISLAM AND CATHOLICISM: SIMILARITIES AND DIFFERENCES

Although Islam and Christianity may seem worlds apart, the two faith traditions do have a core of common beliefs. For example, both worship God as the Creator and consider Abraham their father in faith. Yet, there also are major points of disagreement.

Monotheism. The central belief of Islam is that there is one God (in Arabic, *Allah*) and that Muhammad is Allah's final and most important prophet. Muslims acknowledge Allah as the creator of all things, and a host of names for him describe his nature. Many of the Muslim names for Allah—the Merciful, the Holy, the Almighty, the Creator, the First, the Last, the Eternal, etc.—describe attributes that Christians ascribe to the Triune God.

ST. JOHN PAUL II ON REVELATION IN CHRISTIANITY AND ISLAM

Whoever knows the Old and New Testaments, and then reads the Koran, clearly sees the process by which it completely reduces Divine Revelation. It is impossible not to note the movement away from what God said about Himself, first in the Old Testament through the Prophets, and then finally in the New Testament through His Son. In Islam all the richness of God's self-revelation, which constitutes the heritage of the Old and New Testaments, has definitely been set aside.

Some of the most beautiful names in the human language are given to the God of the Koran, but He is ultimately a God outside of the world, a God who is only Majesty, never Emmanuel, God-with-us. Islam is not a religion of redemption. There is no room for the Cross and the Resurrection. Jesus is mentioned, but only as a prophet who prepares for the last prophet, Muhammad. There is also mention of Mary, His Virgin Mother, but the tragedy of redemption is completely absent. For this reason not only the theology but also the anthropology of Islam is very distant from Christianity.

Nevertheless, the religiosity of Muslims deserves respect. It is impossible not to admire, for example, their fidelity to prayer. The image of believers in Allah who, without caring about time or place, fall to their knees and immerse themselves in prayer remains a model for all those who invoke the true God, in particular for those Christians who, having deserted their magnificent cathedrals, pray only a little or not at all.

The Flagellation by Pacher.
"Jesus is mentioned in the Koran, but only as a prophet. The tragedy of redemption is completely absent." (St. John Paul II)

The Council has also called for the Church to have a dialogue with followers of the 'Prophet,' and the Church has proceeded to do so. We read in *Nostra Ætate*: 'Even if over the course of centuries Christians and Muslims have had more than a few dissensions and quarrels, this sacred Council now urges all to forget the past and to work toward mutual understanding as well as toward the preservation and promotion of social justice, moral welfare, peace, and freedom for the benefit of all mankind' (*Nostra Ætate* 3).

(St. John Paul II, *Crossing the Threshold of Hope* [New York: Knopf Doubleday Publishing Group, 2013], pp. 92-93)

Although Muslims profess a monotheistic religion, their conception of the one God differs significantly from what the Catholic Church teaches that God has revealed about himself. Although Muslims stress the oneness of God, they reject the Revelation of the Blessed Trinity as well as the divinity of Jesus Christ, considering one God in three Persons to be polytheistic. In Islam Jesus Christ is a prophet but not divine and not the Second Person of the Blessed Trinity. (The Koran teaches that an impostor, not Jesus himself, died on the Cross.) The Holy Spirit is regarded not as God himself but as a created being that brings God's life, inspiration, or guidance to people.

God, man, and creation. Islam teaches the absolute separation between God and creation. God can only be known through Revelation, not through reason. Catholics also believe in a separation between God and creation but believe that God can be known to some extent through creation. (We will discuss this later under the heading "Natural law.")

Catholics also believe that God made human beings in his own image and likeness[1] and became man himself in the Person of Jesus Christ, thus uniting himself intimately with the world. Islam rejects these beliefs; instead, it emphasizes the distance between the Creator and creation, like that of a carpenter and the chair he made. These different conceptions of God result in radical differences in how Muslims and Catholics approach God.

Muslims, for example, conceive of God primarily as a master. The word Islam means "submission" to Allah (or "peace through submission" to him), and it is a primary Islamic belief that men and women, creatures totally separated from God, must submit to Allah as their remote master, submitting to his commands out of a sense of duty or obligation. To Muslims God is also a merciful and compassionate master, but he is radically separate from man.

Muhammad Leads Abraham, Moses, and Jesus in Prayer.
Medieval Persian illumination.
In Islam Jesus Christ is a prophet but not divine and not the Second Person of the Blessed Trinity.

Catholics conceive of God first as a Father—a God who brought us into being, nurtures us, and loves us intensely. We also acknowledge God as our master and recognize that we are to submit to the will of God and that serving God is part of our call as disciples of Christ. But our call to submit to and serve God is not to be seen as a burden but rather the joyful duty of a child serving his or her father, motivated by love and responding to love. St. John revealed, "God is love";[2] the essential attribute of God in Catholic theology, therefore, is love.

What's more, for Catholics, God not only is an intimate and loving God but also seeks to draw us ever closer to him. Our ultimate goal in seeking holiness and living virtuously is complete union with God through Christ, who offers the promise of heaven.

Sacred Scripture. The Koran is the primary holy book of Islam. Muslims also accept those parts of the Bible that they believe were revealed to Moses, David, and Jesus, namely, the Pentateuch, the Psalms, and the Gospels. This acceptance, however, is highly conditional; they do not accept these writings in their present form. They claim that the Bible was corrupted over time, so it cannot be fully trusted as God's full and true revelation.

The Gospels are suspect particularly because Muslims believe that the true Gospel—the prophecy God gave to the "prophet" Jesus—has been lost. The ones written by the four Evangelists are not all that reliable. Muslims do not believe, for example, that Jesus was crucified or rose from the dead.

That is why, in the Muslim view, Allah gave the Koran to Muhammad: to correct the errors of the Old and New Testaments so that God's Revelation could be known accurately. Muslims are not encouraged to read the books of the Bible unless they are already well grounded in the Koran so that they can see the perceived errors of the Bible.

Furthermore, Islam teaches that the Koran is the literal word of God, that there was no human involvement in its writing beyond its recording. Koran means "recitation," which refers to the belief that Allah's revelation was recited verbatim to Muhammad. Catholics, however, understand that the biblical writers were the human authors of the Scriptures, who were truly inspired by God but used their human literary styles and devices in order to express what God wished to reveal.

Natural law. Because of their belief in the extreme separation of God and creation, Muslims in general do not acknowledge natural law, the belief that God has implanted knowledge of good and evil in each person. We do not have to be told that stealing is wrong, for example, but know it instinctively in our hearts. But according to Islam, the only way to know God's laws, whether a prohibition on theft or anything else, is through revelation.

Teaching authority. Further complicating matters is that no central authority governs the Islamic religion. In the Catholic Church, the Pope and the Magisterium are the supreme teaching authority and can resolve any disagreements over doctrine or practice in the Church. No such universal authority exists in Islam; there is no real teaching hierarchy. Muslims recognize the Koran as their sole authority, but its interpretation varies widely among Islamic scholars, clerics, spiritual leaders, and individuals and disputes arise over teachings and practice.

Veneration of the Blessed Virgin Mary. Although they do not believe that Jesus is divine, they do accept that he was born of a virgin. Many Catholics are surprised to discover the Muslim veneration of Mary. Since most have encountered a negative Protestant attitude toward the Mother of God and her role in salvation history, they often assume that all non-Catholics—especially those who are not Christians—would share that view of her. In fact, she is held in high esteem in Islam.

Jesus Speaks Immediately After His Birth, book illustration.
Muslims do not believe that Jesus is divine, but they do accept that he was born of a virgin.

The Blessed Virgin Mary is the only woman mentioned by name in the Koran, and she is mentioned more than thirty times (more frequently, in fact, than she is mentioned in the New Testament!). Muslims believe, like Catholics, that she was born without sin and that she is pure like no other woman. In addition, they believe in the Virgin Birth: that Jesus was conceived in her womb by a miracle of God. She is seen as a perfect model of faithfulness, and she is extolled because of her submission to God's will; remember the importance of submission in Muslim thought. Muslims refer to Jesus as the "son of Mary," which emphasizes her importance (as well as rejects the divinity of Christ).

Of course, Catholic and Islamic teaching on the Blessed Virgin Mary is not identical. Because Muslims do not believe in the divinity of Christ, they do not consider her the Mother of God. Islam does not accept her Assumption into heaven either, as that doctrine implies the divinity of Christ and the salvation wrought by his Crucifixion and Resurrection.

Catholic and Muslim veneration of the Blessed Virgin Mary, although distinct in theology and practice, is a beautiful means of bringing people to Christ. By drawing Muslims closer to the Mother of Christ, they will also be drawn closer to Christ himself.

Moral teachings. Similarities can be found in the moral codes of Islam and Catholicism. Many of the immoral practices that modern society has found acceptable—abortion, homosexual acts, sexual relations outside of marriage, etc.—are prohibited or at least strongly discouraged within the Islamic community. Muslims, like Catholics, also place great value on families. Catholicism and Islam, however, are not always in complete agreement on the specifics of these issues, and moral positions sometimes vary even among the various Muslim communities since Islam lacks a single teaching authority.

Nevertheless, as the world at large has become more hostile to traditional morality, Catholics and Muslims have drawn closer together in common cause to uphold several time-tested teachings. This has been true particularly at the United Nations, where the Vatican and Muslim leaders have helped block proposed language in international declarations that have threatened to weaken the family.

Prophet Muhammad Returns from His Night Journey and Ascension, book illustration. Muslims believe the dead will be raised and face a final judgment by God (Allah).

Sacraments. The Sacraments are means by which God makes himself present among us, giving us his grace for the sake of our sanctification and salvation. Islam has no such equivalent of Sacraments or grace; rather, Muslims strive to live according to the Five Pillars of Islam as expressions of their faith and submission to Allah.

Pious practices. In the religious practices of Catholics and Muslims, we find other similarities, particularly prayer, fasting, and almsgiving. These three aspects of the Five Pillars of Islam also form the core of Catholic spiritual practices. Of course, both religions derive these practices from Judaism, which has followed them for thousands of years.

Muslims practice *selah*, in which they pray ritually five times each day. In a similar manner, the Church encourages all Catholics to pray the *Liturgy of the Hours*, which is celebrated seven times throughout the day, as well as to engage in personal prayer and devotions.

Muslims observe *Ramadan*, a month set aside each year for fasting. Catholics each year observe the liturgical season of Lent, of which fasting is a major component.

Muslims must contribute a specific portion of their income to charity. Likewise, Catholics must contribute to the support of the Church and are encouraged to support charitable activities as well.

A term related to Muslim piety, which has become alarming in some contexts, is *jihad* ("struggle"). It is one of the ten principles of Shiite Islam. In its purest context, *jihad* refers to the interior struggle of a person who is striving for purification and virtue, particularly through the Five Pillars. It also can refer to the struggle to practice one's faith amid oppression and persecution, and it can refer to armed conflict against religious oppression. While mainstream Muslim leaders believe such conflict must be limited and aimed solely at ending the oppression, some radical Islamic groups use the idea of *jihad* to justify their acts of terrorism in a "holy war" against non-Muslim regions of the world.

The afterlife. Like Catholics, Muslims believe the dead will be raised and face a final judgment by God (Allah): The good will go to *Jannah* (heaven); the evil will go to *Jahannam* (hell), where they will experience constant shame and suffering. Muslims have no concept of purgatory, and their concept of heaven is not of a spiritual domain but of a very physical one—a lush garden flowing with rivers of milk, honey, and wine where carnal delights will be ever satisfied.

Pope Benedict XVI met with Palestinian Muslims living in the Aida Refugee Camp in Bethlehem during his Apostolic visit to the Holy Land in 2009.

CATHOLIC-MUSLIM DIALOGUE

Catholic and Muslim leaders are engaged in formal dialogue. For example, the Vatican hosted a forum with Muslim representatives in 2008, and regional dialogues in the U.S. have gone on since 1996 with the involvement of the United States Conference of Catholic Bishops.

Dialogue with those of the Islamic faith is essential in today's world. A respectful and peaceful dialogue between leaders in the Catholic and Islamic worlds can do much to advance the cause of faith and human solidarity. Some areas of particular concern for this dialogue include the following:

- How can people of faith work together to promote the role of religion in the world?
- What is the relationship between faith and reason?
- Does violence have a role in religion?
- How are truth and tolerance related?

The Second Ecumenical Council of the Vatican supported Catholic-Muslim dialogue strongly and encouraged efforts to improve interfaith relations. After speaking of "esteem" for the Muslims for their faith in God, their respect for Jesus and Mary, their belief in the resurrection of the dead, and their pious practices, the Council Fathers wrote:

> Since in the course of centuries not a few quarrels and hostilities have arisen between Christians and Moslems, this sacred synod urges all to forget the past and to work sincerely for mutual understanding and to preserve as well as to promote together for the benefit of all mankind social justice and moral welfare, as well as peace and freedom. (*Nostra Ætate*, 3)

FAR EASTERN WORLD RELIGIONS

Christianity is the dominant religion in the West and the most populous in the world. Judaism has had an enormous influence in the history of Western culture. Islam is the most prominent religion in the Middle East and is also influential in Africa and parts of Eastern Europe, Western Asia, and Oceania. However, most of the religious prominent traditions in the Indian subcontinent and the Far East have a history far different than the Abrahamic religions, and most of their beliefs and practices diverge radically from those of the major monotheistic faiths. The Catholic Church desires to engage in dialogue with these faith communities both to promote the common good of the human race and to orient all men and women towards the Gospel.

The major religions coming from the Far East are generally structured more like ethical systems than creedal religions, and there are many similarities among them.

Hinduism

Hinduism, practiced chiefly in India, is the world's third most populous religion after Christianity and Islam, yet it lacks many of the characteristics usually associated with the word "religion." Those who consider themselves Hindu do not claim a unified system of beliefs, though they do share some common themes about why human beings were created and how to live. The origins of Hinduism are unclear, going back thousands of years, and no one person is considered the religion's founder. Rather, it is a religion of gods with origins in unrecorded history.

ST. FRANCIS XAVIER, APOSTLE TO THE EAST

Historically, Christian missionary work in the Far East has been a daunting task. The continents of Europe, North America, South America, Australia, and most of Africa have been permeated with the Gospel, but Christian preaching has not extended as deeply into Asia, especially the Far East. Some notable exceptions include the Philippines, which is one of the most populous Catholic countries in the world; India, where St. Thomas the Apostle may have preached and established a community; and China and Vietnam, where there are sizable Catholic minorities. However, in general the preaching of Christ has been met with resistance or apathy in the countries of the Far East.

St. Francis Xavier (detail) by Salaverra. He has been called the greatest missionary of the Church since St. Paul.

However, St. Francis Xavier one of the first Jesuits and the close friend of the order's founder, St. Ignatius of Loyola, was able to successfully evangelize in his Far East missionary work. He met with severe hardships during his missionary travels, including persecution from many native peoples. However, he preached the Gospel tirelessly and worked among the peoples of these foreign lands, baptizing thousands. He has been called the greatest missionary of the Church since St. Paul.

Unfortunately, the work begun by St. Francis did not continue to flourish in the Far East, where authorities in China and Japan persecuted the budding Christian communities brutally, which continues in recent times by Chinese communists. Small groups of Catholics survived in Japan and China, but these remain a small minority to the present day.

Statue of Lord Shiva at the Murudeshwara Temple.
Shiva ("auspicious one") is a Hindu deity. He is considered the Supreme God within Shaivism, one of the three most influential denominations in Hinduism.

Hindus are not monotheistic. Although they believe in one supreme absolute that encompasses all things, called Brahman, there are countless Hindu gods and goddesses. Hindus are not only polytheistic but also pantheistic, believing that nature and the divine are one. In the traditional monotheistic religions of Christianity, Judaism, and Islam, there is a separation between God and creation, but in pantheism, all things are part of the one absolute.

No concept of heresy or apostasy exists in Hinduism, for all beliefs are accepted as ways to the divine. But there are several major beliefs that most Hindus hold:

Dharma is somewhat comparable to natural law as believed by Catholics. It is the law by which people should abide in order to maintain the natural order of things. It encompasses duty, justice, worship, and other concepts that foster correct behavior.

Karma is the concept of action and reaction in life. It focuses on cause and effect: how one action causes other reactions. Hindus do not agree on the ultimate source of karma; some ascribe the reactions caused by actions to a divine power and others to the way of nature.

Samsara is the Hindu belief in a cycle of birth, life, death, and rebirth—in other words, reincarnation. Samsara is related to karma in that actions lead to reactions that impact the cycle. One common Hindu belief is that a person's own ignorance causes the cycle of samsara and karma to continue and that, when he or she purifies him- or herself—usually through ascetical practices—he or she will be liberated from the cycle.

Buddhism

Buddhism, which like Hinduism began in India, traces its origins to Siddhartha Gautama, commonly known as Buddha, who lived sometime between the sixth and fourth centuries BC. Buddha is not considered a deity or even a prophet but rather an enlightened person whose teachings can help end suffering, ignorance, and hatred.

There is a close relationship between Buddhism and Hinduism: Buddha came from a Hindu family, and the two religions share many of the same teachings and beliefs. Some have compared the relationship between the two to the relationship between Christianity and Judaism, although the analogy is quite imperfect.

Like Hindus, Buddhists are polytheists, but they do not believe in a supreme absolute as Hindus do. Buddhists do hold to the ideas of dharma, karma, and samsara, although the Buddhist concepts of them differ from the Hindu.

The *dharma*, or doctrine, of Buddhism rests on what are called the "four noble truths," namely:

- Life is suffering.
- This suffering is caused by human desire.
- To be freed from suffering requires detachment from desire.
- We can detach ourselves from desire through the "eightfold path" of right thinking, intentions, speech, actions, livelihood, effort, awareness, and concentration.

Buddha's teachings, then, have as their goal the escape from pain and suffering. The state in which there is no suffering is called *nirvana*.

Tibetan Buddhism is an early offshoot of Buddhism that began to develop in the seventh century. It syncretizes early Buddhist ideas with the indigenous religion of Tibet. It is perhaps the best-known version of Buddhism because of the popularity of its spiritual leader, called the Dalai Lama.

Jainism

Jainism, which originated in ancient India, also has conceptual links to Hinduism and Buddhism. It emphasizes nonviolence and self-control as the means to purify the soul (*jiva*) and to be freed from an endless cycle of reincarnation.

In Jain thought the jiva is intrinsically pure and endowed with perfect knowledge, perception, happiness, and energy, but these attributes are corrupted by karma, which happens through interaction with the nonliving universe over many lifetimes. These impurities of karma can be cleansed and refined through right living and ascetic practices. This freedom from karma and achievement of perfect refinement of soul is called *moksha*.

A fundamental doctrine of Jainism is *anekantavada*, the idea that all points of view hold some truth and that absolute truth is unknowable, which thereby calls for religious tolerance for all faiths. It also leaves Jainism as a religion without creed or dogma as it functions more as an ethical system for the liberation of the soul and seeks to ask questions rather than formulate answers.

Shinto

Shinto is a polytheistic Japanese religion that originated around the year 500 BC. It is the *de facto* national religion of Japan, having been intertwined with the Japanese political system historically. Only in the twentieth century has Japanese political life become separated from Shinto.

Most people who practice Shinto also practice Buddhism, often applying Shinto to life situations and Buddhism to things related to death and the afterlife. Shinto itself has no strongly developed theology or moral code. Adherents worship their ancestors, and in fact the purpose of Shinto is to establish a connection between the modern day and Japan's past. The fundamental beliefs of Shinto can be summarized in their "four affirmations":

- Tradition and family. Shinto involves deep reverence for the past, including considering the family to be vital in preserving traditions.
- Love of nature. Followers of Shinto hold nature to be sacred, a means to worship the Shinto gods.
- Ritual purity. Shinto followers engage in ritual bathing in order to be purified before participating in Shinto rituals. They also hold general physical cleanliness in high regard.
- Matsuri. This is the worship of Shinto gods and ancestors.

The Creation Myth of Shinto. Izanagi-no-Mikoto (male) and Izanami-no-Mikoto (female) were called by all the myriad gods and asked to help each other create a new land which was to become Japan.

Sikhism

Sikhism (from the Punjabi *sikh*, "disciple") was founded by Guru Nanak in the 1500s in what is now Pakistan but was then part of India. It represents an effort to syncretize the religions of Hinduism and Islam and is held to have resulted from revelations to Nanak from the one Universal God, usually called *satnam* or *waheguru*. Although it may seem that Sikhism is a monotheistic religion—and it is often characterized as such—it can be described as a *monistic pantheism* because *satnam* is not a personal god. Instead, he is associated with truth and reality and can be manifest in countless ways under countless names and can also be equated with the universe itself.

Sikhism emphasizes the internal religious state of the individual and the value of good works over religious rituals. Its teachings come from the ten gurus, Nanak and his nine successors, all enlightened souls who guided and developed Sikh thought. After the death of the tenth guru in 1708, it was decided that the holy writings they left behind, the *Adi Granth*, would become the eleventh and eternal guru.

Like other major Eastern religions, Sikhs believe in a cycle of birth, life, death, and rebirth (reincarnation). The purpose of this cycle is to draw closer to *satnam* and to become one with him. Because the believer's goal is union with *satnam*, Sikhs desire to avoid anything that separates them from that union. The "five evils" in particular—anger, ego, greed, attachment, and lust—keep a person from divine union. The practice of the "eight virtues"—wisdom, truth, justice, temperance, patience, courage, humility, and contentment—are the prescribed means to combat these evils.

Baha'i

Founded in nineteenth-century Iran, Baha'i is a monotheistic religion. Those who follow Baha'i see religious history as a series of messengers—Moses, Buddha, Jesus, and Muhammad—each establishing his own religion, each of which brings humanity closer to God.

Baha'i stresses the unity of God, the unity of religion, and the unity of the human race. The Baha'i conception of God is very similar to Christian teaching: God is One, personal, All-powerful, All-knowing, and All-present. Because Baha'i followers believe religion has developed through time, they also believe that most religions are valid. Every person has a rational soul, and all are equal before God.

Although Baha'i originated as a syncretistic religion, subscribing to the beliefs of many different faiths, over time it has acquired enough uniqueness to be considered an independent religion. Nevertheless, many Muslims today consider Baha'i to be a breakaway from Islam.

The largest and the oldest surviving Baha'i House of Worship is in Wilmette, Illinois.
Known as the "Mother Temple of the West," the only decorative symbol inside the auditorium is Arabic calligraphy of the "Greatest Name" (O Thou the Glory of the Most Glorious!) in the top center of the inside of the dome.

CATHOLIC DIALOGUE WITH NON-CHRISTIAN EASTERN RELIGIONS

There are many radical differences between the Eastern non-Christian religions and Catholicism, starting with strikingly different conceptions of the divine. Yet, Catholics believe that some elements of truth exist in each of these faiths, including the importance of compassion, moral restraint, spiritual

ARE ALL RELIGIONS A WAY TO HEAVEN?

In pluralistic societies most people have daily encounters with people of other faith traditions. We have friends, neighbors, and even family members who are not Catholic and not even Christian. Because we love the people close to us, we desire their ultimate good, which is union with God in heaven. The desire to see loved ones in heaven—even those who do not follow Christ—might lead us to think that all religions, no matter what they teach, are equally valid and effective paths to heaven. But can a Catholic accept such an idea and still accept the teachings of the Church?

Christ declared, "I am the way, and the truth, and the life; no one comes to the Father, but by me" (Jn 14: 6). The Church has always proclaimed as one of her fundamental teachings that Christ is the *exclusive* means of salvation. Because of this, it would be illogical to claim that Christianity is just one valid religion out of many.

What can be said—and what the Catholic Church teaches—is that Christianity is fully true and that elements of truth are found in other religions. For example, any religion that teaches that there is one God teaches something that is true. Any religion that teaches that we must be compassionate toward those in need teaches something that is true. Truth is truth, no matter where it is proclaimed.

The Catholic Church teaches that we can hope for the salvation of those who do not profess the Catholic faith openly. But the Church also urges Catholics to share their faith with others: "Although in ways known to himself God can lead those who, through no fault of their own, are ignorant of the Gospel, to that faith without

The Ascension (detail) by Colombe.
If a non-Christian is saved,
it is through the work of Jesus Christ.

which it is impossible to please him, the Church still has the obligation and also the sacred right to evangelize all men" (CCC 848).

> **Those also can attain to salvation who through no fault of their own do not know the Gospel of Christ or His Church, yet sincerely seek God and moved by grace strive by their deeds to do His will as it is known to them through the dictates of conscience.[3] (*Lumen Gentium*, 16)**

A non-Christian's salvation would not come about because of the practice of his or her own religion. Instead, if a non-Christian is saved, it is through the work of Jesus Christ and because he or she responded to the graces that were given by God, even if unknowingly. No one comes to the Father except by Christ, but we hope and pray that even those who do not profess Christ might be drawn to him in ways we do not understand.

discipline, and respect for human dignity. These elements of truth can help orient members of these religions toward a more complete reception of the Gospel.

Dialogue with members of most religions outside the Judeo-Christian and Muslim faiths might appear difficult since there is so little in the way of a common foundation on which to build. At the same time, Christianity and the Eastern religions have had scant historical intersection, so there is little or no historical ill will to create divisions and roadblocks to effective dialogue. Furthermore, since most of the main Eastern traditions are focused more on spiritual perfection and tolerance than on creed, there is a natural openness to welcoming good interfaith relationships.

One event that marked a renewed openness to interfaith cooperation was the interfaith World Day of Prayer for Peace hosted by St. John Paul II at the Basilica of St. Francis in Assisi, Italy, in 1986. The gathering brought together leaders from thirty-two Christian religious groups and eleven non-Christian religions, including representatives of Jewish, Muslim, and Far Eastern faiths, including animists. In his remarks to close the assembly, St. John Paul II said:

> For the first time in history, we have come together from everywhere, Christian Churches and Ecclesial Communities, and World Religions, in this sacred place dedicated to Saint Francis, to witness before the world, each according to his own conviction, about the transcendent quality of peace.
>
> The form and content of our prayers are very different, as we have seen, and there can be no question of reducing them to a kind of common denominator. Yet, in this very difference we have perhaps discovered anew that, regarding the problem of peace and its relation to religious commitment, there is something which binds us together.[4]

St. John Paul II greets the Dalai Lama at Assisi in 1986. Dalai Lamas are the head monks of the Gelugpa lineage of Tibetan Buddhism. The 14th Dalai Lama, Tenzin Gyatso (shown above), won the Nobel Peace Prize in 1989 and is also well known for his lifelong advocacy for Tibetans inside and outside Tibet.

The caution against reducing the spiritual expressions and perspectives of diverse faith groups to a "common denominator" echoes our earlier concerns about a "too-easy ecumenism." Although interfaith dialogue can include shared prayer for peace and other objectives of substantial agreement, we cannot simply embrace prayer forms and practices of other religions and somehow incorporate them into Catholic piety. There is a principle in Catholic tradition: *lex orandi, lex credendi*—loosely, "as we pray, so we believe." This means not only that how we pray reflects our beliefs but also that our prayer actually *shapes* our beliefs. Thus, it is important that our spiritual practices harmonize well with our doctrine of faith.

Addressing this issue in his book *Crossing the Threshold of Hope*, St. John Paul II pointed out "an essentially different way of perceiving the world" between Christianity and the Far Eastern religions. He explained that Buddhist forms of meditation and ascetic practices are aimed at achieving enlightenment (nirvana) and liberation through a radical detachment and indifference to the world, which Buddhists perceive negatively as "the source of evil and of suffering for man." It does not seek to draw oneself closer to God. The Christian tradition, meanwhile, is quite different:

> For Christians, the world is God's creation, redeemed by Christ. It is in the world that man meets God. Therefore he does not need to attain such an absolute detachment in order to find himself in the mystery of his deepest self. For Christianity, it does not make sense to speak of the world as a "radical" evil, since at the beginning of the world we find God the Creator who loves His creation, a God who "gave his only Son, so that everyone who believes in him might not perish but might have eternal life" (Jn 3:16).[5]

The Christian spiritual tradition does seek a certain detachment from the world but not as an end in itself. We detach from material things because we desire ultimately the eternal joy of heaven, where we

Pope John Paul II at the interfaith World Day of Prayer for Peace at the Basilica of St. Francis in Assisi, Italy, 1986. "With the other Christians we share many convictions and, particularly, in what concerns peace. With the World Religions we share a common respect of and obedience to conscience, which teaches all of us to seek the truth, to love and serve all individuals and people, and therefore to make peace among nations." (St. John Paul II, *Address to the Representatives of the Christian Churches and Ecclesial Communities and of the World Religions*, October 27, 1986)

will remain forever in the presence of God. Our mission as followers of Christ is to transform and perfect the world, not to abandon it. Detachment is a means to approach God rather than an end in itself. Thus, the Pope issued this warning:

> For this reason it is not inappropriate *to caution* those Christians who enthusiastically *welcome certain ideas originating in the religious traditions of the Far East*—for example, techniques and methods of meditation and ascetical practice. In some quarters these have become fashionable, and are accepted rather uncritically. First one should know one's own spiritual heritage well and consider whether it is right to set it aside lightly.[6]

The Pontifical Council for Interreligious Dialogue oversees the Catholic Church's official relationships with all non-Christian religions worldwide. The Church has ongoing dialogues with many Far Eastern religions at the international level, and a number of national and local churches likewise spons[illegible] dialogues to build understanding and good will.

NON-CHRISTIAN OFFSHOOTS OF CHRISTIANITY

In this chapter we have looked mainly at religions with no direct [illegible]ty. They developed apart from Christian[illegible]ial at best. However, in the [illegible] movements developed that claimed [illegible] Christianity," which was seen as first-century or apostolic Christianity [illegible] these movements formed new Protestant denominations, and some separated themsel[illegible] traditional Christianity entirely, professing belief in Christ but ceasing to be definably Christi[illegible] lack of a valid rite of Baptism.

Tw[illegible] most prominent of these latter movements are the Church of Jesus Christ of Latter-day S[illegible]—better known as the Mormons—and the Jehovah's Witnesses.

Christus statue located in the North Visitors' Center on Temple Square in Salt Lake City, Utah. Mormons believe in the divinity of Jesus Christ and his Resurrection, but they reject the doctrine of the Blessed Trinity. The Father, Son, and Spirit are considered separate beings that form one Godhead.

LATTER-DAY SAINTS

The Church of Jesus Christ of Latter-day Saints was founded by Joseph Smith. According to Smith, he received a book of golden plates from the angel Moroni in the 1820s in western New York State. He then claimed to have translated these plates, which were written in an unknown language; afterward, the angel took back the plates. This text became known as the Book of Mormon, which Mormons consider a sacred text. Like the Koran, the Book of Mormon is alleged to be a new revelation from God that expands and corrects distortions of the Old and New Testaments.

The Book of Mormon is a collection of books that tells the story of how a group of Jews migrated to present-day North America centuries before Christ and established a civilization. It goes on to describe how Christ, after his Resurrection, came to North America to preach the Gospel to them. Traditional Christianity teaches that Christ ascended into heaven forty days after his Resurrection and will not return to earth until the end of time.

Smith developed a strong following and established communities in Ohio and Missouri, which soon faced opposition from their neighbors over their beliefs. Armed clashes led to the Mormon War in Missouri, and the Latter-day Saints were expelled from the state in 1839. They then moved to Illinois and established the city of Nauvoo, where Smith petitioned the U.S. government for status as an independent territory.

The "revelations" to Smith did not end with the Book of Mormon; rather, Smith claimed to have received revelations regularly, and these teachings were later incorporated into a collection called *Doctrines and Covenants*. Other revelations led him to rewrite some of the books of the Torah, sometimes inserting long sections of new material.

When Smith began teaching his associates some of his doctrines—including the allowance of *polygamy*, or "plural marriage," by which a man could have more than one wife—several objected and started a breakaway Mormon denomination. Eventually, the disagreement escalated to the point where the former associates brought charges against Smith, who was imprisoned in nearby Carthage, Illinois. It is there that a mob stormed the prison and killed Smith in 1844.

After Smith's death the Mormons were divided over the issue of a successor and experienced a four-way schism. The largest group accepted as its leader Brigham Young, who over the next few years led a resettlement to what is now Salt Lake City. This group is known as the Church of Jesus Christ of Latter-day Saints (LDS Church).

A smaller group believed that the leadership should remain within the Smith family. They formed the Reorganized Church of Latter Day Saints (RLDS) and established a headquarters in Wisconsin that was moved later to Independence, Missouri. Many of the beliefs of this group, now known as the Community of Christ, have evolved from the more controversial Mormon doctrines—so much so, in fact, that it has restored valid Baptism and can be considered an authentically Christian ecclesial community. (See the section "Are They Christian?")

Other splinter sects of Mormonism exist today, including some known for their practice of polygamy and cult-like control over members.

Beliefs and Practices

Several teachings of the LDS Church differ from the traditional beliefs and practices of Catholicism, Orthodoxy, and mainstream Protestantism:

Concept of God. The LDS Church rejects the doctrine of the Blessed Trinity as formulated in the early Church. They believe that God the Father has a coequal wife, the heavenly Mother, who together generate and raise the spirits of humans before they are sent to earth to be born; Jesus was the first of these created spirits and was given divine status before his human birth. The Father and the Son both have physical, glorified bodies; the Holy Spirit is spirit alone and, like the Son, is a created being. The Father, Son, and Spirit are perfectly united in will and purpose as a Godhead but are separate beings and not consubstantial, often described as "one in purpose, but separate beings," essentially, three gods united as one. Mormons worship and pray to the heavenly Father through Jesus but never directly to Jesus or the Holy Spirit.

Mainline Mormons also believe that the "righteous" among them become gods themselves after death. Just as Christ received his divine status by perfect obedience to the Father, righteous Mormons can achieve divine status, or *exaltation*, through our own obedience and faithfulness.

These complex teachings lead many Christian scholars to describe the Mormon view as polytheism, meaning belief in many gods, or *henotheism*, meaning belief in multiple gods but worship of only one God above the others. Generally, Mormons deny these labels.

The First Vision of Joseph Smith, stained glass. Mormons believe that Joseph Smith received revelations from God and that his successors continue to receive revelations, including new doctrines.

Continuing Revelation. The Catholic Church teaches that public Revelation—God's Revelation of himself and his saving plan—ended with the death of the last Apostle. Mormons believe that Joseph Smith received revelations from God and that his successors continue to receive revelations, including new doctrines.

Church governance. The LDS Church has a hierarchy led by a president who is assisted by two counselors; together these three men comprise the First Presidency. The next level of the hierarchy is the Quorum of the Twelve Apostles, whose members oversee various specific areas of ministry. Below them are the First and Second Quorum of the Seventy, which oversee specific geographic areas of the world, followed by several levels of intermediate hierarchy. The basic local LDS community is the ward, which is headed by a bishop. Most males over the age of twelve are considered priests.

It should be noted here that the Church of Jesus Christ of Latter-day Saints is not a "church" in the true sense, even though it uses the term in its official name. We know this from our earlier reading on what defines a church: Apostolic Succession, which thereby means a valid priesthood and valid Sacraments. Mormons lack these elements and thus do not constitute a church.

Sacrament. The LDS Church observes several rites called *ordinances*. Five of these ordinances—baptism, confirmation, ordination (for men only), temple endowment, and sealing of marriage—bear a resemblance to the Christian Sacraments. Other ordinances include "the sacrament," which resembles a communion service; administration to the sick; blessing of children; and blessing of graves.

The LDS Church baptizes adults using the Trinitarian formula, but their baptisms are not considered valid as they do not believe in the Blessed Trinity. They partake of "the sacrament" at their weekly "sacrament meeting" by consuming blessed bread and water symbolic of the Body and Blood of Christ. Marriage sealing and endowment are performed at the temple in Salt Lake City.

A Mormon bishop hears "confessions" but does not forgive sins. Rather, he facilitates the process by which God forgives.

Baptism of the Dead. Mormons believe that people who have already died can be "baptized," allowing them to become Mormons posthumously. This is done by baptizing someone here on earth as a proxy for a person who has already passed away. That is why the Latter-day Saints are known for their immense genealogical work: They gather names of deceased non-Mormons so they can be baptized by proxy as Mormons.

JEHOVAH'S WITNESSES

The Jehovah's Witnesses was founded by Charles Taze Russell in the late nineteenth century. Like Mormonism, this organization believes itself to be a restoration of first-century Christianity. Russell was raised a Protestant, became agnostic for a time, and then regained interest in religion, especially in the return of Christ at the end of the world. In 1879 he started the Watch Tower, which eventually became known as the Watchtower Bible and Tract Society, the teaching organ of the Jehovah's Witnesses.

Charles Taze Russell, 1911.
Jehovah Witnesses derive their name from the Book of Isaiah: "You are my witnesses."

Jehovah's Witnesses, often called simply Witnesses, derive their name from the Book of Isaiah, which declares:

> **"You are my witnesses," says the Lord, "and my servant whom I have chosen, that you may know and believe me and understand that I am He. Before me no god was formed, nor shall there be any after me. I, I am the Lord, and besides me there is no savior. I declared and saved and proclaimed, when there was no strange god among you; and you are my witnesses," says the Lord.** (Is 43:10-12)

Witnesses consider the Bible to be inspired and their source of authority but only accept as valid a specific translation known as the New World Translation. This version has certain unique translations of important Scriptural passages that support the Witnesses' doctrinal views. For example, Witnesses reject the doctrine of the Blessed Trinity, teaching that Jesus is a creation, not the eternal Son of God. Thus, their translation of the first verse of St. John's Gospel reads, "In [the] beginning the Word was, and the Word was with God, *and the Word was a god*" [emphasis added]. Catholic and most Protestant Bibles correctly translate this last phrase, "...and the Word was God."

In addition to their rejection of the Blessed Trinity and the divinity of Christ, Jehovah's Witnesses have many distinctive beliefs and practices:

The name of Jehovah. Witnesses stress the importance of the name "Jehovah" for God. When Moses asked God for his name, God told him "I AM WHO I AM."[7] This was represented by the tetragrammaton YHWH, but out of respect for the name of God, the Israelites normally referred to God as *Adonai*, meaning "Lord." Due to differences in translations and languages over time, the tetragrammaton was also rendered JHVH, and approximating the vowels from *Adonai* produces *Jehovah*. According to Jehovah's Witnesses, the Holy Spirit is simply God's power, not a person of the Godhead.

The afterlife. Witnesses reject the concept of hell and believe that the soul can die just like a body can die. Based on their reading of the Book of Revelation, they believe that exactly 144,000 people will be taken up to heaven to rule with Jesus.[8] Other followers of Jesus have the possibility of being raised to live on a cleansed earth free from sin and corruption.

Rejection of blood transfusions. One of the most peculiar and well-known practices of Jehovah's Witnesses is their absolute rejection of blood transfusions, even if it means death for a loved one. They base this practice on Scripture verses: "Only you shall not eat flesh with its life, that is, its blood,"[9] and "For the life of every creature is the blood of it; therefore I have said to the people of Israel, You shall not eat the blood of any creature, for the life of every creature is its blood; whoever eats it shall be cut off."[10]

ARE ONLY 144,000 SAVED?

One of the more interesting beliefs of the Jehovah's Witnesses is their teaching that only 144,000 people will be taken by God into heaven. What is the significance of that number, and why do the Witnesses believe this?

Scriptural support for this unique belief is two passages from the Book of Revelation. In the first, taken to be a vision of the end of the world, the angels delay the destruction of the earth "till we have sealed the servants of our God upon their foreheads," and the number of those to be sealed is given as 12,000 from each of the Twelve Tribes of Israel, which is 144,000.[11] The second passage seems to paint a picture of the Last Judgment:

> I looked, and lo, on Mount Zion stood the Lamb, and with him a hundred and forty-four thousand who had his name and his Father's name written on their foreheads. (Rev 14:1)

Jehovah's Witnesses take the 144,000 number in this passage literalistically, claiming it to be the exact number of souls that will be in heaven at the end of time.

There are several problems with this interpretation. First, we must be aware of the meaning and use of numbers in the Bible. Numbers have symbolic meaning in the Scriptures and are not always intended to be taken literalistically. This is something that the biblical authors knew and their readers understood, too. The number forty, for example, is frequently used in the Bible, and it symbolizes the length of one generation (forty years) or a "complete time" (such as forty days). The number twelve also has profound symbolism: It is both the number of tribes of Israel and the number of Apostles and thus represents the complete People of God. In addition, the number 1,000 is used to represent a large number, no matter what the actual number really is.

Thus 144,000, which is 12 x 12 x 1000, represents the complete and great numbers of the heavenly People of God. It is not intended to be a literalistic figure but to represent the vast reach of God in salvation history.

This is a prime example of the danger of interpreting Scripture apart from the Church, whose teaching authority is guaranteed by the Holy Spirit to be free of error. By misunderstanding an admittedly difficult passage, the Jehovah's Witnesses have created a core doctrine where none really exists.

The Adoration of the Trinity (detail) by Durer.
Mormons and Jehovah's Witnesses reject the doctrine of the Blessed Trinity, the full divinity of Jesus Christ, and many other fundamental teachings of traditional Christianity.

ARE MORMONS AND JEHOVAH'S WITNESSES CHRISTIAN?

One of the most common questions when discussing Mormons and Jehovah's Witnesses is very basic: Are they Christian?

This can be a controversial question. On the one hand, Mormons and Jehovah's Witnesses claim to be Christian on the principle that they follow Christ and accept on some level the authority of what he revealed in the New Testament. On the other hand, they reject the doctrine of the Blessed Trinity, the full divinity of Jesus Christ, and many other fundamental teachings of traditional Christianity.

So, are they Christian? To answer this we must recall our discussion from an earlier chapter of what defines a Christian. The Church maintains a very specific definition for Christian: a person who is *validly baptized*. Although a baptized person may not necessarily be a good Christian, an informed Christian, or even a practicing Christian, he or she, by the mere fact of a valid Baptism, has become a member of the Family of God, the Church, and is a Christian.

Although Mormons and Jehovah's Witnesses do practice a ritual called baptism, the Catholic Church does not recognize these as valid. Remember that according to the Church, a valid Baptism must be administered using water and the Trinitarian formula: "...in the name of the Father, and of the Son, and of the Holy Spirit." The person who administers the Baptism intends to do what the Church does in Baptism. A valid Baptism, then, presumes belief in the Blessed Trinity: three divine Persons in one God.

The Jehovah's Witnesses are monotheistic but reject the Trinity outright, acknowledging only the Father as divine. Their baptism does not use the Trinitarian formula. The LDS Church baptizes with water and uses a Trinitarian formula, but their doctrines regarding the Father, Son, and Holy Spirit deviate too radically from Christian belief. Neither the LDS Church nor the Jehovah's Witnesses, then, practice a valid Baptism. Thus, they are not considered Christian ecclesial communities or Christians.

The Community of Christ, formerly called the Reorganized Church of Jesus Christ of Latter-day Saints, has a Christian understanding of Baptism and the Trinity and therefore practices a valid Baptism and is considered a Christian ecclesial community.

Certain other religious groups that may appear to be Christian or have "Christian" in their name are in fact not Christian ecclesial communities, properly understood. Some of these include Christian Science (no baptismal rite; baptism is an internal "purification by spirit"), the Salvation Army (dedication service but no water baptism), and Unitarian Universalists (dedication service but no baptism).

Whenever a person presents himself or herself to enter full communion with the Catholic Church and it cannot be determined whether he or she was validly baptized or not, the Church will perform a *conditional Baptism* ("If you have not already been baptized, I baptize you...") in order to ensure that Baptism has been received.

The fact that the Catholic Church does not accept certain religions as Christian, however, is not an excuse for disrespect or lack of charity. Like all people, adherents of these religions deserve respect due to their dignity as creatures made in the image and likeness of God, and dialogue between their faiths and the Catholic Church can be productive in finding common ground for the good of all people.

CONCLUSION

The vast breadth and diversity of religious faith represented by the religions of the world present a major challenge to the Church. The mission of the Church is to bring all people to knowledge and acceptance of the Gospel in hopes that all will unite within the one Church instituted by Christ, which subsists in the Catholic Church. Christianity itself, as we saw in earlier chapters, is fractured by disagreements that are historical, cultural, and doctrinal in nature, which presents already a formidable task as ecumenical dialogue seeks to overcome differences that in some cases have existed for several centuries. Interfaith dialogue with adherents of other world religions, although perhaps an effort that meets with still greater obstacles, is no less critical to our obligation to work toward the complete unity that Christ so desired for all people. Christianity shares much in common with non-Christian religions such respect for the family, the dignity of human beings, and a desire for peace. The dialogue between the Catholic Church and other religions can do much to improve mutual respect and to promote peace in the world.

No one, no matter how distant from full communion with the Catholic Church one may be, is beyond the reach of God's infinite mercy and redemption. So even as the Church, in fulfillment of her sacred mission, strives to bring all people into her fold as Christ so intensely desires, she prays also that even those who do not respond to this call may ultimately be saved by the grace and mercy of God.

Neither the LDS Church nor the Jehovah's Witnesses practice a valid Baptism. Thus, they are not considered Christian ecclesial communities or Christians.

CHALLENGES:

If our ultimate goal is to unite all people in faith, then why can each side not compromise its beliefs when it comes to ecumenical and interreligious dialogue?

Oftentimes when two parties are in conflict, they sit down and hammer out a solution. One side gives in a little, the other side gives in a little, and somewhere in the middle they meet. Neither side gets everything it originally wanted, but both sides come away gaining something and feeling reconciled. It is a win-win situation for everyone involved. Would that not be a great way to achieve Christian unity?

What God has revealed to his Church is objectively true. Objective truth is something that is true for everyone at all times; it is not a matter of personal preference or perspective. There can be a plurality of opinion on a number of issues and beliefs, but when it comes to objective truth, there can be no compromise.

There is no real unity apart from unity in the truth. Any "unity" derived on the basis of what is false is itself a false unity. That is why the Catholic Church must always stand up for the truth that has been revealed by God, the doctrinal and moral truth that is guaranteed and guided by the Holy Spirit.

Catholic belief in the Real Presence of Christ in the Eucharist is not an issue on which there can be compromise.

Take, for example, Catholic belief in the Real Presence of Christ in the Eucharist. Many Protestant ecclesial communities believe that the Eucharist is only a symbol, that Christ is not truly present in the Sacrament. This is not an issue on which there can be compromise. The Church cannot decide that Christ both is and is not really present in the Eucharist at the same time, or that every person is free to believe in the Real Presence or to believe it is just a symbol. The only way to realize unity on this issue is to guide the separated Christian communities to understand Christ's Eucharistic presence as we do and, moreover, to understand that this Eucharist is validly consecrated only through the actions of a priest who has received the Sacrament of Holy Orders in a Church that has preserved Apostolic Succession.

That illustrates how, when there are conflicting beliefs that contradict one another intrinsically, only one belief can be true. In other instances, however, dialogue may uncover how other churches and Christian ecclesial communities also reflect part of the truth and can help provide balance to how the fullness of truth is presented.

One example of this is in the *Joint Declaration on the Doctrine of Justification*, in which the positions of both the Catholic Church and the Lutheran World Federation were found to be in essential harmony as to the importance of both faith and works. Another example pertains to the *Filioque* controversy, which the *Catechism of the Catholic Church* and, increasingly, Orthodox scholars characterize more as a disagreement over semantics rather than the actual substance of doctrine (cf. CCC 248). The fruits of the Catholic-Anglican dialogue, too, show how the serious, respectful, and loving pursuit of the totality of truth—and how best to express that truth—can help provide such balance.

There is a wonderful expression, often attributed to St. Augustine (but probably not originating with him), that summarizes this centrality of objective truth in ecumenical dialogue: "In essentials unity, in nonessentials liberty, in all things charity." Proclamation of the truth goes together with dialogue.

PILLARS OF THE FAITH

ST. JOHN PAUL II

More than any Pope in recent memory, St. John Paul II was known for his outreach not only to other Christian communities but also to non-Christian religions. Through his statements, documents, joint prayer meetings, and personal visits, he sought to open doors of dialogue in order to increase understanding and peace among the religions.

Although the Church's relationship with Islam has often been difficult, St. John Paul II made a point of visiting mosques and meeting with Muslim leaders and groups during his international trips. At the same time he decried Muslim violence in the world, shed light on persecutions of Christians under Islamic law, and insisted on full religious freedom in predominantly Muslim countries.

He made similar efforts to build bridges with Jews and Judaism, which he considered the elder brother of Christianity, blessed with the original and irrevocable covenant with God.

St. John Paul II believed strongly that shared prayer can unite believers. That is why he invited leaders of Judaism, Islam, Buddhism, Hinduism, Zoroastrianism, Unitarianism, traditional African and Native American religions, and many others to join Catholic, Orthodox, and Protestant leaders in the 1986 World Day of Prayer for Peace in Assisi, Italy.

In many other gatherings, meetings, and addresses during his pontificate, St. John Paul II sought to draw representatives of all religions into deeper mutual respect and understanding, encouraging dialogue about shared values and beliefs. He never watered down Catholic belief, however, and always called upon Catholics engaged in such dialogues to represent the Gospel and Church teachings with complete fidelity.

Continued

ST. JOHN PAUL II

Continued

Pope Benedict XVI beatified Pope John Paul II before 1.5 million faithful in St. Peter's Square and surrounding streets on May 1, 2011. "He restored to Christianity its true face as a religion of hope," Pope Benedict said in his homily.

After the 2001 attacks against the World Trade Center and Pentagon by radical Islamists with ties to terrorist organizations, St. John Paul II continually assured the Muslim world that the Church did not view terrorism perpetrated by Islamist groups and the "war on terror" waged against such groups largely by Western nations as a religious war between Muslims and Christians.

When St. John Paul II passed away in 2005, Muslims around the world paid him tribute. Among these were President Hosni Mubarak of Egypt, the most populous Arab country, who declared three days of mourning for the Pope and praised him for his "long journey of giving, during which he remained a symbol of love and peace and one who called for dialogue between religions."[12] Meanwhile, Sheikh Tantawi, the highest religious authority of Sunni Islam, characterized the Pope's death as "a great loss for the Catholic Church and the Muslim world....He was a man who defended the values of justice and peace and worked for the victory of relations between the Muslim and Christian people based on friendship and love."[13]

"His profound humility, grounded in close union with Christ, enabled him to continue to lead the Church and to give to the world a message which became all the more eloquent as his physical strength declined... Blessed are you, beloved Pope John Paul II, because you believed!" (Pope Benedict XVI Homily, May 1, 2011)

SUPPLEMENTARY READING

Muslim and Christian Communities Should be in Respectful Dialogue

Both Muslims and Christians prize their places of prayer, as oases where they meet the All Merciful God on the journey to eternal life, and where they meet their brothers and sisters in the bond of religion. When, on the occasion of weddings or funerals or other celebrations, Christians and Muslims remain in silent respect at the other's prayer, they bear witness to what unites them, without disguising or denying the things that separate.

It is in mosques and churches that the Muslim and Christian communities shape their religious identity, and it is there that the young receive a significant part of their religious education. What sense of identity is instilled in young Christians and young Muslims in our churches and mosques? It is my ardent hope that Muslim and Christian religious leaders and teachers will present our two great religious communities as communities in respectful dialogue, never more as communities in conflict. It is crucial for the young to be taught the ways of respect and understanding, so that they will not be led to misuse religion itself to promote or justify hatred and violence. Violence destroys the image of the Creator in his creatures, and should never be considered as the fruit of religious conviction.

— St. John Paul II, *Address to the Muslims of Damascus*. (May 6, 2001) no. 3

Three Worshipers Praying in a Mosque by Gerome. "Both Muslims and Christians prize their places of prayer, as oases where they meet the All Merciful God on the journey to eternal life." (St. John Paul II)

Multireligious and Interreligious Prayer

In the age of dialogue and of the encounter between religions, the question has necessarily arisen as to whether we can pray with each other. Nowadays people make a distinction here between multireligious and interreligious prayer.... Multireligious prayer [is when] people belonging to various religious affiliations meet together....They pray—albeit simultaneously—in separate places, each in his own fashion.... I see two basic conditions [for multireligious prayer]:

1. Such multireligious prayer cannot be the normal form of religious life but can only exists as a sign in the unusual situations, in which, as it were, a common cry for help rises up, stirring the hearts of men, to stir also the heart of God.
2. Such a procedure almost inevitably leads to false interpretations...that is why...these procedures must remain exceptional and why a careful explanation, of what happens here and what does not happen, is most important....

While in multireligious prayer this is done in fact within the same context, yet separately, interreligious prayer means people or groups of various religious allegiances praying together.... Three elementary conditions have to be set, without which such prayer would become a mere denial of faith:

1. We can pray with each other only if we are agreed who or what God is and if there is therefore basic agreement as to what praying is: a process of dialogue in which I talk to a God who is able to hear and take notice....
2. Yet there must also be fundamental agreement—on the basis of the concept of God—about what is worth praying about and what might be the content of prayer....
3. The whole thing must be so arranged that the relativistic misinterpretation of faith and prayer can find no foothold in it.

—Joseph Cardinal Ratzinger, *Truth and Tolerance*, (San Francisco: Ignatius Press) 2004. pp. 106-109

VOCABULARY

ABRAHAMIC RELIGIONS
Those religions that claim to originate with the Old Testament figure of Abraham. Judaism, Christianity, and Islam are considered the most significant Abrahamic religions.

ADI GRANTH
The sacred writings of Sikhism, regarded as the eleventh and final guru.

ALLAH
The name commonly given to the one God worshiped by Islam. The word is simply the Arabic word for "God" and is thus even used by Arabic non-Muslims for God.

ASBAB AL-NUZEL
The name given to passages in the Koran that are believed to come later than other passages on the same subject and, thus, supersede those previous passages.

BOOK OF MORMON
A holy book of Mormonism that is believed to have originated from golden tablets given to Joseph Smith by an angel called Moroni. It contains the story of a group of Israelites who travelled to America before the time of Christ and were then visited by Christ after his Ascension.

BRAHMAN
The supreme absolute of Hinduism. Brahman is believed to encompass all things.

CALIPH
Literally, "successor." The caliphs were the successors of Muhammad and, thus, the leaders of the early Muslim community.

DHARMA
Similar to natural law, it is the law by which people should abide in order to maintain the natural order of things. Both Hindus and Buddhists teach the importance of dharma.

EXALTATION
In Mormon belief, the divine status, or salvation, achieved after death by righteous Mormons through their obedience and faithfulness to the Father.

GURU NANAK
A sixteenth-century religious leader who founded Sikhism, which emphasizes the internal religious state of the individual and the value of good works over specific religious rituals.

HADITH
A written version of an Islamic tradition associated with the life and words of Muhammad. These traditions are influential in determining Islamic beliefs and practices, but the Koran is held in higher regard.

HAJJ
The pilgrimage to Mecca required of each Muslim at least once during his lifetime.

HENOTHEISM
The belief in the existence of many gods only one of whom is worshiped. Mormons claim this was the practice of the early Jews and practice it today.

HIJRA
The event of Muhammad's migration from Mecca to Medina (Yathrib) in 622, regarded as the founding of Islam.

JAHANNAM
Muslim term for a place of punishment that is similar in some ways but not the same as the Christian idea of hell.

JANNAH
Muslim term for heaven.

JIHAD
Arabic for "struggle." A religious war of Muslims against religious oppression. While mainstream Muslim leaders believe such conflict must be limited and aimed solely at ending the oppression, radical Islamic groups use the idea of *jihad*, or "holy war," to justify their acts of terrorism against the non-Muslim world.

KARMA
The concept of action and reaction in life—how one action impacts future actions. Both Hindus and Buddhists teach the importance of Karma.

LEX ORANDI, LEX CREDENDI
Latin for "as we pray, so we believe," a reference to how prayer both reflects and shapes our beliefs.

VOCABULARY Continued

LITURGY OF THE HOURS
A collection of Psalms, other biblical passages and prayers that have been organized by the Catholic Church as a means of daily prayer. They are divided into different "offices" that are prayed at specific times of day.

MATSURI
The worship of gods and ancestors in the Shinto religion.

MECCA
The birthplace of Muhammad, it is therefore considered the holiest city in the religion of Islam. It is located in modern-day Saudi Arabia.

NATURAL LAW
The participation of man in the plan of God in relation to human life and action, insofar as the mind can understand it. The objective order established by God that determines the requirements for people to thrive and reach fulfillment. Natural law "enables man to discern by reason the good and the evil, the truth and the lie" (CCC 1954).

NIRVANA
The state of being free from suffering, which is the goal of Buddhists and Hindus.

PANTHEISM
The belief that everything is part of God. In pantheism, the universe and God are identical.

POLYGAMY
Attempted marriage between more than two people (one man and one woman) at the same time. Polygamy refers to a man attempting marriage with more than one wife; polyandry refers to a woman attempting marriage with more than one husband. This is a sin against the unity of marriage and forbidden by the Sixth Commandment.

KORAN
The holy book of Islam. The Koran is considered to contain the visions of Muhammad, which were written down by his followers. Muslims consider the Koran to be completely inerrant and to literally contain the words of God.

RADICAL SECULARISTS
Those who wish to eliminate completely the role of God and religion in public life.

RAMADAN
The holy month of Islam commemorating the time during which Muslims believe the Koran was given to Muhammad. Celebrated in the ninth lunar month of each year, a strict fast is observed from sunrise to sunset each day.

REINCARNATION
The belief that after this life, one will be reborn into another life in the future. Also known as samsara, it is accepted by Hindus and Buddhists.

SAMSARA
The belief in a cycle of birth, life, death, and rebirth. Also known as reincarnation, it is taught by both Hindus and Buddhists.

SELAH
Ritual prayer of the Muslims, accomplished five times daily.

SHAHADA
The first pillar and credal statement of Islam: "There is no God but Allah, and Muhammad is his prophet."

SIDDHARTHA GAUTAMA
Also known as "Buddha," he is the founder of Buddhism who taught the importance of overcoming suffering in this world.

SYNCRETIC RELIGION (SYNCRETISM)
The combining of different religious beliefs, even contradictory ones, by an individual or group.

STUDY QUESTIONS

1. If there is only one true religion, are all other religions completely false? Why or why not?
2. Who founded Islam? When and where did he found it?
3. What was the initial reaction to Muhammad's teachings?
4. What is the significance of the town once known as Yathrib?
5. What is a caliph?
6. What is the origin of the schism between the Sunni and Shiite Muslims?
7. How far into Europe did the original Muslim conquests reach?
8. Why was the first Crusade called?
9. How have the Crusades led to a strain in the relations between Christians and Muslims even today?
10. What is the origin of the Koran?
11. What are the *asbab al-nuzel*, and how do they impact relations between Muslims and Christians and Jews?
12. What are the Five Pillars of Islam?
13. List at least three similarities between Islam and Christianity.
14. How do Muslims view Jesus differently than Christians?
15. What does the word "Islam" mean, and how does that reflect the Muslim view of Allah (God)?
16. How does the Catholic view of biblical inspiration differ from the Muslim view of the Koran's inspiration?
17. Do Muslims have a figure like the Pope as an authority? If not, how are they assured of properly interpreting the Koran?
18. What are some subjects for dialogue between Christians and Muslims today?
19. What are the three major beliefs that Hindus share?
20. Who is the founder of Buddhism and from what religion did Buddhism originate?
21. What is the primary problem Buddhism addresses?
22. What are the four affirmations of Shinto?
23. Who founded Sikhism and when and where did he found it?
24. Describe the key teachings of Sikhism. Who or what is the eleventh and eternal guru?
25. What do Sikhs consider the five evils?
26. What does it mean that Baha'i is a syncretic religion?
27. What are some similarities between Catholicism and the religions of the Far East?
28. What are some beliefs of Mormons that differ from traditional Christianity?
29. Where do Jehovah's Witnesses derive their name?
30. How does the Bible translation used by the Jehovah's Witnesses differ from other Bible translations?
31. Why is the number 144,000 important to Jehovah's Witnesses?
32. Why are the Church of Jesus Christ of Latter-day Saints (Mormons) and Jehovah's Witnesses not considered Christian religions by the Catholic Church?

PRACTICAL EXERCISES

1. Explain the difference between the Catholic and Muslim views of their holy writings, the Bible and the Koran. Who wrote the Koran? How? Why?

2. How do you explain the teaching *extra ecclesiam nulla salus* ("Outside the Church there is no salvation") while recognizing the teaching that a non-Catholic may be saved.

3. Choose a Muslim-run country and research its laws. Find out about its civil rights, morality, political process, and government.

4. Choose a religion mentioned in this chapter other than Islam. Research its origins. Who founded it? When and where was it founded? How did it grow? How many members does it currently claim worldwide and in your country?

5. Explain why an LDS Church (Mormon) baptism is not a valid Christian Baptism.

FROM THE CATECHISM

39 In defending the ability of human reason to know God, the Church is expressing her confidence in the possibility of speaking about him to all men and with all men, and therefore of dialogue with other religions, with philosophy and science, as well as with unbelievers and atheists.

841 *The Church's relationship with the Muslims.* "The plan of salvation also includes those who acknowledge the Creator, in the first place amongst whom are the Muslims; these profess to hold the faith of Abraham, and together with us they adore the one, merciful God, mankind's judge on the last day."[14]

842 *The Church's bond with non-Christian religions* is in the first place the common origin and end of the human race:

> All nations form but one community. This is so because all stem from the one stock which God created to people the entire earth, and also because all share a common destiny, namely God. His providence, evident goodness, and saving designs extend to all against the day when the elect are gathered together in the holy city...[15]

843 The Catholic Church recognizes in other religions that search, among shadows and images, for the God who is unknown yet near since he gives life and breath and all things and wants all men to be saved. Thus, the Church considers all goodness and truth found in these religions as "a preparation for the Gospel and given by him who enlightens all men that they may at length have life."[16]

844 In their religious behavior, however, men also display the limits and errors that disfigure the image of God in them:

> Very often, deceived by the Evil One, men have become vain in their reasonings, and have exchanged the truth of God for a lie, and served the creature rather than the Creator. Or else, living and dying in this world without God, they are exposed to ultimate despair.[17]

FROM THE CATECHISM Continued

845 To reunite all his children, scattered and led astray by sin, the Father willed to call the whole of humanity together into his Son's Church. The Church is the place where humanity must rediscover its unity and salvation. The Church is "the world reconciled." She is that bark which "in the full sail of the Lord's cross, by the breath of the Holy Spirit, navigates safely in this world." According to another image dear to the Church Fathers, she is prefigured by Noah's ark, which alone saves from the flood.[18]

856 The missionary task implies a *respectful dialogue* with those who do not yet accept the Gospel.[19] Believers can profit from this dialogue by learning to appreciate better "those elements of truth and grace which are found among peoples, and which are, as it were, a secret presence of God."[20] They proclaim the Good News to those who do not know it, in order to consolidate, complete, and raise up the truth and the goodness that God has distributed among men and nations, and to purify them from error and evil "for the glory of God, the confusion of the demon, and the happiness of man."[21]

World Day of Prayer for Peace in Assisi, October 27, 2011.
Pope Benedict XVI invited nearly 300 representatives of the religions of the world as well as agnostics to participate in the 25th anniversary of the World Day of Prayer for Peace: A Day of Reflection, Dialogue and Prayer for Justice and Peace in the World, on the theme *Pilgrims of Truth, Pilgrims of Peace*. The representatives attending the gathering included Catholics, Orthodox and Protestant Christians, Muslims, Buddhists, Jews, Hindus, Shintos, Sikhs, agnostics, Confucists, Taoists, Jainists, Baha'is, and Zoroastrians.

ENDNOTES – CHAPTER EIGHT

1. Cf. Gn 1:26-27.
2. 1 Jn 4:8.
3. Cfr. Epist. S.S.C.S. *Officii ad Archiep.* Boston.: Denz. 3869-72.
4. St. John Paul II, *Address to the Representatives of the Christian Churches and Ecclesial Communities and of the World Religions*, October 27, 1986.
5. St. John Paul II. *Crossing the Threshold of Hope.* (Vatican City: Alfred A. Knopf) 1994, p. 89.
6. Ibid, p. 89-90.
7. Ex 3:14.
8. Cf. Rev 14:1-5.
9. Gn 9:4.
10. Lv 17:14.
11. Rev 7:1-8.
12. *www.hurriyetdailynews.com/default.aspx?pageid=438&n=muslims-hail-popes-efforts-to-build-ties-with-islam-2005-04-04* [retrieved 7/25/2015].
13. *www.nbcnews.com/id/7359150/ns/world_news-one_year_later_remembering_pope_john_paul_ii/* [retrieved 7/25/2015].
14. *LG* 16; cf. *NA* 3.
15. *NA* 1.
16. *LG* 16; cf. *NA* 2; *EN* 53.
17. *LG* 16; cf. Rom 1:21, 25.
18. St. Augustine, *Serm.* 96, 7, 9: PL 38, 588; St. Ambrose, *De Virg.* 18, 118: PL 16, 297B; cf. already 1 Pt 3:20-21.
19. Cf. *RMiss* 55.
20. *AG* 9.
21. *AG* 9.

CHAPTER 9

Proclamation and Dialogue: The New Evangelization

As Catholics we are called to participate in the ecumenical mission of the Church both in the witness of our lives and in our words.

Ecumenism and Interreligious Dialogue

CHAPTER NINE

Proclamation and Dialogue: The New Evangelization

INTRODUCTION

When St. John Paul II was elected to the papacy and delivered his inaugural homily, he offered a startling exhortation: "Do not be afraid to welcome Christ and accept his power. Open wide the doors to Christ!"

That call—to "open wide the doors to Christ"—is the fundamental call of every Christian. But it is a particularly urgent call for the Catholic faithful who, as baptized members of the common priesthood in full communion with the Church founded by Christ himself, have a sacred obligation to draw others toward Christ by their lived witness.

The Church is duty-bound to proclaim salvation through Christ to the ends of the earth. Entrusted with the keys of the kingdom, the Church founded upon St. Peter "opens wide the doors to Christ" for the whole world. Nevertheless, most of the world follows religions or traditions other than Catholicism. The Church dialogues with these faiths, striving together for a deeper appreciation and knowledge of the truth. Both duties—proclamation and dialogue—are necessary and intrinsic aspects of the Church's relations with the world.

Yet, although the "official" ecumenical dialogue of the Church is the work of relatively few Catholics—Popes, Vatican officials, bishops, appointed theologians, and so on—the actual work of ecumenism belongs to all of us. Formal Christian unity at the organizational level will take place when leaders of the Church find the necessary theological and practical consensus with leaders of other churches and ecclesial communities, but informal Christian unity happens one soul at a time, as other Christians, non-Christians, and nonbelievers come to know the Catholic faith better through our own words, deeds, and lived witness.

In this final chapter, we will survey and revisit:

- The role of the Catholic Church in God's plan of salvation and the status of other Christians, non-Christians, and nonbelievers in relation to this plan;
- The forms of interreligious dialogue by which we may draw persons of other faiths closer to the Gospel and the truth proclaimed by the Church;
- The relationship of ecumenism with evangelization, the proclamation of the Gospel;
- The role of individual Catholics, and in particular young Catholics, in ecumenism, interfaith dialogue, and the New Evangelization.

Sacred Heart of Jesus by Chambers.
"Open wide the doors to Christ!"

THE CHURCH AND SALVATION

Earlier we looked at the often misunderstood statement, "Outside the Church there is no salvation." Cited often by the Church Fathers and repeated for centuries, these words, when taken out of context, sound as if only Catholics will go to heaven1. That, however, is not what the statement means.

PROCLAMATION: *DOMINUS IESUS*

In 2000 the Congregation for the Doctrine of the Faith—the Vatican office responsible for the proper teaching and proclamation of the Catholic faith—released a document titled *Dominus Iesus* ("The Lord Jesus") with the subtitle, "On the Unicity and Salvific Universality of Jesus Christ and the Church." The document was drafted under the supervision of Joseph Cardinal Ratzinger—later elected Pope Benedict XVI—and approved by St. John Paul II.

Dominus Iesus reaffirmed the constant teaching of the Church that Jesus Christ is necessary for salvation and that the Catholic Church is the instrument used by Christ to bring about that salvation. While affirming the importance of interreligious dialogue, the document nonetheless emphasized the deficiency of non-Christian religions.

> **With the coming of the Saviour Jesus Christ, God has willed that the Church founded by him be the instrument for the salvation of all humanity (cf. Acts 17: 30-31).[1] This truth of faith does not lessen the sincere respect which the Church has for the religions of the world, but at the same time, it rules out, in a radical way, that mentality of indifferentism "characterized by a religious relativism which leads to the belief that 'one religion is as good as another.'"[2] If it is true that the followers of other religions can receive divine grace, it is also certain that *objectively speaking* they are in a gravely deficient situation in comparison with those who, in the Church, have the fullness of the means of salvation.[3] However, "all the children of the Church should nevertheless remember that their exalted condition results, not from their own merits, but from the grace of Christ. If they fail to respond in thought, word, and deed to that grace, not only shall they not be saved, but they shall be more severely judged."[4] (*Dominus Iesus*, 22).**

Dominus Iesus combats the danger of *indifferentism*, which can infect both ecumenical and interreligious talks. This is the error of seeing all faith traditions as equally valid and equally able to lead a person to salvation. While respecting the importance of ecumenism and interreligious dialogue, the Church reaffirmed the proclamation of Jesus Christ as the Savior of the world and the Church as the instrument used by him for salvation.

What it does mean is that all salvation comes from Jesus Christ through the Church that he established, which is the Catholic Church.[5] St. Paul identifies the Church as the Body of Christ and Christ as the Head of his Church; he also identifies the Church as the Bride of Christ. When Christ appeared to St. Paul, who was persecuting members of the Church, the Lord asked, "Why are you persecuting *me*?"[6] Such images associate the Church intimately with Christ himself, the same Christ whose Death and Resurrection brought salvation to the world.

Therefore, given this relationship, we cannot speak of salvation through Christ without also speaking of salvation through the Church.

Likewise, because Christ is identified with his Church, to embrace Christ is to embrace the Church. By the same token, to reject the Church is to reject Christ. Consequently, to reject the Church is to reject the salvation offered by Christ through his Church:

> **Basing itself upon Sacred Scripture and Tradition, [this Council] teaches that the Church, now sojourning on earth as an exile, is necessary for salvation. Christ, present to us in His Body, which is the Church, is the one Mediator and the unique way of salvation. In explicit terms He Himself affirmed the necessity of faith and baptism[7] and thereby affirmed also the necessity of the Church, for through baptism as through a door men enter the Church. Whosoever, therefore, knowing that the Catholic Church was made necessary by Christ, would refuse to enter or to remain in it, could not be saved. (*Lumen Gentium*, 14)**

In order to be saved, one cannot knowingly and willfully reject the Church. Because Christ is so completely identified with his Church, we can say that to reject the Church is to reject Christ. As St. Cyprian wrote, "He can no longer have God for his Father who has not the Church for his mother." To know that the Catholic Church is the Church established by Jesus Christ for our salvation and yet reject that Church is to reject salvation as it has been offered by God.

SALVATION AND NON-CHRISTIANS

We return to the question of salvation for non-Christians and nonbelievers in light of the larger question as to why, if salvation can be attained apart from communion with the Church, we should even bother with evangelization and the proclamation of our faith.

We have seen and discussed how other Christians share in an imperfect communion with the Catholic Church, something less than full communion. To be a Christian, however, means to have experienced a Baptism recognized by the Church as sacramentally valid. This is what unites us on a fundamental level as Christians.

Baptism, as Christ himself taught, is essential to salvation: "Truly, truly, I say to you, unless one is born of water and the Spirit, he cannot enter the kingdom of God" (Jn 3: 5). The *Catechism of the Catholic Church* affirms the same:

> The Lord himself affirms that Baptism is necessary for salvation.[8] He also commands his disciples to proclaim the Gospel to all nations and to baptize them.[9] Baptism is necessary for salvation for those to whom the Gospel has been proclaimed and who have had the possibility of asking for this sacrament.[10] (CCC 1257)

Baptism of the Eunuch by Rembrandt. Baptism, as Christ himself taught, is essential to salvation.

Non-Catholic Christians, then, can find salvation even though they have an imperfect communion with the Church. But what does this mean for non-Christians, or even nonbelievers?

Note the wording of the above passage: "Baptism is necessary for salvation for those to whom the Gospel has been proclaimed and who have had the possibility of asking for this sacrament." The *Catechism* stipulates two conditions:

- ✠ The unbaptized individual has heard the Gospel preached or taught; and
- ✠ Baptism is available to him or her.

This opens the possibility of salvation to those who have never been evangelized. Even people in the remotest tribe or village, who may be unaware of the Good News of Jesus Christ, are not excluded from the scope of God's mercy and redemption.

The same *Catechism* paragraph continues:

> The Church does not know of any means other than Baptism that assures entry into eternal beatitude; this is why she takes care not to neglect the mission she has received from the Lord to see that all who can be baptized are "reborn of water and the Spirit." *God has bound salvation to the sacrament of Baptism, but he himself is not bound by his sacraments.* (CCC 1257)

What this means is that God has revealed the way to salvation, which always begins with Baptism. This is the *ordinary* way in which people are saved, and no other way has been revealed to the human race. Therefore, we, who have heard the message of Christ, are bound to the sacramental system that he instituted.

Walking on Water by Aivazovsky.
The miracles performed by Christ were possible because God is not bound by the laws of nature.

However, God can supersede the laws that he himself has established. The miracles performed by Christ—such as healing the sick, calming the storm, or multiplying the loaves and fishes—were possible because God is not bound by the laws of nature, which he created. So although God instituted the Sacraments as the ordinary means by which he would dispense his saving grace, he is free to grant salvation while bypassing the Sacraments as well, even without the Sacrament of Baptism. Yet, even when salvation comes in an *extraordinary* way, apart from the physical administration of the Sacraments, it is still a matter of salvation coming through the Church, the Body of Christ, because all salvation is through Christ.

THE RESPONSIBILITY OF CATHOLICS TO EVANGELIZE

> **"Go therefore and make disciples of all nations, baptizing them in the name of the Father and of the Son and of the Holy Spirit, teaching them to observe all that I have commanded you; and lo, I am with you always, to the close of the age."** (Mt 28:19-20)

Even if he or she has not received Baptism, a person who sincerely seeks the truth and follows the dictates of conscience in regard to that truth can still be saved.

> Those who, through no fault of their own, do not know the Gospel of Christ or his Church, but who nevertheless seek God with a sincere heart, and, moved by grace, try in their actions to do his will as they know it through the dictates of their conscience—those too may achieve eternal salvation.[11] (CCC 847)

This raises a question that has been asked with some frequency in recent Church history: If a person can be saved by following his or her conscience—with or without Baptism, with or without even hearing the Gospel—then what is the urgency of spreading the Catholic faith "to the end of the earth"? Why preach the Good News if salvation can be achieved without it?

Although salvation is possible outside visible membership in the Catholic Church and even apart from the Christian faith and the reception of Baptism, all salvation ultimately is the work of Christ, and he calls us into an intimate communion with himself. Thus, the call of Christ to evangelize the world remains our sacred obligation.

In 2007 the Congregation for the Doctrine of the Faith, correcting those who might use ecumenism as a pretext for failing to proclaim the fullness of the Catholic faith, taught:

> Ecumenism does not have only an institutional dimension aimed at "making the partial communion existing between Christians grow towards full communion in truth and charity."[12] It is

also the task of every member of the faithful, above all by means of prayer, penance, study and cooperation. Everywhere and always, each Catholic has the right and the duty to give the witness and the full proclamation of his faith. With non-Catholic Christians, Catholics must enter into a respectful dialogue of charity and truth, a dialogue which is not only an exchange of ideas, but also of gifts,[13] in order that the fullness of the means of salvation can be offered to one's partners in dialogue.[14] In this way, they are led to an ever deeper conversion to Christ. (*Doctrinal Notes on Some Aspects of Evangelization*, 12)

FUNDAMENTALS OF THE PROCLAMATION

The salvation of the world, as we have seen, is the very reason for the existence of the Church. Jesus Christ came to earth to make salvation possible for every human person throughout time, from the creation of Adam and Eve to the end of the world. His one sacrificial act provides superabundant graces, more than sufficient for the redemption of every person who ever lived and who ever will live.

The Lord's Prayer (detail) by Tissot. It is the teaching of the Catholic Church that the fulfillment of all that is good in other religions can be found in the proclamation of the Gospel of Jesus Christ.

Yet, the public ministry of Christ lasted only three years. He preached and taught as many people as he could during his earthly mission before enduring the suffering and Death for which he was made incarnate. With his Resurrection and Ascension into heaven, he fulfilled his saving mission.

And yet, before he returned to the Father, he handed on his saving mission to us. He did this by establishing his Church, led by the Apostles with St. Peter primary among them. He gave them the power to baptize, to forgive sins, to turn bread and wine into his own Body and Blood—in short, he gave his Church the Sacraments, by which he has continued to pour forth his grace into the world. And he commissioned his Apostles to preach the Gospel throughout the world, making disciples of all nations through the Sacrament of Baptism. He also sent the Holy Spirit upon this Church so his truth may be proclaimed forever through the teaching authority he established in his Apostles and their successors.

The fullness of this Church founded by Christ comes to us today in the Catholic Church, the Church united under the leadership of the successors of St. Peter and the Apostles. The Catholic Church has always held, based on the words of her founder and the events of salvation history, that she possesses the fullness of the means of salvation willed by God as the ordinary way of saving all people. By availing ourselves of these "means of salvation," each of us has access to the graces necessary to complete the pilgrimage to our heavenly home.

Salvation comes to us through the Church, and the Church proclaims this salvation to the world. This proclamation consists fundamentally of the following points, which can be found in the Apostles' Creed:

God is One and Triune. The Revelation of the Blessed Trinity is the essential component of the Revelation given to the world by God. It reveals *who God is* and thus informs our worship and proclamation of him.

Jesus Christ is the Son of God and the Second Person of the Trinity become man. The entire Christian proclamation centers on the historical fact that God became man in Jesus of Nazareth. The Church has defended—and proclaimed—the truth that Jesus Christ is fully God and fully man.

Salvation is a gift of God by grace through Jesus Christ. Due to the Fall at the beginning of human history, the human race is incapable of attaining complete fulfillment with God in heaven. But God in his mercy has made salvation available to us through the life, Death, and Resurrection of his Son, Jesus Christ.

The Holy Spirit—whose mission is inseparable from Christ's—builds, animates, and sanctifies the Church. Before he ascended into heaven, Christ promised his Apostles that he would send them the Holy Spirit. This was fulfilled at Pentecost. We receive the Holy Spirit primarily in Baptism and a strengthening in the gifts of the Holy Spirit in Confirmation.

Christ established the Church to continue his salvific mission until he comes again. We become members of the Catholic Church, the Mystical Body of Christ, in Baptism. Through the Eucharist, which is the Sacrament of the Church's Unity, our union with Christ and our communion with the other members of his Body is strengthened. Christ established one Church and desires that his disciples be unified in her.

The Institution of the Eucharist (detail) by Poussin. The Church has defended—and proclaimed—the truth that Jesus Christ is fully God and fully man.

Each person is called to holiness now and eternally by participation in God's love. The Church proclaims boldly that our true calling is to be like God, to partake of the divine nature.[15] Through Baptism we are sanctified and are called to become, by God's grace, more and more like Christ. God desires that we have eternal life with him in heaven.

It is the teaching of the Catholic Church that the fulfillment of all that is good in other religions can be found in the proclamation of the Gospel of Jesus Christ. These essential elements of the story of the salvation of humanity are ultimately what all religions seek. Thus, the Catholic Church is in dialogue with many world religions not only to discover common beliefs and to seek the common good but also to lead all people to Jesus Christ and his Church.

OUR CALL TO EVANGELIZATION

If, therefore, the Catholic Church is the full and ordinary means of salvation, each member of the Church has an obligation to proclaim this truth to the world. Not doing so would be both unjust and a serious lapse of charity. The Church teaches the truth that the world needs to hear, the truth that leads to eternal happiness; if we truly have love and compassion for our neighbor, we will share the truth with them so that they may enjoy this eternal happiness, too. Christ is the remedy for our sinfulness, our chance for victory over death; if we do not evangelize others, then it is as though we have the life-saving cure for a serious illness but refuse to share it with those who need it most. The Gospel is "good news," and good news must be shared.

For St. Paul, who endured many hardships and sufferings to proclaim the salvation won by Christ, the desire to evangelize was so embedded in his faith that he wrote, "Woe to me if I do not preach the gospel!"[16] St. Paul serves as a model for all faithful followers of Christ: Evangelization is an integral part of the Christian faith, no matter the cost.

> **The mission of evangelization, a continuation of the work desired by the Lord Jesus, is necessary for the Church: it cannot be overlooked; it is an expression of her very nature.** (Pope Benedict XVI, *Ubicumque et Semper*)

Although evangelization is of necessity an essential element of each person's Catholicism, this does not mean that it is practiced using the same means in each person's life. Like St. Paul, some are called to travel to foreign lands to preach the Gospel. Others are called to teach the Catholic faith to children or adults wanting to know more about Catholicism. Additionally, each Catholic is called to evangelize those around him: family, friends, neighbors, schoolmates, co-workers, etc. Our great desire in life should be to lead others to have the life-giving relationship with Christ in the Catholic Church that we have been given.

THEN WHY DO SOME NOT BELIEVE?

We know that man is a religious being who seeks God naturally. The many and varied expressions of religious faith found throughout the world attest to this reality. Every culture in every time has been filled with religious people, and the very design of creation provides abundant evidence that there is a Supreme Being behind it all.

Why, then, do some people still deny the existence of God?

The modern era in particular has seen the rise of *atheism*, the rejection of belief in God. Many people today claim that there is no God or any superior spiritual being, a denial that constitutes a belief system in itself.

People embrace atheism for various reasons. The *Catechism* points out some of the common factors:

> The name "atheism" covers many very different phenomena. One common form is the practical materialism which restricts its needs and aspirations to space and time. Atheistic humanism falsely considers man to be "an end to himself, and the sole maker, with supreme control, of his own history."[17] Another form of contemporary atheism looks for the liberation of man through economic and social liberation. "It holds that religion, of its very nature, thwarts such emancipation by raising man's hopes in a future life, thus both deceiving him and discouraging him from working for a better form of life on earth."[18] (CCC 2124)

In atheism we find an exaggerated sense of our self-sufficiency [19]: An atheist might not arrive necessarily at a philosophical or scientific conclusion that God does not exist but rather admit of no need or desire for God. An honest evaluation of an atheistic perspective will often find that it is grounded at least in part in a rejection of any moral law outside of one's own making as though the commandments and traditional faith-based ethics represent an unjust restriction on human, personal freedom.

A related lack of faith is manifest in *agnosticism*, which does not directly deny the existence of God but is indifferent to his existence. An agnostic may say, "If God does happen to exist, he is so unknowable, remote, or detached from the world that he is irrelevant to humanity."[20]

> Agnosticism can sometimes include a certain search for God, but it can equally express indifferentism, a flight from the ultimate question of existence, and a sluggish moral conscience. Agnosticism is all too often equivalent to practical atheism. (CCC 2128)

To these we can add a troubling trend that exists among an increasing number of Christians—what Pope Benedict XVI called a "practical" atheism, in which a person professes belief in God but does not live and act as though this faith really matters:

> A particularly dangerous phenomenon for faith has arisen in our times: indeed a form of atheism exists which we define, precisely, as "practical," in which the truths of faith or religious rites are not denied but are merely deemed irrelevant to daily life, detached from life, pointless. So it is that people often believe in God in a superficial manner, and live "as though God did not exist" (*etsi Deus non daretur*). In the end, however, this way of life proves even more destructive because it leads to indifference to faith and to the question of God. (General Audience, November 14, 2012)

This practical atheism is often the result of *secularization*, a loss of the religious sense in a society that once embraced Christian moral principles to some degree. Secularism—and the practical atheism to which it leads—is one of the major obstacles to as well as targets of the New Evangelization.

St. Paul VI and *Evangelii Nuntiandi*

Evangelization and proclamation of the Gospel have always been part of the mission of the Church. The inclusion of every member of the faithful in this call, however, has gained a renewed emphasis within the last century.

The reforms of the Second Vatican Council—coupled with certain adverse social and cultural trends that gained momentum in the 1960s—gave rise to some confusion among many Catholics over the nature of the Church and her teaching authority. This led to a certain apathy toward the value of evangelization and efforts to lead others to the Catholic faith. Stressing religious freedom and toleration, some even began to believe that one religion or Christian denomination was as good as another, so there was no reason to share our faith with others who were happy with their own beliefs.

St. Paul VI recognized the seriousness of the situation. He called a synod of bishops to discuss the importance of evangelization in the Church's life as well as ways to promote it. After the synod, St. Paul VI wrote the apostolic exhortation *Evangelii Nuntiandi* ("The Proclamation of the Gospel").

In this document St. Paul VI declared that the Church "exists in order to evangelize,"[21] noting how Christ, who was the first evangelizer, called his Apostles and all who would follow them to evangelize as he did.

The Pope identified three "burning questions" regarding evangelization in the modern world—questions that still demand answers today:

> — "In our day, what has happened to that hidden energy of the Good News, which is able to have a powerful effect on man's conscience?
>
> — "To what extent and in what way is that evangelical force capable of really transforming the people of this century?
>
> — "What methods should be followed in order that the power of the Gospel may have its effect?" (*Evangelii Nuntiandi*, 4)

Reflecting on these three questions, St. Paul VI got to the heart of the work of evangelization: *Evangelization must begin with us*. There is an old rule of thumb: "You cannot share what you do not have." If we are to share our Catholic faith, then we must be strong and "on fire" with the Catholic faith already.

Pope Paul VI at the opening of the Second Vatican Council.
St. Paul VI identified three "burning questions" regarding evangelization in the modern world—questions that still demand answers today.

Interior Conversion Is Necessary

The Catholic faithful need to experience internal conversion *within themselves* in order to proclaim the Gospel energetically; this is the aforementioned "hidden energy of the Good News" about which St. Paul VI inquired. The Gospel has the power to change people's lives because through it the Holy Spirit can change people's hearts and turn them toward Christ and his truth. In order to be effective instruments through which the Holy Spirit can accomplish this work, we must proclaim the truth in love both in our words and our actions.

Evangelization is not just about what we say but what we do: the witness we give by the virtues we exhibit in our daily and ordinary lives. Our lived example is as necessary to the work of proclaiming our Catholic faith as any explanation we can offer. Evangelization is only successful when it is carried out by those who have already been converted, who trust in the Holy Spirit to do the work of conversion, and who reach out to those around them in a style that is natural to their peers. The Pope went on to say:

> The purpose of evangelization is therefore precisely this interior change, and if it had to be expressed in one sentence the best way of stating it would be to say that the Church evangelizes when she seeks to convert, solely through the divine power of the message she proclaims, both the personal and collective consciences of people, the activities in which they engage, and the lives and concrete milieu which are theirs. (*Evangelii Nuntiandi*, 18)

THE NEW EVANGELIZATION

In a sense St. Paul VI rediscovered for us the importance of evangelization, an importance that had been forgotten in some corners of the Church. His call to reembrace evangelization in *Evangelii Nuntiandi* introduced the idea of a "new period of evangelization" in the Church. That call of his led to a movement popularized later during the papacies of St. John Paul II and Benedict XVI: the *New Evangelization*.

What is the New Evangelization, and what makes it different from the "old" evangelization?

ST. JOHN PAUL II TO YOUTH: "PREACH IT FROM THE ROOFTOPS"

When St. John Paul II celebrated Mass at Denver's Cherry Creek State Park during World Youth Day in 1993, he issued a strong challenge to the assembled youth to carry on the work of the New Evangelization boldly:

> Do not be afraid to go out on the streets and into public places like the first Apostles who preached Christ and the Good News of salvation in the squares of cities, towns and villages. This is no time to be ashamed of the Gospel. It is the time to preach it from the rooftops.
>
> Do not be afraid to break out of comfortable and routine modes of living, in order to take up the challenge of making Christ known in the modern metropolis....
>
> Young people of World Youth Day, the Church asks you to go, in the power of the Holy Spirit, to those who are near and those who are far away. Share with them the freedom you have found in Christ.
>
> People thirst for genuine inner freedom. They yearn for the life which Christ came to give in abundance. Christ needs laborers ready to work in his vineyard. May you, the Catholic young people of the world, not fail him.

Pope John Paul II preaching the Gospel "from the rooftops."
The New Evangelization consists of an effort to energize the Church from within
so she may in turn be transformed into a more effective witness to the faith in the midst of the world.

Since the beginning of her mission following Pentecost, the Church has been engaged in evangelization. Historically, this has occurred primarily by reaching out to new empires, nations, and lands, preaching the Gospel and baptizing new converts until a society could be considered Christian. This is how the Roman Empire, much of Europe, Russia, and many countries in South America were evangelized. The introduction of Christianity did not make these societies perfect by any means, but they did tend to be governed by a system of laws that more or less reflected Christian principles.

Over the course of time, however, many nations have experienced a loss of their Christian character. The faith has becomes stagnant or has been challenged by the introduction of other belief systems. In many places there has been an increasing secularization of society—a tendency to move away from Christian religious values in legal and cultural views of morality and justice. Such societies can tend to become more and more "nonreligious" as they extract any hint of religious influence from public policy and practice, even to the point where freedom of religious expression is threatened.

When a people, even one that is still nominally Christian, no longer practices the faith, it presents a major challenge to the Church today. This is the situation that characterizes much of Europe and North America.

That is precisely the challenge of the New Evangelization: Just as evangelization begins with the interior conversion of the individual Catholic, who must be firm in faith in order to share the faith with others, the New Evangelization is a renewed evangelization of those already baptized—those who were never properly taught the faith, those who have drifted away from the faith, and those who are lukewarm in their practice of the faith. It consists of an effort to energize the Church from within so she may in turn be transformed into a more effective witness to the faith in the midst of the world.

When Benedict XVI established the Pontifical Council for the New Evangelization in 2010, he described its mission in a homily on, significantly, the Eve of the Solemnity of the Apostles Sts. Peter and Paul, the founders of the Church of Rome:

> There are regions of the world that are still awaiting a first evangelization; others that have received it, but need a deeper intervention; yet others in which the Gospel put down roots a long

> time ago, giving rise to a true Christian tradition but in which, in recent centuries with complex dynamics the secularization process has produced a serious crisis of the meaning of the Christian faith and of belonging to the Church.
>
> From this perspective, I have decided to create a new body, in the form of a "Pontifical Council," whose principal task will be to promote a renewed evangelization in the countries where the first proclamation of the faith has already resonated and where Churches with an ancient foundation exist but are experiencing the progressive secularization of society and a sort of "eclipse of the sense of God," which pose a challenge to finding appropriate to propose anew the perennial truth of Christ's Gospel.[22]

The New Evangelization embraces new ways of proclaiming the Gospel. The modern age has seen an avalanche of new communications technologies, and the Church seeks to use these means to repropose the Gospel to all peoples. From her beginning Christianity has always used modern communications to spread the faith, and today should be no different.

The work of the New Evangelization falls on each one of us. Since the missionary field of the New Evangelization is countries like the United States, we are missionaries in that field. We must be examples of holiness in the world and share with others the joy that the practice of the Catholic faith gives to us.

The Four Evangelists by Jordaens.
We must be examples of holiness in the world and share with others the joy that the practice of the Catholic Faith gives to us.

> The Church always evangelizes and has never interrupted the path of evangelization. She celebrates the eucharistic mystery every day, administers the sacraments, proclaims the word of life—the Word of God, and commits herself to the causes of justice and charity. And this evangelization bears fruit: It gives light and joy, it gives the path of life to many people; many others live, often unknowingly, of the light and the warmth that radiate from this permanent evangelization.
>
> However, we can see a progressive process of de-Christianization and a loss of the essential human values, which is worrisome. A large part of today's humanity does not find the Gospel in the permanent evangelization of the Church: That is to say, the convincing response to the question: How to live?
>
> This is why we are searching for, along with permanent and uninterrupted and never to be interrupted evangelization, a new evangelization, capable of being heard by that world that does not find access to "classic" evangelization. Everyone needs the Gospel; the Gospel is destined to all and not only to a specific circle and this is why we are obliged to look for new ways of bringing the Gospel to all. (Cardinal Joseph Ratzinger, *Address to Catechists and Religion Teachers*, Jubilee of Catechists, December 12, 2000)

We, the faithful of the Church, participate in this missionary endeavor when we "proclaim the Good News to those who do not know it, in order to consolidate, complete, and raise up the truth and the goodness that God has distributed among men and nations, and to purify them from error and evil 'for the glory of God, the confusion of the demon, and the happiness of man.'"[23]

PUTTING INTERRELIGIOUS DIALOGUE INTO PRACTICE

In light of the truth that Catholics are called to proclaim the Gospel to the whole world, we return to the subject of the relation of the Catholic Church with other religions. The dialogue with the religions of the world can occur on many levels at once, levels that are mirrored to some degree in ecumenical relations with other Christian churches and ecclesial communities. It begins by recognizing what is good and true about other faith traditions but always involves the honest proclamation of the truths of the Gospel.

> The missionary task implies a *respectful dialogue* with those who do not yet accept the Gospel.[24] Believers can profit from this dialogue by learning to appreciate better "those elements of truth and grace which are found among peoples, and which are, as it were, a secret presence of God."[25] They proclaim the Good News to those who do not know it, in order to consolidate, complete, and raise up the truth and the goodness that God has distributed among men and nations, and to purify them from error and evil "for the glory of God, the confusion of the demon, and the happiness of man."[26] (CCC 856)

Dialogue and proclamation are compatible, for both have the same goal: to seek the truth. In the interfaith initiatives of the Church, both dialogue and proclamation have as their final goal the full communion of all peoples in Christ.

FORMS OF DIALOGUE

Dialogue, like evangelization, is about more than words. Although the term "interfaith dialogue" brings to mind a formal discussion among religious leaders, theologians, and scholars, this is only one aspect of the fullness of dialogue. Dialogue seeks not compromise but understanding.

Dialogue between various faith traditions is the respectful and prayerful exchange of ideas and beliefs with the goal of articulating the objective truth, and it is something that involves both talk and action. Following are a few ways in which it is carried out; these means are useful both in interreligious relations and in ecumenical outreach with other Christians.

World Youth Day in Madrid, Spain, August 2011.
Nearly 2,000,000 young pilgrims attended WYD 2011 in Madrid, the last WYD to be attended by Pope Benedict XVI.
The theme was "Rooted and Built Up in Jesus Christ, Firm in the Faith" (cf. Col 2:7).
Dialogue and proclamation are compatible, for both have the same goal: to seek the truth.

DIALOGUE: ST. JOHN PAUL II CALLS FOR RETHINKING THE PAPACY

In ecumenical relations, whether between Catholics and Orthodox or Catholics and Protestants, one of the main obstacles to union is the office of the papacy. Orthodox Christians disagree with the specific prerogatives that the Catholic Church ascribes to the Pope, and most Protestant Christians reject the necessity of the office itself. What is particularly unfortunate about this situation is that one of the most important roles of the Pope is to be a source of *unity* among Christians. What the Lord set up to unite his followers has become a reason for division.

In 1995 St. John Paul II released the encyclical *Ut Unum Sint* ("That They May Be One") in which he wrote about the work of ecumenism and specifically the role of the Pope in the reuniting of Christendom.

In this letter the Pope recounted the reasons for divisions within Christianity and called for greater ecumenical work to bring about reunion. But what is most noteworthy about this encyclical is that the Pope recognized that the papacy has been a source of division and called on both Catholic and non-Catholic theologians, scholars, and leaders to discuss with him a rethinking of how the papacy could be practiced such that it would be a source of unity again.

In 1995 St. John Paul II released the encyclical *Ut Unum Sint* ("That They May Be One").

> **All this however must always be done in communion. When the Catholic Church affirms that the office of the Bishop of Rome corresponds to the will of Christ, she does not separate this office from the mission entrusted to the whole body of Bishops, who are also "vicars and ambassadors of Christ."[27] The Bishop of Rome is a member of the "College," and the Bishops are his brothers in the ministry.**
>
> **Whatever relates to the unity of all Christian communities clearly forms part of the concerns of the primacy.... I am convinced that I have a particular responsibility in this regard, above all in acknowledging the ecumenical aspirations of the majority of the Christian Communities and in heeding the request made of me to find a way of exercising the primacy which, while in no way renouncing what is essential to its mission, is nonetheless open to a new situation.** (*Ut Unum Sint* 95-96)

St. John Paul II was not suggesting that the doctrines surrounding the papacy, such as infallibility and universal jurisdiction, are false or should be ignored. Rather, he was calling on all Christians to meditate on how those gifts of the papacy should be used responsibly in modern times. This call was a beautiful example of the humility needed for successful ecumenical discussions.

Witness in daily life. In most modern, pluralistic societies it is common to interact with people of other faith traditions on a regular basis. We have passed the days when religious groups lived in isolated neighborhoods without any contact with outsiders. In most parts of the United States, especially in larger towns and metropolitan areas, Catholics and fellow Christians live and work right alongside Muslims, Jews, Mormons, and people who follow Far Eastern religions. Even if one were to live in an area that is not religiously diverse, it is nearly impossible to travel far without having the opportunity to interact with people of other faith traditions. Such interactions can open doors to dialogue and witness.

If someone knows that we are serious about our Catholic faith, they may ask questions about our beliefs or practices. They may ask why we make the Sign of the Cross when we pray before a meal, what we do when we go to confession, or why we receive ashes on our forehead on Ash Wednesday. Such questions give us opportunities to express something about our faith. The inquirer may be motivated by nothing more than curiosity and might not necessarily even question us with complete sincerity and respect, but the opportunity for us to witness in some appropriate way is there all the same.

Catholic missionaries in Mexico.
It is a beautiful witness whenever people of diverse backgrounds come together for a common cause.

Since dialogue is a two-way street, it works in the other direction as well. We might have a Jewish friend who mentions a religious holiday, tradition, or belief in the course of a conversation or wears a distinctive article of clothing in our presence. Approached with courtesy, such matters can serve as conversation starters by which we can learn more about a faith tradition different from our own. Such inquiries can help to build a level of trust and exchange that allows us to speak freely about our Catholic faith in return.

We may not know that anyone is watching us, but we must remember that our lived witness is vital to any effort of evangelization. For anyone who knows that we are Catholic or Christian, we represent an example of what Catholicism or Christianity is all about. That is why we must model our behavior always according to the example of Christ.

Shared service. All major religions emphasize the importance of compassion and caring for those in need. This shared service to the poor and needy is an opportunity for dialogue. Even when people of different religious traditions do not agree on matters of faith, we can often find common ground as to how we put our faith into practice in caring for the weaker and less fortunate among us.

Any concerted interreligious initiative should include working together in this kind of service. It is a beautiful witness whenever people of diverse backgrounds come together for a common cause. Many larger population centers have interfaith hospitality networks in which members of various religious groups participate in an organized outreach to the poor, the sick, and the homeless. Soup kitchens, tutoring services, programs for people with developmental disabilities, and other such initiatives lend themselves readily to cooperation among persons of various faiths. The prolife movement and its defense of unborn human life is one that has been a particularly strong vehicle for drawing together supporters across religious traditions.

Such efforts facilitate what has been called "dialogue in the trenches." This refers to the discussions that come about during shared activities. Uniting in a common and just cause tends to break down barriers and increase comfort levels among people of different religions so their interactions about the cause they support can lead to conversations about faith. Even though such activities do not constitute ecumenism and religious dialogue in a formal sense, improved ecumenical and interfaith relations can be a positive side effect.

Supper at Emmaus (detail) by Lhermitte.
All interreligious dialogue hinges on a mutual search for truth undertaken with respect and understanding of our differences in both religious belief and culture.

Theological dialogue. Theology is the most important science, for it is the study of what we believe about God and what he has revealed to us. Every major religion has theologians, who study the doctrines of their religion and teach those doctrines to others. The dialogue between theologians of different religions is essential in the search for truth.

The history of relations between different religions has all too often been marked by misunderstandings and uninformed accusations. These misunderstandings often result from a lack of charity, for charity desires the truth. Fruitful dialogue seeks the truth through the interaction of Catholic experts with those of other faiths with the goal of accurate understanding. Theologians of the Catholic Church have been engaged for decades in this dialogue with all the major faith traditions.

We may never be called to take up the academic study of theology and earn an advanced degree that would enable us to carry on intense interfaith theological discussions. However, we ought to know our own faith well—and live it—so we can present our faith accurately, and we ought to study other faiths as well so we can become that much closer to understanding their beliefs. Thus, we may be well prepared to tackle the ecumenical and interreligious dialogue opportunities that will come our way.

Shared spiritual experience. Human beings are both matter and spirit, and we all share this twofold reality. Just as a baseball player and a relay swimmer can share in the experience and exhilaration of athletic competition despite the obvious differences in their respective sports, the experience of prayer and spiritual reflection has certain commonalities across the spectrum of religious traditions.

This shared experience can be a basis for dialogue: How do you pray? Why do you pray? For what do you pray? To whom do you pray? These questions and others like them can lead us to a deeper appreciation of the spiritual life in general and its importance in the life of all people. Due to the connection between doctrine and prayer—remember *lex orandi, lex credendi* in the previous chapter—we must be careful not to borrow uncritically from the spiritual experiences of others. Still, we can find room for dialogue on matters such as the distractions to prayer, dealing with grief or anxiety, and other issues related to the human condition.

United fundamentally in our status as religious beings—our innate search for God and for meaning in life—we can share common experiences and thus learn from persons of diverse religious beliefs and traditions even as we pray that the friendships thus formed may lead them closer to Christ and his Church.

REQUIREMENTS FOR DIALOGUE

Finally, when it does come down to words, all interreligious dialogue—as well as ecumenical dialogue—hinges on a mutual search for truth undertaken with respect and understanding of our differences in both religious belief and culture.

Dialogue between diverse religious traditions is a mutual search for the truth: What do you believe and why? What evidence supports your beliefs? These questions and others like them help to inform and make interreligious dialogue and ecumenism productive.

EXAMPLE OF PROCLAMATION: WORLD YOUTH DAY

St. John Paul II loved young people. Before becoming Pope, he was active as a priest and bishop in reaching out to youth and helping them in their walk with God. He did not coddle young people or treat them as unintelligent or "less Catholic" than adults. No, he challenged them and treated them as young adults, calling them to a deeper commitment to Christ.

However, becoming the Supreme Pontiff of the Catholic Church brings countless responsibilities and obligations. No one thought that he would continue to focus on working with young people after he had been elected Pope, but St. John Paul II was committed to helping young people, whom he recognized as the future of the Church. One of his lasting contributions was the creation of World Youth Day, which has impacted millions over the years.

St. John Paul II celebrated the first World Youth Day (WYD) in Rome in 1985 to encourage young people to live the Catholic faith boldly in the face of severe opposition from the world. Initially a diocesan event in Rome, WYD soon became an international event. The first WYD in the United States was in Denver in 1993. In the weeks leading up to that WYD, many predicted that the young people of America, disenchanted with religion, would ignore the event or attend in small numbers; instead, more than 500,000 young adult pilgrims converged on the city for the weeklong event.

Two years later WYD was held in Manila and was attended by over 5,000,000 people—recognized as the largest crowd ever by the *Guinness Book of World Records*. Since then WYD has continued to draw large crowds, and many religious and clerics cite WYD as the place where they first heard their vocation call.

The Church has designated St. Teresa of Calcutta and St. John Paul II as the patron saints of WYD.

LIST OF WORLD YOUTH DAYS

Year	Location	Attendance
1985	Rome, Italy	300,000
1987	Buenos Aires, Argentina	1,000,000
1989	Santiago de Compostela, Spain	400,000
1991	Czestochowa, Poland	1,600,000
1993	Denver, Colorado, USA	500,000
1995	Manila, Philippines	5,000,000
1997	Paris, France	1,200,000
2000	Rome, Italy	2,000,000
2002	Toronto, Canada	800,000
2005	Cologne, Germany	1,200,000
2008	Sydney, Australia	400,000
2011	Madrid, Spain	2,000,000
2013	Rio de Janeiro, Brazil	3,700,000
2016	Krakow, Poland	3,500,000
2019	Panama City, Panama	700,000
2022	Lisbon, Portugal	*future event*

Knowledge and understanding of the religious faith of others help us to recognize the positive elements in the doctrine and practice of others and to appreciate the fact that we share them:

> **The Church, therefore, exhorts her sons, that through dialogue and collaboration with the followers of other religions, carried out with prudence and love and in witness to the Christian faith and life, they recognize, preserve and promote the good things, spiritual and moral, as well as the socio-cultural values found among these men.** (*Nostra Ætate*, 2)

The Church has always recognized that God has planted "seeds of the Word" throughout the world. Jesus Christ, who is the Word and is the Truth, has been acknowledged in incomplete ways even in non-Christian religions. For example, the Sikh religion emphasizes the quest for union with God and that certain evils in this world—especially anger, ego, greed, attachment, and lust—hinder that quest for divine union. This thought has many parallels in Catholic teaching, which holds that Jesus Christ is our means of union with God and that he has come to destroy the power of sin and evil in this world. By dialoguing with the Sikh religion, the Catholic Church can appreciate the truth of their deepest longings and proclaim that the Church believes Jesus Christ to be the fulfillment of them.

Ecumenically speaking, the beliefs and practices of other Christian traditions can help to deepen the Church's appreciation for her own teachings. For example, Protestantism has from its beginnings emphasized the importance of Sacred Scripture, and Christians in Protestant ecclesial communities have generally a great devotion to regular reading and study of the Bible. This has not always been a point of emphasis in Catholic practice, largely because Catholics have a magisterial teaching authority and tradition that complements Scripture, whereas Protestants base their beliefs on their interpretations of the Bible. Ecumenical relations as well as the encouragement of the Church over the last century have helped Catholics come to a greater appreciation of Sacred Scripture both for study and for devotional use.

If dialogue between diverse religious traditions is oriented toward the mutual search for truth, then it stands to reason that anyone involved in such dialogue must be both well informed about other religions and deeply knowledgeable about his or her own faith. Ignorance is the enemy of both proclamation and dialogue. As stated earlier, a thorough understanding of the teachings and practices of Catholicism is a prerequisite for sharing our Catholic faith with others and for engaging in fruitful dialogue with those of other faiths. For a well-informed Catholic, dialogue breeds more knowledge.

Suffer the Little Children to Come unto Me by Van Dyke.
Catholic teaching holds that Jesus Christ is our means of union with God and that he has come to destroy the power of sin and evil in this world.

THE GOAL OF UNITY IN JESUS CHRIST

Proclamation and dialogue are presented sometimes as diametrically opposed ideas. Proclamation is sometimes confused with proselytization, which is an overt effort to convert someone to a particular religious faith; sometimes dialogue, on the other hand, is erroneously assumed to mean a meeting of minds in which ideas are exchanged but there is no objective truth to be found and therefore all points of view are deemed equally valid. Both conceptions are incorrect as far as Catholic ecumenical and inter-religious relations are concerned.

Pope Benedict XVI and Archbishop of Canterbury Dr. Rowan Williams pray together.

When the Church proclaims what she believes, she does so both in fulfillment of her apostolic mission and with the utmost respect for the freedom of each person. When she engages in dialogue, this respect is reflected in an appreciation for the elements of truth that exist within other churches, ecclesial communities, and religions and for the ways in which the lived expressions of these elements of truth enrich her own understanding of truth. She knows that, while it is her obligation to speak the revealed truths that she has received according to the teachings and example of Christ, the real work of conversion belongs to the Holy Spirit. Only through the Holy Spirit can hearts and souls be turned ultimately toward Christ and his Church.

Proclamation and dialogue ought to be oriented toward the hope that all peoples might one day be united in full communion with Jesus Christ through his Church. This has been the plan of God from the beginning of time, and it is the ultimate fulfillment of the human race.

> *For man*, this consummation will be the final realization of the unity of the human race, which God willed from creation and of which the pilgrim Church has been "in the nature of sacrament."[28] Those who are united with Christ will form the community of the redeemed, "the holy city" of God, "the Bride, the wife of the Lamb."[29] She will not be wounded any longer by sin, stains, self-love, that destroy or wound the earthly community.[30] The beatific vision, in which God opens himself in an inexhaustible way to the elect, will be the ever-flowing well-spring of happiness, peace, and mutual communion. (CCC 1045)

This unity, at last, is the ultimate goal of all ecumenical and interfaith dialogue.

CONCLUSION

"Salvation is found in the truth," teaches the *Catechism of the Catholic Church*.[31] In this statement we see again the link between the unique institution of the Catholic Church and the apostolic mission that she received from Jesus Christ, the Redeemer of the world: The Church is the instrument of salvation for the world, and her sacred commission is to transmit the truth of Christ to all people so they may be united in the Church, which is the Body of Christ. Because of this, neither this mission nor the truth it proclaims can be compromised.

> Those who obey the prompting of the Spirit of truth are already on the way of salvation. But the Church, to whom this truth has been entrusted, must go out to meet their desire, so as to bring them the truth. Because she believes in God's universal plan of salvation, the Church must be missionary. (CCC 851)

As Catholics we are called to participate in the ecumenical mission of the Church both in the witness of our lives and in our words. The essential point of beginning, if progress is to be made, is to know our own faith and to live it authentically. This sacred mission of ecumenism is not one born of a triumphalistic spirit as though we were God's privileged elite, for if we do not speak "the truth in love,"[32] then we do not reflect the attitude of Christ, who alone can bring about the unity in faith that we seek.

CHALLENGES:

How can I, as a young Catholic, take an active role in witnessing to my faith among other Christians, people of other religions, and even my fellow Catholics?

This is a vital question for every young Catholic. How do I live my faith? Even the fact a young person might ask this question reveals that he or she is taking the faith very seriously.

The question pertains to the role of every baptized person in evangelization. Note that we said "every baptized person." Everyone who is baptized is called to evangelize others—to be a Christian witness—regardless of age or state in life.

If we truly want to be witnesses for our faith, then first we must know and live our faith. Remember the slogan, "You cannot give what you do not have." If we do not understand the truths of our faith and strive to live by them, then we will not be very effective witnesses of Christ to others. So an important first step is to study the Catholic faith. We must learn what the Church teaches and why she teaches it. We should read Scripture, the *Catechism of the Catholic Church*, and good spiritual books: the lives of the saints, the documents of the Church, the writings of Popes, and other authentic teachers of the Catholic faith.

If we are to evangelize others, we must be evangelized ourselves. We must experience an interior conversion so as to live our faith with great love and commitment. This is the "hidden energy of the Good News" of which St. Paul VI wrote in *Evangelii Nuntiandi*. The evidence of this interior conversion is our commitment to regular prayer, our participation in the Mass and the Sacraments, and the integration of our Catholic faith into every aspect of our lives. Faith is not one "compartment" of our lives—separated from school, work, family, sports, leisure, and other concerns—but must permeate everything that we do. That does not mean we should walk around with a holier-than-thou attitude or communicate with others by reciting Scripture verses only, but it does mean that the spiritual and moral truths of our faith guide our thoughts, words, and actions whether we are in church, in the classroom, on the playing field, or in our own living rooms.

The goal of evangelization is to help to bring about an interior conversion in others so they might embrace the truth and live their own lives according to this truth. When we try to accomplish this among other Catholics who have grown perhaps lukewarm in their faith or have abandoned it to a large degree, we call this the New Evangelization. When we do this among other believers or nonbelievers, this is simply evangelization, the proclamation of the Gospel.

Evangelization involves both words and actions. Our example ordinarily will draw people to (or away from) Christ and his Church far more effectively than anything we might say. So by living faithful lives as Catholics—treating others with the love and compassion that Christ showed to the people that he met—we are already engaged in evangelization. When opportunities present themselves whereby we may be called upon to speak or write the truth in love, we also evangelize with our words. Often, our lived example may lead people to ask us about the faith that we have, or to want to get to know us better so they can learn what inspires our lives. Those are prime invitations to talk about our Catholic faith.

The various levels of ecumenical and interreligious dialogue about which we read in this chapter apply on the personal level. In addition to the "dialogue of witness in daily life," we have opportunities to evangelize through the "dialogue of shared service," whereby we work together alongside other Christians and non-Christians on charitable causes of common concern. We may not be theologians, but we can engage in theological "dialogue" insofar as we are competent whenever we discuss the doctrines of our faith and explain them to others. (This effort is greatly helped if we take the time to study and understand the core doctrines of other Christians and religions and show an interest in conversing about what others believe.) Also, we can be part of the "dialogue of shared spiritual experience" whenever we discuss problems and commonalities of the human condition and how faith helps us cope with the issues that arise from these experiences.

As Cardinal Ratzinger—later elected Pope Benedict XVI—once cautioned, we must be careful of falling into a "too-easy ecumenism" in the course of seeking unity and friendship. All of our relationships with others must be oriented toward the truth: proclaiming the truth taught by Christ and his Catholic Church and dialoguing with others so they may come to know this same truth, which all human persons seek, however consciously or deficiently.

PILLARS OF THE FAITH

MSGR. LUIGI GIUSSANI

As a young priest in the 1950s, Msgr. Luigi Giussani noticed something about the young people with whom he was coming in contact. While many of them identified themselves as Catholic and attended Mass regularly, very few had a firm grasp of even the fundamental teachings of the Church and of how to apply those teachings in their everyday lives. There was a grave disconnect, it seemed, between the faith they had and the way they perceived the world. Their outlook was extremely secularized; they looked at questions of right and wrong and the very purpose of their lives as though God did not exist.

Msgr. Giussani realized that young people needed to receive an education in the faith that would permeate their very lives with the understanding that Christ is the center of their lives. Such a Christ-centered awareness must shape their entire outlook so all their daily activity is lived for Christ. Thus, by their lived example, their lives would help evangelize others.

A professor, he challenged the secularism of the culture that oppressed the Catholic believer from all sides. He taught his students how to examine the conscience and to use it to enter into true friendship with Christ. God infuses the human heart with a desire to seek him, and every person needs to be awakened to that call. And the best and surest way to come to know God and to draw ever nearer to him is through his Church and Sacraments.

Msgr. Giussani founded several Catholic youth and student organizations to help young people live as committed Christians in the modern world. In the late 1960s as the prevalent radical ideas of the decade meant the spread of Marxist ideology throughout many Italian universities, Msgr. Giussani's students at the University of Milan published a manifesto titled *Comunione e Liberazione* ("Communion and Liberation") in which they stated that a human person can only be truly free if he or she lives in communion with Christ and his Church. This gave rise to an international movement by the same name that gradually began taking its message of Catholics engaging their culture beyond the university and into their everyday lives.

In 1983 Fr. Giussani was given the title of Monsignor by St. John Paul II.

When Communion and Liberation (CL) took the lead in supporting an Italian referendum in 1974 to repeal legislation that had legalized divorce three years earlier, leftist agitators committed more than 100 acts of violence against the offices and members of the movement. The movement's courage in standing up for Catholic moral values won the admiration of St. Paul VI.

Continued

MSGR. LUIGI GIUSSANI

Continued

Later, CL earned the attention and encouragement of St. John Paul II, who in 1982 called upon the members of CL to "go into all the world and bring the truth, the beauty, and the peace which are found in Christ the Redeemer." The Pope saw CL as an instrument of the New Evangelization throughout the world. With this level of approval, Communion and Liberation won support from many bishops as it grew in popularity across Europe. CL also embarked on numerous missionary initiatives that resulted in the movement taking root in some eighty countries around the world, including in the United States. Although CL does not involve formal membership, it is one of the largest lay ecclesial movements in the Church, with more than 100,000 lay people participating regularly in CL activities.

Msgr. Giussani passed away on Feb. 22, 2005. In the homily at his funeral Mass, Joseph Cardinal Ratzinger—who two months later was elected Pope Benedict XVI—recalled the wisdom of CL's founder as his members first came face to face with extreme poverty:

> Father Giussani really wanted not to have his life for himself, but he gave life, and exactly in this way found life not only for himself, but for many others. He practiced what we heard in the Gospel: he did not want to be served but to served...This centrality of Christ in his life gave him also the gift of discernment, of deciphering correctly the signs of the times in a difficult time, full of temptations and of errors, as we know....Think of 1968 and the following years. A first group of his followers went to Brazil and found itself face to face with extreme poverty, with extreme misery. What can be done? How can we respond? And there was a great temptation to say, "For the moment we have to set Christ aside, set God aside, because there are more pressing needs, we have first to change the structure, the external things, first we must improve the earth, then we can find heaven again."...
>
> Monsignor Giussani, with his fearless and unfailing faith, knew that, even in this situation, Christ, the encounter with Him, remains central, because whoever does not give God, gives too little, and whoever does not give God, whoever does not make people find God in the face of Christ, does not build, but destroys, because he gets human activity lost in ideological and false dogmatisms.
>
> Father Giussani kept the centrality of Christ and, exactly in this way, with social works, with necessary service, he helped mankind in this difficult world, where the responsibility of Christians for the poor in the world is enormous and urgent.

Msgr. Giussani was greatly interested in promoting the New Evangelization and, beginning in the early 1980s, spoke of a Pontifical Council that could assist in its activities. This idea bore fruit in 2010 when Pope Benedict XVI established the Pontifical Council for the New Evangelization.

In February 2012, seven years after Monsignor Giussani's death, the Archdiocese of Milan opened the cause for his beatification, the first step toward a declaration of sainthood.

SUPPLEMENTARY READING

Dialogue and Proclamation

Among the reasons that make the relationship between dialogue and proclamation a relevant theme for study, the following may be mentioned:

a) In the world of today, characterized by rapid communications, mobility of peoples, and interdependence, there is a new awareness of the fact of religious plurality. Religions do not merely exist, or simply survive. In some cases, they give clear evidence of a revival. They continue to inspire and influence the lives of millions of their adherents. In the present context of religious plurality, the important role played by religious traditions cannot be overlooked.

b) Interreligious dialogue between Christians and followers of other religious traditions, as envisaged by the Second Vatican Council, is only gradually coming to be understood. Its practice remains hesitant in some places. The situation differs from country to country. It can depend on the size of the Christian community, on which other religious traditions are present, and on various other cultural, social, and political factors. A further examination of the question may help to stimulate dialogue.

c) The practice of dialogue raises problems in the minds of many. There are those who would seem to think, erroneously, that in the Church's mission today dialogue should simply replace proclamation. At the other extreme, some fail to see the value of interreligious dialogue. Yet others are perplexed and ask: If interreligious dialogue has become so important, has the proclamation of the Gospel message lost its urgency? Has the effort to bring people into the community of the Church become secondary or even superfluous? There is a need therefore for doctrinal and pastoral guidance to which this document wishes to contribute, without pretending to answer fully the many and complex questions which arise in this connection.

As this text was in its final stages of preparation for publication, the Holy Father, Pope John Paul II, offered to the Church his Encyclical *Redemptoris Missio* in which he addressed these questions and many more. The present document spells out in greater detail the teaching of the Encyclical on dialogue and its relationship to proclamation (cf. *RMiss* 55-57). It is therefore to be read in the light of this Encyclical.

Dialogue can be understood in different ways. Firstly, at the purely human level, it means reciprocal communication, leading to a common goal or, at a deeper level, to interpersonal communion. Secondly, dialogue can be taken as an attitude of respect and friendship, which permeates or should permeate all those activities constituting the evangelizing mission of the Church. This can appropriately be called "the spirit of dialogue." Thirdly, in the context of religious plurality, dialogue means "all positive and constructive interreligious relations with individuals and communities of other faiths which are directed at mutual understanding and enrichment," in obedience to truth and respect for freedom. It includes both witness and the exploration of respective religious convictions. It is in this third sense that the present document uses the term dialogue for one of the integral elements of the Church's evangelizing mission.

Proclamation is the communication of the Gospel message, the mystery of salvation realized by God for all in Jesus Christ by the power of the Spirit. It is an invitation to a commitment of faith in Jesus Christ and to entry through baptism into the community of believers which is the Church. This proclamation can be solemn and public, as for instance on the day of Pentecost (cf. Acts 2: 5-41), or a simple private conversation (cf. Acts 8: 30-38). It leads naturally to catechesis which aims at deepening this faith. Proclamation is the foundation, centre, and summit of evangelization (cf. *EN* 27).

— Pontifical Council for Inter-religious Dialogue, *Dialogue and Proclamation: Reflection and Orientations on Interreligious Dialogue and the Proclamation of the Gospel of Jesus Christ.* (May 19, 1991) nos. 4, 9-10

SUPPLEMENTARY READING Continued

On the Unicity and Salvific Universality of Jesus Christ and the Church

The *Lord Jesus*, before ascending into heaven, commanded his disciples to proclaim the Gospel to the whole world and to baptize all nations: "Go into the whole world and proclaim the Gospel to every creature. He who believes and is baptized will be saved; he who does not believe will be condemned" (Mk 16: 15-16); "All power in heaven and on earth has been given to me. Go therefore and teach all nations, baptizing them in the name of the Father, and of the Son, and of the Holy Spirit, teaching them to observe all that I have commanded you. And behold, I am with you always, until the end of the world" (Mt 28: 18-20; cf. Lk 24: 46-48; Jn 17: 18, 20, 21; Acts 1: 8).

The Church's universal mission is born from the command of Jesus Christ and is fulfilled in the course of the centuries in the proclamation of the mystery of God, Father, Son, and Holy Spirit, and the mystery of the incarnation of the Son, as the saving event for all humanity. The fundamental contents of the profession of the Christian faith are expressed thus: "I believe in one God, the Father, Almighty, maker of heaven and earth, of all that is, seen and unseen. I believe in one Lord, Jesus Christ, the only Son of God, eternally begotten of the Father, God from God, Light from Light, true God from true God, begotten, not made, of one being with the Father. Through him all things were made. For us men and for our salvation, he came down from heaven: by the power of the Holy Spirit he became incarnate of the Virgin Mary, and became man. For our sake he was crucified under Pontius Pilate; he suffered death and was buried. On the third day he rose again in accordance with the Scriptures; he ascended into heaven and is seated at the right hand of the Father. He will come again in glory to judge the living and the dead, and his kingdom will have no end. I believe in the Holy Spirit, the Lord, the giver of life, who proceeds from the Father. With the Father and the Son he is worshiped and glorified. He has spoken through the prophets. I believe in one holy catholic and apostolic Church. I acknowledge one baptism for the forgiveness of sins. I look for the resurrection of the dead, and the life of the world to come."

In the course of the centuries, the Church has proclaimed and witnessed with fidelity to the Gospel of Jesus. At the close of the second millennium, however, this mission is still far from complete. For that reason, Saint Paul's words are now more relevant than ever: "Preaching the Gospel is not a reason for me to boast; it is a necessity laid on me: woe to me if I do not preach the Gospel!" (1 Cor 9: 16). This explains the Magisterium's particular attention to giving reasons for and supporting the evangelizing mission of the Church, above all in connection with the religious traditions of the world.

In considering the values which these religions witness to and offer humanity, with an open and positive approach, the Second Vatican Council's Declaration on the relation of the Church to non-Christian religions states: "The Catholic Church rejects nothing of what is true and holy in these religions. She has a high regard for the manner of life and conduct, the precepts and teachings, which, although differing in many ways from her own teaching, nonetheless often reflect a ray of that truth which enlightens all men." Continuing in this line of thought, the Church's proclamation of Jesus Christ, "the way, the truth, and the life" (Jn 14: 6), today also makes use of the practice of inter-religious dialogue. Such dialogue certainly does not replace, but rather accompanies the *missio ad gentes*, directed toward that "mystery of unity," from which "it follows that all men and women who are saved share, though differently, in the same mystery of salvation in Jesus Christ through his Spirit." Inter-religious dialogue, which is part of the Church's evangelizing mission, requires an attitude of understanding and a relationship of mutual knowledge and reciprocal enrichment, in obedience to the truth and with respect for freedom.

—Congregation for the Doctrine of the Faith, *Declaration "Dominus Iesus" on the Unicity and Salvific Universality of Jesus Christ and the Church* (August 6, 2000) nos. 1-2

VOCABULARY

ASH WEDNESDAY
The first day of Lent, on which Catholics receive ashes on their foreheads with the reminder, "Remember that you are dust and to dust you shall return." It begins the penitential life of the season of Lent.

CATECHESIS
From the Greek for "instruction by word of mouth," this constitutes Christian education, especially of young people and those preparing for Baptism.

INDIFFERENTISM
A form of religious relativism that considers all religions and faiths to be of equal or subjective value.

PROCLAMATION
Announcement of the Good News of Jesus Christ to others. All followers of Christ are obligated to proclaim his saving works to the world and to spread the Gospel to all lands.

SANCTIFICATION
Process of being made holy, which begins with Baptism and continues by giving glory to God, regularly receiving the Sacraments, and growing in grace. It is completed when a person enters heaven and becomes united with God in the Beatific Vision.

UNIVERSAL SALVATION
The belief that all of humanity will ultimately be saved based on the revealed truth that "God wills the salvation of everyone through the knowledge of the truth" (CCC 851). Nonetheless, God grants all men and women the freedom to choose him or to reject him; he offers the gift of salvation but does not force it upon a person against his will.

Religious representatives from all over the world gathered together
at the the interfaith World Day of Prayer for Peace
at the Basilica of St. Francis in Assisi, Italy, 1986 organized by St. John Paul II.

STUDY QUESTIONS

1. What does it mean that "outside the Church there is no salvation?"
2. What is indifferentism and why is it dangerous?
3. What does it mean that the Catholic Church possesses the full and ordinary means of salvation?
4. What does it mean that "God has bound salvation to the sacrament of Baptism, but he himself is not bound by his sacraments" (CCC 1257)?
5. What are the six fundamentals of the Church's proclamation?
6. What is evangelization?
7. What are some ways that Catholics are called to evangelize?
8. What role do young people play in the New Evangelization?
9. What is the New Evangelization?
10. What is the goal of both dialogue and proclamation?
11. How can movements such as the pro-life movement help advance ecumenism?
12. How can Catholics dialogue with non-Catholics in daily life?
13. How can theologians help advance dialogue between religions?
14. How can Catholics be helped by a mutual search for truth with non-Catholics?
15. Why is it necessary to have knowledge of one's faith to dialogue with others?
16. What are some misconceptions today about dialogue and proclamation, and what do these terms actually mean?
17. What are some meanings of the word "dialogue?" What does it mean when it comes to interreligious dialogue?

PRACTICAL EXERCISES

1. Throughout Church history men and women have given their lives to missionary work. Why does the Church need missionaries if she recognizes elements of truth in other religions?

2. Find two Scripture verses supporting each of the six fundamentals of the Church's proclamation.

3. Organize a door-to-door project with your class to tell people about the Catholic faith.

4. Choose one non-Christian religion other than Judaism and Islam—other than the one you researched in an earlier chapter—mentioned in this book. Research its teachings and explain how five of its beliefs are compatible with Catholic teaching.

FROM THE CATECHISM

848 "Although in ways known to himself God can lead those who, through no fault of their own, are ignorant of the Gospel, to that faith without which it is impossible to please him, the Church still has the obligation and also the sacred right to evangelize all men."[33]

855 The Church's mission stimulates efforts *towards Christian unity*.[34] Indeed, "divisions among Christians prevent the Church from realizing in practice the fullness of catholicity proper to her in those of her sons who, though joined to her by Baptism, are yet separated from full communion with her. Furthermore, the Church herself finds it more difficult to express in actual life her full catholicity in all its aspects."[35]

899 The initiative of lay Christians is necessary especially when the matter involves discovering or inventing the means for permeating social, political, and economic realities with the demands of Christian doctrine and life. This initiative is a normal element of the life of the Church:

> Lay believers are in the front line of Church life; for them the Church is the animating principle of human society. Therefore, they in particular ought to have an ever-clearer consciousness not only of belonging to the Church, but of being the Church, that is to say, the community of the faithful on earth under the leadership of the Pope, the common Head, and of the bishops in communion with him. They are the Church.[36]

900 Since, like all the faithful, lay Christians are entrusted by God with the apostolate by virtue of their Baptism and Confirmation, they have the right and duty, individually or grouped in associations, to work so that the divine message of salvation may be known and accepted by all men throughout the earth. This duty is the more pressing when it is only through them that men can hear the Gospel and know Christ. Their activity in ecclesial communities is so necessary that, for the most part, the apostolate of the pastors cannot be fully effective without it.[37]

905 Lay people also fulfill their prophetic mission by evangelization, "that is, the proclam ation of Christ by word and the testimony of life." For lay people, "this evangelization...acquires a specific property and peculiar efficacy because it is accomplished in the ordinary circumstances of the world."[38]

> This witness of life, however, is not the sole element in the apostolate; the true apostle is on the lookout for occasions of announcing Christ by word, either to unbelievers...or to the faithful.[39]

2044 The fidelity of the baptized is a primordial condition for the proclamation of the Gospel and for the Church's mission in the world. In order that the message of salvation can show the power of its truth and radiance before men, it must be authenticated by the witness of the life of Christians. "The witness of a Christian life and good works done in a supernatural spirit have great power to draw men to the faith and to God."[40]

2145 The faithful should bear witness to the Lord's name by confessing the faith without giving way to fear.[41] Preaching and catechizing should be permeated with adoration and respect for the name of our Lord Jesus Christ.

2472 The duty of Christians to take part in the life of the Church impels them to act as *witnesses of the Gospel* and of the obligations that flow from it. This witness is a transmission of the faith in words and deeds. Witness is an act of justice that establishes the truth or makes it known.[42]

> All Christians by the example of their lives and the witness of their word, wherever they live, have an obligation to manifest the new man which they have put on in Baptism and to reveal the power of the Holy Spirit by whom they were strengthened at Confirmation.[43]

Christ Carrying the Cross by Titian.
Evangelization involves both words and actions. Our example ordinarily will draw people to (or away from) Christ and his Church far more effectively than anything we might say. So by living faithful lives as Catholics—treating others with the love and compassion that Christ showed to the people that he met—we are already engaged in evangelization.

ENDNOTES – CHAPTER NINE

1. *LG* 17; *RMiss* 11.
2. *RMiss* 36.
3. *Mystici Corporis*: DS 3821.
4. *LG* 14.
5. Cf. CCC 846.
6. Acts 9:4; emphasis added.
7. Cf. Mk 16:16; Jn 3:5.
8. Cf. Jn 3:5.
9. Cf. Mt 28:19-20; cf. Council of Trent (1547) DS 1618; *LG* 14; *AG* 5.
10. Cf. Mk 16:16.
11. *LG* 16; cf. DS 3866-3872.
12. *Ut Unum Sint* 14; AAS 87 (1995), 929.
13. Ibid., 28: AAS 87 (1995), 939.
14. *UR* 3, 5.
15. Cf. 2 Pt 1:4.
16. 1 Cor 9:16.
17. *GS* 20 § 1.
18. *GS* 20 § 2.
19. Cf. CCC 2126.
20. Cf. CCC 2127.
21. *EN* 14.
22. Benedict XVI, *Homily at First Vespers*, June 28, 2010.
23. CCC 861; *AG* 9.
24. Cf. *RMiss* 55.
25. *AG* 9.
26. Ibid.
27. *LG* 27.
28. Cf. *LG* 1.
29. Rev 21:2, 9.
30. Cf. Rev 21:27.
31. CCC 856.
32. Eph 4:15.
33. *AG* 7; cf. Heb 11:6; 1 Cor 9:16.
34. Cf. *RMiss* 50.
35. *UR* 4 § 8.
36. Pius XII, Discourse, February 20, 1946: AAS 38 (1946) 149; quoted by St. John Paul II, *CL* 9.
37. Cf. *LG* 33.
38. *LG* 35 § 1, § 2.
39. *AA* 6 § 3; cf. *AG* 15.
40. *AA* 6 § 2.
41. Cf. Mt 10:32; 1 Tm 6:12.
42. Cf. Mt 18:16.
43. *AG* 11.

ART AND PHOTO CREDITS

Cover

Pope Benedict XVI at the Western Wall of Jerusalem, May 12, 2009, Holy Land Visit; ©L'Osservatore Romano

Front Pages

iii See Cover Credit
iv *The Holy Trinity*, Andrea Previtali; Accademia Carrara, Bergamo, Italy

Introduction

2 *The Last Supper* (detail), Benjamin West; Detroit Institute of Arts, Detroit, Michigan
3 *Jerusalem, Jerusalem*, James Tissot; Brooklyn Museum, New York
4 *Archbishop of Canterbury Dr. Rowan Williams and Pope Benedict XVI*; Private Collection

Chapter 1

7 *The Two Trinities*, Bartolome Esteban Murillo; National Gallery, London
8 *God the Father with Sts. Catherine of Siena and Mary Magdalen*, Fra Bartolomeo; Museo e Pinacoteca Nazionale di Palazzo Mansi, Lucca, Italy
9 *Sermon on the Mount*, Rudolf Yelin; Reinerzau Church, Germany
11 *Moses Crossing the Red Sea*, Raphael; The Raphael Loggia, Palazzi Pontifici, Vatican
12 *The Annunciation*, Francesco Albani; The Hermitage, St. Petersburg, Russia
13 *Creation of the Sun, Moon, and Planets*, Michelangelo; Sistine Chapel, Vatican
14 *Eve, the Serpent, and Death* (detail), Hans Baldung Grien; National Gallery of Canada, Ottawa, Canada
15 *Paradise*, Lucas Cranach the Elder; Kunsthistorisches Museum, Vienna, Austria
16 *The Last Supper*, Carl H. Bloch; Frederiksborg Palace Chapel, Denmark
17 *The Creation of Adam in the Garden of Eden*, Jan Brueghel the Younger, Stedelijk-Museum, Leuven, Belgium
18 *Noah Sacrificing after the Deluge*, Benjamin West; The San Antonio Museum Association, Texas
19 *Isaac Bears the Wood for His Sacrifice*, James Tissot; Brooklyn Museum, New York
20 *Abraham, Sarah, and the Angel*, Jan Provost; Musée du Louvre, Paris, France
21 *Joseph Explains the Dreams of Pharaoh*, Jean-Adrien Guignet; Musee des Beaux-Arts, Rouen, France
22 *Moses and the Burning Bush*, Raphael; The Raphael Loggia, Palazzi Pontifici, Vatican
23 *Moses Receiving the Tablets of Law*, F.W. McCleave & Co. ca.1877; Library of Congress Prints & Photographs Division, Washington, D.C.
24 *Adoration of the Golden Calf*, Nicolas Poussin; National Gallery, London
25 *Anointing of David* (detail), Felix-Joseph Barrias; Musee du Petit-Palais, Paris, France
26 *Jeremiah Lamenting the Destruction of Jerusalem*, Carl Ebert, ca.1869; Private Collection
27 *Baptism of Christ*, Pieter de Grebber; St. Stephanus Church, Beckum, Germany
28 *The Holy Trinity* (detail), Francesco Cairo; Museo del Prado, Madrid, Spain
29 *Adoration of the Magi* (detail), Monaco Lorenzo; Galleria degli Uffizi, Florence, Italy
30 *St. John the Evangelist's Vision of Jerusalem* (detail), Alonso Cano; Wallace Collection, London
31 *Christ Handing the Keys to St. Peter*, Peter Paul Rubens; Gemaldegalerie, Berlin, Germany
32 *Pope Emeritus Benedict XVI*; Private Collection
33 *Pope Emeritus Benedict XVI and Pope Francis*; Private Collection
35 *St. Peter*, Peter Paul Rubens; Museo Nacional del Prado, Madrid, Spain
38 *The Resurrected Christ*, Salvator Rosa; Musée Condé, Chantilly, France

Chapter 2

41 *Christ Handing the Keys to St. Peter*, Master of the Legend of the Holy Prior; Wallraf-Richartz Museum, Cologne, Germany
42 *Feed My Lambs*, James Tissot; Brooklyn Museum, New York
43 *St. Peter's Basilica and Square, the Canonization of St. Josemaria Escriva*; Wojciech Dubis, Photographer; MTF Archives
44 *The Israelites' Camp and Wilderness Tabernacle at Mount Sinai*, French School, Eighteenth Century; Private Collection
45 *Joshua Passing the River Jordan with the Ark of the Covenant*, Benjamin West; Art Gallery of New South Wales, Sydney, Australia
46 *Christ's Charge to Peter*, Raphael; Tapestry Cartoon, Victoria and Albert Museum, London, England
47 *Pentecost* (detail), Juan de Flandes; Museo del Prado, Madrid, Spain
48 *St. Paul*, Antonio del Castillo; Cordoba Museum of Fine Arts, Cordoba, Spain; Archivo Oronoz
49 *The Transfiguration*, Lodovico Carracci; Pinacoteca Nazionale, Bologna, Italy

ART AND PHOTO CREDITS

50 *St. Peter Preaching in the Presence of St. Mark*, Fra Angelico; Museo di San Marco, Florence, Italy
51 *Apostle Peter*, Anton Raphael Mengs; Kunsthistorisches Museum, Vienna, Austria
52 *Christ's Charge to Peter*, Paolo Veronese; Private Collection
53 *St. Peter Enthroned*, Guido di Graziano; Pinacoteca Nazionale di Siena, Italy
54 *Appearance on the Mountain in Galilee* (detail), Duccio; Museo dell'Opera del Duomo, Siena, Italy
55 *St. Matthias*, Workshop of Simone Martini; The Metropolitan Museum of Art, New York
56 *The Four Evangelists*, Abraham Bloemaert; Princeton University Art Museum, Princeton, New Jersey
57 *St. Paul*, Andrea di Bartolo; Private Collection
58 *Pentecost*, Fray Juan Bautist Maino; Museo Nacional del Prado, Madrid, Spain; Archivo Oronoz
59 *St. Peter Preaching*, Masolino; Cappella Brancacci, Santa Maria del Carmine, Florence, Italy
60 *The Resurrection*, Tintoretto; Gallerie dell'Accademia, Venice, Italy
61 *The Ascension*, John Singleton Copely; Museum of Fine Arts, Boston, Massachusetts
62 *Apostles Peter and Paul*, El Greco; The Hermitage, St. Petersburg, Russia
63 *The Martyrdom of St. Paul*, Tintoretto; Madonna dell'Orto, Venice, Italy
64 *The Nativity*, Bicci di Lorenzo; Wallraf-Richartz-Museum, Cologne, Germany
65 *Annunciation*, Nicolas Poussin; National Gallery, London

Chapter 3
69 *Last Supper*, Jaume Huguet; Museu Nacional d'Art de Catalunya, Barcelona, Spain
71 *St. Paul of the Cross Church*, Park Ridge, Illinois; Julie Koenig, Photographer
72 *Pope Francis and the College of Cardinals, March 13, 2013*; ©L'Osservatore Romano
73 *Pope Benedict XVI and Patriarch Theophilos, May 15, 2009*; Private Collection
74 *First Council of Nicæa*, Icon; MTF Archives
75 *The Baptism of Christ*, Joachim Patinir; Kunsthistorisches Museum, Vienna, Austria
76 *Supper at Emmaus*, Jacopo Pontormo; Galleria degli Uffizi, Florence, Italy
77 *Baptism*, St. Thomas the Apostle Church, Naperville, Illinois; Photo Courtesy of Debbie Snyder
78 *Adoration of the Lamb* (detail), *The Ghent Altarpiece*, (central panel, lower tier), Jan Van Eyck; Cathedral of St. Bavo, Ghent, Belgium
79 *Appearance While the Apostles Are at Table*, Duccio; Museo dell'Opera del Duomo, Siena, Italy
80 *Pope Paul VI and Patriarch Athenagoras I*; Archivo Oronoz
82 *Communion of the Apostles* (detail), Luca Signorelli; Museo Diocesano, Cortona, Italy
83 *Baptism of the Ethiopian* [or *Eunuch*], Rembrandt; Private Collection
84 *Good Friday Morning: Jesus in Prison*, James Tissot; Brooklyn Museum, New York
85 *Parable of the Lost Sheep*, Alford Usher Soord; *Standard Bible Story Readers, Book One* by Lillie A. Faris, The Standard Publishing Company, 1925
86 *Henri Cardinal de Lubac, SJ*; Private Collection
87 top left: *The Last Supper*, Francisco Ribalta; Museo de Bellas Artes de Valencia, Valencia, Spain
bottom right: *Pope Benedict XVI Celebrates Mass, November 5, 2009*; ©L'Osservatore Romano
92 *The Last Supper* (detail), Pascal-Adolphe-Jean Dagnan-Bouveret; Private Collection

Chapter 4
93 *Christ Pantocrator,* Deesis Mosaics (detail); Hagia Sophia, Istanbul, Turkey; Wikipedia Commons: Edal Anton Lefterov, Photographer
94 *Christ Pantocrator*, Greek Icon, Elias Moskos; Icon Museum, Recklinghausen, Germany
95 *Altarpiece of St. Philip and St. James*; Catedral de Huesca, Museo de Arte Cataluña, Barcelona, Spain; Archivo Oronoz
96 *Last Prayers of the Christian Martyrs*, Jean-Leon Gerome; Walters Art Museum, Baltimore, Maryland
97 *Emperor Constantine and the Council of Nicæa*, Illustration from MS CLXV, *Biblioteca Capitolare, Vercelli*, a Compendium of Canon Law, Northern Italy, ca.825; *Europe in the Dark Ages,* p. 143 (London: Thames & Hudson, 1969)
98 *St. Ambrose Converting Theodosius*, Pierre Subleyras; Galleria Nazionale, Perugia, Italy
99 *Virgin Mary and Christ Child,* Southwestern Entrance Mosaics, Hagia Sophia, Istanbul, Turkey; Wikipedia Commons: Myrabella, Photographer
101 *St. Athanasius* (detail), Alonso Sanchez Coello; Royal Monastery of St. Lawrence of Escorial, Madrid, Spain; Archivo Oronoz
102 *St. Cyril of Alexandria*, Osorio Meneses; Museum of Fine Arts, Seville, Spain; Archivo Oronoz
103 *The Transfiguration*, Icon attributed to Theophanes the Greek; State Tretyakov Gallery, Moscow, Russia
104 *St. John Chrysostom*, Northern Tympanon Mosaics (detail); Hagia Sophia, Istanbul, Turkey
106 *The Divine Liturgy*, Byzantine Catholic Church; The Catholic Knight, www.catholicknight.blogspot.com
108 *Early Church Fathers*, Icon; MTF Archives
109 *The Holy Trinity* (detail), Hendrick van Balen; Sint-Jacobskerk, Antwerp, Belgium

ART AND PHOTO CREDITS

110 *Hagia Irene Interior*, Istanbul, Turkey; Wikipedia Commons: Gryffindor, Photographer
111 *Coronation of Charlemagne* (detail), *Great Chronicles of France*, Illuminated by Jean Fouquet; Paris, BnF, Manuscripts Department, French 6465, fol. 89v. (*Second Book of Charlemagne*)
112 left: *The Taking of Constantinople*, Palma il Giovane; Palazzo Ducale, Venice, Italy
right: *Constantinople's Bronze Horses*, St. Mark's Basilica, Venice, Italy; Wikipedia Commons: Nino Barbieri, Photographer
114 left: *St. Mark the Archbishop of Ephesus*, Icon; The Orthodox Church in America, oca.org
right: *The Entry of Mehmet II into Constantinople*, Jean-Joseph Benjamin-Constant; Musee des Augustins, Toulouse, France
116 left: *Procession of the Palms, Vigil Service, Entry into Jerusalem*; Russian Orthodox Church; Public Domain Photograph
right: *Procession of the Palms led by Pope Francis*, St. Peter's Square, April 2013; ©L'Osservatore Romano
117 *The Immaculate Conception*, Francisco de Zurbaran; Museum of Fine Arts, Budapest
118 *Pope Benedict XVI and Patriarch Bartholomew I*, November 2006; Private Collection
119 *Three Holy Hierarchs*, Seventeenth Century Icon; Historic Museum, Sanok, Poland
121 *Iconostasis*, Greek Catholic Cathedral, Hajdudorog, Hungary; Wikipedia Commons: Jojojoe, Photographer
122 *Pope St. Leo IX*; St. Kilian Church of Dingsheim, Alsace, France
123 *Interior of Hagia Sophia*, Istanbul, Turkey; Wikipedia Commons: Sheba, Photographer
124 *Sts. Cyril and Methodius*, Jan Matejko; Public Domain
125 *The Baska Tablet*; Croatian Academy of Sciences and Arts, Zagreb, Croatia; Public Domain Photograph
129 *Christ Pantocrator*, Imperial Gate Mosaics, Hagia Sophia, Istanbul, Turkey; Wikipedia Commons: Myrabella, Photographer
132 *Pope John Paul II and Archbishop Christodoulos*, May 4, 2001; Private Collection

Chapter 5
133 *King Henry the VIII*, Hans Holbein; Barberini Palace, Rome, Italy; Archivo Oronoz
134 *Palais des Papes*, Avignon, France; Wikipedia Commons: Jean-Marc Rosier, Photographer
135 *Emperor Charlemagne*, Albrecht Dürer; German National Museum, Nuremburg, Germany
137 *Jan Hus at the Council of Constance*, Carl Friedrich Lessing; Stadelsches Kunstinstitut und Stadtische Galerie, Frankfurt, Germany
138 *Martin Luther as an Augustinian Monk*, Cranach Workshop; German National Museum, Nuremburg, Germany
139 *New Testament in German*, Martin Luther Translation, 1522; Woodcuts by Lucas Cranach the Elder, British Library, London
140 *Martin Luther at the Diet of Worms*, Anton von Werner; Staatsgalerie, Stuttgart, Germany
141 *Apostle St. James the Less*, El Greco; Museo de El Greco, Toledo, Spain
142 *Desiderius Erasmus*, Hans Holbein the Younger; National Gallery, London
143 left: *Portrait of Young John Calvin*, Unknown Flemish Master; Library of Geneva, Geneva, Switzerland
right: *Looting of the Churches of Lyon by the Calvinists, 1562*, Antoine Caron; Public Domain
144 top right: *Ulrich Zwingli*, Hans Asper; Kunstmuseum Winterthur, Winterthur, Switzerland
bottom left: *Heinrich Bullinger*, Hans Asper; *History of the Canton of Zurich*, Vol. 2; Public Domain
145 top: *Thomas Cranmer*, Gerlach Flicke; National Portrait Gallery, London
bottom: *John Wesley*, Unknown Master; Public Domain
146 *St. Thomas More*, Hans Holbein the Younger; The Frick Collection, New York
147 *The Wedding*; Stockbyte, Stock Photography
148 *Pope Paul III*, Titian; Toledo Cathedral, Toledo, Spain; Archivo Oronoz
149 *St. Ignatius of Loyola*, Peter Paul Rubens; Brukenthal National Museum, Sibiu, Romania
150 *The Savior*, Juan de Juanes; Museo del Prado, Madrid, Spain; Archivo Oronoz
151 *Pope Benedict XVI Baptizing an Infant*, Feast of the Baptism of the Lord, Vatican; ©L'Osservatore Romano
152 *The Crucifixion*, Giambattista Tiepolo; St. Louis Art Museum, St. Louis, Missouri
153 *The Holy Trinity*, El Greco; Museo del Prado, Madrid, Spain; Archivo Oronoz
154 *The Last Supper* (detail), Dieric Bouts the Elder; Sint-Pieterskerk, Leuven, Belgium
155 *The Elevation*; Restored Traditions; MTF Archives
156 *St. Matthew and the Angel*, Guido Reni; Pinacoteca, Vatican
157 *Rest on the Flight into Egypt* (detail), Caravaggio; Galleria Doria Pamphilj, Rome, Italy
158 *Ordination of Twenty-nine Deacons*, April 27, 2008, St. Peter's Basilica, Vatican; ©L'Osservatore Romano
159 *Virgin and Child in Glory with Saints*, Giovanni Battista Carlone; Private Collection
160 *Pope Benedict XVI and the Archbishop of Canterbury Dr. Rowan Williams*, September 17, 2010; ©L'Osservatore Romano
161 *Martin Luther Nailing His Ninety-five Theses to the Wittenburg Church Door*, Hugo Vogel; Archiv für Kunst und Geschichte, Berlin, Germany
162 *Pope Paul VI*; Archivo Oronoz
163 *Second Vatican Council*, St. Peter's Basilica, Vatican; Archivo Oronoz
165 *St. Peter Enthroned and Four Saints*, Marco Basaiti; San Pietro di Castello, Venice, Italy
171 *St. Peter's Square, the Canonization of St. Josemaria Escriva*; Wojciech Dubis, Photographer; MTF Archives
172 *The Throne of St. Peter*, St. Peter's Basilca, Vatican; ©L'Osservatore Romano

ART AND PHOTO CREDITS

Chapter 6

173 *Pope Benedict XVI Visits the Basilica of the Holy Sepulchre*, May 15, 2009, Jerusalem; ©L'Osservatore Romano
174 *Pope Benedict XVI and Archbishop of Canterbury Dr. Rowan Williams*, March 10, 2012; ©L'Osservatore Romano
175 *The Last Sermon of Our Lord*, James Tissot; Brooklyn Museum, New York
177 *Pope Leo XIII*, Official Portrait, Vatican Album of the Ecumenical Council; U.S. Library of Congress Prints and Photographs
178 *Beatification of Cardinal John Henry Newman*, September 19, 2010; ©L'Osservatore Romano
179 *Cardinal John Henry Newman*, Emmeline Deane; National Portrait Gallery, London
180 *The Lamentation of Christ*, Sir Anthony Van Dyck; Koninklijk Museum voor Schone Kunsten, Antwerp, Belgium
181 *Our Lady of the Atonement Statue*; The Shrine Chapel, Our Lady of the Atonement Church, San Antonio, Texas
182 *Pope John XXIII*; Archivo Oronoz
183 *Elevation of the Chalice during a Tridentine Mass by the Priestly Fraternity of Saint Peter*; http://fssp.org
184 *Second Vatican Council* (detail); St. Peter's Basilica, Vatican; Archivo Oronoz
185 *Statue of Patriarch Athenagoras I and Pope Paul VI*; Arcade in the Church of the Annunciation, Nazareth, Israel
186 *Pope John Paul II and Patriarch Teoctist*, 1999; Private Collection
187 *Pope Benedict XVI and Archbishop of Canterbury Dr. Rowan Williams*, November 2009; Private Collection
188 *Pope Francis and Archbishop of Canterbury Justin Welby*, June 14, 2013; ©L'Osservatore Romano
189 *Sermon on the Mount* (detail), Carl H. Bloch; Frederiksborg Palace Chapel, Denmark
190 *Pentecost*, Luis Tristan; Museum of Fine Arts, Bucharest, Romania
191 *The Way to Calvary*, Domenichino; J. Paul Getty Museum, Los Angeles, California
192 *Pope Benedict XVI Celebrates Holy Mass in the Valley of Josaphat*, May 12, 2009, Jerusalem; ©L'Osservatore Romano
193 *The Repentant Peter*, El Greco; The Phillips Collection, Washington, D.C.
194 *Sts. Peter and Paul Present God's Temple*, Byzantine Icon; Scuola Cretese Veneziana; Public Domain
195 *Pope Benedict XVI and Bishop Dr. Munib Younan*, December 2010; Private Collection
196 *Bl. Maria Gabriella Sagheddu*, Icon; www.365rosaries.blogspot.com
197 *Christ Taking Leave of the Apostles*, Duccio; Museo dell'Opera del Duomo, Siena, Italy
199 *Archbishop Christodoulos of Athens*; Public Domain
200 *Archbishop of Canterbury Dr. Rowan Williams and Pope Benedict XVI*, September 2010; Private Collection
202 *Christ Handing the Keys to St. Peter* (detail), Pietro Perugino; Sistine Chapel, Vatican

Chapter 7

203 *Jesus Unrolls the Book in the Synagogue*, James Tissot; Brooklyn Museum, New York
204 *The Presentation of Jesus in the Temple*, Ambrogio Lorenzetti; Uffizi Gallery, Florence, Italy
205 *World Day of Prayer for Peace*, Assisi, Italy, October 27, 1986; ©L'Osservatore Romano
206 *Pope Benedict XVI Baptizing an Infant*, Feast of the Baptism of the Lord, Vatican; ©L'Osservatore Romano
207 *Moses on Mount Sinai*, Jean-Leon Gerome; Private Collection
208 *Jesus Among the Doctors*, Jean Auguste Dominique Ingres; Musee Ingres, Montauban, France
210 top right: *Sefer Torah* in the former Glockengasse Synagogue, Cologne, Germany; Willy Horsch, Photographer
bottom left: *Moses Mendelssohn* (copy of portrait by Anton Graff at University of Leipzig); Jewish Museum, Berlin, Germany
211 *Allegory of the Old and New Testaments*, Hans Holbein the Younger; National Gallery of Scotland, Edinburgh, Scotland
212 *The Last Supper* (detail), Bartolomeo Carducci; Museo Nacional del Prado, Madrid, Spain; Archivo Oronoz
216 *Sermon on the Mount* (detail), Altarpiece, Henrik Olrik; Sankt Matthæus Kirke, Copenhagen, Denmark
217 *Destruction of the Temple in Jerusalem by Titus* (detail), Nicolas Poussin; Kunsthistorisches Museum, Vienna, Austria
219 *Christ Before Caiaphas* (detail), Giotto; Cappella Scrovegni (Arena Chapel), Padua, Italy
220 *St. Paul Preaching in Athens* (detail), Raphael; Victoria and Albert Museum, London, England
221 *Pope John XXIII*; Vatican Archives
222 *Pope Pius XII*; Vatican Archives
223 *Jesus Wept*, James Tissot; Brooklyn Museum, New York
224 *Pope John Paul II leaves a letter at the Western Wall, Jerusalem*, March 2000; *John Paul II: A Light for the World*; ©L'Osservatore Romano
225 *Yad Vashem Hall of Remembrance*, Jerusalem, Israel; Pictorial Library of Bible Lands; Todd Bolen, Photographer
226 *St. Teresa Benedicta of the Cross*; Archivo Oronoz
227 *Elevation of the Cross*, Peter Paul Rubens; Musee du Louvre, Paris, France
229 *Pope John Paul II Visits the Great Roman Synagogue*, April 13, 1986; Private Collection
231 *Reconstruction of Jerusalem and the Temple of Herod*, James Tissot; Brooklyn Museum, New York
inset: *Western Wall in Jerusalem at Night*; Wikipedia Commons, Wayne McLean, Photographer

ART AND PHOTO CREDITS

Chapter 8

235 *Dome of the Rock*, Jerusalem, Israel; Wikipedia Commons, Victor Grigas, Photographer
236 *Standing Buddha* (Stopping the Ocean), Rattanakosin style (in royal attire), Wat Arun, Bangkok, Thailand; Wikipedia Commons, Heinrich Damm, Photographer
237 *Prayer in Cairo, 1865*, Jean-Leon Gerome; Hamburger Kunsthalle, Hamburg, Germany
238 *The Battle of Poitiers* (detail), Charles de Steuben; Palace Art Collection, Versailles, France
239 *The Taking of Jerusalem by the Crusaders*, Emile Signol; Salles des Croisades, Palace of Versailles, France
240 *St. Francis: Trial by Fire Before the Sultan*, Domenico Ghirlandaio, Fresco; Santa Trinità, Florence, Italy
241 *Battle of Lepanto*, Luca Cambiaso; Royal Monastery of St. Lawrence of Escorial, Madrid, Spain; Archivo Oronoz
242 *The Kaaba at the Al-Masjid al-Haram Mosque during the Hajj*, Mecca, Saudi Arabia; Wikipedia Commons source: Al Jazeera
243 *Muslims Praying Towards Mecca*, Umayyad Mosque, Damascus, Syria; Antonio Melina/Agencia Brasil, Photographer
244 *The Flagellation*, Michael Pacher; Osterreichische Galerie, Vienna, Austria
245 *Muhammad Leads Abraham, Moses, and Jesus in Prayer* (retouched to fit), Medieval Persian Manuscript; Reference: *The Middle Ages. An Illustrated History* by Barbara Hanawalt, Oxford University Press, 1998
246 *Jesus Speaks Immediately After His Birth*; Illustration from *Prophets in the Quran: An Introduction to the Quran and Muslim Exegesis*, by Brandon Wheeler; Continuum, 2002
247 *Prophet Muhammad Returns from His Night Journey and Ascension*; Illustration from *Prophets in the Quran: An Introduction to the Quran and Muslim Exegesis*, by Brandon Wheeler; Continuum, 2002
248 *Pope Benedict XVI at the Aida Refugee Camp*, May 13, 2009, Holy Land Visit; ©L'Osservatore Romano
249 *St. Francis Xavier* (detail), Elias Salaverra; Javier Castillo Church, Navarra, Spain; Archivo Oronoz
250 *Lord Shiva at the Murudeshwara Temple*, Karnataka, India; Wikipedia Commons, Prashant Sahu, Photographer
251 *The Creation Myth of Shinto: Izanagi and Izanami*, Kobayashi Eitaku, ca. 1885; Public Domain
252 *Baha'i House of Worship*, Wilmette, Illinois; Wikipedia Commons, Jeff3000, Photographer
253 *The Ascension* (detail), Jean Colombe; Illumination, *Tres Riches Heures du Duc de Berry*; Musee Conde, Chantilly, France
254 *Pope John Paul II and the Dalai Lama*, Assisi 1986; Private Collection
255 *World Day of Prayer for Peace*, Assisi, Italy, October 27, 1986; ©L'Osservatore Romano
256 *Christus Statue*; North Visitor's Center, Temple Square, Salt Lake City, Utah; Public Domain
257 *The First Vision of Joseph Smith*, Stained Glass 1913; Museum of Church History and Art, Salt Lake City, Utah
258 *Charles Taze Russell, 1911*; United States Library of Congress's Prints and Photographs Division, Washington, D.C.
260 *The Adoration of the Trinity* (detail), Albrecht Durer; Kunsthistorisches Museum, Vienna, Austria
261 *Pope John Paul II Baptizes an Infant*; Sistine Chapel, Vatican; ©L'Osservatore Romano
262 *Daily Mass*, Northridge Preparatory School, Niles, Illinois; Julie Koenig, Photographer
263 top right: *Pope John Paul II*, 1999; Beatification Mass for Anton Martin Slomek, Maribor, Slovenia; Gabriel Bouys/AFP, Photographer
bottom left: *Pope John Paul II*; Private Collection
264 top left: *Beatification of Pope John Paul II*, May 1, 2011; St. Peter's Square, Vatican; Private Collection
bottom right: *Pope John Paul II*; Private Collection
265 *Three Worshipers Praying in a Corner of a Mosque*, Jean-Leon Gerome; Private Collection
270 *World Day of Prayer for Peace in Assisi*, October 27, 2011; Private Collection

Chapter 9

271 *Ananias Restoring the Sight of St. Paul*, Jean Restout; Musee du Louvre, Paris, France
272 *Sacred Heart of Jesus*, Charles Bosseron Chambers; restoredtraditions.com
274 *Baptism of the Eunuch*, Rembrandt [copy of a lost Rembrandt ca. 1631]; The Kremer Collection, Fondation Aetas Aurea
275 *Walking on Water*, Ivan Aivazovsky; Private Collection
276 *The Lord's Prayer* (detail), James Tissot; Brooklyn Museum, New York
277 *The Institution of the Eucharist* (detail), Nicolas Poussin; Musee du Louvre, Paris, France
279 *Pope Paul VI Opening the Second Vatican Council*; St. Peter's Basilica, Vatican; Archivo Oronoz
281 *Pope John Paul II in Assisi, Italy*, 2002; *John Paul II: A Light for the World*; ©L'Osservatore Romano
282 *The Four Evangelists*, Jacob Jordaens; Musee du Louvre, Paris, France
283 *World Youth Day 2011*; Madrid, Spain; ©L'Osservatore Romano
284 *Pope John Paul II*; Private Collection
285 *Catholic Youth Service Project in Mexico*; Luke Mata, Photographer; MTF Archives
286 *Supper at Emmaus* (detail), Leon Augustin Lhermitte; Private Collection
288 *Suffer the Little Children to Come unto Me*, Anthony Van Dyke; Museo del Prado, Madrid, Spain
289 *Pope Benedict XVI and Archbishop of Canterbury Dr. Rowan Williams*; Private Collection
291 *Pope John Paul II and Fr. Luigi Giussani*, 1983; Private Collection
295 *World Day of Prayer for Peace*, 1986, Assisi; ©L'Osservatore Romano
298 *Christ Carrying the Cross*, Titian; Museo del Prado, Madrid, Spain

INDEX

INDEX

INDEX

G

H

I

INDEX

INDEX

INDEX

INDEX

The Good Shepherd, Russian icon, 19th century; Private collection.